2003

Plate 1. Vauxhall Motors body shop 1910.

THE PUBLICATIONS OF THE BEDFORDSHIRE
HISTORICAL RECORD SOCIETY
VOLUME 82

VAUXHALL MOTORS AND THE LUTON ECONOMY 1900–2002

Len Holden

THE BEDFORDSHIRE HISTORICAL RECORD SOCIETY

THE BOYDELL PRESS

First published 2003

A publication of
Bedfordshire Historical Record Society
published by The Boydell Press
an imprint of Boydell & Brewer Ltd
PO Box 9, Woodbridge, Suffolk IP12 3DF, UK
and of Boydell & Brewer Inc.
PO Box 41026, Rochester, NY 14604–4126, USA
website: www.boydell.co.uk

ISBN 0 85155 068 1

Details of previous volumes are available from
Boydell & Brewer Ltd

A catalogue record for this book is available
from the British Library

This publication is printed on acid-free paper

Typeset by Joshua Associates Ltd, Oxford
Printed in Great Britain by
The Cromwell Press Ltd, Trowbridge, Wiltshire

Contents

Page

List of Plates   ix

List of Tables and Charts   xi

Acknowledgements   xiii

Abbreviations   xv

Introduction   xvi

Part One

Chapter One
The Evolution of Vauxhall: The 1890s to 1925   1

Chapter Two
The American Takeover of Vauxhall   28

Chapter Three
The Rise of Vauxhall to the 'Big Six': 1930–1950   37

Chapter Four
Financial, Marketing and Export Strategies   61

Chapter Five
Management and Labour Relations to 1929   87

Chapter Six
The Bartlett Years: Industrial Relations Policies 1929–1950   117

Chapter Seven
The Growth of Luton: From Hats to Cars   137

Chapter Eight
Vauxhall and the Luton Economy to the 1950s   159

Part Two

Chapter Nine
Vauxhall and Luton 1950–1970: Boom and Affluence   177

Chapter Ten
Acme to Nadir: The Decline of Vauxhall in Luton 1970–2002   203

Appendix A
Managing Directors of Vauxhall   227

Appendix B
Luton and Bedford Companies referred to in the book   229

Appendix C
Explanation of Conference Terms   231

Bibliography   233

Index   241

List of Plates

Page

Frontispiece
1. Vauxhall Motors body shop 1910   iv

Chapter One
2. The first Vauxhall motor car 1903   2
3. 1903 5hp four seater – price 130 guineas   5
4. 1905 visit to Vauxhall, Luton   6
5. 1906 18hp model   8
6. F.W. Hodges, Chief Engineer and designer of the early Vauxhall models   9
7. 1908 12–16hp Vauxhall. Percy Kidner and A.J. Hancock   10
8. Laurence Pomeroy at the wheel of a prototype Prince Henry in Lynmouth, Devon   12
9. 1911 C-type Prince Henry   13
10. Laurence Pomeroy, designer of the Prince Henry and the 30/98   14
11. General Allenby's entry into Jerusalem in a Vauxhall D-type, December 1917   17
12. 1923 Wensum, one of the famous 30/98 designs of Laurence Pomeroy   22
13. Awaiting a royal visit to the Vauxhall works, Luton 1926   23
14. Leslie Walton, Chairman and Managing Director from 1907 to the late 1940s   25

Chapter Three
15. Cadet 1930, the first visible outcome of the General Motors takeover   39
16. Bedford 2-ton truck 1931, described by Reg Pearson as a 'life saver'   44
17. 1931 WHG Waveney bus   47
18. The Luton site in the mid-1930s   49
19. 1938 H-type 10hp, the 'first modern British car' with its integral body and chassis   51
20. Vauxhall Velox (L-type) 1948   58

Chapter Five
21. The Vauxhall and West Hydraulic Engineering Company works, Luton 1905   91
22. The forge shop in Luton 1910   93
23. Engine assembly shop, Vauxhall Motors, Luton 1910   94

24. Erecting shop 1910   95
25. Paint shop 1910   96
26. Running shop 1911   97
27. Erecting shop highway 1913   98
28. Mounting shop 1914   99

Chapter Six
29. Sir Charles Bartlett, Managing Director Vauxhall Motors 1929–
    1953   118
30. Sir Reginald Pearson   133

Chapter Nine
31. 1951–1957 E-type Cresta – the new look   180
32. 1957–1961 F Victor   180
33. The 'American Look' showing the influence of designer Harley
    Earl   181
34. 1961–1964 FB Victor   182
35. 1963–1966 HA Viva – the 1960s best-selling Vauxhall car   183
36. The AC paint shop in 1961   184
37. Bedford CA camper van in Prague 1957   185
38. Vauxhall Motors Luton planned expansion in the early 1950s   186
39. Charles Bartlett and his replacement as Managing Director, Walter
    Hill, in 1953   188
40. P.W. Copelin, who replaced Walter Hill as Managing Director of
    Vauxhall in 1955   189
41. D. Jones (designer), M. Platt (Chief Engineer), J. Alden (Chief
    Engineer after Platt's retirement) and W. Swallow (Managing
    Director 1961–1966)   190
42. Velox E-type assembly line 1952   196

Chapter Ten
43. 1970–1979 HC Viva, keeping Vauxhall afloat in the 1970s   206
44. 1972–1976 FE Victor – the last 'British' Vauxhall car   207
45. The Chevette, the replacement for the Viva model in 1978   210
46. Mark I Astra Saloon, part of the 'mass Opelisation' of Vauxhall   211
47. The first UK-built Cavalier 1977   212
48. The 'marriage' of a Mark III Cavalier body with mechanical
    components in 1993   216
49. Nick Reilly, Managing Director of Vauxhall 1996–2001   219

I would like to thank the Vauxhall Motors Archive for allowing permission to reproduce these photographs.

Tables and Charts

Page

Tables
1. Vauxhall models 1903–1913 — 10
2. Total output, employees and floor area, Vauxhall 1903–1913 — 15
3. Sales and pre-tax profits of Vauxhall 1909–1914, and a comparison with Sunbeam — 15
4. Vauxhall sales, profit and capital 1914–1929 — 18
5. Output of cars, number of employees and floor area of Vauxhall Motors 1919–1930 — 21
6. Vauxhall models 1919–1930 — 22
7. Percentage of car output held by car producers 1929–1939 — 37
8. Vauxhall car models 1931–1939 — 40
9. Total output of cars and CVs, number of employees and floor space, Vauxhall Motors 1929–1938 — 41
10. Chassis prices of 2 ton and 30 cwt trucks 1931–1933 — 46
11. Bedford percentage of CV output 1931–1938 — 46
12. 10hp model competition 1938 and 1939 — 52
13. Vauxhall output 1946–1950 — 56
14. Vauxhall share of the car and CV market 1946–1950 — 56
15. Percentage share of total production of cars 1946–1950 — 57
16. Capital investment, Vauxhall Motors 1925–1938 — 62
17. Vauxhall profits and turnover 1929–1948 — 62
18. Profits as percentages of assets, Vauxhall, Austin and Morris 1931–1938 — 63
19. Profit per unit, Vauxhall, Morris and Austin 1931–1938 — 64
20. Dividends on preference and ordinary shares and interest on first mortgage 7 per cent debenture stock 1927–1938 — 65
21. Vauxhall exports 1908–1912 — 78
22. Vauxhall exports 1919–1930 — 79
23. Vauxhall vehicle exports 1930–1950 — 82
24. AEU membership figures for Luton 1920–1934 — 109
25. Unemployment in Luton 1920–1934 — 110
26. AEU membership figures for Luton 1933–1950 — 126
27. Comparison of numerical and percentage rise of AEU membership in Luton and Coventry 1934–1940 — 127
28. NUVB membership in Luton 1916–1958 — 128
29. Population of Luton in relation to national growth 1821–1951 — 138
30. Population and workforce of Luton 1911, 1921 and 1931 — 139
31. Size of major non-hat firms in Luton to 1914 — 142
32. Unemployment in Luton 1920–1924 — 145

33. Insured and occupied workforce in Luton 1901–1948   146
34. Size of Luton firms 1919–1950   147
35. The five largest firms in Luton 1900–1950   148
36. Birth-place of total Luton population 1945   149
37. Bedfordshire district index of wages in BEEA firms   167
38. Local negotiations of the BEEA 1937–1949   168
39. Vauxhall production, exports, employees and site acreage 1950–1970   178
40. Main Vauxhall car models 1948–1970   181
41. Vauxhall net profit (after tax) and total sales figures 1952–1970   192
42. 'Equivalent' motor vehicles produced per employee per annum 1955–1976   192
43. Strikes and man hours lost 1962–1964   193
44. Luton population 1951   198
45. Luton profile by sector and occupation 1951 and 1961   199
46. Days lost in car manufacturing 1974–1983   205
47. Vauxhall vehicle sales, profits after tax and total employees 1970–1989   208
48. Percentage share of the British car market of the main producers 1970–1989   209
49. Vauxhall output per employee 1984–2000   216
50. Vauxhall net profit, market share, employees and output 1990–2000   217
51. Sectoral structure of Luton 1981–2000   225

Charts

1. Vauxhall's new sales organisation 1929   71
2. Potential sales prospects for Bedford light trucks, GM-style market analysis 1929   72

Acknowledgements

In writing such a history of an important company and town one is conscious
of relying on the knowledge and cooperation of many people. I would like to
record my appreciation for the help given by Mr. Glyn Davies, Vauxhall Press
Officer until his retirement in 1981, who made available the Reports to the
Directors and many Vauxhall publications housed in the archives.

I must also express gratitude to Mr. Eric Wooding, Director of the Mid-
Anglian Engineering Employers' Association, for allowing me access to the
archives of the Association and also for his invaluable advice and comments.
Mr. H.K. Mitchell allowed permission to view the Engineering Employers'
Federation National Archives at Broadway House, where Lilly Cartwright and
her staff were ever-pleasant guides through the labyrinth of microfilm and
written material. Likewise I am grateful to the librarians and archivists of the
Amalgamated Union of Engineering Workers at Peckham Road, and of the
Trades Union Congress, at Congress House.

Mr. Brook, Librarian of the Vintage and Veteran Car Club, and members
gave enthusiastic advice on the technical merits of Vauxhall vehicles before
1930 and readily made available the library and archives at the club headquarters in Ashwell, Herts. Richard Storey, Archivist of the Modern Records
Centre, University of Warwick, kindly informed me of the existence of the
Young Papers, which contain correspondence between A.P. Young and Sir
Charles Bartlett.

Much local information was gleaned from Luton Chamber of Commerce
archives, for which I am grateful to Mr. P.A. Hoskins, Secretary-General, for
permission to peruse the early minutes and the journals. Particularly helpful
were the staffs of Luton Reference Library and Luton Museum, who made
available to me the extensive local collections. Miss Pat Bell and staff did
likewise in the Bedfordshire County Records Office, Bedford.

Much of this book rests on the memories of ex-Vauxhall employees whose
names are recorded in the Bibliography. Insights on local matters, particularly
the hat trade, were given by Dr. J.G. Dony, an acknowledged expert on the
Straw Trade and the history of Luton itself.

I am much indebted to the Car Workers' Group, which met at the London
School of Economics in the 1980s, and whose members researched industrial
relations in the motor vehicle industry. Particular thanks are due to Dave
Lyddon for his help on the National Union of Vehicle Builders, Adrian
Thornhill for his advice concerning references to Vauxhall in the Engineering
Employers' Federation Archives, Paul Thompson of Essex University for
advice on the use of oral sources, Richard Whiting of Leeds University for
sending me proofs of his now published work on Cowley, Oxford; Howard
Gospel of the University of Kent for allowing me the use of his own files on
Vauxhall, and particularly Steve Tolliday of King's College, Cambridge, for

reading the drafts of the thesis and offering invaluable advice on the chapters referring to industrial relations.

Thanks also to my external tutor of the original thesis, Professor Roy Church of the University of East Anglia, and to Dr. Tony Aldgate, my internal tutor at the Open University.

For the latter part of the book which takes the Luton Vauxhall story up to the present I would also like to thank Bryan Millin, Editor of *The Vauxhall Mirror* and Internal Communications Manager, Vauxhall Motors. Of immense help was Dennis Sherer, Vauxhall Archivist and photographer, who not only furnished me with many magnificent pictures of Vauxhall throughout the 20th century but provided an inordinate amount of data on prices of model types.

At Luton Borough Council I would also like to thank Paul Barton and Stuart Cuff of the Department of Environment and Regeneration for their knowledge and advice.

Particular acknowledgement is due to Gordon Vowles who, as editor of the Bedfordshire Historical Record Series, provided immense help and advice in the processes leading towards this book. Also particular appreciation goes to James Collett-White of the Bedfordshire County Records Office for his unstinting faith in my work and his encouragement.

I would also like to thank Margaret Spence, Leicester Business School Secretary, who provided an excellent secretarial service which has saved me an enormous amount of time and effort.

I also add my thanks and appreciation of the efforts of Sylvia Woods in compiling the index, a task that requires an inordinate amount of concentration and skill.

Finally, enormous gratitude to my wife whose help and encouragement have made me conscious of the reasons why so many writers praise their wives after such projects.

Dr. Len Holden
Leicester Business School
De Montfort University
Leicester

October 2002

Abbreviations

AEU	Amalgamated Engineering Union
ASE	Amalgamated Society of Engineers
AUEW	Amalgamated Union of Engineering Workers
BEEA	Bedfordshire Engineering Employers' Association
BLMC	British Leyland Motor Corporation
BL	British Leyland
CEO	Chief Executive Officer
CKD	Completely knocked down parts of cars
CV	Commercial Vehicle
EEC	European Economic Community
EEF	Engineering Employer's Federation
EU	European Union
GM	General Motors
GMAC	General Motors Acceptance Corporation
GMOO	General Motors Overseas Operations
HP/hp	horse power
IBC	Isuzu Bedford Corporation
MAC	Management Advisory Committee
MD	Managing Director
NUMMI	New United Motor Manufacturing Incorporated
NUVB	National Union of Vehicle Builders
OPEC	Organisation of Petroleum Exporting Countries
PIAE	*Proceedings of the Institute of Automobile Engineers*
PIPE	*Proceedings of the Institute of Production Engineers*
PRO	Public Record Office
TGWU	Transport and General Workers' Union

Introduction

The main theme of this work is the history of Vauxhall Motors and its impact on Luton in the 20th century. An earlier volume in this series (*Strawopolis*, by Stephen Bunker) explored the relationship of the hat trade with Luton in the 19th century, and this volume takes further the theme of one dominant industry and its impact on the local economy.

When I first began researching and writing about Vauxhall Motors and Luton back in the late 1970s and early 1980s, Luton and its environs was still very much dominated by Vauxhall and its plants at Luton and Dunstable. Since being asked to extend that work, which was completed in 1983 and took the Vauxhall story up to the 1950s, Vauxhall and Luton have changed considerably. I ended my thesis by stating that the aims of the New Industries Committee of the late 1890s had not been fulfilled. They wanted Luton to move away from reliance on one trade, that of hats, and to diversify into other industries so that the people and economy of Luton would not be at the mercy of the shocks to which the millinery trade was prone. Bouts of unemployment had caused hardship for hat employees and those reliant on the trade. As a result the whole town entered into recession, causing misery and difficulties for many Lutonians and the populace in the surrounding area. The New Industries Committee was to prevent this from happening by encouraging other industries to come to the town and provide work so that recessions in one trade would not have such a devastating impact.

The New Industries Committee set about encouraging emerging industries, one of which was Vauxhall, to locate to Luton. Vauxhall and other companies (notably Electrolux, SKF, George Kent, Hayward-Tyler and Laporte Chemicals) became important industries to the town's development. As we are aware, Vauxhall became a massive success story and bolstered the town's prosperity considerably, causing it to grow enormously. By the 1960s concerns were once again being expressed that Luton was becoming a 'one industry town' with the predominance of vehicle production. The local authorities addressed their attention to encouraging diversification. Meanwhile Vauxhall, along with the rest of the motor vehicle industry, began to experience the first shocks of the oil crisis in the 1970s. The increased intensity of competition with many new car-producing nations entering the market led the company to develop new strategies. The obvious one was to globalise operations, initially into regions and then into an international network of production plants and global markets. The success of the Cavalier (Vauxhall's first attempt at a 'world car' – 'J' car) was one enormous step towards this.

Meanwhile other industries in Luton were experiencing similar pressures. Electrolux has moved most of its manufacturing facilities overseas, SKF has been subsumed under several companies since then and has reduced its presence in Luton, and Brown Bouvri, now also part of an industrial giant, has long since diminished in the local business environment. By the 1990s it looked as though Luton Borough Council's concerns were being addressed by forces beyond their control – globalisation.

Vauxhall remains important to the town albeit with a reduced presence. Luton itself has diversified and there has been a considerable growth in service industries, such as Luton Airport, Luton University and an amazing variety of small business concerns. Thus we have seen in the space of 30 years the transformation of the town, once reliant on motor vehicle production, now diversified into many smaller concerns. This may cause consternation for opposite reasons. Will these concerns be able to sustain the Luton economy into the 21st century? With unemployment being recorded in Luton as the highest in the county of Bedfordshire at nearly 4 per cent this may well require larger industries to be attracted into Luton once more. Whatever the outcome, as I write in 2002 I am sure that Luton will survive and indeed prosper as it has done in the past. Perhaps this modest history will serve to give instruction to the Local Authority, concerned local bodies and others that a template for Luton's growth had already been made over one hundred years ago. Is it time to dust it off for another revamp?

The majority of this book is devoted to the history of Luton and Vauxhall to the 1950s and the careful reader will note that the last two chapters that bring the story up to the present day are much shorter and therefore less detailed. I apologise for this in advance but the General Editor of the Bedfordshire Historical Record Society, Gordon Vowles, was conscious of the importance of Vauxhall to Luton and that its decline could equally have a considerable impact, albeit negatively. These last chapters then serve to bring the story up to date as the ceasing of car production this year (in March 2002) at the Luton plant has meant a significant end to an important period in Luton's, and indeed Vauxhall's, history.

The development of the motor vehicle industry in the 20th century has proved to be of great importance to both the British economy and the economies of the major industrialised nations of the world. Vauxhall Motors has played a significant part in that growth and occupies a place as one of the largest vehicle manufacturers in Britain. It is surprising, therefore, that the development of the company has not, hitherto, been the subject of detailed research. Consequently, the main objective of this study is to attempt to remedy this omission. Several books have been published on the history of the company which emphasise the technical developments of car and commercial vehicle design. While a history of Vauxhall cannot ignore these aspects, particular emphasis in this study has been placed on the economics of vehicle production: finance, marketing, management and labour relations, and the impact of Vauxhall's growth on the development of the local economy. Chapter 1 is concerned with the origins and growth of Vauxhall until 1925, and attempts to analyse the reasons for the company's initial success in the years before the First World War and its financial troubles, which eventually led to its acquisition by General Motors in 1925.

Chapter 2 examines the takeover by General Motors and endeavours to show the relationship of the new owners to the British subsidiary and the consequent effects on the character and development of Vauxhall with special reference to the amount of autonomy which the parent company accorded to Vauxhall.

Chapter 3 charts the expansion of Vauxhall in the 1930s and 1940s, and an attempt is made to explain how and why it entered into the ranks of the six largest vehicle producers in Britain, collectively known as the 'Big Six'. A more detailed examination is undertaken in Chapter 4 of the financial, marketing and export performance of the company, reinforcing the analysis in Chapter 3. Chapters 5 and 6 are devoted exclusively to management–labour relations and are divided into developments before and after 1929. The controversial period before 1929 is closely examined and involves an analysis of the management's sudden change of policy towards the workforce which coincided with the company's withdrawal from the Engineering Employers' Federation in 1921. These developments offer the opportunity to evaluate the theory that has categorised those changes as representing a move by managers towards securing direct control over the workforce.

The post-1929 period has been entitled the 'Bartlett Years', and Chapter 6 explores the reason why Vauxhall had such tranquil industrial relations during Charles Bartlett's period as Managing Director. Vauxhall's labour relations after 1929, a period of relative tranquillity, also raise the question of job control and trade union policies

Chapters 7 and 8 consider the development of Vauxhall Motors in the context of the Luton economy. Chapter 7 examines the growth of Luton from the 19th century, when the hat trade grew to become the dominant industry, leading Luton Town Council and the Chamber of Commerce to promote diversification of the town's economic base in order to escape from excessive reliance upon an industry which predominantly employed female labour. The creation of a New Industries Committee succeeded in attracting engineering industries, including that of Vauxhall, and an assessment of its impact on the local economy is undertaken, in particular regard to its effects on female labour.

Chapter 8 considers the influence of Vauxhall on the policies of other local employers, for example the effects on trade union organisation and upon wages and conditions between 1930 and 1950.

In the second part of the book Chapters 9 and 10 bring the Vauxhall story up to date. They describe the predominance of the company's influence from the 1950s through to the ebbing of its influence as the company gradually cut back its factory sites and workforce. With the cessation of Vectra car assembly in 2002 so ended nearly 100 years of car production in Luton. An attempt is made in the final chapter to draw the strands of the main themes together to make an overview of the Vauxhall–Luton story and pose some questions for the future.

PART ONE

Chapter One

The Evolution of Vauxhall: The 1890s to 1925

The pattern of development of Vauxhall Motors epitomises the growth of much capitalist enterprise, starting as a small company owned and run by one man, growing into a limited company; thence into a subsidiary of a multi-national organisation. The continuity of the firm remains only in the associations of the name 'Vauxhall.' In this chapter the process of change in the nature and size of the company will be examined, outlining the reasons for Vauxhall Motors' success up to 1919. In addition an analysis will be made as to why the company ran into difficulties in the 1920s which eventually led to its acquisition by General Motors in 1925.

In 1857 Alexander Wilson, a Scottish engineer, founded Alex. Wilson and Company to produce marine engines used in river tugs and pinnaces (a large row boat, usually eight oared and part of a warship, driven by steam and then petrol engines from the 19th century) for which it gained a number of Admiralty contracts.[1] The firm was located near the River Thames at Wandsworth Road, Lambeth, close to Vauxhall Gardens and Vauxhall Bridge, and was thus known locally as the Vauxhall Works. By the 1880s and the 1890s Wilson had diversified into the production of dry air refrigeration plant, used for large scale storage, and donkey engines for boiler water feeders.

Despite Wilson's ability as an engineer he was weak on the financial and managerial side of the business.

> Wilson's desk, according to one of his employees, was usually a mass of papers which nobody dared tidy or disturb. Old envelopes and the backs of letters were used for making notes and rough engineering drawings, and were stuffed into Wilson's pockets for further reference.[2]

The Vauxhall Iron Works was an example of enterprise run by capable engineers, unconscious of the growing importance of financial and managerial techniques. It was, however, a small firm employing no more than 150 men in the 1880s.[3]

In the early 1890s the firm ran into difficulties and the receiver, appointed a

---

[1] There are no records of this company and information rests heavily on the memory of T.W. Holtom, who served with the company and the subsequent Vauxhall Company from 1888 to 1938. His early accounts are to be found in L.C. Derbyshire *The Story of Vauxhall 1857–1946* (Luton, 1946) and 'Early Memories of Vauxhall,' *Luton Saturday Telegraph*, 23 November 1935, p. 6.

[2] Quoted in K. Ullyett, *The Vauxhall Companion* (Stanley Paul, 1971), p. 16.

[3] Derbyshire, op. cit., p. 9.

Plate 2. The first Vauxhall motor car 1903, a 5hp model driven by Vauxhall Managing Director W. Gardner (left) and A.E. Ash, also a Board director.

Mr. John Chambers, an engineer, to run the firm. In 1892 Vauxhall became a limited company and a Mr. William Gardner took the position of Joint Managing Director with Chambers while Alexander Wilson remained on the Board for another two years.[4] In 1894 Wilson left and set up as a consulting

---

[4] Derbyshire, op. cit., p. 9. Neither Companies House nor the *Investors' Monthly Manual* have any

engineer in Fenchurch Street, London. Two years later the company was reformed and renamed the Vauxhall Iron Works Co. Ltd. and it was essentially this Board which was to take the company into car manufacture.[5]

Under the Memorandum of Agreement the Wilson Company was purchased for £9,480 which also meant paying off Wilson's outstanding debts.[6] The nominal capital of the company was to be £20,000 divided into £1 shares, but in April only 9,000 had been taken up by the public and 10,000 in July.[7] Even by 1901 only 18,000 of the £20,000 issue had been taken up.[8] Chambers and Gardner owned over a quarter of the shares, although a Robert Everett, a chartered accountant, was the major shareholder with 4,170.[9] Much of the subsequent capital of the firm was to be accumulated internally and very slowly, in a rather similar fashion to that of Standard Motors. In many respects this was not a disadvantage as many early car companies tended to become rapidly over capitalised and consequently ran into difficulties when the market contracted, as in the case of Argyll and Humber. The most significant, if untypical, case was that of Harry Lawson and the comparatively huge capitalisation of the Daimler Motor Company and its eventual collapse in 1902.[10] Interestingly, Daimler produced marine engines and tested prototype petrol engines in river launches before installing them in cars[11] as Vauxhall was to do under the engineering guidance of Frank William Hodges. Like William Gardner, Hodges was an ex-apprentice of Alex Wilson, and it was he who obtained a car which was thoroughly examined with the idea of producing an independent and improved design. The faith of Hodges in his own work was sufficient for him to purchase over 3,000 Vauxhall shares, acquire a position on the Board of Directors and take up the appointment of Chief of the Drawing Office and Principal assistant to the Works Managing Director, at a salary of £100 per annum.[12]

Tests of a petrol engine in a river launch led to the production of a prototype engine in 1902. The 1-cylinder engine proved satisfactory enough for it to be put into a light car chassis in 1903.[13] This light car was in effect a voiturette, or four-wheeled cycle car. Nevertheless, Autocar described it as 'neat, efficient and cheap . . . which should find many friends.'[14] It cost £150. Interestingly, Vauxhall was never to mass produce a car below 10hp, and yet it began production at the lightest end of the market.

record of this company and Derbyshire has once more been used. The PRO, BT 31 file has no record of this company either.

[5] Vauxhall Iron Works Co. Ltd., Articles of Association, 31 March 1896. PRO, BT 31, 15593. Co. no., 47433.

[6] Memorandum of Agreement, 9 April 1898. PRO, BT 31, 15030.

[7] Nominal Capital Statement, 31 March 1896, PRO, BT 31, 15593; Memorandum of Agreement, ibid.; Summary of Capital and Shares, 31 July 1896, ibid.

[8] Summary of Capital and Shares, 21 February 1901, Ibid.

[9] Ibid., Summary of Capital and Shares, 31 July 1896.

[10] S.B. Saul, 'The Motor Industry in Britain to 1914,' Business History V (1962), p. 31.

[11] David Burgess Wise, 'Daimler: Limousines Fit for Kings and Nobility,' The World of Automobiles: An Illustrated Encyclopaedia of the Motor Car (no date: late 1970s), p. 1484.

[12] Hodges took up the post in 1898. Special Resolution, 28 March 1898, PRO, BT 31. He purchased shares in 1901. Summary of Capital and Shares, 21 February 1901, PRO, BT 31 file.

[13] Derbyshire, op. cit., pp. 10 and 11.

[14] Autocar, 31 October 1903, pp. 536–9.

Vauxhall entered the motor vehicle industry at a time when a large number of firms were starting up. Between 1901 and 1905 over 220 firms were founded of which only 22 were to be still in existence by 1914.[15] In many respects its very survival after the failure of so many car companies can be said to have been an achievement in itself.

Five basic reasons lay behind the company's success: firstly, a steady but not over extended rate of capital accumulation and expansion of productive capacity; secondly, a balanced managerial board and management staff, ensuring the co-operation of engineering skill and commercial expertise; thirdly, a solid engineering background which virtually enabled the total production of engine and chassis; fourthly, adaptability to changing market conditions; and, fifthly, the inestimable influence of Laurence H. Pomeroy.

The first factor: has already been partly examined and we have seen that slow capital accumulation was not a problem peculiar to Vauxhall. In fact, investors were often suspicious of a new industry such as motor vehicle manufacture, and the example of Daimler was a reminder of the possible dangers of such 'follies.' As late as 1907 financial journals were warning investors of the problems of over production in the car industry.[16] Slowness of capital accumulation was therefore a result of depending heavily on internal expansion.

Of the twelve owners of the 18,000 Vauxhall shares, the five largest share-holders were the directors, owning 14,720 shares between them, who also held managerial posts in the firm.[17]

In 1904 the firm issued 6 per cent preference shares at £1 each and by the end of the year 3,000 had been taken up, of which Rudolph Selz, an engineer, and a coal and iron master named John Lancaster, had 1,000 each.[18]

A fundamental development took place in the following year when Vauxhall amalgamated with the West Hydraulic Company. The capital was increased from £20,000 to £30,000, but that the increased issue was not readily taken up is evidenced by the fact that a debenture of £15,000 was taken out in July, with the obvious intent of financing the move from London to Luton, to share the West Hydraulic's premises there.[19]

It would be interesting at this point to ask the question why Vauxhall decided to move from London to Luton. According to T.W. Holtom, the lack of space at the Lambeth works was an important factor.[20] The West Hydraulic Company owned 6 acres of land, of which three were offered to Vauxhall, a significant increase on the quarter acre plot allocated to car production at the London works. Although the plot was not to be fully used until after the First World War, immediate expansion could take place in a modest way. In addition reorganisation of production along more efficient lines was possible,

---

[15] S.B. Saul, op. cit., table I, p. 23.
[16] See for example *Investors' Chronicle* (November 1907), p. 231.
[17] PRO, BT 31: Summary of Capital and Shares, 21 February 1901. These directors were Chambers, £2,000 shares; Everett, £4,170; Gardner, £2,600; Hodges, £3,000 and Rudolph Selz, £3,000, also an engineer who joined the firm in December 1900 and was appointed a director and an assistant manager.
[18] Ibid.: Preference Share Certificates, 25 February 1904, 18 July 1904.
[19] Ibid.: Debenture Certificate, 12 July 1905.
[20] Op. cit., *Luton Saturday Telegraph*, 23 November 1935.

Plate 3. 1903 5hp four seater – price 130 guineas.

with separate workshops for each stage: including an engine shop, a fitting shop, test benches and a frame shop. A running shop, a pattern shop and a body, trimming and paintshop were also planned.[21] At this time, however, the Vauxhall coach work was custom made by Messrs. Morgan and Company of Long Acre,[22] a general practice in the car industries at this time.

Cheaper rates of pay for labour was another possible factor in the move. A Guildford firm (probably Dennis Motors) had moved from London for this reason and had influenced Vauxhall to do likewise.[23] Shortly after its arrival in Luton Vauxhall was plunged into a dispute involving the Amalgamated Society of Engineers, which was demanding extra payment for night shift work. Alfred Ash, the works manager, was the major spokesman for the firm at the Engineering Employers – ASE tribunal held at York.[24] From this dispute we learn that the West Hydraulic Company had been paying time and a half in Bradford, and had abolished that practice on moving to Luton in 1903. The Luton New Industries Committee mentioned in trade journals the lower wage rates of the district, coupled with a lack of unionism, as specific attractions for firms moving to the town.[25] *The Engineer* also mentions 'high wages' as a strong reason for Vauxhall and other London companies to 'move

[21] *The Engineer*, 31 March 1905; *Luton News*, 30 March 1905, p. 3 col. 1.
[22] Mentioned in numerous advertisements in *Autocar*, 1904.
[23] *Luton News Supplement on Industry*, 26 March 1964, p. 4. No source is indicated by the writer.
[24] Engineering Employers' Federation Archives, May 1905: Microfilm ref. N (2) 7.
[25] Thomas Keens, 'Luton as an Industrial Centre,' *Engineering*, 13 April 1900, p. 10.

Plate 4. 1905 visit to Vauxhall, Luton. This shows the first three Vauxhall cars produced.

from the Metropolis.'[26] In 1906 Commercial Cars moved from London to Luton where it also achieved comparable growth to that of Vauxhall in the pre-1914 period.[27]

The New Industries Committee proclaimed reduced rates as an additional incentive to move to Luton, as well as cheap electricity (Luton was an early town to have electrification), cheap gas, and the availability of sidings on the main London-Midland railway.[28] Other towns offered some of the favourable conditions but the shared site was probably the main attraction for Vauxhall.

One intriguing question must be asked. Why did a marine engine firm move to a town which was not on or near a navigable river? There are no documents available which answer this. The Grand Union canal passed through neighbouring Leighton Buzzard but Vauxhall did not choose to move there. It seems likely that the distance from navigable waterways was not important. Many Midland firms such as Humber and Daimler in Coventry produced marine engines without their works being located near large or navigable rivers. The engines could be bench tested and taken by railway to their customers. The Vauxhall works had its own railway sidings off the main London–Midland line.

T.W. Holtom informs us that by 1905 the company felt it was making too many different products 'and this diversity did not work out too well.'[29] We must assume that they were unsure which direction the firm was going to take. In that year the company formally amalgamated with the West Hydraulic to form the Vauxhall and West Hydraulic Company Ltd, and the Board was increased from six to nine.[30]

This meant that cars, pumps, refrigerator equipment and hydraulic machinery was being produced as well as marine engines. The solution to the problem was to legally separate the car side of the business in 1907 to form Vauxhall Motors Limited.[31] The Vauxhall management was uncertain on which products to concentrate in those early erratic days of the car industry; they did not want to put all their eggs into one basket. Events proved that the future lay with motor cars and by 1908 the Vauxhall and West Hydraulic parent company had had its capital reduced in value from £50,000 to £25,000.[32] The company limped on through the First World War but was finally wound up in 1918; the only two directors left being William Gardner, of the original Vauxhall Iron Works, and Benjamin Todhunter, one of the original owners of the West Hydraulic works.[33] That the original firm's product, marine engines, faded because it moved to Luton is doubtful. The more likely explanation is that the car side became comparatively more successful. By 1911 marine engines were only built

[26] *The Engineer*, 31 March 1905, vol. XCIX, no. 2570.
[27] The Empire Trade League, *Progressive Luton* (Luton, 1933), p. 19; *Luton News*, 17 August 1911, p. 7 col. 4.
[28] Thomas Keens, ibid., p. 3.
[29] T.S. Holtom, 'Memories of Vauxhall: Part Two,' *Luton Saturday Telegraph*, 3 April 1936, p. 7.
[30] PRO, BT 31: Special Resolution, 17 April 1905.
[31] *The Times*, 15 April 1907, p. 14 col. 1. The announcement is the only contemporary documentation available of this separation. Vauxhall themselves have no record, and the Companies House Vauxhall file only begins in 1914, when the motor car side was reconstituted once again. The PRO Vauxhall file does not contain references to this either.
[32] PRO, BT 31: Affidavit to Reduce Capital, 11 November 1908.
[33] Ibid.: Special Resolution, 9 July 1918; Return of the Final Winding Up Meeting, 24 Sept. 1919.

Plate 5. 1906 18hp model. The first serious offering from the now Luton based Vauxhall factory.

to order and they were advertised with designs and estimates for aeronautical engines, not a side of the business that developed.[34]

The formation of Vauxhall Motors in 1907 gave a balanced leadership to the company for the first time. Leslie Walton was appointed Chairman and Joint Managing Director with Percy Kidner. Walton was very much a financial man. He was born in 1882 in Croydon, and was educated at Eton, after which he received commercial training in a private bank in the City of London. He later joined his father's business as a hop merchant before taking up his Vauxhall posts.[35] He owed his position not only to his financial experience but also because he was a major shareholder.[36] Percy Kidner had joined the Vauxhall Iron Works in London in 1903, had purchased 2,000 preferential shares, and had replaced John Chambers as Joint Managing Director after Chamber's resignation from the firm in that year.[37] He was an engineer and later became a works driver in competitions. The other major force on the Board was Frank Hodges, who was appointed Consulting Engineer.[38] It was Kidner and Hodges who undoubtedly pushed the motor car side of the firm before forming the separate company for this purpose. This breed of men strove for engineering

[34] *Vauxhall Motor Carriages*, Vauxhall Motors catalogue (Luton, 1911), p. 60.
[35] *Who's Who in the Motor Trade*, ed. P. Peters and H. Thornton Rutter (1934), p. 155.
[36] Although no evidence has been unearthed as to how many shares he owned at this time, *The Car Super Excellent*, Vauxhall Motors (1914) Ltd. indicates a large holding.
[37] PRO, BT 31: Register of Directors, 28 December 1903.
[38] Derbyshire, op. cit., p. 18.

Plate 6. F.W. Hodges, Chief Engineer and designer of the early Vauxhall models until he was replaced by Laurence Pomeroy.

worthiness but like the relationship between Rolls and Royce, Walton, the businessman, attempted to keep them on the road of solvency and profitability. Both types of specialist were needed, and unfortunately too many car firms placed much emphasis on engineering excellence rather than vehicle production as a viable commercial venture.[39]

Royce in his search for technical perfection was constantly holding up the flow of production, and was removed to a small research establishment. Lanchester's ideas, though excellent, were often too far in advance of commercial developments within the industry. Hodges was not in the class of such men as Royce and Lanchester. Under his engineering leadership 'the company had been making cars of no particular distinction.'[40] Table 1 overleaf hints at this change of engineering style from 1906 onwards when Laurence H. Pomeroy's influence on the firm begins.

Despite the pedestrian qualities of Hodges cars they proved to be profitable for the company. The price of the early voiturettes, ranging between £150 and

[39] Saul, op. cit., p. 41.
[40] Kent Karslake and Laurence Pomeroy (Jnr.), *From Veteran to Vintage* (1956), p. 86.

Plate 7. 1908 12–16hp Vauxhall. First car to make a nonstop run of 2,000 miles. Percy Kidner (left), Vauxhall director and trials driver, described by Maurice Platt as 'opinionated, inflexible, robustly extrovert, not particularly intelligent but a motor enthusiast'. A.J. Hancock (right), although adept at road trials and racing, was not suited to the routine of factory management. Both men resigned from the Vauxhall Board in 1927 after strong disagreements with the new American owners.

Table 1. Vauxhall Models 1903–1913[41]

Year	Year ceased	Name/Type	HP	Cyls.	Price
1903	1904	—	5	1	£150
1904	1905	—	6	1	£150
	1908	12/14	12	3	£375
1905	1905	—	7/9	3	—
	1907	—	18	4	£475
1906	1908	12/16	21	4	£375
	1907	—	9	3	—
1907	1907	12/14	16.8	4	—
1908	1910	12/16	21	4	£350
	1911	A09	20	4	£465
	1911	B09	16	4	£390
1910	1910	B10	27	6	£535
	1912	A11	20	4	£525
	1912	B11	29	6	£665
1911	1912	C10	20	4	£485
1912	1912	S	20	4	—
	1913	A12	20	4	—
	1915	'Prince Henry'	25	4	£565
	1915	A	16/20	4	(£375)
	1916	B12	35	6	£650
	1922	D	25	4	£465
1913	1915	E	30/98	4	

[41] 'Vauxhall Facts and Figures' (Vauxhall Motors, 1966).

£375, suggests that the company was aiming at the professional class, which at the time was the lower end of the market. One of Vauxhall's first recorded customers was a doctor.[42] At the Olympia Show of 1905, 434 types of car were displayed, at an average price of £600 with the most expensive costing £2,500.[43] The Edwardian car market and the growth of engineering knowledge soon influenced Hodges to build more elaborate and larger cars. The market demand was dominated by the wealthy who mostly regarded motoring as a leisure and sporting pursuit, and wanted good performance and ostentation rather than economy. Body work was becoming increasingly heavy as tops, sides and windscreens were fitted, resulting in the need for stronger chassis and more powerful engines. One notable failure which originated in an attempt to cater for the upper class market was based on an idea by Lord Ranfurly. A hansom cab body was imposed on a 5hp chassis, and the chauffeur was to be seated at the back of the vehicle exposed to the elements, while his employers rode in comfort in the cab section.[44]

More significantly, Hodges produced the 3-cylinder 12/14 model, which priced at £375 was a £225 increase and heralded the departure from the inexpensive light car class.

Once Vauxhall had settled in Luton, towards the end of 1905 a 4-cylinder 18hp model was produced, priced at £475, and in the following year a 21hp 12/16 came on the market. After this time Vauxhall rarely produced a car below 20hp until the First World War.

While Hodges was not a great innovator he did succeed in adapting to the changing market and incorporated some of the new features which were constantly being introduced by the industry. In 1906 the 12/16, with a 4-cylinder engine, was basically a new design. It was in the main the work of L.H. Pomeroy, a man whose engineering design skill was to elevate Vauxhall from a run of the mill car producer to a firm with an enviable reputation.

Laurence Henry Pomeroy was born in 1883, and became apprentice at the age of 16 to the North London Locomotive Works in Bow; simultaneously he commenced a four year engineering course at East London Technical College. In 1903 he won a Whitworth Exhibition, and by the age of 20 'he had a formidable knowledge of mathematics, science and engineering.'[45] In searching for early jobs he found his academic qualifications of little account, and it was not until he mentioned that he was capable of working in the shops if necessary that he found himself acceptable.[46] After working briefly with a London civil engineering firm and a Basingstoke vehicle company, he took up a post at Vauxhall in 1905 as a junior draughtsman, and in 1906 was promoted to assistant chief engineer to Hodges. Vauxhall's strong tradition of building and designing engines enabled the firm to attract such a talent as Pomeroy's and allow it scope to develop. Many other car firms at this time were simply assembly plants.[47] The first fillip which

---

[42] Letter to *Autocar*, May 1904. Quoted in Derbyshire, op. cit., p. 13.
[43] Karslake and Pomeroy, op. cit., p. 53.
[44] Derbyshire, op. cit., p. 12.
[45] Karslake and Pomeroy, op. cit., p. 85.
[46] Karslake and Pomeroy, op. cit., p. 85.
[47] 'Argyll, Dennis and Clement cars bought their engines from Aster and White and Poppe, for

Plate 8. Laurence Pomeroy at the wheel of a prototype Prince Henry in Lynmouth, Devon, probably in 1908.

Pomeroy gave to Vauxhall's fortunes was in 1908 when a new car was needed to enter the 2,000 mile RAC Trials. Hodges, the chief engineer, 'was away in Egypt' and Pomeroy was not slow to seize the opportunity presented to him. By the time of Hodges return, Pomeroy's design was well on the way to completion but 'not without opposition from many of the older members of the firm.'[48] The car went on to win the trial for its class, and earned the distinction of the least stoppages of all cars in any class. The next lowest to the 20hp Vauxhall was the Rolls-Royce 'Silver Ghost.' *The Auto Motor Journal* summed up by saying; 'That the 1908 performance brought the 20hp Vauxhall a comparatively uninteresting background into the full glare of public interest.'[49] The opposition within the firm was no doubt quelled by the fact that Percy Kidner, the Joint Managing Director, drove the car in the trial and from this time it appears that Kidner, Pomeroy and A.J. Hancock pushed the old members of the firm, such as Hodges and Ash, into the background.

Alfred Hancock came from a similar background to that of Pomeroy. He was born in 1884, attended St. Olave's Grammar School, London and the Borough Polytechnic, and was apprenticed for five years at the Vauxhall Iron Works. Under the tutelage of Kidner and Pomeroy he was to emerge as the main works driver for Vauxhall and participated in over 120 races both

example, and merely produced the chassis. Singer and Norris also began in a similar fashion': Saul, op. cit., pp. 34 and 35.

[48] Derbyshire, op. cit., p. 19.

[49] Quoted in Karslake and Pomeroy, op. cit., p. 87.

Plate 9. 1911 C-type Prince Henry, the Pomeroy designed car that helped build Vauxhall's early reputation.

nationally and internationally. In 1914 he was appointed General Works Manager, the post previously held by Hodges.[50]

In the next six years Pomeroy produced two outstanding vehicles based on the development of the 20hp car of 1908. They were the C-type, also known as the Prince Henry, and the 30/98. The technical advances in the industry were rapid from 1907 onwards, and by 1914 the car had much more in common with the model of 1934 than it had with the design of 1904.[51] The 30/98 though first built in 1913 is regarded as a vintage rather than a veteran car as the major part of production took place in the years after the First World War. It remained in production in various forms until 1926, strongly rivalling Bentley products.

Pomeroy was regarded as 'one of the most influential engineers in the industry',[52] and therefore comparable with Lanchester and Royce, but his closest rival was Louis Coatalen of Sunbeam in terms of racing designs and prowess. Both men had a fundamental influence on the direction and development of their firms, creating a respected marque through reputations gained in competitions. Both firms expanded as a result of the excellence of their designers. Table 2 illustrates the expansion of Vauxhall, which was marked from 1909.

[50] *Who's Who in the Motor Trade*, ed. P. Peters and H. Thornton Rutter (1934), p. 63.
[51] Karslake and Pomeroy, op. cit., p. 5.
[52] N. Seth-Smith, *The Long Haul: A Social History of the British Commercial Vehicle Industry* (1975), p. 109.

Plate 10. Laurence Pomeroy, the brilliant and far-sighted engineer who designed the Prince Henry and the 30–98hp Vauxhall.

The fivefold increase between 1907 and 1913 seems impressive. Although one of the 29 major car producers, Vauxhall's output was small.[53]

[53] Sunbeam's output was as follows:

Year	Output	
1909	100	
1910	515	
1911	853	
1912	2,350	
1913	1,700	Source: Saul, op. cit., p. 29.

The steep rise in Sunbeam's output between 1909 and 1910, and its continuing increase, is attributed to Coatalen's 12–16hp model: Saul, ibid., p. 29

Table 2. Total Output, Employees and Floor Area of Vauxhall: 1903–1913[54]

Year	Car output	Employees	Floor area	Output per employee
1903	43	150*	½ acre	.28+
1904	76	180*	½ acre	.42+
1905	1	180*	1 acre	change of site
1906	15	180*	1 acre	.08+
1907	69	200*	1½ acres	.34+
1908	94	250*	2 acres	.37+
1909	195	350*	2½ acres	.55+
1910	243	460*	3 acres	.52+
1911	265	500*	3 acres	.53+
1912	302	560*	4 acres	.53+
1913	387	575	4 acres	.67+

* Estimated figures (no records).
+ Calculated from columns 2 and 3.

The 'Model T' factory at Manchester had an output of 6,000 vehicles in 1913, which would have accounted for just under one-fifth of the total British vehicle output of 34,000. Wolseley was the second largest producer with 3,000, and the other leaders were Humber 2,500, Sunbeam 1,700, Rover 1,600 and Austin with 1,500 cars.[55] These six firms accounted for nearly 50 per cent of British vehicle production. Vauxhall's expansion had been slow by comparison with Sunbeam. The first Sunbeam car had been produced in 1899, four years before Hodge's 1-cylinder voiturette, but even by 1906 Sunbeam's output was only 161 cars.[56] At this time the two firms were fairly comparable in size but Sunbeam expanded rapidly after 1908. The authorised capital of Sunbeam was only £40,000 in 1905.[57]

Pomeroy's son reminds us, however, that size and output are not necessarily synonymous with profitability, and that Vauxhall 'made a net profit of about 10 per cent on the catalogue price of the car.'[58]

Table 3 indicates the annual breakdown of profits and sales before director's fees and income tax were deducted.

Table 3. Sales and Pre-Tax Profits of Vauxhall 1909–1914 and a comparison with Sunbeam[59]

Year	Sales	Profits	Capital	Sunbeam profits	Capital
1909	£89,786	£12,939	n/a	£90	n/a
1910	£120,326	£18,722	n/a	£20,700	n/a
1911	£127,539	£7,651	n/a	£41,000	n/a
1912	£176,217	£16,984	n/a	n/a	n/a
1913	£220,690	£30,868	n/a	£94,909	£120,000
1914	£260,670	£21,173	£200,000	n/a	n/a

[54] 'Vauxhall Facts and Figures' (Vauxhall Motors, 1966). There is no indication as to how these estimates were calculated.
[55] Saul, op. cit., table 3, p. 25.
[56] Saul, op. cit., table 2, p. 24.
[57] David Scott-Moncrieff, *Veteran and Edwardian Motor Cars* (Batsford, 1955), p. 156.
[58] Karslake and Pomeroy, op. cit., p. 90.
[59] Vauxhall Auditor's Report, 27 April 1914: Companies House, Vauxhall file no. 135767, for the years ending 31 December 1909–1913. Report to the Directors 1914, Vauxhall Motors Archives. Sunbeam figures are quoted in Karslake and Pomeroy, op. cit., p. 92.

Because of expenses involved in works reorganisation, profits fell in 1911. Sunbeam's profits of £94,909 in 1913 on a capital of £120,000 can only be described as spectacular, and by such comparisons Vauxhall's progress seems somewhat sluggish. Obviously concerned that it was producing below works capacity, despite the expansion and the use of modern machinery,[60] the firm was reconstituted and recapitalised in 1914 under the title of Vauxhall Motors (1914) Ltd.[61] Hodges had been more sceptical of the commercial value of sporting successes than Pomeroy and Kidner[62] but Sunbeam had pursued a competitive racing policy.

Pomeroy was aware of the means to attain efficient production. He sought to achieve this by ensuring that machinery was up to date and that work flowed well, and was organised on a card-indexing system of job allocation which involved the timing of jobs.[63]

The major reason for its lack-lustre sales performance compared with that of Sunbeam has been ascribed to lack of business acumen.[64] This is rather a vague concept and the writer does not elaborate. Vauxhall vehicles were in great demand after the success achieved by Pomeroy's cars, but they could not meet that demand. The potential works capacity was present but external capital was lacking. Vauxhall was singularly unsuccessful in attracting capital and much of its expansion was reliant on debenture issues and the ploughing back of profits, as in the case of the Vauxhall expansion of 1911. Even before reorganisation in 1914 shareholdings only amounted to £19,297 of a possible issue of £30,000.[65] A slow accumulation of capital could not be regarded as a disadvantage up to 1908, but thereafter when Vauxhall vehicles were in demand, it was a hindrance.

The Board of the reorganised company sought to rectify this position. The nominal capital of Vauxhall Motors (1914) Ltd. was issued at £200,000 in ordinary shares, of which £66,000 were to be taken in part purchase of the old company. This left £134,000 to be issued, of which £44,000 had been taken up by the directors;[66] thus was effected a considerable rise in Vauxhall's capital.

Company reorganisation was accompanied by the removal of all existing directors who were replaced by Leslie Walton, his brother Alfred, Laurence Pomeroy, and John Maitland, a banker. Walton and Kidner were the joint managing directors of the new company.[67]

Considerable optimism was expressed by the Board concerning the new venture, and projected profits for 1914 were expected to top £40,000, and be even higher in 1915.[68] The initial effects of the war were to thwart these hopes,

[60] 'A Visit to the Vauxhall Works,' *Luton News*, 2 November 1911, p. 7 cols. 4, 5 and 6; *Luton News*, 14 November 1912, p. 7 cols. 6 and 7; *The Car Super Excellent*, Catalogue of the Vauxhall Motor Carriage (Luton, 1914), pp. 43, 44 and 46.
[61] Memorandum and Articles of Association, 12 May 1914, Companies House, Vauxhall file no. 135767.
[62] K. Ullyett, *The Vauxhall Companion* (Stanley Paul, 1971), p. 54.
[63] *The Car Super Excellent*, op. cit., p. 47.
[64] S.B. Saul, 'The Motor Industry in Britain to 1914,' *Business History* V (1962), p. 34.
[65] Valuation of Vauxhall Motors Ltd., 10 March 1914, Companies House, Vauxhall file no. 135767.
[66] 'Nominal Capital Vauxhall Motors (1914) Ltd.,' 1 May 1914, Vauxhall file no. 135767.
[67] 'Articles of Association,' op. cit. in n. 61 above.
[68] *The Times*, 18 May 1914, p. 20 col. 6.

Plate 11. General Allenby's entry into Jerusalem in a Vauxhall D-type, December 1917.

despite the fact that the previous year was its most successful in racing and competitions. Profits fell to £21,173. Walton, who was appointed Chairman following Maitland's death in 1914, reported that this was mainly due to '150 men out of a staff of 700 joining the colours, and consequently the rate of production was affected.'[69] The company was saved by orders from the War Office which took Vauxhall's entire output; but only one car, the 25hp model, was to be built and used as an army staff car. In addition, the Admiralty and War Office awarded large contracts to Vauxhall for the manufacture of fuses, which was to require the equipping and building of an entire factory.[70] By 1916 all available land adjoining the works was purchased with a view to extensions.[71] In order to finance the extensions a further 100,000 ordinary shares were issued. New offices and stores were erected and extensions made to the running shop.[72] Guaranteed sales slightly higher than pre-war market prices, together with the sales resulting from the fuse department, ensured healthy profits. By the end of the war a further £100,000 of shares had been issued bringing a total £400,000; meanwhile, since 1915, shareholders had received an annual dividend of 10%.[73] Profits in 1919, however, provided an indication of the problems which Vauxhall was to face in the 1920s, as Table 4 on the following page reveals.

The 1919 downturn in profits was viewed as temporary and attributed to

[69] 'Report of the 1st Ordinary General Meeting,' *The Times*, 9 April 1915, p. 6 col. 4.
[70] Ibid., p. 6 col. 4.
[71] 'Report of the 2nd Ordinary General Meeting,' *The Times*, 14 April 1916, p. 14 col. 5.
[72] Ibid., p. 14 col. 5.
[73] Extraordinary Resolution, Nominal Capital Increase, 19 November 1919, Companies House, Vauxhall file no. 135767.

Table 4. Vauxhall Sales, Profit and Capital 1914–1929[74]

Year	Motor dept. sales £s	Fuse dept. sales £s	Issued capital	Actual profits £s	Profit on trading £s
1914	260,000	—	200,000	21,173	n/a
1915	411,584	—	200,000	56,028	n/a
1916	315,896	216,074	300,000	70,000	n/a
1917	376,579	239,135	300,000	79,327	n/a
1918	483,698	418,263	300,000	67,100	n/a
1919	595,590	50,087	400,000	25,800	
1920	812,579	—	600,000	35,222	53,179
1921	519,240	—	600,000	−221,758 (loss)	None
1922	542,127	—	600,000	−76,710 (loss)	−49,000 (loss)
1923	983,790	—	600,000	54,132	105,459
1924	1,000,528	—	600,000	50,066	101,279
1925	n/a	—	300,000*	36,082	91,283
1926	n/a	—	600,000	36	36
1927	n/a	—	668,000	−320,943 (loss)	−320,943 (loss)
1928	n/a	—	750,000	−266,340 (loss)	−195,114 (loss)
1929	n/a	—	750,000	−283,791 (loss)	−209,913 (loss)

* Capital halved into 300,000 ordinary shares @ 10 shillings each, and 300,000 Preferential shares @ 10 shillings each.

excess profit tax, the change over from war to peace time production and the loss of war contracts in the fuse department.[75]

In addition the Russian Branch, which had been opened in 1911 (after royalty and nobility had shown an interest in Vauxhall cars), lost money regularly, beginning in the revolutionary year of 1917. Finally in 1922 the Board decided to write off the sum of £18,305 as it was unable to continue trading 'in view of the present uncertain state of affairs in Russia.'[76]

The struggle for survival 1920–1925

During the First World War Vauxhall had built nearly 2,000 staff cars for the British Army, and possessed, as did the Crossley Car Company, the major advantage of having been in continuous vehicle production since 1914; reconversion seemed to present few problems which prompted considerable optimism for future prospects. Far from such hopes being realised however, the company began to sink deeply into financial crisis from 1921, and by the middle 1920s the firm's continued existence was under threat.

There are a number of reasons for this, including unsound managerial policies which were manifested in over expansion at the end of the war, the resumption of competitive racing at a time of slump, and the production of the

[74] Sources: Companies House, Vauxhall file no. 135767; Reports to the Directors 1914–1929, Vauxhall Company Archives; Reports of the Ordinary General Meetings, *The Times*, 1914–1925.
[75] Report to the Directors, 1922, p. 5.
[76] Report to the Directors for the Year Ending 31 December 1921, presented at the 8th Ordinary General Meeting, 27 April 1922.

wrong type of models.[77] Vauxhall was not alone in suffering from such defects – some of which had been part of a success story in the pre-war years. The basic reasons lay in the effects of the post-war depression, and the fundamental change in the motor car market during the 1920s, led by the large producers such as Ford, Morris and Austin. Of these, the change in the car market was by far the most important, and this development was not to be fully recognised until well into the decade. Such developments were therefore not apparent to car producers in the seller's market that prevailed in the immediate post-war years. Anxious to cash in on the boom of a vehicle starved market, many new firms entered the industry and those in existence planned extensive expansion programmes between 1918 and 1921. Vauxhall's capital was increased by £200,000 in 1920 to £600,000[78] and an additional 1½ acres of floor space was added. This more than doubled the size of the Vauxhall works of 1914. Kimpton Road, which serviced the works, was metalled and 320 workmen's houses were built on a site nearby. In addition an apprentice scheme had been introduced with classes in various trades.[79] In 1921 17 acres of playing fields with attendant facilities had been opened 'as comprehensive provision for workers' recreation.'[80] Finance was provided by bank overdrafts to the value of £246,000 in 1919[81] and by the issue of £300,000 on short term notes, repayable in 1925.[82] Perhaps the most unwise of Vauxhall's moves was to invest £90,000 in S.F. Edges, A.C. Cars Ltd.[83], which was to go into liquidation along with numerous other firms during the 1920s The consequence of the boom conditions included high car prices which were caused by the rapid increase in labour and material costs.

Prices rose from a pre-war peak of £650 for a Vauxhall 35hp 6-cylinder model to £1,960 for the 4-cylinder 30/98 model in 1919.[84] The 25hp D-type, which had been the only car to be produced during the war, was to be marketed at £875 in 1918 but in 1919 was selling at the much higher price of £1,450.[85] Despite the buoyant post-war market, firms could only be profitable if enough cars could be sold with a wide profit margin on each model. At that time those such as Vauxhall, Daimler, Sunbeam and Crossley could not achieve these ends. This was because the handcraft methods of production, which these firms, and most others, employed, were unable to produce vehicles in large enough numbers.[86] This would entail a change to mass production methods. Therefore, when the boom collapsed in 1920/21, demand for cars fell away by almost 50

---

[77] This can be 'summed up as weak management and weak management policies,' and the 1920s market starkly revealed this 'lack of business acumen' to which Saul refers: S.B. Saul, 'The Motor Industry in Great Britain to 1914,' *Business History* V (1962), p. 34.

[78] Extraordinary Resolution, 12 February 1920, Companies House, Vauxhall file no. 135767.

[79] *Luton News*, 11 December 1919, p. 5, and 24 January 1918, p. 7.

[80] *Luton News*, 7 July 1921, p. 4.

[81] 'Report to the Directors of 6th Ordinary General Meeting', 20 April 1920.

[82] *The Times*, 7 October 1920, pp. 14 and 15.

[83] 'Report of 8th Ordinary General Meeting,' *The Times*, 28 April 1922, p. 23 col. 5. The Company was named by Michael Sedgwick in *Vauxhall: A Pictorial Tribute* (London: Beaulieu Books, 1981), p. 17. No evidence is available as to why this investment was made.

[84] 'Vauxhall Facts and. Figures' (Vauxhall Motors, 1966).

[85] Sedgwick, op. cit., p. 30.

[86] R.J. Overy, *William Morris: Viscount Nuffield* (London: Europa, 1976), p. 16.

per cent while prices remained high, and profitability evaporated quickly. Even a relatively large producer such as Austin ran into serious financial difficulties.[87] However, Austin was already planning to produce a 7hp mass produced car in the summer of 1920.[88] The Austin Seven was to retail at £225 in 1922, which was soon to fall to £165 by December 1923.[89] By mass producing low priced cars such as the 'Seven' and 'Morris,' the 8hp 'Cowley,' large profits could be realised by catering for a cheaper and wider market.

Vauxhall and its rivals, which were producers of cars in the medium luxury and touring range, immediately felt the slump in the market. Despite Walton's proclamation in 1920 that 'high prices will rule in our industry . . . Even if there was overproduction it will certainly not be in the type of car that we manufacture,'[90] by the end of the year the £1,300 model had been reduced to £1,050 and the £1,950 model to £1,675.[91] All firms did likewise, following the example of Morris which had cut prices of the Cowley two-seater from £465 in 1920 to £299 in October 1921, the Oxford two-seater from £535 to £415. By 1928 the Cowley two-seater and four-seater and the Oxford two- and four-seaters were respectively priced at £210 and £225.[92] Such price decreases could only be achieved by mass production methods and the wholesale buying out of components, a further feature of which was the manufacture and assembly of the car as a whole, including the body work and finish.

The medium luxury car firms of which Vauxhall was representative could not hope to compete and this type of producer suffered quite severely as the mass producers making efficient, reliable and cheap cars, squeezed them out. Vauxhall, Sunbeam and similar firms were either forced to compete, by adopting such methods, or had to become producers of high quality vehicles for a limited market in which high prices could be profitable. In effect, such firms fell between two stools.

These trends were not to be fully appreciated until later in the decade, but even in 1922 Vauxhall management still expressed a belief in the market for the larger car once that trade had revived sufficiently.

> Everyone who has purchased a small car to do the work of a big car is going to buy the 25hp Vauxhall or something similar, as soon as he is once again able to afford it . . . the uses to which a small car can be put are relatively limited.[93]

Such desperate optimism was held in the knowledge that Vauxhall sustained losses of £221,758 in 1921.[94] With heavy capital commitments and debts in the form of bank overdrafts and short term notes, the Vauxhall Board reluctantly turned to the production of a smaller vehicle which they hoped would increase

[87] Roy Church Herbert, *Austin: The British Motor Car Industry to 1941* (London: Europa, 1979), p. 50.
[88] R.J. Wyatt, *The Austin Seven: The Motor for the Million* (1968), p. 19.
[89] Wyatt, ibid., pp. 22 and 24.
[90] 'Report of the 6th Ordinary General Meeting,' *The Times*, 20 April 1920, p. 25 col. 5.
[91] *The Times*, 4 October 1920, p. 10 col. 5.
[92] R.J. Overy, op. cit., table 5, p. 132.
[93] 'Report of the 8th Ordinary General Meeting,' *The Times*, 28 April 1922, p. 23 col. 5.
[94] See Table 4 above.

sales. The results of this policy change was the production of the N-type 14/40 in 1922 retailing at £650 – a considerable drop in the normal Vauxhall price. The firm, no doubt, took comfort in the fact that Sunbeam, Crossley and Humber also began production of 14/40s, although these rivals would narrow that market considerably.

The interesting thing is that firms of a like nature responded in a similar fashion to the market change. The number of car sales increased in each of these companies, as the following table indicates, but 'alas the market for these steadily dried up, and slowly the ranks of the specialist producers withered.'[95]

Table 5. Output of cars, number of employees and floor area of Vauxhall Motors 1919–1929[96]

Year	Car output	Employees	Floor area (acres)
1919	565	750*	8½
1920	689	1023	9
1921	479	1210*	9½
1922	637	1390*	9½
1923	1462	1570*	10
1924	1366	1750*	10
1925	1388	1820*	10½
1926	1516	1934	10½
1927	1654	2277	11
1928	2589	1477	11½
1929	1278	1552	11½

The 14/40 was one of the fruits of C.E. King's work as Chief Engineer. King was a capable engineer and had served his apprenticeship in Adams Motors in nearby Bedford, later becoming their designer and then moving to the post of Assistant to the Directeur Technique, Société Lorraine de Dietrich in Paris. He joined Vauxhall in 1914, first as a designer and then as Assistant Chief Engineer, under Pomeroy, and became Chief Engineer on the resignation of Pomeroy in 1919.[97]

King was content, in the main, to improve rather than innovate and this conservative approach contrasted strikingly with that of Pomeroy.

Nevertheless, the 14/40, the OE and the OD, his two other designs, based heavily on Pomeroy's work, were considered to be excellent examples of the good vintage car and well within the tradition of Vauxhall 'Super excellence.'[98] The 14/40, however, became the mainstay of the factory until 1925, from which came 30 cars a week, a high rate by Vauxhall's previous standards and providing employment for 2,000 workers.[99] The following table of Vauxhall vehicles in the 1920s clearly indicates that they still produced predominantly more powerful vehicles other than the 14/40 for the rest of the decade.

[95] Lord Montagu of Beaulieu, *Lost Causes of Motoring* (1960), p. 5.
[96] 'Vauxhall Facts and Figures' (Vauxhall Motors, 1966) * Estimated figures (no records). It is not known which month's figures for car output and employees are taken for a 12 month period.
[97] P. Peters and H. Thornton Rutter (eds.), *Who's Who in the Motor Trade* (Temple Press, 1934), p. 82.
[98] M. Sedgwick, *Vauxhall* (London: Beaulieu Books, 1981), p. 17.
[99] C. Clutton and J. Stanford, *The Vintage Motor Car* (Batsford,1961 edition, 1st pub. 1954), p. 156.

Table 6. Vauxhall models 1919–1930[100]

Year	Year ceased	Name/Type	HP	Cyls.	Price
1919	1922	D Type	25	4	£1,300–1,050
	1922	E Type	'30/98'	4	£1,960–1,350
1922	1925	M Type	'14/40'	4	£650
	1926	OD Type	23/60	4	£695
1923	1926	OE Type	30/98	4	—
1924	1927	LM Type	14	4	£815–495
1925	1927	25/70	25	6	£1,675–1,350
1927	1928	R Type	20	6	—
	1929	20/60	20	6	£475–375
1929	1929	R Type	21	6	—
1930	1933	Silent 80	23	6	£750–565

Plate 12. 1923 Wensum, one of the famous 30/98 designs of Laurence Pomeroy.

While Vauxhall cars were well made and enjoyed a considerable reputation they lagged behind in some areas of technical development. The first 14/40s produced, for example, had side valves, as did the E-type, when rivals were installing over-head valves which gave better performance. The E-type front wheel brakes were always suspect, especially in a car which had a powerful engine. Four wheeled brakes and overhead valves were not incorporated until

[100] 'Vauxhall Facts and Figures' (Vauxhall Motors,1966).

Plate 13. Awaiting a royal visit to the Vauxhall works, Luton 1926.

the middle of the decade; but by 1925 the 14/40 'had developed into a very pretty touring car.'[101]

The 30/98 was always highly regarded, but by the middle of the decade the original 1913 design was becoming outmoded. Price cutting exerted additional pressure. The 14hp LM-type, which was a modified 14/40 and priced at £495 in 1927[102] stood up well to the slightly superior Sunbeam 14/40 priced at £625 in the same year.[103] The Humber 14/40 at £460 performed less well than the Vauxhall.[104] None however could compete with the Morris Oxford tourer at £300, and even though its performance was inferior to that of the Vauxhall and Sunbeam, the car was reliable, easy to maintain and, above all, cheap.

In the larger car market Vauxhall also found considerable competition. The 6-cylinder 25/70 or S-type was an attempt to maintain a position in the market

---

[101] Clutton and Stanford, op. cit., p. 157.
[102] See Table 6 above.
[103] G. Bishop, 'Sunbeam: Milestones of Motoring History' in *The World of Automobiles: An Illustrated Encyclopaedia of the Motor Car*, ed. I. Ward (no date, late 1970s), p. 2250.
[104] G. Bishop, 'Humber: Quality and Comfort before Performance' in ibid., p. 985. Rover, Crossley, Bean all produced 14hp cars, and Star, Singer and Straker Squire produced 15hp models. This middle range market was heavily competitive in what was to become a relatively declining market.

after 1925 but retailed at between £1,675 and £1,350; whereas the Sunbeam 20/60 handled better and had better brakes and sold for only £950 in 1926.[105] In terms of reliability and performance neither car could compete with the Rolls-Royce 20hp which retailed at a similar price to the Vauxhall S-type, but combined superb workmanship and finish in body and trim. Attempts to compete in the large and small medium range markets were unsuccessful. The basic problem for Vauxhall, Humber, Sunbeam and similar companies was their low productivity which prevented effective price competition with producers such as Morris, Ford and Austin.

By the mid 1920s Vauxhall had made an attempt to remedy low productivity by reorganising the works along a quasi-assembly line for the insertion of the engine and other adjacent parts of the chassis.[106] It was, however, ponderously slow compared with mass producer companies, and was in reality a more efficient version of the old batch system of production. The faint praise given by the *Automobile Engineer* after a correspondent had visited the reorganised works was almost a condemnation.

> The Company have managed to introduce some of the best features of mass production into an organisation which preserves individuality, and is sufficiently flexible to cater for the customer who is prepared to pay rather more than the price of a mass produced car.[107]

In 1925 Leslie Walton stated the Vauxhall dilemma in bold words which could equally have applied to Sunbeam, Humber, Crossley and other firms:

> We are not equipped, we have not had the training and we have no desire to produce large quantities of cars on mass production principles. We are equipped for, and we do produce a reasonable number of high class cars at a moderate price, and this must always be our policy.[108]

Even had there been the desire to change to mass production, the struggling concern simply did not have the capital with which to carry it out. In 1925, with the prospect of the redemption of the £300,000 Short Term Notes taken out in 1920, and large bank overdrafts, the company was in desperate financial straits. At a special shareholders meeting Walton stated that although profits had improved during the previous two years 'it had not been enough to reduce our overdraft, or allow us to set aside a fund to repay these notes.'[109] It was proposed at the meeting to create and issue First Mortgage Debenture Stock for a total sum of £350,000 which in crude terms was tantamount to mortgaging the firm's fixed capital and assets. After seeing the capital reduced from £600,000 to £300,000, by writing off 10 shillings on each share in 1923[110] and having received no dividend since 1919, the shareholders not surprisingly,

---

[105] I am grateful to Mr. Brook, Librarian of the Veteran Car Club, for this information, and some members who spent time debating the merits of Vauxhall vehicles and their rivals in the 1920s. Robert Gray, *Rolls on the Rocks: The History of Rolls Royce* (Salisbury, 1971), p. 54.

[106] 'The Works of Vauxhall Motors Ltd.,' *Automobile Engineer* vol XV, no. 207 (October 1925), pp. 341–7.

[107] Ibid., p. 347.

[108] 'Report to the 11th Ordinary General Meeting,' *The Times*, 1 May 1925, p. 21 col. 3.

[109] 'Special Shareholders Meeting Report,' *The Times*, 3 July 1925, p. 24 cols. 1, 2 and 3.

[110] 'Report to the 9th Ordinary General Meeting,' *The Times*, 13 April 1923, p. 21 col. 1.

Plate 14. Leslie Walton, Chairman and Managing
Director from 1907 to the late 1940s, making him
the longest serving director of the company.

raised a number of questions notably concerning the consequences of rejecting
the proposal. Walton's reply was candid: the company would have to go into
liquidation.[111]

Had not General Motors stepped in, in 1925, it is possible that Vauxhall
could have limped on throughout the decade as did Crossley, Sunbeam,
Humber and others, which were either taken over or ended in the bankruptcy
courts.

An interesting speculative point is whether Pomeroy's resignation in 1919
really spelt the doom of Vauxhall. Laurence Pomeroy, his son, who later
became the technical editor of *The Motor*, is clearly convinced that Vauxhall's
pre-war success was largely due to his father's designs.[112] When Pomeroy
resigned Frederick Lanchester wrote, 'If I had shares in the Vauxhall Company
I would sell them quick . . . It was nearly a one man show as anything in the
country.'[113] Few would disagree that up to the 1930s Pomeroy 'was one of the

---

[111] Special Shareholders Meeting Report, *The Times*, 3 July 1925, p. 24 cols. 1, 2 and 3.
[112] K. Karslake and L. Pomeroy, *From Veteran to Vintage* (1956), p. 90.
[113] Letter: Frederick Lanchester to Percy Martin, Feb. 1919, Daimler MSS, box file 28. Quoted in
K. Richardson, *The British Motor Industry: A Social and Economic History 1896–1939* (1977),
p. 33.

best automobile engineers in the country.'[114] It is highly doubtful that had Pomeroy stayed Vauxhall would have taken a radically different course. Whereas it is true that one man can influence a firm's fortunes, as in the case of Henry Ford, William Morris and Herbert Austin, the essential difference was that their respective firms became committed to a different philosophy of car making which was to become the major force in the 1920s: that of the mass produced family car. Louis Coatalen remained with Sunbeam until the middle 1920s, but this did not prevent that firm from running into financial difficulties. Pomeroy himself went to Daimler, another firm which had a reputation based on engineering prowess, and yet in 1936 when it was running into difficulties, he was not re-elected to the Board.[115] King, who took over the Pomeroy mantle at Vauxhall, was a good designer very much in the Pomeroy mould; and the 3 litre car produced for the Isle of Man Tourist Trophy in 1922, was partly designed by Dr. H.R. Ricardo, as consultant engineer – another man who enjoyed an enviable reputation in engineering design. The Vauxhall 'easily beat the Sunbeam' in that event.[116]

Racing ventures, however, were no longer regarded as essential for commercial success. This was a common view during the pioneering pre-war years, and proved to be an expensive side issue to the major business of producing cheaper cars for middle class family use.[117] In recognition of this fact Vauxhall withdrew from competitive racing in 1923[118] as did Sunbeam in 1927.[119]

Pomeroy was primarily an excellent engineer and designer and as such was committed to making high quality cars. Vauxhall, through King continued this work, but to no profitable end in the 1920s. Other firms such as Sunbeam, Bentley, Crossley, Humber and others, all produced good cars but were unable to survive. Thus, it was not engineering creativity that Vauxhall required but a change of commercial and production policy; either to concentrate in the high quality market, as Rolls-Royce had successfully done or to join Morris Austin and Ford in the mass producer market.

The old British management, of which Pomeroy had been a central part, did not fully realise why Vauxhall was unprofitable until faced with complete bankruptcy in 1925. Like many managements they were waiting for the market to become buoyant again after the 1921 depression and had over extended between 1919 and 1921. They were forced to reduce prices to compete and this

---

[114] M. Seth-Smith, *The Long Haul: A Social History of the British Commercial Vehicle Industry* (1975), p. 109.

[115] Richardson, op. cit., p. 33.

[116] Laurence Pomeroy, *The Grand Prix Car 1906–1939* (1949), p. 141.

[117] There is no doubt that in pre-war years racing had considerable merits in making a reputation, advertising the firm and consequently attracting custom. Even Henry Ford made enormous use of his record breaking '999' car to attract capital to enable him to found the Ford Motor Company. That he went on to produce the 'Model T' marks the essential differences of approach between the commercially minded Americans and the engineering perfectionists such as Pomeroy and Vauxhall. See Henry Ford, *My Life and Work* (1922, 7th ed. 1924), pp. 51 and 52, and Pomeroy's view in L.H. Pomeroy, 'Automobile Engineering and the War,' *Proceedings of the Institute of Automobile Engineers* (*PIAE*) IX (1914). Pomeroy states 'Great Britain . . . is a land of culture, and because of this demands a certain exclusiveness of product which is against quantity production on anything like the American scale,' p. 343.

[118] L.C. Derbyshire, *The Story of Vauxhall 1857–1946* (Luton: Vauxhall Motors, 1946), p. 39.

[119] C. Clutton and J. Stanford, *The Vintage Motor Car* (Batsford, 1961), p. 99.

had the effect of reducing profit margins which led to an inability to pay debts. Vauxhall therefore remained troubled until 1925, and even after General Motors had taken over and sorted out the debts, the firm continued to make losses, because it adhered to the same model and production policies until 1928. The market for large and middle range models, although growing, was relatively small. Production of the 14hp model ceased at Vauxhall in 1927 and the company relied on models of 20hp and over, a class which had an even smaller appeal.

In addition, the competition between firms in these ranges grew more intense as it became clear that the price cutting practices followed by Morris and Austin would influence reduction in prices at the larger end of the market, as buyers became attracted to cheaper models. In order to remain profitable there was a need to sell more cars, and although Vauxhall increased its annual output fivefold between 1921 and 1928, from approximately 500 to 2,500 units, it was not enough to allow sufficient economies of scale to be made in terms of profit per unit.

Hamstrung by weak policies in the early 1920s the Vauxhall management was never able to overcome these difficulties, while large debts acted as a drain on profitability. One commentator on the 1920s British car industry has suggested that the sales department was able to obtain orders, 'but the production department did not seem to have been able to cost their production adequately. This includes a failure of control and co-ordination at managerial level.'[120] Inadequate costing, however, would seem to have been of marginal importance compared with the error of producing the wrong models. Unfortunately, Vauxhall suffered from a good reputation and this blinded its management to the necessity for change.

---

[120] A. Holme, 'Some Aspects of the British Motor Manufacturing Industry during the Years 1919 to 1930' (Sheffield University M.A. thesis, 1964), p. 80. Holme does not furnish any evidence for these conclusions.

Chapter Two

The American Takeover of Vauxhall

Vauxhall's continued existence beyond the mid-1920s could only be assured if production and model policies changed and if it attracted sufficient capital. The acquisition of Vauxhall by General Motors in 1925 was the fertile seed of an overseas manufacturing division which was to make Vauxhall one of the six largest motor vehicle producers in Britain in the late 1930s.

The history of the purchase was not without controversy and this was to hinder greatly policy-making and development in the company until the end of the decade. Within the British motor industry resentment focussed on the acquisition of a respected marque by an American mass producer. The Vauxhall Board clearly did not want the reputation of Vauxhall diminished under its new owners; and the members of the GM Board wrangled amongst themselves about what to do with this unpromising, relatively small company and whether a large injection of capital would be worthwhile. Ford did not arouse the same hostility because he had established a British base well before the War when the car industry was in its infancy; but of more importance Ford did not purchase any established British car companies. GM's acquisition of Vauxhall was seen by many as cynical commercialism in order to avoid tariff duties, and thence to turn the company into a 'dismal' mass producer of 'unworthy successor (s) to the immortal 30/98.'[1]

Conscious of these criticisms particularly in the climate of British economic nationalism fostered by William Morris, among others, GM developed a managerial policy whereby Vauxhall was seen to be run by British management, employing a British workforce and making a British product. This also had the effect of allowing Vauxhall to have considerable autonomy in running its own affairs within the GM structure.

The motivation behind the General Motor's purchase was to secure an industrial base behind British tariff barriers which had been increasingly difficult to breach after the slump in car prices in 1921.[2] In the post-war boom American car exports had sold well in Britain; and 420,000 GM cars and trucks had been sold abroad, mainly in Britain, France and Germany in 1920.[3]

In that year General Motors Overseas Operations (GMOO) felt sufficient optimism about the British market to open an assembly plant at Hendon Aerodrome in the London suburbs.[4] The plant imported CKDs (completely

[1] C. Clutton and J. Stanford, *The Vintage Motor Car* (Batsford, 1961), p. 158.
[2] Alfred P. Sloan, *My Years With General Motors* (London: Sidgwick & Jackson, 1965), p. 315.
[3] Ibid., p. 315.
[4] Taped interview with Jack West who began work at the plant in 1920 and remained with the firm and Vauxhall until 1965, when he retired. He was born in 1900. Interviewed January 1981.

knocked down parts of cars) from the USA, including Buicks, La Salles, Cadillacs, Oaklands and Chevrolets, which were all subsidiaries of the General Motors empire.[5] Parts and CKDs though taxed on import, paid a lower tariff than complete vehicles. Despite this advantage over most other foreign importers, the American success followed the path of other producers of large cars. The radical price reductions of the 1921 depression was the first blow, followed by the growth in popularity of smaller horse power vehicles on the British market, led by Morris and Austin. A British survey, commissioned by GM in 1924, and conducted by James D. Mooney, Head of GMOO, clearly pointed to tax on engine size, plus 'fees, insurance and garage charges' as placing Chevrolet (the cheapest GM car import) at a 112 dollar disadvantage compared with the Austin equivalent; which, of course, was cheaper in price.[6]

GMOO, therefore, was given a directive: to seek acquisition of a suitable production plant in Britain.[7] Meanwhile, the Hendon plant was primarily turned over to the assembly of Chevrolets with locally made commercial vehicle bodies, in order to keep the plant busy.[8] Ironically, it was this very type of product which was to play such a large part in the Vauxhall success story of the 1930s with the production of the Bedford truck, which could trace its origins back to the converted Chevrolet.[9]

Logically, the ideal British company GM hoped to acquire was an established one with a fairly large capacity (at least in British terms) to enable a relatively smooth transition to GM production requirements. That company proved to be Austin Motors. Herbert Austin was amenable to General Motors overtures as the company was having difficulty raising capital to cope with its mass production expansion programme.[10] Negotiations opened in 1924, but were conducted against a background of criticism, particularly from the motoring press, which resented a well-known British firm passing into the hands of Americans.[11] Eventually, in October 1925 'dissenting (Austin) directors favoured a considerably more modest capital reconstruction scheme and avoiding American acquisition.'[12]

In the same month in which Austin negotiations had broken down, General Motors opened talks with Vauxhall Motors. As we have already seen, Vauxhall was in severe financial difficulties and was forced to raise loan capital by the issue of £350,000 mortgage debenture stock at 7 per cent.[13] The issue had not

[5] Sloan, op. cit., p. 318.
[6] Sloan, op. cit., p. 318.
[7] In 1919 GM had tried to gain an industrial base in Europe by attempting to acquire The Citroen Car Company, but the French Government opposed this: ibid., p. 317. Germany was probably not considered due to the economic difficulties and uncertain political climate there until 1924.
[8] Jack West interview, op. cit.
[9] M. Sedgwick, *Vauxhall* (London: Beaulieu Books, 1981), p. 7.
[10] Roy Church, *Herbert Austin: The British Motor Car Industry to 1941* (London: Europa, 1979), p. 103.
[11] An example of this kind of criticism at its most vociferous appeared in *The Motor* where such editorial headlines as 'The British Motor Industry for the British Nation' led blistering attacks on the negotiations: 27 October 1925, vol. XLVIII, no 1245.
[12] Church, op. cit., p. 104.
[13] Prospectus, 21 September 1925, Companies House, Vauxhall file no. 135767/52.

been particularly successful and in October, the Vauxhall Board was more than willing to entertain the General Motors offer of 2,575,291 dollars for the purchase of the ordinary shares.[14] This enabled the 300,000 ordinary shares to return to their pre-1923 value of £1 each.[15] Former shareholders had the option of purchasing 300,000 preference shares at £1 each with a guaranteed dividend of 6 per cent.[16] Old ordinary shareholders were paid a £210,000 bonus, making a total, in British terms, of '£510,000 invested in the company.'[17]

The new Board of Directors numbered seven in all, including Leslie Walton, who was to remain as Chairman; Percy Kidner, Mr. Bisgood and Mr. Petch; and three Americans, namely James D. Mooney, Edward Riley and Alfred Swayne.[18] Mooney, who had conducted the negotiations on behalf of GMOO, was to remain on the Vauxhall Board until the 1940s. Riley was brought in from the Hendon operation, but in 1926 he left the Board, and for the following 13 years worked in GM plants in Europe and Australia, before replacing Mooney as Head of GMOO in the 1940s thereby becoming overlord of Vauxhall. Swayne was brought in from New York, the GMOO headquarters.[19] Some members of the GM Board were disappointed at the purchase of Vauxhall. Alfred Sloan, the GM Chairman, euphemistically described the acquisition as 'a kind of experiment in overseas manufacturing,' and that compared with the proposed Austin purchase was much 'less controversial.'[20] This falls short of the truth as vociferous disagreements over Vauxhall continued within GMOO and the Detroit HQ until 1928.

Though Vauxhall was a tiny part of the GM empire, the arguments surrounding its future were important as this was the first overseas manufacturing operation acquired by the Corporation inside Europe; and, as Jim Mooney had previously pointed out, inside the British Empire.[21] Such policy decisions, and the results therefrom, would undoubtedly set the pattern for future GM ventures abroad.

The questions at issue were whether Vauxhall was to be expanded or written off as a bad investment? Was it really necessary to manufacture in Europe? Or could a modified Chevrolet, exported from the USA, compete with European cars in European markets?'[22]

The two chief opponents to the Vauxhall venture were Charlie and Fred Fisher, who had brought the Fisher Body Company into GM and were powerful in the inner circle.[23] The pro-Vauxhall view was strongly presented by Mooney and according to Hartnett (a British employee of GMOO who ran

[14] Sloan, op. cit., p. 320.
[15] Special Resolution, 16 November 1925, Companies House, Vauxhall file no. 135767/52.
[16] Companies House, Vauxhall file no. 135767/52, 16 November 1925.
[17] Report to the Directors, 31 December 1926, Vauxhall Motors Archive.
[18] List of Directors, 16 November 1925, Companies House, Vauxhall file no. 135767/53. Nothing is known of the two British Directors, Bisgood and Petch.
[19] Information taken from Companies House file, ibid.; M. Platt, *An Addiction to Automobiles* (Warne, 1980), p. 148, and Sloan, op. cit., ch. 18.
[20] Sloan, op. cit., p. 320.
[21] 'The British Market: An American View', speech by J.D. Mooney reported in *The Times*, 18 November 1925, p. 8 col. 6.
[22] Sloan, op. cit., pp. 320 and 321.
[23] Laurence Hartnett, *Big Wheels and Little Wheels* (1965), pp. 34 and 35.

Nordiska GM in Stockholm, and a friend of Mooney) was 'being given hell over it.'[24] The delay in making a policy decision was caused by Sloan who wanted to move slowly and cautiously 'until we had worked out a clear policy of overseas operations.'[25]

Meanwhile, Vauxhall continued producing large cars and continued making losses until 1929. The last 30/98 was produced in 1926 and the 14hp LM-type was phased out in 1927, after which Vauxhall concentrated on the production of 6-cylinder models of 20hp above. They were sound enough cars in their way[26] but even the 20/60 model, which was aimed at the family market, still retailed at around £500, and was expensive when compared with the Vauxhall Cadet which retailed at half that price in the early 1930s. Though competitive with the Austin 20hp models[27] in the late 1920s, they were out of date in design and not as good performers[28] added to which was the relative decline in growth of this sector of the market in favour of the smaller mass produced cars. The obvious difference was that the Austin 20hp car was a small part of its production, whereas in Vauxhall it was the predominant production model. Vauxhall car production peaked at 2,589 for the decade in 1928, and, although the workforce fell by 800 to approximately 1,500 employees in 1928,[29] losses of £320,000 and £266,000 were respectively recorded for 1927 and 1928, and the decade ended with a loss of £283,000 in 1929.[30]

Not surprisingly these losses led the GM Executive Committee to reformulate policy concerning Vauxhall's future. However, the problem was complicated by the entry into the picture of the possible purchase of Adam Opel, the German car company. GM had established an assembly plant in Germany in the 1920s and discussion turned on whether that should be combined with a German manufacturing base.[31]

Throughout 1928 the Executive Committee discussed whether manufacture in Europe should take place at all. This was dependent on the future feasibility of the GM Export Company. In a memorandum to Sloan in July, Mooney argued that it was not. GM exports had impressively risen from 20 million to 250 million dollars in the five years before 1928, but Mooney felt that because of the relative high price of the Chevrolet further rapid expansion would be difficult. He felt that the largest volume area for the Chevrolet was in the USA and not in the world market.[32] In Europe, in particular, it was at a disadvantage because of the high tax on engine size, which in Britain favoured producers of smaller cars such as Austin and Morris.

Most influential in the case for retention and expansion of Vauxhall was the importance of the British Empire, 'which covered 38 per cent of the world

[24] Hartnett, ibid., p. 34.
[25] Sloan, op. cit., p. 320.
[26] C. Clutton and J. Stanford, *The Vintage Motor Car* (Batsford, 1961) p. 157.
[27] R. Church, *Herbert Austin: The British Motor Car Industry to 1941* (London: Europa, 1979), table 10, p. 131.
[28] Clutton and Stanford, op. cit., p. 157.
[29] See Table 5, above.
[30] See Table 4, above.
[31] Sloan, op. cit., p. 321.
[32] Sloan, ibid., p. 322.

market outside the USA and Canada.'[33] Mooney sensed that 'the dollar was moving away from the British pound', and having a manufacturing base within the Sterling area would act, 'as an insurance policy in the form of a British product which could flow into these British countries if the people of these areas find it impossible to get dollars to buy American cars.'[34] In addition Mooney pointed out that Vauxhall 'had already started on a manufacturing programme and we have a large and growing distribution system in England, and an investment in the Vauxhall plant that had to be safeguarded.'[35]

Interestingly, the possibility of a German manufacturing base was not seen as an alternative to Vauxhall but as a parallel development establishing a continental manufacturing base for the European market. Vauxhall was to be a manufacturing base for the British Empire markets.

Mooney's views were clearly vindicated by the experience of the international market in the 1930s. The McKenna Tariff in Britain, and the move towards smaller vehicles in terms of mass production, had held US car exports at a disadvantage towards the end of the 1920s.[36]

With the onset of depression, and the rise of economic nationalism, as many nations receded behind high tariff barriers, home markets became very important. It was then that these GM industrial bases came into their own, particularly that of Vauxhall.[37] Another influence on the future direction of Vauxhall policy was the controversy engendered in the British motoring press over the acquisition by GM. This was to have a fundamental effect on the leadership of the company, its advertising and sales promotion, and its industrial relations.

The most vociferous critic of the acquisition was Edmund Dangerfield, the editor of *The Motor*. He attacked the 'persistent efforts of American motor interests to secure holdings in British and continental concerns,'[38] and even urged state intervention to ensure that 'such things do not come to pass.'[39] In the following edition he presented a scathing analysis of General Motor's practices, attacking the American corporation for wanting to 'obtain complete control' through the ownership of the ordinary shares and then giving smaller dividends to the (British) preferential shareholders. A speech by Leslie Walton was quoted at length which, though out of context, provided support for Dangerfield's criticism.[40]

---

[33] Sloan, op. cit., p. 322.
[34] Hartnett, op.cit., p. 36.
[35] Sloan, op. cit., p. 322.
[36] Miller and Church clearly show the predominance of British car manufacture in the British market in the second half of the 1920s and that British car exports increased by a third between 1924 and 1929. By contrast 'net imports rose by only 2,500 units while British car sales rose from 123,000 to 168,000 units for the 1924–29 period' and 'British firms supplied 94 per cent of this growth.' A manufacturing base in Britain would therefore be the correct policy at this time, as Mooney had urged. M. Miller and B.A. Church, 'Motor Manufacturing' in N.K. Buxton and D.H. Aldcroft (eds.), *British Industry between the Wars: Instability and Industrial Development* (Scolar, 1979) p. 186.
[37] A more thorough examination of Vauxhall's export performance is carried out in Chapter 4.
[38] 'The British Motor Industry for the British Nation', editorial in *The Motor*, 27 October 1925.
[39] Ibid.
[40] Editorial in *The Motor*, 3 November 1925.

Maurice Platt, who was a correspondent with *The Motor* (and ironically was to join Vauxhall in 1937 as a sales and service contract engineer later rising to a directorship and Chief Engineer),[41] stated in his memoirs

> We had hundreds of letters from readers deploring the sale . . . one result of all this clamour was that the General Motors connection was never mentioned in Vauxhall advertising and sales promotion for many years.[42]

Such remained the policy until the 1960s.

The strong reaction worried the Vauxhall directors sufficiently for them to place a double page advertisement in *The Motor* which emphasised that it would 'remain a 100 per cent British institution,' and that the managing directors, the staff, workmanship and product were British. Significantly, it was signed by Walton and Kidner, the two remaining British directors on the Board.[43]

In this atmosphere GM obviously felt it wise to have the figureheads of the company as British nationals; but despite the uncertainties as to the future of the company before 1928, Mooney was anxious to have a senior GMOO man 'to look into the Vauxhall show and do what he could to save it.'[44] In 1927 he appointed Bob Evans, an American who was Regional Director for Europe, as Managing Director of Vauxhall. Evans replaced Walton, who became Chairman of the company, and this meant that Evans would share the managing director-ship with Percy Kidner. The British and American directors shared the respon-sibilities of Vauxhall uneasily. Kidner had obviously continued at Vauxhall as he had been very much part of the growth of the company, and hoped that American capital would see the company through a bad patch and continue producing high quality and performance vehicles with a high reputation. It must have become clear to him with the appointment of Evans, that this was not to be the case. A 'robust car enthusiast,' Kidner was described by Platt, as 'opinionated, inflexible and not particularly intelligent';[45] and after a trip to GM's Detroit HQ described by Platt as 'disastrous' he commented that 'anyone less likely to get on with middle western Americans it would be difficult to imagine.'[46] Not surprisingly, early in 1928 Kidner resigned and took A.J. Hancock with him.[47]

The departure of Kidner left GM in the uncomfortable position of having an American in the Managing Director's chair, and rumblings of protest over the 1925 acquisition still occasionally echoing through the columns of the motoring press.[48]

[41] M. Platt, *An Addiction to Automobiles* (Warne, 1981), p. 95.
[42] Platt, op. cit., p. 90.
[43] L. Walton and P. Kidner, 'The Future of Vauxhall Motors,' *The Motor*, 1 December 1925.
[44] Hartnett, op. cit., p. 39.
[45] Platt, op. cit., p. 91.
[46] Platt, op. cit., p. 91.
[47] Kidner resigned in 1928 and A.J. Hancock in March 1929: *Luton News*, 11 April 1929, p. 4 col. 4. In later years Kidner and Hancock became influential in the Institute of Automobile Engineers. In 1935 Hancock was appointed President, and in his Inaugural Address attacked mass producers of cars, and looked back to a time when reputation counted for more than large sales. No doubt he had Vauxhall in mind: A.J. Hancock, 'Presidential Address,' *PIAE* XXX (1935). Kidner eventually joined L.H. Pomeroy at Daimler.
[48] C. Clutton and J. Stanford, *The Vintage Motor Car* (Batsford, 1961), p. 157. As late as the 1950s these two authors stated that 'the Vauxhall story is rounded off in a rather dismal fashion with the G.M. purchase in 1925.'

Once the decision had been made to give the Vauxhall expansion the go
ahead, Sloan personally told Mooney to pick an Englishman to run Vauxhall.
A story at the time, according to Platt, was that Mooney replied 'Well I guess it
had better be Charlie Bartlett; he's about as English as they come.'[49]

Bartlett was born in Gloucestershire in 1889 and he completed his formal
education at Bath Technical College, where he trained in business methods and
accounting. In 1914 he enlisted in the Devonshire and Dorsetshire Regiment in
which he saw active service throughout the war. Demobilised in 1919 with the
rank of sergeant, he joined General Motors (Hendon) Limited in the following
year as an accounting clerk. At Hendon Bartlett's managerial potential was
recognised, his promotion rapid, and in 1926 he became Managing Director. It
was at Hendon that he undoubtedly saw the great potential for the light truck
market which was later to play a major role in the expansion of Vauxhall in the
1930s. In 1929 he was appointed Managing Director of Vauxhall.[50]

Apart from his obvious abilities shown at Hendon, and the fact that he was
British, it has also been stated that his capabilities were noted during the
investigations and the financial planning which preceded the acquisition of
Vauxhall by GM in 1925.[51]

Bartlett's appointment was an inspired one. Though very much a GM man,
and in tune with the financial and managerial policies of the American
company, he possessed the essential ability to interpret the American company
policy into a British context. This success in guiding the progress of Vauxhall
into the ranks of the 'Big Six' British car producers in the 1930s impressed GM
sufficiently to allow Vauxhall 'to enjoy considerable autonomy . . . and (GM)
delegated many responsibilities to the Vauxhall management in Luton.'[52]

One of the successful areas in which the Bartlett hand was clearly in evidence
was in industrial relations;[53] and while General Motors in the USA was battling
with the United Auto Workers Union in 1936 and 1937[54] Vauxhall enjoyed
unprecedented peaceful industrial relations. Even in the British context,
Vauxhall was seen as a 'model' of industrial relations and this reputation
was to last well into the 1960s.[55]

The degree of autonomy which GM allowed Vauxhall was in line with its
established policy in relation to its subsidiaries in the USA. To understand the
development of General Motors it is helpful to contrast it with that of Ford.
Since the foundation of the General Motors Company in 1908 by W.C. Durant,
it had been significantly different in structure from Ford. Fords was much more
like a pyramid with Ford himself at the apex; GM can be seen as a number of

---

[49] Platt, op. cit., p. 93.
[50] Sources: Obituaries in *The Times*, 11 August 1955; *Luton News*, 11 August 1955; *Who Was Who 1951–60*.
[51] Mentioned by Eric Bates in a typed and taped interview, March 1980. Bates began work at Vauxhall in 1931.
[52] Platt, op. cit., p. 91.
[53] See Chapters 5 and 6 for a detailed review of Bartlett's managerial policies.
[54] R.O. Boyer and H.M. Morais, *Labor's Untold Story* (New York, 1955; 3rd edition 1972), 'Sit Down in Flint,' pp. 298–309.
[55] 'Sir Charles,' ch. 6 in Kenneth Ullyett, *The Vauxhall Companion* (London, 1971), pp. 81–93; 'The Turnip Patch: Industrial Relations at Vauxhall,' in Graham Turner, *The Car Makers* (1963; Penguin edition 1964), pp. 122–129.

satellites guided by the HQ at Flint, Michigan. By 1919 Durant's organisation included the Olds, Oakland (Pontiac), Cadillac, Buick and Chevrolet car companies, as well as the AC Spark Plug Company, the Fisher Body Company, the Frigidaire Company and tractor concerns.[56] Though it had become the fifth largest of all industrial concerns in the USA,[57] it had run into financial difficulties which eventually led to the removal of the flamboyant Durant and his replacement by the austere and phlegmatic Sloan.

Both men knew that it was impossible to run the General Motors Corporation in the centralised and dictatorial style of Henry Ford. Sloan had to face the problem of how to maintain control centrally and at the same time allow flexibility within the divisions to enable them to respond to changing market conditions. Ford did not learn this invaluable lesson, and while his production techniques were progressive in terms of productivity, his management remained under his autocratic control, and in the 1930s, when his major rivals had adopted similar production techniques, the Ford Company suffered accordingly. 'At managerial level, Henry failed to create a system of administration which could guide the company efficiently through the labour problems and style changes of the 1930s.'[58] The decentralised policies followed by Durant were far too lax and lacked cohesion: Sloan's remarkable plan for the Corporation was to allow the divisions autonomy but in a much more controlled manner. Each 'division headed by its chief executive shall be complete in every function and enabled to exercise its full initiative and logical development.'[59] Sloan recognised that 'certain central organisation functions are absolutely essential to the logical and proper control of the Corporation's activities.'[60] This idea of divisional autonomy helped GM to win the largest share of the automobile market in the USA and administer successfully its overseas manufacturing and marketing.[61]

The degree of autonomy allowed to Vauxhall was not surprising as it was compatible with evolved GM policy.[62] The effect of the controversy over the acquisition probably ensured a much lower GM profile than originally envisaged, although technical innovation, marketing and financial expertise were made available to Vauxhall by the parent company throughout the 1930s. How much independence Vauxhall was to enjoy varied with the economic and political climate and the Vauxhall performance in relation to British and world markets. The rapid growth of Vauxhall in the 1930s was helped considerably by GM but the company did not want to spoil the success by revealing too much of the American associations. Autonomy was enhanced to a greater degree by the Second World War, when Vauxhall production was turned over to

[56] Sloan, op. cit.; chs. 1 and 2 outline the acquisition of these companies.
[57] Alfred D. Chandler, *Strategy and Structure: Chapters in the History of the American Industrial Enterprise* (Cambridge, Mass., 1962; paperback edition 1980), p. 115.
[58] Roy Church, 'Men, Myths and Motor Cars: A Review Article,' *The Journal of Transport History* vol. IV, no. 2 (September 1977), p. 106.
[59] 'General Motors Corporation-Organisation Study'. DE GM I quoted in Chandler, op. cit., p. 133.
[60] Chandler, op. cit., p. 134.
[61] Frederic G. Donner, *The World Wide Industrial Enterprise: Its Challenge and Promise* (New York: McGraw Hill, 1967), pp. 29–31.
[62] The Vauxhall's policy was similarly applied to Opel's in Germany.

government contract work, and, given the difficulties of international economic relations, Bartlett was to enjoy an independent role. The wresting back of American control through the GMOO organisation in the post-war years provided a scenario for personal conflict between Bartlett and the new GMOO head, Ed Riley.[63] On the retirement of Bartlett in the early 1950s, American control of the Vauxhall Board considerably increased, mainly in response to intensified competition in the automobile markets of that time, and the perceived need for a tighter overall worldwide strategy.

---

[63] M. Platt, *An Addiction to Automobiles* (Warne, 1980), p. 148.

Chapter Three

The Rise of Vauxhall to the 'Big Six': 1930–1950

Vauxhall's remarkable achievement in the 1930s was to secure a place among the ranks of the largest British car and commercial vehicle producers. By the end of the decade Vauxhall had joined Austin, Morris, Ford, Standard and Rootes, known as the 'Big Six'. Particularly impressive was the exceptional growth of Vauxhall's light commercial vehicle production, sold under the trade name of 'Bedford.' Sales of Bedford trucks provided much of the source for the company's profits before the introduction of a truly all-British car in 1933 in the form of the 'Light Six' and the even more popular 'Vauxhall Ten' which commenced mass-production in 1938.

This achievement was largely due to the backing of General Motors which was able to invest finance in Vauxhall, build up the subsidiary's capital equipment, reorganise production along mass assembly lines, introduce intensive marketing techniques and enable the firm to benefit from the technical expertise and mechanical and design innovations of the American parent company. The skill in applying these assets to the British context in a successful manner rested heavily with the British management team led by Charles Bartlett. At the end of the 1920s the car industry was in a state of 'near duopoly' with Austin and Morris dominant.[1] The following table shows that by the end of the decade a marked increase in the share of the market had been taken by Vauxhall, Standard, Rootes and Ford, rising from a combined percentage share of 11 per cent in 1929 to a peak of 48 per cent in 1938.

Table 7. Percentage of car output held by car producers 1929–1939

Year	Vauxhall	Standard	Rootes	Ford	Morris	Austin	'Others'
1929	0.75	3.3	3.0	3.8	34.8	25.3	29.0
1930	5.10	4.4	4.8	6.0	34.4	32.2	13.0
1931	4.50	7.5	4.8	2.4	27.4	24.2	29.2
1933	4.97	6.2	6.4	13.2	19.9	20.1	29.1
1934	6.96	6.9	6.9	12.4	23.7	23.2	19.8
1935	8.01	7.0	7.5	15.6	29.7	21.8	10.2
1936	5.80	8.9	8.6	20.4	27.3	21.3	7.7
1937	7.40	8.9	8.7	20.5	25.3	20.9	8.3
1938	10.40	9.9	10.2	17.5	23.6	20.4	8.0
1939	9.40	11.5	9.8	13.2	24.2	21.9	10.0

Sources: This is a modified version of the table published in A. Silberston and G. Maxcy, *The Motor Industry* (1959), p. 107. Revision by D.G. Rhys in 'Concentration in the Inter-War Motor Industry', *The Journal of Transport History* vol. 111, no. 4 (September 1976), table L, p. 246.

[1] D.G. Rhys, 'Concentration in the Inter-War Motor Industry,' *The Journal of Transport History* vol. III, no. 4 (September 1976), p. 253.

By the mid-1930s the car industry had developed into a form of oligopoly and the performance of the two American-owned firms was impressive, particularly that of Ford. Their combined share of the market rose from 4.55 per cent in 1929 to 27.9 per cent in 1937 and 1938. Morris, and to a lesser degree Austin, lost ground, but the sharpest decline was in the percentage share of the market held by firms outside the top six, which transformed duopoly into oligopoly. The reasons for these developments lay in the changing nature of the car market and the responses of each firm. The home market grew by 124 per cent in the period 1931–37 but net imports managed to capture only a tenth of the increase. Export success also added to British car sales and the height and peaks depended on them.[2] The bulk of the expansion rested, however, in the home market due to the increases in real income, particularly that of the middle class, and reduction in the costs of owning a car.[3] Fuel costs, taxation, upkeep and maintenance expense ensured that demand increased for the smaller vehicle, but a vehicle 'without loss of comfort, reliability and performance.'[4] The Austin 12 and Morris Cowley, which had been the mainstay of these firms in the latter half of the 1920s was replaced by the 10hp car, which was still 'up market' compared to the Austin Seven and the Morris Eight, though the latter models enjoyed considerable popularity whilst in production. The demand, therefore, lay in a mass-produced car which was cheap, but with additional features which created extra appeal. Price-cutting tendencies which were characteristic of competition in the 1920s were replaced by price-model competition. While low prices were important to sales, mass producers, such as Austin and Morris, realised that profit margins were becoming dangerously low and would hurt them in the long run. With the entry into the field of Ford, Standard, Rootes and Vauxhall as mass producers this might be permanently damaging. Ford's new integrated production plant at Dagenham, which began production in 1931, was potentially the most efficient plant outside the USA[5] and proved to be an aggressive adversary.

More pertinent to Vauxhall was the dramatic decline in the large car market of 14hp and above. A total failure to read these trends by the General Motors management led to poorer sales of Vauxhall mass-produced cars than envisaged.

The initial choice of production models was not satisfactory. Americans wanted to produce a big car, which they thought would sell in export markets. The first car product of the reorganised assembly line was the 26hp Cadet which was mainly for export, and a 17hp version designed for the home market. The sales can only be described as disappointing, particularly when the large investment in reorganisation is taken into account.

The Cadet was chosen because the Americans, and Sloan in particular, believed 'in the persistent but mistaken notion that Europeans would prefer to own larger and more powerful cars if they were given the chance to buy

[2] M. Miller and R.A. Church, 'Motor Manufacturing' in N.K. Buxton and D. Aldcroft (eds.), *British Industry between the Wars* (Scolar, 1979; paperback edition 1982), p. 186.
[3] Miller and Church, ibid., p. 188.
[4] Miller and Church, op. cit., p. 188.
[5] Rhys, op. cit., p. 247.

Plate 15. Cadet 1930, the first visible outcome of the General Motors takeover. Based on an Opel Kadet it was produced in a 17hp and 26hp version aimed at the cheaper market. The 17hp version retailed at £280.

them at competitive prices.'[6] This was totally at odds with the changing state of the British car market. The idea of a kind of European Buick was dropped, but the 17hp and 26hp were still too large. Its chief rivals were the Austin 16, the Hillman Wizard and the Morris Oxford Six, and though the Cadet was competitive in price and incorporated synchromesh gears (the first to do so in Britain), this sector of the market could absorb at the most 5,000 units a year in a worldwide depression.[7] The Cadet according to Eric Bates, who began work in the Vauxhall engineering office in 1930, was based heavily on the Opel Kadet: 'They were using the Kadet drawings and modifying them.'[8] In production terms this would seem logical as the recently purchased GM German subsidiary already possessed the designs and experience of mass production which could be transferred to Vauxhall with relative ease.[9]

The GM Vauxhall production policies paralleled those of Ford's British operation, and displayed the necessity of appointing sound British management which was close enough to the market to perceive changes and initiate appropriate model designs.

[6] M. Platt, *An Addiction to Automobiles* (London: Warne, 1980), p. 92.
[7] M. Sidgwick, *Vauxhall* (London: Beaulieu Books, 1981), p. 42.
[8] Interview with Eric Bates, March 1980; retired from Vauxhall 1979.
[9] Opel's output in 1928 was 43,000 vehicles compared to approximately 2,000 produced by Vauxhall. Opel was the largest car manufacturer in Germany and produced 44 per cent of all German-made cars sold in Germany in 1928: A.P. Sloan, *My Years with General Motors* (London, 1965), pp. 326 and 327.

At the end of the First World War, Ford had been the largest British producer of cars but had lost that lead to Morris and Austin in the 1920s. The main problem was its reliance on the large-horse-power Model T, and in 1928 on the Model A, which became its replacement. The decision to produce these rested with Henry Ford himself, who was much more concerned with his US operations and large production runs than with changing British market demands. By the end of the decade Austin sales were mainly of 12hp models, and in the 1930s there was a shift to the 10hp car in the highest sales bracket. The re-appointment of Sir Percival Perry, the British Managing Director of Ford, led to a small-bore Model A for the European market but it did not sell well enough to justify the huge investment in the Dagenham works. In 1931 Perry was forced to ask for the production of a smaller model, which led to the creation of the 8hp Model Y,[10] which enabled Ford to reclaim a significant slice of the British car market.

The Cadet was the Vauxhall equivalent of the Model A and the model policy of each company shows the American production at the same time suffering from an inadequate perception of the consumer preference in the local market. Charles Bartlett was the Vauxhall equivalent of Ford's Perry, and it was these two men who had to convince their respective American parent companies of the need for a smaller British model for the British and European markets.

Under Bartlett's influence Vauxhall turned to the production of the Light Six, a 6-cylinder model with 12 or 14hp engines retailing at £195 and £215 respectively. Thereafter the model leaders were to have much lower horse power ratings than in the 1920s, culminating in the Vauxhall Ten in 1938. (See Table 8.)

Table 8. Vauxhall car models 1931–1939

Year	Year ceased	Name/Type	HP/capacity	Cyls.	Price
1931	1933	Cadet VX	17	6	£280
		Cadet VY	26	6	
1933	1934	Light Six ASY	12	6	£195
		Light Six ASX	14	6	£215
1934	1936	Big Six BY	20	6	£325
		Big Six BX	26	6	£550
1935	1938	Big Six DY	12	6	£205
		Big Six DX	14	6	£225
1937	1939	GY & GL	25	6	£330–£615
1938	1940	H & I	10 & 12	4	£168–£198
1939	1940	J14	14	6	£189

Sources: *Vauxhall Facts and Figures* (Luton: Vauxhall Motors, 1966); L.C. Derbyshire *The Story of Vauxhall* (Luton: Vauxhall Motors,1946) pp. 54, 55.

[10] This information rests heavily on R. Church and M. Miller, 'The Big Three: Competition, Management and Marketing in the British Motor Industry, 1922–1929' in Barry Supple (ed.), *Essays in British Business History* (Oxford, 1977), p. 171.

It was the Light Six and the British management's decision to produce it which brought Vauxhall much more in line with the market trend. Bartlett described the Light Six as 'a dream come true.'[11] The *Luton News* commented that 'a notable feature of the car is the roominess and leather upholstery – unusual in cars of this price and gives a touch of luxury.'[12] The Deluxe 14hp model also had a no-draught ventilation system and incorporated synchromesh gears, both innovations which came originally from the GM parent company.[13]

Here can be observed the emerging features of motor vehicle competition in which styling, technological innovation and optional extras became important in securing sales. In price terms the Vauxhall Light Six 12hp was far cheaper than the Austin 12, which retailed at £225, although only £7 more expensive than the 1933 price of the light 'Austin 12' introduced a year earlier. The Morris 12 also retailed at £195 in 1933. Thus, while there was little attempt by Vauxhall to undercut rivals in price, efforts were spent on trying to ensure superiority of design, the offer of optional extras and additional attractive features and on vigorous marketing methods.[14] Signs that such policies were successful are to be found in the sudden jump in Vauxhall car sales from 3,600 in 1932 to over 11,000 in 1931. By 1935 Vauxhall car sales had more than doubled, to over 26,000.

Table 9. Total output of cars and CVs, number of employees and floor space, Vauxhall Motors 1929–1938

Year	Total Output	Cars	CVs	Employees	Total floor area in acres	
1929	1278	1278	—	1552	11½	
1930	8930	8930*	—	2725	12½	
1931	15152	3927	11225	2458	13	7 acre increase
1932	16918	3679	13239	3268	20¼	
1933	27636	11106	16530	5200	20¼	
1934	40455	11816	21639	6352	25¼	5 acre increase
1935	48671	26240+	22431	6726	34¼	9 acre increase
1936	50703	21319	29384	7660	41¼	7 acre increase
1937	59744	28076	31668	8669	43¼	
1938	60111	35415+	24696	8589	53¼	10 acre increase

* The figure for 1930 must have included Chevrolet trucks assembled for the first time at Luton.
+ Years when car output exceeded CV output.
Source: 'Vauxhall Facts and Figures' (Vauxhall Motors, 1966)

The Light Sixes heralded the entry of Vauxhall into the ranks of the mass car producers. However, it was still a comparatively small car producer, and though comparable with Standard and Rootes its output was only half that

[11] *Luton News*, 21 September 1933, p. 11.
[12] *Luton News*, 15 June 1933, p. 8.
[13] Synchromesh gears were developed by the Cadillac Company in 1928 and the No-Draft Ventilation system was developed by the Fisher Body Company and fitted to all GM American models in 1933: 'About General Motors Corporation,' Public Relations typescript (London, 1977), pp. 5 and 6.
[14] A.F. Palmer-Phillips, 'Arguments against Price Cutting,' *General Motors News* (November 1929), p. 123. Palmer-Phillips was Director of Vauxhall Sales Department.

of Ford, a quarter of Austin and a quarter of Morris.[15] The Light Six seems to have taken from the top end of the growing middle class market.

Much of the initial reorganisation and expansion of the Vauxhall works, however, was due to the production of light trucks, which must take a large part of the credit in explaining the success of the company in the 1930s.

At the time of the GM takeover of Vauxhall in 1925 a kind of quasi-assembly line was in existence, but there were no automatic conveyors and much of the work was manhandled into assembly position. Much bench and batch production work was carried out and the capacity of the works was at 25 to 30 chassis a week.[16]

The reorganisation for mass production required considerable investment by GM and this was tentatively started in 1927 when £250,000 additional capital was provided to finance extensions to the factory.[17] An indicator of large scale expansion was given in 1929 when GM acquired 276,202 preference shares, of which 23,798 remained in the hands of the Board members.[18] All the ordinary shares had been acquired in 1925.

The beginnings of a modern mass assembly line were installed in 1929 once GM had agreed to the expansion of Vauxhall. Two problems faced the Vauxhall/GM management at this time: which vehicle to produce, and what to do with the GM organisation at Hendon?

Although over 1,000 people were employed at Hendon the works did not have the same potential for expansion as the Vauxhall works. In addition, the Chevrolet truck assembled from CKDs was immediately available for mass production and enjoyed considerable sales in Britain and abroad. For these reasons the decision was taken to transfer the whole of the GM Hendon manufacturing operations to Luton, and to make Hendon a centre for sales distribution and service operations after the amalgamation of the hitherto separate organisations.[19]

By the summer of 1930 'radical changes had been effected both in the layout of the works and the equipment employed.'[20] Conveyors were used in engine and chassis assembly though moving assembly lines were not introduced until 1933.[21] The plant was capable of producing 75 chassis per day, and 85 per cent of production was devoted to Chevrolet trucks.[22]

In retrospect, the decision to produce the Chevrolet truck was not surprising. The engine and chassis had been designed in USA specifically for mass production and the expertise in assembly gained at Hendon throughout the 1920s could easily be applied to the newly reorganised works at Luton. During the years 1925 to 1932 no fewer than 17,884 cars including Cadillac, Buick, Chevrolet, La Salle, Oldsmobile, Pontiac, Oakland and Marquette, were

[15] See Table 7, above.
[16] *Automobile Engineer* vol. XV, no. 207 (October 1925). How Vauxhall changed to mass production is important to the argument on labour control in Chapter 6.
[17] Report to the Directors for the Year Ending 31 December 1927.
[18] Report to the Directors for the Year Ending 31 December 1929.
[19] *General Motors News* vol. 11, no. 3 (September 1929), p. 57.
[20] 'The Works of Vauxhall Motors Limited,' *Automobile Engineer* vol. XX, no. 270 (August 1930).
[21] 'The Vauxhall Works,' *Automobile Engineer* (September 1933), pp. 319 and 320.
[22] *Automobile Engineer* (August 1930).

assembled at Hendon. In addition, 54,462 commercial vehicles were assembled there during the same period, including 5,986 Bedfords in 1931.[23] This averaged 2,235 cars, and about 6,800 trucks, per year. The average yearly output of each of the eight models of GM cars (although the cheaper Chevrolets would sell more than the Cadillacs) equals 280 – not an impressive figure as the basis for GM's entry into the mass production market in Britain and this not surprisingly prompted consideration of the production of one or two car and truck models. The production of the Chevrolet truck at Luton had solved temporarily the problem of a CV model for the British market, and in 1930 greater urgency was seen to be the need to mass produce a Vauxhall car resulting in the Cadet in 1931. However, criticism in the motoring press of Vauxhall's American connection continued and in the economic nationalist climate of the depression it became clear to Vauxhall/GM management that the name Chevrolet would have to be expunged and replaced by a suitable British substitute.[24] The outcome was the mass production of the 'all British' Bedford truck. A 2-ton model was produced in 1931, followed by the extremely popular 30cwt model in 1932, which was to enjoy enormous sales throughout the 1930s. Once again, it was the British management's suggestions that led to the production of the right model; and Sir Reginald Pearson recalls:

> The Americans at first wanted to build a wide range of cars but there was no call for this in Great Britain in the 1930s. Bartlett said 'What was needed was a good truck'. Bartlett convinced Sloan that a truck was the best thing for Vauxhall. It was a life saver.[25]

Additional weight was given to the idea of an all British truck when Bill Knudsen, the President of Chevrolet, who was visiting England in 1930, reacted angrily when he discovered that Chevrolet truck production had gone ahead without his permission. Immediately he ordered Vauxhall to cease manufacturing Chevrolet components.[26] Bartlett had learnt from Hendon in the 1920s that as a result of placing truck bodies on the Chevrolet chassis, GM trucks sold better than the cars. The Ford company in England had followed a similar policy when saddled with the increasingly outmoded and comparatively large Model T.[27] Some market potential existed in the 1920s for a lightweight truck,

[23] 'Vauxhall Facts and Figures' (Vauxhall Motors, 1966), p. 3.

[24] Frequent claims in the press by Vauxhall that the Chevrolet was made up of 80 per cent British labour and materials, and soon to be 95 per cent, shows the sensitivity of Vauxhall management to these criticisms: *Luton News*, 27 March 1930, p. 20. As late as 1932 Walton, Vauxhall Chairman, stated that 'the name General Motors has been associated in this country with the sale of imported cars and commercial vehicles and in consequence our position as builders of British products has been somewhat prejudiced': 'Report of the 18th Ordinary General Meeting,' *The Times*, 13 April 1932, p. 21 col. 3.

[25] Interview with Sir Reginald Pearson, February 1979. Sloan's desire to build a wide range of cars was an extension of GM's successful policy in competing against Ford in the 1920s. It would therefore have seemed to Sloan that this policy would work in Britain as well. In fact what was needed was one successful CV and car model to penetrate into the ranks of mass producers. Model diversification could come once a model leader was established.

[26] L. Hartnett, *Big Wheels and Little Wheels* (1965).

[27] The Model T incorporated an ingenious innovation whereby a saloon body could be clipped on in place of a lorry body at the whim of the owner: A. Holme, 'Some Aspects of the British Motor Manufacturing Industry during the Years 1919–1930' (unpublished M.A. thesis, Sheffield University, 1964), p. 109.

Plate 16. Bedford 2-ton truck 1931, described by Reg Pearson as a 'life saver', and a consistent profit maker throughout the 1930s.

and Ford, and particularly GM, began to exploit this by adapting their large cars to meet these potential home and overseas markets.[28]

Throughout the 1920s most commercial vehicle companies produced for the heavier end of the market, which was much more a bespoke business, producing vehicles in batches which ensured high prices beyond the pocket of the small trader and businessman. In addition, hire-purchase and other credit facilities were not available to the extent they were to become a decade later.

For much of the decade British CV producers were fending off the problems of insolvency coming immediately after the war when the home market was flooded with ex-army lorries, affecting new sales drastically. Retrenchment ensued to ensure survival, and profitability only began to rise again with the onset of the 'bus boom' associated from 1926 with the rapidly growing charabanc market.

One of the major obstacles to change was the batch methods of production. It was difficult and too expensive to produce both large vehicles of 2 tons and above, and cater for the light truck market. With the entry of Morris Commercial in 1924, commercial vehicle companies found difficulty competing. Leyland, for example, produced a 30cwt truck in 1923 costing £560, but could

---

[28] Sir Raymond Dennis, of Dennis Motors, reported as early as 1920–21, after a world tour, that 'the light American commercial vehicle would be preferred to the heavy duty CVs produced in Britain': Holmes, op. cit., p. 74.

not compete with the Morris van and Ford Model T retailing at around £200 in 1924.[29] Leyland's vehicle sizes increased in the second half of the decade, as a reaction to previous failure in this sector of the market. Other companies rejected attempts at mass production and proclaimed engineering perfection as their objective. Foden continued to produce steam vehicles up to the early 1930s as the main part of its works output, when it was clear that these beautifully made but heavy and slow monsters were an anachronism.[30]

Morris Commercial clearly showed that the advantage of the light truck lay with the mass producer, as it was 'produced largely with the same equipment as that used in the production of passenger cars.'[31] The gain in economies of scale reduced costs and lowered prices significantly. Whilst this process had been influential in the car market in the 1920s, with the mass production policies of Morris and Austin, these changes were not introduced to commercial vehicle production until the 1930s, a development of the two American companies as innovators.[32]

The assembly line in Vauxhall's Luton works was initially set up for the Chevrolet truck; but this was regarded primarily by the Americans as an interim measure. They mistakenly identified a need for the main thrust of Vauxhall's expansion to be centred on the production of large cars. The assessment of Jim Mooney as Head of General Motors Overseas Operations was that a manufacturing base was needed in Britain. This was proved correct when American imports fell sharply after the boom of 1928/29. In 1930, 80 per cent of all goods vehicles produced in the UK fell in the up to 50cwt class, and 22 per cent within that category had a capacity of less than 15cwt.[33] The trend was obviously towards lightweight vehicles, and significantly the empire market was to be a fruitful export area (another Mooney prediction) – but the vehicle produced was the 26hp Cadet.

In early 1931 the first Bedford truck appeared on the market. It was a 2-ton model and boosted Vauxhall CV sales from 7,590[34] in 1930 to 11,225 in 1931. Keen prices helped to secure this success. The short wheel-base chassis/cab cost £198 and the larger model £210. The complete factory built drop-side trucks cost only £240 and £260 respectively.[35] Their closest rival was the Ford 2-ton which was £10 cheaper. (See Table 10 overleaf.)

Of the 18 British and foreign firms which competed in this sector of the market the two American subsidiaries led the field in both types of wheel base. The price of the more expensive 2-ton trucks reached almost £500 and not surprisingly Vauxhall and Ford led the field in sales.

At the end of 1931 Vauxhall unveiled the 30cwt truck which was a modified and cheaper version of the 2-tonner and replaced the Chevrolet. Despite a 3.0 per cent national fall in production of commercial vehicles in 1931 and another

[29] Holmes, op. cit., p. 109.
[30] Pat Kennet, *The Foden Story* (Cambridge, 1978), p. 119.
[31] Miller and Church, 'Motor Manufacturing,' op. cit., p. 205.
[32] Miller and Church, op. cit., p. 205.
[33] Miller and Church, op. cit., p. 205.
[34] i.e. 85 per cent of the 8,930 Vauxhall output was Chevrolet trucks in 1930: see Table 9.
[35] *You See Them Everywhere: Bedford Commercial Vehicles since 1931* (Luton: Vauxhall Motors,1979), p. 3.

Table 10. Chassis prices of 2 ton and 30 cwt trucks 1931–33

	2ton*		30cwt**
	Short wheel base	Long wheel base	
Bedford	£198	£210	£175
Ford	£188	£197	£189
Karrier	£198	£235	—
Willy's Overland	£224	—	—
Morris Commercial	£226	—	£198
Commer	£248	£265	£210
Dennis	£385	—	£300

* 1931   ** 1933
Sources: *Commercial Motor*, 3 November 1931, pp. 406–408; 5 May 1933, p. 409.

drop of 8.9 per cent in 1932, Bedford truck sales continued to rise and by 1932 had risen by 18 per cent, and in 1933 by a further 25 per cent. Between 1931 and 1937 the output of Bedfords had nearly tripled. Meanwhile from 1933 Bedfords accounted for over 25 per cent of British CV output.

Table 11. Bedford percentage of CV output 1931–1938

Year	CV output GB	Bedford output	% of GB output
1931	67,003	11,225	16.7
1932	61,756	13,239	21.4
1933	65,221	16,530	25.3
1934	85,134	21,639	25.4
1935	105,456	22,431	21.2
1936	108,000	29,384	27.2
1937	118,000	31,668	26.8
1938	97,000	24,696	25.4

Sources: G. Maxcy and A. Silberston, *The Motor Industry* (1959), table 1, p. 223; 'Vauxhall Facts and Figures' (Vauxhall Motors, 1966).

The 30cwt Bedford's success was not only that it was the cheapest in its range at £175, but that it was a strong and reliable vehicle. Its payload, for example, could be exceeded by as much as 50 per cent[36] and the robust quality of this vehicle proved popular with the businessman. In addition, Vauxhall was able to increase output by the adaptation and exploitation of GM marketing techniques thereby widening potential market sales. Much in the same way the model policies of Singer, Standard and Hillman helped to stimulate the market for 10hp cars in the early 1930s.[37] Intensive advertising, the employment of trained salesmen in the field, an increase in outlets and the extension of credit facilities through the General Motors Acceptance

---

[36] *You See Them Everywhere*, p. 3. Much was made in Vauxhall advertisements of the time of the ability of Bedford trucks to exceed their payload.
[37] Church and Miller 'The Big Three,' op. cit., p. 175.

Plate 17. 1931 WHG Waveney bus, a successful by-product of the move into the commercial vehicle sector. This 14-seater proved a popular seller and was fitted with a Waveney body.

Corporation[38] and British credit companies were also important.[39] Particularly after 1929 when depression caused vehicle replacement to slow down, owners hung on longer to their old models. Credit and HP inducements given by GMAC would persuade a quicker replacement than otherwise would have taken place and hopefully customers would switch to Bedford trucks. GMAC first opened a British branch in 1928.[40] By contrast Austin and Morris sales techniques appeared pedestrian, and Henry Ford had always placed more emphasis on the production side of the business. Equally influential in Vauxhall's success was its impressive increase in overseas sales, particularly of the 30cwt truck[41] facilitated by excellent sales and maintenance services. Once again GM was able to help considerably by making available its extensive overseas outlets based in 104 countries.[42] In these areas British commercial vehicle producers noticeably lagged behind.[43] The lightweight truck was preferred in less developed countries and the large payload in comparison to its size, combined with a sturdy chassis frame and springing, made them ideal for rough roads.

In Britain light truck sales were given a considerable fillip by the incorporation of the Salter Report proposals into the Road Traffic Act of 1933, which penalised heavy commercial vehicles by high taxation.[44]

---

[38] A GM credit company began in the USA in 1919: A.R. Sloan, *My Years with General Motors* (1965), p. 152.

[39] This is more fully discussed in Chapter 4 under Marketing.

[40] *General Motors News* 1 (July 1928), p. 10.

[41] Vauxhall's export performance is examined in Chapter 4.

[42] 'This is General Motors,' *General Motors News* (June 1930), pp. 330–331.

[43] See *Commercial Motor*, 10 February 1931, p. 912, in which British CV companies' failure in overseas markets is examined.

[44] *Commercial Motor*, 28 April 1933, p. 379. E.g. a £7 increase was put on vehicles below two tons and thereby increased by each ton. Ten ton vehicles and above had a £177 increase.

Vauxhall also achieved success in the light passenger commercial vehicle market. In the last quarter of 1931 no fewer than 52 per cent of all 14 to 20-seater buses and coaches registered in Britain were Bedford:[45] a remarkable rise as it was not launched until August of that year. In 1932, 65 per cent of all buses and coaches sold in the 9 to 20-seater category were Bedford[46] and by 1939 5,500 commercial passenger vehicles had been sold; of all the small buses and coaches operating in Britain 70 per cent were Bedfords.[47] Impressive though these figures appear to be it must be remembered that in the market for 14-seater buses in 1931 Bedford only had two rivals whose chassis prices were £450 compared to that of £250 for the Bedford.[48] In the 20-seater bus range competition was greater with about 12 firms in the market, but neither Morris-Commercial nor Ford, Bedford's main mass producer rivals, had a model in this range. The Bedford chassis was by far the cheapest at £265 with Commer (also a Luton firm) second at £295; the rest were priced between £400 and £600.[49] Ford did compete with Bedford in the 12cwt van range and was £10 cheaper at £135, but the Bedford was attractive to buyers as it incorporated synchromesh gears, using the Cadet 17hp engine and transmission.[50]

The preparation for production of the Light Sixes and the need for greater capacity to fulfil the increased demand of Bedfords entailed a further reorganisation and expansion of the Luton plant. While Vauxhall had taken advantage of the ability of the plant to produce cars and lightweight trucks with much the same equipment, the existence of a single assembly line created unnecessary delays. The 1929 reorganisation had laid the foundation of a modern assembly line, but it was small by comparison with that of Ford, Morris and Austin. Components of each type of vehicle had to be manufactured in batches and commercial vehicles were produced 'for some days, or possibly weeks, before tooling was changed for the production of the Vauxhall model.'[51]

During the erection both commercial vehicles and cars were assembled on the chassis line simultaneously, 'although separate frame assembly lines and body building shops (were) provided.'[52] In February 1933 £500,000 was invested in reorganising the works to expand capacity.[53] Two parallel assembly lines were installed; one for passenger cars and one for commercial vehicles, both of which incorporated machine operated continuous conveyors for engine, chassis and final assembly.[54]

By comparison Morris did not introduce moving assembly lines at Cowley until 1933[55] though certain lines for the Morris Minor were propelled by chains

---

[45] *Bedford Buses and Coaches since 1931* (Luton: Vauxhall Motors, 1979), p. 5.

[46] Ibid., p. 6.

[47] *Bus Fayre* vol. 1, no. 1 (April 1978), p. 11.

[48] *Commercial Motor*, 31 November 1931, pp. 406–408.

[49] Ibid., pp. 406–408.

[50] *Commercial Motor*, 5 May 1931, p. 409.

[51] 'The Works of Vauxhall Motors Limited,' *Automobile Engineer* (August 1930).

[52] Ibid.

[53] *Luton News*, 9 February 1933, p. 8 col. 3.

[54] *Luton News*, 16 March 1933, p. 9 col. 4.

[55] P. Andrews and E. Brunner, *The Life of Lord Nuffield* (1955), p. 197, quoted in D. Lyddon, 'Workplace Organisation in the British Car Industry: A Critique of Jonathan Zeitlin', *History Workshop Journal* no. 15 (Spring 1983), p. 132.

Plate 18. The Luton site in the mid-1930s.

in early 1929.[56] Ford's Dagenham plant had fully automated conveyors in 1931 after its move was completed. This had the effect of speeding up production considerably. Though the floor space was increased by 17 per cent, output was improved by 50 per cent, and the works capacity was raised to 150 chassis a day.[57] This was double the 1930 capacity of 75 chassis a day. Bartlett saw the reorganisation as the last stage in the transformation of Vauxhall into a mass producer and stated that the replanned works were the final break with the company's past association with 'old selective and expensive private cars.'[58] The 'Silent 80' retailing at £750 was phased out of production ending the line of Vauxhall cars with a direct pedigree from the old company.

Much of the reorganised production facilities catered for the Light Sixes[59] and the Bedford 30cwt truck, but in 1934 the Vauxhall management felt the need to have a model in the larger car market. These were the Big Sixes and due to increased productivity, the 20hp and 26hp 6-cylinder models retailed at £325 and £550 – a considerable drop on the 'Silent 80' price. Michael Sedgwick wryly comments 'its appeal was to the captains of industry with fleets of Bedfords.'[60] Vauxhall also entered into the larger commercial vehicle market in 1934 with the introduction of a 3-ton truck priced at between £245 and £260. It was the cheapest in this range and only Morris Commercial at £276 and Fordson at £307 could come close to competing in price terms.[61] The effect of Vauxhall's price lead was to induce price reductions in the commercial vehicle field thereby creating a similar kind of price competition to that which had taken place in the car market in the 1920s. A close comparison is, however, difficult as there were considerable differences in commercial vehicle and car production. Despite moves toward mass production led by Morris-Commercial, Ford (Fordson) and Vauxhall (Bedford), this could only truly be effected in engine and chassis production. Body building was still very much a specialised part of the final stages of completion and was expensive because it was largely carried out by skilled manual labour. In fact Vauxhall offered over 44 variations of its seven basic commercial vehicle models: from vans to ambulances. Along with other major car producers, Vauxhall had moved into 'factory custom' body production, but where the demand for a body style was limited they commissioned it from specialists. Salmons-Tickford of Newport Pagnell, and Grosvenor, both of which had long associations with Vauxhall stretching back to before the First World War, were two of the seven outside firms with whom contracts for such work were pursued.[62] The trend towards the end of the decade was to eliminate these expensive sidelines, and Vauxhall led the way in 1937 with the production of the 10hp H series, which was the first British integral all

---

[56] *Automobile Engineer* (June 1929), p. 225, quoted in Lyddon, ibid., p. 132.
[57] 'The Vauxhall Works,' *Automobile Engineer* (September 1933), pp. 319–325.
[58] *Luton News*, 30 March 1933, p. 11.
[59] 80 per cent of Vauxhall car deliveries were Light Sixes in 1935: M. Sedgewick, *Vauxhall* (1981), p. 57.
[60] Ibid., p. 56.
[61] *Commercial Motor*, 27 April 1934, p. 385. Of the ten makes in the 3-ton category held up for price comparison, most were well over £300 and one over £400.
[62] Sedgwick, op. cit., p. 42.

Plate 19. 1938 H-type 10hp, called the 'first modern British car' with its integral body and chassis. Selling at £168 it was the cheapest Vauxhall car produced to that date and sold over 55,000 before the outbreak of war in 1939.

steel saloon body which needed no separate frame or chassis.[63] Once again, Vauxhall drew on the technical expertise of its American parent company, and much of the initial design work, drafting, and body tooling was carried out in the USA, as 'Vauxhall resources were inadequate at the time for such a heavy undertaking.'[64] Maurice Olley and Alex Taub, two senior GM engineers, were transferred from Detroit to advise on the mechanical and design aspects involved in production.[65] Indeed, it was Taub who worked on its most outstanding sales feature, that of fuel economy. Working with the Zenith Carburettor Company he was able to produce an engine performance of over 40 miles to the gallon much to the initial disbelief of the motoring press. It was on proving this to be true that A.F. Palmer-Phillips, the sales distribution manager, based much of the 'Ten' publicity programmes, with successful results.

Another noticeable sales feature was independent springing, on which Olley had worked at the Cadillac Company. The advertising incorporated the phrase 'Riding changed to gliding,' emphasising the ease and comfort in handling of the vehicle.[66] Fuel consumption, innovatory features and style were emphasised

[63] L.C. Derbyshire, *The Story of Vauxhall* (Luton: Vauxhall Motors, 1946), p. 43.
[64] M. Platt, *An Addiction to Automobiles* (London: Warne, 1980), p. 98.
[65] Platt, ibid., p. 98.
[66] Vauxhall advertisements and publicity in Vauxhall archives, Luton, and The National Motor Museum Library archives, Beaulieu.

in the publicity campaign launched against Morris, Austin, Ford and Standard, which were the Vauxhall Ten's mass producer rivals, and it was priced at a competitive £168.

Table 12. 10hp model competition in 1938 and 1939

	Morris	Austin	Standard	Ford	Vauxhall
1938	£185	£175	£172	£145	£168
1939	£175	£175	£169	—	£168

Sources: R. Church, *Herbert Austin* (1979), table 9, p. 129, taken from *The Motor Car Index 1928–1939* (Norwich: Fletcher & Son Ltd., 1939) and 'Vauxhall Facts and Figures' (Vauxhall Motors, 1966).

The success of the Vauxhall Ten is evidenced by the rise in Vauxhall car sales, which topped 35,000 in 1938, outstripping commercial vehicle sales by over 10,000. More significantly, it helped cushion Vauxhall against the recession in the motor vehicle trade which took place in 1938 and was more damaging to the industry than the depression in 1931. British car production fell from 390,000 in 1937 to 341,000 in 1938, a drop of 12½ per cent.[67] Vauxhall car production by contrast rose from 28,076 in 1937 to 35,145 in 1938, a rise of 26½ per cent.[68] British commercial vehicle production fell by 12 per cent between 1937 and 1938, whilst Bedford truck production fell by 22 per cent.[69] Vauxhall combined car and commercial vehicle output nevertheless increased by 0.6 per cent; an infinitesimal increase, but an increase all the same when the output of the other Big Six producers was falling in absolute terms. Vauxhall accounted for 10.4 per cent of British car output for 1938, the highest it was to achieve in the years up to the Second World War and ample testimony of the importance of the Ten to Vauxhall. Morris and Standard attempted to counteract falling sales by cutting their model prices by £10 and £3 respectively, but the Vauxhall was still cheaper and superior. Only the Ford was lower priced but was still of comparatively inferior design.[70] It is interesting to speculate on the potential sales of the Vauxhall Ten had not the war intervened in the following year, causing Vauxhall to switch to truck and Churchill tank production.

Between 1933 and 1937 Vauxhall reorganised and extended its plant continually and during that time floor space doubled from 20 to 41 acres.[71] In 1935 K Block was built covering 6½ acres and was mainly concerned with machining and assembly of axles, body finishing and general assembly.[72] In 1936 £200,000 was invested in a 7 acre increase in the works but capacity was still not enough to meet demand, and the proposals to bring the remaining sales and services from Hendon to Luton had to be postponed.[73] By 1936 Bartlett announced that

[67] Calculated from G. Maxcy and A. Silberston, *The Motor Industry* (1959), p. 223, table 1.
[68] Calculated from figures in Table 9, above.
[69] Calculated from table 1, Maxcy and Silberston, op. cit., p. 223, and Table 9, above.
[70] See Table 12.
[71] See Table 9, above.
[72] *Luton News*, 22 August 1935, p. 9 col. 6.
[73] *Luton Evening Telegraph*, 29 January 1936, p. 1 cols. 2 and 3. After the war Hendon became the HQ for the GM subsidiaries of Frigidaire, U.K. Open Marketing and AC Delco European Replacement Parts Operation.

the company had spent over £2 million on the Luton factory, a very great deal of which had gone in machines and machine tools.[74] However, the production of the Ten was to demand the largest single capital investment programme since the company's inception, costing a million pounds.[75] The Luton plant was extended by another ten acres to over 53 by 1938, and was the single largest increase in floor space up to that time. More significant was the reorganisation of the production processes to incorporate the new integral body shell construction, which made Vauxhall the most advanced plant in Europe in this respect. The most interesting feature was the great advance in welding technique and the entire body shell was built without rivets or bolts by a series of flash welding operations. This was organised on a continuous basis with a time cycle of 6 minutes per shell, and the majority of operations mechanised to eliminate human error. Not surprisingly, output and productivity were considerably increased and the welding on a 25hp model was reduced from 35 minutes to 2 minutes.[76] In 1933 the Luton plant was producing 150 chassis per day;[77] in 1936 this was raised to 225 vehicles per day[78] and after the 1937 reorganisation 197 cars a day could be produced on a two shift system, and 272 on a three shift day. Estimating truck production at 41 per cent of output in 1938 this would give a total vehicle output per day of 333 vehicles on a 2 shift day, and 461 on a 3 shift day – an increase of between 48 and 105 per cent, depending on the number of shifts.

Another indication of the increased efficiency of the plant was that although trading profits per vehicle fell from £36 to £26 between 1936 and 1938 total vehicle output increased by 18 per cent and car output by 66 per cent.[79] The reduction in profit per vehicle was the result of price reductions on those vehicles which mass production could allow while maintaining overall profits. Despite Vauxhall's impressive performance it retained a number of weaknesses unique to the company and some that it shared with the industry as a whole. The Vauxhall site was unsuitable for a large modern factory as it was situated on the lower slopes of the Chiltern Hills which skirted Luton. This made expansion difficult and large volumes of earth had to be removed from the gradients to erect new buildings. The presence of Kimpton Road, which at one time was on the periphery of the works, but as a result of extensions became a central thoroughfare, necessitated bridge construction for the conveyance of vehicle units from one site to another.[80] Thus the organisation of production at Vauxhall was unique due to geographical location and hindered the attainment of maximum utilisation of the works. Such considerations led to a decision in 1938 to purchase land in nearby Dunstable for the erection of a plant devoted to commercial vehicles[81] though in fact this was not implemented until the 1950s.

[74] Ibid., p. 1. col. 3.
[75] *Luton News*, 25 March 1937, p. 11 cols. 6 and 7.
[76] 'Producing the Vauxhall Ten All Steel Body,' *Automobile Engineer* (January 1938).
[77] 'The Vauxhall Works,' *Automobile Engineer* (September 1933).
[78] 'The Vauxhall Works,' *Automobile Engineer* (August 1936).
[79] Calculated from Vauxhall Trading profits in Report to the Directors for 1936 and 1938 and 'Vauxhall Facts and Figures,' (Vauxhall Motors, 1966).
[80] 'Producing the Vauxhall Ten All Steel Body,' *Automobile Engineer* (January 1938).
[81] *Luton News*, 14 July 1938, p. 10. col. 2.

A feature of the move toward mass production is the reliance on outside suppliers of components, and manufacturing processes in car factories became largely replaced by assembly.[82] Vauxhall's reliance on supplies was greater than most, particularly those of the Big Three (Austin, Morris and Ford), and caused a number of weaknesses. Vauxhall had no foundry, all castings, stampings and forgings being bought in rough form to be machined at Luton.[83] A small output compared to those produced by the Big Three meant that orders were smaller and contracts were consequently less valuable to suppliers such as Lucas and Smiths, who would naturally give priority to Vauxhall's larger rivals. This would have the effect of causing bottlenecks in production and delays in deliveries to dealers.

Morris had the advantage that it had pursued a policy of acquiring as many of its component suppliers as possible in the 1920s.[84] Though other firms purchased their castings from outside, Austin made a deliberate decision to manufacture as many as was possible from the mid 1920s, saving up to 50 per cent of the cost in this way.[85] Ford had its own foundry at Dagenham.

Charles Bartlett deplored Vauxhall's excessive reliance on external suppliers because it forced the company into the arms of suppliers and placed it at a competitive disadvantage. Criticism was aimed in particular at highly priced and inferior quality sheet metal and the price fixing of safety glass, paint, copper, nickel and lamp bulbs.[86] He viewed the monopolistic position of manufacturers as obstacles to lower costs in the car industry and thus as a barrier to lower priced vehicles.[87] Certainly A.P. Young of the B.T.H. Company Limited, with whom he corresponded, did not share these views[88] and Bartlett standing alone in this indicates the vulnerability of Vauxhall in this respect.[89]

A third problem which affected Vauxhall, as well as the British car industry as a whole, was the failure to gain real economies of scale. Maxcy and Silberston estimated that a firm would need at least a run of 60,000 vehicles to achieve this[90] but models would need to have enough similarities to allow the use of the same assembly lines. One corollary of the price-model competition which became the characteristic of the 1930s British market was the annual model change which was usually revealed at the Olympia Show in the Autumn. This increased costs and prevented long runs of production. Morris attempted

---

[82] Eric Bates, interview March 1980. He described Vauxhall in the 1930s as much more a giant assembly plant than a manufacturing centre.

[83] This was still the case in the 1970s: K. Ullyett, *The Vauxhall Companion* (Stanley Paul, 1971), p. 44.

[84] R.J. Overy, *William Morris, Viscount Nuffield* (Europa, 1976), p. 28.

[85] R. Church, *Herbert Austin* (Europa, 1979), p. 102.

[86] M. Platt, *An Addiction to Automobiles* (Warne, 1980), p. 93. Letter from Bartlett to A.P. Young of the B.T.H. Co., Ltd., 4 November 1942: the Young Papers, MS 242: T.26 Modern Records Centre, University of Warwick.

[87] Letter to A.P. Young, 23 November 1942: the Young Papers, ibid.

[88] Letter from Young to Bartlett, 9 December 1942: the Young Papers, ibid.

[89] In 1954 the AC Delco division was formed, which produced engine components, and a factory was opened at Dunstable: 'About General Motors Limited,' GM Ltd. PR Department typescript (1977), p. 2.

[90] M. Maxcy and A. Silberston, *The British Motor Industry* (1959), p. 79.

to overcome this in 1935 with 'series' production where small technical changes might be made but the model remained constant over a number of years.[91] Morris claimed success, but other producers did not follow this practice until after the Second World War.

This dilemma led to conflicts of interest among Vauxhall departments. A.F. Palmer-Phillips, the Sales Director, was insistent that frequent changes in specifications would make Vauxhall cars and Bedford trucks more attractive to buyers. After the Olympia Show of 1938 he met with strong resistance from the cost-conscious production team led by Reg Pearson, A.W. Laskey, the supply manager, and the Chief Engineers.[92] Bartlett himself, parsimonious in business matters, sided with the production team, but the intervention of war in the following year caused Vauxhall to turn to other matters for the duration.[93]

Vauxhall in the 1940s

With the onset of war, Vauxhall concentrated on fulfilling government contracts for the War Department, and between 1939 and 1946 produced nearly a quarter of a million trucks, 5,640 Churchill tanks, and various other war materials ranging from 5 million jerrycans to steel helmets.[94] Car production which was limited to one hundred for military use had virtually ceased.[95]

Peacetime production was not resumed until 1946 and because of the preoccupation with war time orders, the continual and unremitting use of plant and capital equipment and steel shortages, the company was in no position to embark on a new peacetime car model programme: a situation shared by the industry as a whole. In addition, the change over from War to peacetime production took some reorganisation, and it was not until well into 1946 that new cars were leaving Luton in significant numbers.[96] Given the circumstances it is not surprising that Vauxhall resumed production of its tried and tested pre-war models, the Ten, Twelve and Fourteen, and it was not until 1948 that the first post-war-designed car emerged.

In the post-war years a sellers market prevailed. European producers had been hard hit by the War and many plants lay in ruins. American plants were working flat out to fulfil home demand. The Labour Government with balance of payments problems, and in particular the need for dollars explains why exporting was accorded the highest priority with motor vehicles singled out as a special spearhead in the export drive.[97] This, too, played a role in delaying the introduction of new models.

Vauxhall followed the national trend in production as pre-war peaks were reached and surpassed by 1948, but with one difference: commercial vehicle output once again exceeded car output at Vauxhall for the years 1946 and 1947,

[91] R.J. Overy, *William Morris, Viscount Nuffield* (Europa, 1976), pp. 57 and 58.
[92] L. Platt, op. cit., p. 116.
[93] Ibid., pp. 115 and 116.
[94] W.J. Seymour, *An Account of our Stewardship* (Luton: Vauxhall Motors Ltd, 1946), pp. 3 and 4.
[95] *A History of Vauxhall* (Luton: Vauxhall Motors, 1980), p. 47.
[96] Ibid., p. 49.
[97] Graham Turner, *The Car Makers* (Penguin, 1963; paperback 1964), p. 30.

mainly because the works were fully tooled-up for this since war time production. From 1948 to 1950, however, car production exceeded that of commercial vehicles mainly as a consequence of the export drive and the resumption of pre-war car sale trends of Vauxhall vehicles, as may be seen in Table 13.

Table 13. Vauxhall output 1946–1950

	Total output	Cars	CVs	Employees	Total floor area (acres)
1946	53,586	19,772	33,864	11,588	64
1947	61,453	30,376	31,077	11,773	64
1948	74,576	39,566	35,010	11,943	64¼
1949	84,167	45,366	38,801	12,003	80
1950	87,454	47,025	40,429	12,659	80

Source: 'Vauxhall Facts and Figures' (Vauxhall Motors,1966).

In terms of percentage share of the market Vauxhall was back to its pre-war peak of 10.5 per cent (achieved in 1930) by 1947 and increased by about 1 per cent in the following year. Though overall output increased, Vauxhall's share of the car market fell below 10 per cent in 1950. The Bedford share of the commercial vehicle output shows a marked fall. From a pre-war peak of 27 per cent of the market in 1937, Bedford's share dropped from 22 to 15 per cent between 1946 and 1950. This was due to the concentration of Vauxhall production on car output as works capacity was pushed to the limit in trying to meet orders, and priority was given to cars which afforded a larger profit per unit. However, plans were in the pipeline to set up a separate commercial vehicle assembly plant at Dunstable.

Table 14. Vauxhall share of the car and CV market 1946–1950

	Vauxhall Share of GB Car output (%)	Bedford share of GB CV output (%)	Vauxhall vehicle output as share of GB output (%)
1946	9.0	22.8	14.6
1947	10.6	19.6	13.8
1948	11.8	19.7	14.5
1949	11.0	17.7	13.3
1950	9.0	15.3	11.1

Source: G. Maxcy and A. Silberston, *The British Motor Industry* (1959), table 1, p. 223; calculated with 'Vauxhall Facts and Figures' (Vauxhall Motors, 1966).

Of the other car firms the combined share of the market of Austin and Nuffield also fell to below 40 per cent; a drop of 6 per cent on their combined percentage in 1939. Ford increased its share the most, regaining the ground lost in the latter part of the 1930s; by the end of the decade the Rootes group increased their percentage share by 3 per cent over the pre-war peak. (See Table 15 facing.)

However, the changes of percentage share did not alter as radically as in the

Table 15. Percentage share of total production of cars 1946–1950

	Vauxhall	Austin-Nuffield	Ford	Rootes	Standard	Others
1946	9.0	43.4	14.4	10.7	11.6	11.0
1947	10.6	39.3	14.8	10.5	12.9	12.0
1948	11.8	40.2	19.8	10.3	11.2	6.7
1949	11.0	39.4	18.7	13.3	11.1	6.5
1950	9.0	39.4	19.2	13.5	11.1	7.8

Source: G. Maxcy and A. Silberston, *The British Motor Industry* (1959), table 3, p. 117.

1930s, and the gains made by the American-owned subsidiaries and by Rootes and Standard were consolidated in this period.[98] The falling share of the market was experienced by those companies outside the Big Six which had been able to gain some ground in the immediate post-war years, but which as the major companies began to plan large investment programmes from 1948, subsequently experienced the effects of their competitive disadvantages. By the mid-1950s their share was just above 4 per cent.[99]

Another feature of the post-war years was increased government involvement, a trend which was to continue. Apart from measures intended to stimulate exports, Stafford Cripps, the Chancellor of the Exchequer, attempted to increase standardisation to enhance greater efficiency in the industry. In 1948 the Big Six Standardisation Committee was set up in anticipation of such government controls. The aim of the committee was to attempt to standardise components and ease interchangeability of company model parts.[100] The results were rather mixed, as strong opposition was encountered from Smiths (the clock and panel instrument makers) and the GM subsidiary of AC Delco.[101]

More important for Vauxhall was the abolition of the horse power system of car tax, and the introduction of a new flat rate system in the budget of 1947. Charles Bartlett said in 1944 'Were it not for this tax, on units of horse power, car manufacturers would list fewer models and produce each one more cheaply than at present.'[102] A long term aim of the budget proposals was to do just this, the intention being to reduce model competition and provide a market structure which would provide greater incentive for achieving economies of scale.

Vauxhall's immediate response was to drop the production of the Ten in the knowledge that the Twelve could be built and operated at much the same cost. In the following year two new models appeared in the form of the 6-cylinder Velox with a 2½ litre engine, the 4-cylinder Wyvern with a 1½ litre engine.[103] In

[98] In the 1950s and 1960s, however, Rootes and Standard were to experience severe financial problems in the losing race to reap economies of scale: D.G. Rhys, 'Concentration in the Inter-War Motor Industry,' *The Journal of Transport History* (September 1976), p. 258.

[99] G. Maxcy and A. Silberston, *The British Motor Industry* (1959), table 3, p. 117.

[100] M. Platt, *An Addiction to Automobiles* (Warne, 1980), p. 152.

[101] Platt, ibid., p. 153. Austin and Nuffield agreed to standardise parts, which proved to be the prelude to the formation of BMC: R.J. Overy, *William Morris: Viscount Nuffield* (Europa, 1976), p. 63.

[102] Sir Charles Bartlett, 'Taxation and the Motor Industry' (publication source unknown, 1944), quoted in Platt, op. cit., p. 147.

[103] *A History of Vauxhall* (Luton: Vauxhall Motors, 1980), p. 51.

Plate 20. Vauxhall Velox (L-type) 1948. The bridgehead between 'sit up and beg' 1930s designs and the 1960s modern models.

essence, they were restyled 12 and 14 hps with origins in the 1930s Light Sixes; but the new styling and bodywork heralded the new look which was to emerge in the following decade.[104]

The discussion of the production of the Wyvern and Velox revealed a new trend in Vauxhall management. Ed Riley, a tough negotiator, had replaced Jim Mooney as head of GMOO in 1941. He had a 'formidable personality (and) an unequivocal belief in the validity of a bold post-war policy to increase GMs manufacturing capacity overseas, especially in England.'[105]

Throughout the war years Vauxhall had enjoyed almost complete autonomy and one of Riley's aims was to relocate control in the American parent company. The fundamental conflict between Riley and Bartlett, which had been submerged in the hectic post-war years, was revealed over major new policy decisions suited to new economic conditions, for whereas Riley wished to inaugurate an entirely new model Bartlett wanted to revamp the Twelve.[106] Bartlett, approaching 60 years of age, succeeded in securing a compromise but it became clear that soon there would be a removal of the relative independence which the British managers had enjoyed in the 1930s.

[104] Platt, op. cit., p. 149.
[105] Platt, op. cit., p. 139.
[106] Platt, op. cit., p. 148.

During the war there had been much enthusiasm generated for a forward-looking planned economy embracing a welfare system which, it was hoped, would prevent a return to the pessimism of the 1930s. Bartlett shared this viewpoint but with one difference. He wanted to see large companies such as Vauxhall sharing this role. The key to ensuring that the post-war economy did not generate large scale unemployment lay in expansion of industry through the adoption of new methods of production which lowered prices by creating large economies of scale.[107] This he constantly preached and in 1948 Vauxhall, with the full approval of General Motors, embarked on a huge reorganisation programme in which £14 million was invested.[108] The floor space of the Luton works was increased by 30 per cent, and production streamlined.[109] This was accomplished by the production of only two car models (Velox and Wyvern), and alone among the large producers Vauxhall was committed to a programme of one hull, one wheel base and a choice of only two engines. This 'was in stark contrast to the complicated line up offered by Nuffield' for instance.[110] Though they may have not realised it at the time, Vauxhall was preparing for the intensities of competition from home and overseas producers which were to take place in the following decades.

In explaining the success of Vauxhall in the 1930s many historians of the vehicle industry have stressed the advantages bestowed on it by its American parent company.[111] While this is undoubtedly true both for Ford as well as for Vauxhall, success was not automatic. While the availability of capital, technical expertise, national and international dealer outlets and marketing expertise (particularly in the case of Vauxhall) were vitally important, the Americans failed to perceive the divergences and dissimilarities between the American and British market. In America huge factory capacity and home demand enabled US manufacturers to achieve economies of scale but the emphasis in the British market came to be in price-model competition, modified by taxation which influenced manufacturers to turn towards smaller engine models. As we have seen both Ford and Vauxhall owed much to their British managements in demanding suitable vehicles for the British market. The attempt to foist the Model A on the British market met with failure, and the Vauxhall Cadet was a disappointment. It was the Ford Model Y and the Vauxhall Light Sixes and Tens which made the impact and these models conformed to prevailing British market trends.

Penetration by the American companies was also made easier by the inability

[107] 'Bold Planning Needed to find New Jobs After the War,' a report of a Bartlett speech, *Luton News*, 26 August 1943, p. 8 col. 3; 'New Attitude to Industry,' a report of a Bartlett speech, *Luton News*, 6 December 1945, p. 6 col. 5.

[108] In the post-war years all expenditure of £1 million pounds or more had to be approved by General Motors (interview with Sir Reginald Pearson). Thus while the expansion seems to have been a Bartlett initiative, its approval rested with GM, who saw this as part of their overseas policy. Bartlett's power was gradually removed in the early 1950s and in 1953 he was given the post of Chairman, which was seen as a figurehead position rather than one vested with power: *Who Was Who 1951–60*.

[109] *A History of Vauxhall* (Vauxhall Motors, Luton. 1980), p. 68.

[110] M. Sedgwick, *Vauxhall* (London: Beaulieu Books, 1981), p. 66.

[111] R.J. Overy, *William Morris: Viscount Nuffield* (Europa, 1976), p. 43; R. Church, *Herbert Austin* (Europa, 1979), p. 20 for example.

of Austin and Morris to capitalise on their success in the 1920s. This has been attributed to management problems, particularly at Morris, and Austin's lag in car design in the 1930s, which was only remedied in 1939.[112] Rhys claims that because of this failure the tendency towards concentration of the 1920s was actually reversed and had much to do with the unique nature of price-model competition in the 1930s, which in many ways was unhealthy, and delayed the final 'shake out' to the 1950s and 1960s.[113] Such factors allowed the American-owned British subsidiaries to capture a considerable percentage of the expanding car market from 1934.

Nevertheless, the performances of Vauxhall and Ford could have been better. Ford's preoccupation with price, in a price-model market did not create long term sales, and the attempts to sell a £100 car in 1935 proved as unsuccessful as were those of Morris and Austin in the small horse power range. The gains made by Ford in the earlier part of the decade were eroded after 1937, the Dagenham works never achieving full peacetime capacity until after the Second World War. Vauxhall car output was small compared to the Big Three (Austin, Morris and Ford) and most of its success rested on its commercial vehicle sales. Its emphasis on large car models until 1933 ensured a late entry into the mass producer market, and its really successful car, the Ten, commenced production in 1938 but within two years war broke out. The main success story for Vauxhall was the 30cwt truck which found great popularity at home and abroad, and it was the profits of the sales of this vehicle, more than any other, which enabled Vauxhall to plough back its returns in expansion programmes, a strategy more closely examined in the next chapter.

[112] R. Church and M. Miller, 'The Big Three: Competition, Management and Marketing in the British Motor Industry, 1922–1939,' in B. Supple (ed.), *Essays in British Business History* (Oxford, 1977), pp. 167 and 173.

[113] D.G. Rhys, 'Concentration in the Inter–War Motor Industry,' *The Journal of Transport History* (September 1976), pp. 247–249.

Chapter Four

Financial, Marketing and Export Strategies

Financial strategies

It is not difficult to surmise that with the takeover of Vauxhall by General Motors much of the capital investment which was needed would be provided by the American parent company. The initial purchase price of 2½ million dollars (approx. £½ million) was supplemented by the acquisition of the ordinary shares which were increased in value from 10 shillings to a £1 each. The preference shares were also increased from 10 shillings to £1. The total shares were thus 600,000 made up of 300,000 shares of each type.[1] The debenture stock raised in 1925, just prior to the GM purchase, remained on the books and totalled £350,000 at 7 per cent interest redeemable in 1928 and 1952.[2]. Thus of the £950,000 in shares and debentures, GM only held £300,000 in 1926. The strategy of GM was to increase its holdings by expanding the ordinary shares while the preference shares and debentures remained unchanged. In 1927 the ordinary shares were increased by 68,000[3] and in 1928 increased by another 82,000 to give a total of 450,000 GM owned ordinary shares.[4] This situation was to remain until 1936 when the ordinary shares were increased to 1,000,000 because it was felt necessary 'to bring the issued capital of the company more into line with the capital actually employed in the business.'[5] The shares were, of course, totally GM owned.

The 'capital normally employed in the business' had been enormously expanded in the interim period in order to precipitate the rapid expansion of Vauxhall to cope with mass production. The additional capital investment came from two sources, initially from General Motors and after 1934 from profits, once all previous debts had been paid off.[6] Internal financing was also a predominant feature of Austin, Morris and Ford. Both Vauxhall and Ford achieved this by making heavy provisions for depreciation[7] as Table 16 shows.

The share capital of the firm was not increased until after the war and expansion was financed mainly through retained earnings and depreciation. In 1948, despite having only 1½ million ordinary shares, the company report states that 'the true capital is over £7 million.'[8] In 1949 the ordinary shares were

[1] Report to the Directors for Year Ending 31 December 1925.
[2] Ibid.
[3] Companies House, Vauxhall file no. 135769.
[4] Ibid.
[5] Report of Extraordinary Meeting Vauxhall Motors, *The Times*, 7 February 1936, p. 19 col. 6.
[6] Report of Vauxhall for 1933, *The Times*, 9 March 1934, p. 20 col. 3.
[7] Maxcy and Silberston, *The Motor Industry* (1959), table 9, p. 163.
[8] Report of Ordinary General Meeting 1948, *The Times*, 13 April 1948, p. 9 col. 9.

Table 16. Capital investment, Vauxhall Motors 1925–1938[9]

Year	Ord. shares	Pref. shares	GM invest. (millions of £s)	Assets	Depreciation £s
1925	300,000 (@10 shillings)	300,000 (@10 shillings)	0.50	1.2*	28,713
1925	300,000 (@ £1)	300,000 (@ £1)			
1926	300,000	300,000		1.1 *	40,689
1927	368,000	300,000	0.25	1.4 *	51,866
1928	450,000	300,000	—	1.2 *	47,019
1929	450,000	300,000	0.25	1.4 *	50,040
1930	450,000	300,000	0.16	1.7 *	60,513
1931	450,000	300,000	—	1.5 *	230,909 +
1932	450,000	300,000	0.50	1.6 *	229,077 +
1933	450,000	300,000	0.25	1.7 *	388,818 +
1934	450,000	300,000	—	2.3 *	529,213 +
1935	450,000	300,000	—	3.0 *	513,539 +
1936	1,000,000	300,000	—	4.0 *	543,702 +
1937	1,500,000	300,000	1.0 ++	4.5 *	710,930 +
1938	1,500,000	300,000	—	5.2 *	815,993 +

Assets included are land, buildings, plant, machinery, special tools, jigs, dies and current assets.
 + These figures include depreciation on buildings, plant, equipment; amounts written off for special tools, jigs and dies; maintenance of buildings and equipment and replacement of tools; plant rearrangement expense.
++ The £1,000,000 investment in 1937 came out of profits and increase of GM ordinary shares.

increased to 3½ million to finance an expansion programme totalling £10 million, of which 'the balance will be provided out of the company's own resources.'[10] The ability to finance much of its own expansion is true testimony of the success which Vauxhall experienced in the 1930s. This can be clearly evidenced by the profits on trading and net profits.

Table 17. Vauxhall profits and turnover 1929–48[11]

Year	Profit on trading (£)	Actual profit (a) (£)	Turnover (£ million)	Profit retained(b) (£)
1929	–320,943 (loss)	–283,791 (loss)	—	–283,791 (loss)
1930	–4,079 (loss)	–88,536 (loss)	—	–382,348 (loss)
1931	310,460	56,039	—	–392,344 (loss)
1932	375,453	123,034	2	–268,995 (loss)
1933	873,749	461,426	4	192,431
1934	1,371,481	837,909	7	956,091
1935	1,535,276	1,012,721	8	1,514,359

 [9] Compiled from Vauxhall Companies House file no. 135769; Reports to the Directors 1925–1938; Report of Ordinary General Meetings, *The Times*, 1925–38.
[10] Announcement in *The Times*, 5 October 1949, p. 9 col. 2.
[11] Sources: Reports to the Directors 1929–1938; *The Times* Reports of Ordinary General Meetings 1929–1948; 'Vauxhall Facts and Figures,' (Vauxhall Motors, 1966).

Table 17. (*cont.*)

Year	Profit on trading (£)	Actual profit (a) (£)	Turnover (£ million)	Profit retained(b) (£)
1936	1,759,281	1,214,550	9	1,161,581
1937	1,905,760	1,159,752	11	1,534,863
1938	1,622,336	743,293	10	1,226,949
1945	2,309,247	597,327*	—	—
1946	1,535,378	817,096	20	—
1948	3,060,178	957,781	26	—

* Low actual profit due to high taxation, shortage of materials (which increased their price) and change from war to peacetime production.[12]

Vauxhall's success is indicated plainly by their profits in relation to their assets, and using this as a yardstick compare more than favourably with the two leaders of the Big Six – Austin and Morris.

Table 18. Profits as percentage of assets, Vauxhall, Austin and Morris 1931–1938[13]

Year	Vauxhall a	Vauxhall b	Austin[14] a	Austin[14] b	Morris[15] b
1931	20	3.7	32.0	23.7	3.5
1932	23	7.6	25.3	19.2	7.2
1933	51	27.1	27.5	21.9	6.4
1934	59	36.4	31.9	25.4	10.5
1935	51	33.7	29.1	23.2	12.4
1936	43.9	30.3	28.8	22.3	6.3
1937	42.3	25.7	30.8	22.8	1.1
1938	31.1	14.2	34.5	15.8	−1.1

a Trading profit as % of assets.
b Net profit as % of assets.

In 1931 the newly reorganised and capitalised Vauxhall does not compare favourably with Austin, and is more on a par with the troubled Morris concern which was witnessing its 1920s lead diminishing. By 1933 Vauxhall was outstripping Austin and peaked in 1934, though the percentages remained healthy until the end of the decade. Austin regained its lead in 1938 but only marginally.

The above statistical table shows the high comparative return on capital assets of the Vauxhall organisation, particularly compared to Morris. For

[12] *The Times*, 4 May 1946, p. 9 col. 7, Report of Ordinary General Meeting.
    (a) Net profits before tax, i.e. trading profits, plus other income, less depreciation, director's salaries, debenture interest, before deduction of preference and ordinary dividends.
    (b) After payment of all debts plus previous year's sums brought forward and after deduction of preference and ordinary shares dividends.
[13] Vauxhall figures calculated from Table 17.
[14] Austin figures taken from Roy Church, *Herbert Austin* (1979), table 14, p. 143.
[15] Morris figures calculated from R.J. Overy, *William Morris: Viscount Nuffield* (1976), table 2, appendix one, p. 129.

example, although Morris output was nearly twice that of Vauxhall, its trading profit was on a par with Vauxhall (£1,442,000)[16] and its retained profit only slightly more at £1,083,000.[17] Vauxhall, of course, pursued a policy of writing off as much depreciation as possible even when not fully justified.

Thus Vauxhall's economic performance in the 1930s was, in terms of expansion and return on capital assets, quite remarkable and the peak reached in 1938 of 11.3 per cent of the car market was not bettered throughout the 1950s.[18] A further indicator of this success is profit per unit which averaged £28.8 on trading profit and £15.5 on actual profit in the years from 1931–38. Vauxhall's performance measured in these terms was consistently better than Morris and had surpassed Austin by 1934, although Austin performed better in this respect in 1938 as the following table demonstrates.

Table 19. Profit per unit, Vauxhall, Morris, Austin 1931–38

Year	Vauxhall[19]		Morris[20]		Austin[21]
	a	b	a	b	b
1931	£20	£ 4	£17.2 +	£ 5.6 –	£24 –
1932	£22	£ 7	£19.2 +	£10.9 –	£23 –
1933	£31	£16	£19.1 +	£11.0 +	£18 –
1934	£34	£21	£20.0 +	£14.1 +	£19 +
1935	£31	£21	£14.9 +	£11.2 +	£15 +
1936	£34	£24	—	— *	£16 +
1937	£32	£19	—	—	£14 +
1938	£27	£12	—	—	£14 –

a Profit per unit on trading profit.
b Profit per unit on actual profit.
+ Vauxhall has greater profit per unit.
– Vauxhall has less profit per unit.
* No output figures available.

Compared with Vauxhall's profit per unit in 1913, at £50 on actual profit, the 1930 figures may seem small, but the nature of production in Vauxhall (and most other car firms) until the mid-1920s was to achieve greater profits per unit on lower output. In the 1930s the object was to achieve economies of scale and with a far greater output at lower profit per unit gain greater overall trading and actual profits. Thus profits in relation to output were more efficient in terms of marginal cost. Compared to American companies, British manufacturers never achieved the full potential of economies of scale in the 1930s.[22] This was partly due to the limited size of the British market but also hindered by model competition which caused manufacturers in Britain to produce too much variety at the expense of large production runs. It has been calculated that a firm would need to produce at least 60,000 vehicles to achieve true economies of

[16] Overy, op. cit., table 2, p. 129.
[17] Overy, op. cit., table 2, p. 129.
[18] Maxcy and Silberston, op. cit., ch. VII, table 2, p. 107 and table 3, p. 117.
[19] Calculated from figures in Table 9 and Table 16, above.
[20] Calculated from Overy, op. cit., figures in tables 1 and 2, pp. 128 and 129.
[21] Taken from Church, op. cit., table 8, p. 114.
[22] Maxcy and Silberston, op. cit., p. 79.

scale.[23] Vauxhall's peak production year in the 1930s was 60,111 but this was combined cars and CV output, and 5 car models and CV models. It was not until the 1950s that Vauxhall began to achieve true economies of scale.

For General Motors, as the major shareholder of Vauxhall, a prime consideration was the return on capital in the form of dividends. This was the form in which they received their profits from Vauxhall. No dividends were paid until 1934 because it was not until that year that the directors could finally write off the remaining outstanding deficit of £268,996.[24] In 1933 arrears of dividend to preference share holders amounted to £90,000.[25] The 1934 £870,000 trading profit allowed Vauxhall to pay off these preference share arrears and to pay an ordinary share dividend of £261,562 to GM. Until 1938 the preference share dividend at 6 per cent averaged £13,000 per annum while the ordinary share dividend averaged £220,000 per annum, as the following table details.

Table 20. Dividends on preference and ordinary shares, and interest on first mortgage 7 per cent debenture stock 1927–38[26]

Year	Depenture-stock redeemed by trustees £	Interest £	Pref. div. £	Ord. div. £	%
1927	5,000	—	18,000	—	
1928	10,000	—	22,000	—	
1929	16,740	—	—	—	
1930	23,161	22,500	—	—	
1931	29,225	22,760	—	—	
1932	37,395	22,274	—	—	
1933	44,885	21,751	—	—	
1934	52,902	21,358	90,000	261,562	75%
1935	61,402	20,796	13,950	343,125	45%
1936	70,402	20,918	13,837	228,750	50%
1937	80,102	20,290	13,612	225,000	45%
1938	91,102	19,572	13,275	217,500	20%

It is to be noted that dividends throughout the war years on ordinary shares were 15 per cent rising again to 20 per cent in 1945.[27] The £275,937 ordinary share dividend totals for 1934 to 1938 seem to prove correct the critical analysis of *The Motor* when GM took over Vauxhall in 1925.[28] Ordinary shares were expanded while previous holders took preference shares at a fixed 6 per cent. *The Motor*, however, was not correct in one respect – it only put the percentage dividend at 10 per cent.

Such facts are open to interpretation, but while it is true that GM took total control of the company, it was their risked capital investment which was primarily responsible for its continued existence and expansion, which was by

[23] Ibid., p. 79.
[24] Report in *The Times*, 9 March 1934, p. 20 col. 3.
[25] Report to the Directors for the Year Ending 1933.
[26] Source: Reports to the Directors 1927–38.
[27] Reports to Ordinary General Meetings, *The Times*, 1940–45, each April.
[28] *The Motor*, 3 November 1925.

no means certain in the late 1920s or the early 1930s. Between 1925 and 1938 GM invested approximately £2 million in Vauxhall of which it had gained in return £275,937 in dividends. Add to this £1½ million in ordinary shares and approximately £5 million in assets, and it can be seen that General Motors held a company worth approximately £8 million: an increase in value of over £7 million on the pre-purchase figure of 1925.

In concluding this section it is worth quoting Frederic G. Donner, Chairman of GM Board and Chief Executive Office, in 1967 in reference to GM's overseas financial strategy:

> While development programmes generally have often focused on the transfer of capital, hopefully accompanied by the transfer of skills and methods, the emphasis in the General Motors experience has been just the reverse. It took a commitment of capital to get started, but increments to the initial investment generally have been self-generated or locally financed rather than provided through additional funds from the parent company. What have been continuously transferred in very large quantities are the policies, practices, and the skills that have so successfully applied in the parent organisation, modified of course, to adapt to local conditions.[29]

This can clearly be seen to have been the Vauxhall experience.

Marketing strategies
One important area where policies, practices and skills have been transferred from GM to Vauxhall is in marketing and distribution. The leading British car manufacturers in the 1920s, Ford, Morris and Austin, had merchandising techniques which differed 'from American practice more in degree of advancement than in principle.'[30] While this was true of the leaders in this decade the changes experienced by Vauxhall in the interwar years under GM influence were quite radical in terms of marketing and distribution. In this section an attempt will be made to answer the question of the relationship between GM and Vauxhall. The main periods of Vauxhall development of marketing can be divided into three: from 1905 to 1922/3; from 1923 to 1929; and from 1929. The major division is, of course, from the late 1920s when Vauxhall began to make major use of the GM Hendon sales and service experience. Marketing relies on the size and nature of the vehicle market and in the years before the First World War this was limited by the high cost of the product to a comparatively small wealthy clientele.[31] This initial demand market[32] meant that the major task of the manufacturers was to publicise their vehicles so that potential buyers were

---

[29] Frederic G. Donner, *The World-wide Industrial Enterprise: Its Challenge and Promise* (New York: McGraw Hill, 1967), pp. v and vi.
[30] Roy Church, 'The Marketing of Automobiles in Britain and the United States before 1939,' in *Development of Mass Marketing: Proceedings of the 7th Conference on Business History*, ed. A. Okochi and K. Shimokawa (Tokyo, 1980), p. 72.
[31] Ibid., p. 64.
[32] Ibid., pp. 65 and 66. Roy Church describes initial demand as 'that which is attributable to the purchases made by those consumers who could afford to buy motor vehicles and realised their utility and desirability. In this phase, elasticities of income and price are likely to be less important, at least directly, than what might be called elasticities of product improvement.'

aware of their existence and their merits. In this respect Vauxhall was no different from other car firms at this time. Advertisements were placed in trade and car journals, which had grown up from the 1890s, and also newspapers and magazines. The major event to exhibit cars was the Olympia Motor show, and although this did not have the significance which it was to assume in the interwar years, when companies used this as a means to unveil annual models, it was a focal point for the developments within the motor trade. The first reference to Vauxhall exhibiting there was in 1905[33] and it was to continue to do so throughout this period.

As a result of the limited nature of the market which was confined to upper and upper middle classes, price was of less importance than technological development, comfort and performance. Vauxhall began by manufacturing light cars between 5 and 12hp retailing at between £150 and £375, which was relatively cheap for those days. However, from 1905 the size of Vauxhall vehicles steadily increased together with the price, reaching a maximum 35hp and prices reached above £600.[34] This was truly reflective of the initial demand nature of the market.

Little is known of the early Vauxhall distribution and customer services. Initially, most customers actually purchased at the factory where closer attention could be given to individual customer requirements but from 1908 this became increasingly difficult as sales expanded, but direct contact was maintained with the owners of sporting cars which they were starting to develop.[35] After the move to Luton in 1905, Vauxhall still maintained a London office at Leadenhall Street. This was its London office for sale of its marine engines as well. It is interesting to speculate whether Vauxhall made use of its customer contacts in this side of the business, as other car manufacturers had used bicycle outlets for their initial sales.[36] Unfortunately no records remain to provide such information. One of the major forms of publicising vehicles in this period and in the 1920s was participation in reliability trials and races, in which the prestige of a company could be enhanced overnight. In this way technical innovations 'not visible to potential buyers'[37] could be demonstrated effectively. Hill climbs, endurance runs, stunts, races and trials drew considerable public attention in the media, which was fascinated by the exciting novelty of record breaking which racing car drivers and, indeed, aeronauts were attempting at this time. For the comparatively young members of the Board of Vauxhall the attraction was no less magnetic. A.J. Hancock, Kidner and Pomeroy, all in their twenties or thirties, threw themselves into such activity to an absorbing degree.

Vauxhall first entered such events in 1904 in which it participated in the Glasgow to London endurance run[38] with a light car driven by Percy Kidner. In 1905 a car was entered for the Isle of Man TT, and in 1908 Vauxhall

---

[33] 'Olympia Show Report,' *Autocar*, 25 November 1905, p. 685.
[34] See Table 1.
[35] Derbyshire, *The Story of Vauxhall 1837–1946* (Luton, 1946), p. 17.
[36] Church, op. cit., p. 62. Humber, Rover and Singer are particular examples in this respect. Morris began as manufacturer and repairer of bicycles.
[37] Church, op. cit., p. 67.
[38] Derbyshire, op. cit., p. 14.

successfully participated in the RAC 2,000 mile Reliability Trials. In that year Vauxhall gained successes in three trials and four hill climbs. In 1909 a car was entered for races at Brooklands and in 1912 a Prince Henry was entered for the French Grand Prix. Vauxhall's most successful year was in 1913 when the 30/98 was winner of many events in its category. There is no doubt that these activities elevated the reputation of Vauxhall cars in the public eye. Both the Prince Henry and the 30/98 were produced as normal road vehicles and their reputations no doubt stimulated the sale of less high performance Vauxhall models. From 1910 Vauxhall entered international car events, including Russia, Germany, Scandinavia, France, New Zealand, and Australia.[39] It was Vauxhall's successes in Russia in 1911 and 1912 which led to numerous sales there and the eventual opening of an office in Petrograd (St. Petersburg).

After the First World War Vauxhall resumed participation in trials and races in 1920 but not to the same degree. In 1919 Vauxhall announced that 'a change in their policy in the marketing of their cars in England has been decided upon.'[40] The London show rooms, which they had acquired in Great Portland Street in 1912 were to be handed over to their London agents, Messrs. Shaw and Kilburn Ltd of 114, Wardour Street, W1, 'thus relinquishing definitely their handling of retail trade. The present officials in the sales department will continue in the service of the company.'[41] By doing this Vauxhall hoped to concentrate their efforts purely on production and leave the marketing and distribution to those who had the knowledge and resources to handle this side of the business. In some respects this was a wise move, the market had begun to change, speeded by the Depression of 1921 which hit the car industry particularly severely. In addition Morris and Ford had laid the groundwork for mass production which many other car firms would be forced to imitate or go under. This process was to come to maturity in the 1930s, and the changes taking place were slow to be assimilated by car companies including the Vauxhall Board. By 1922 Vauxhall had come to realise the need for greater sales at lower prices of car, as the full effects of price competition adversely affected profits. In 1923 Vauxhall withdrew from sporting events and concentrated on car production.

The second phase of Vauxhall marketing from 1922/3 to 1929 can only be described as years of uncertainty. Price competition was pre-eminent and the market was slowly percolating down to lower income levels as mass production made car prices more within the reach of the middle classes. Vauxhall's general sales policy had to come in line with demand and from 1922 began to produce a 14hp car priced from £495 – a considerable drop in price compared with immediate post-war prices at nearly £2,000. In the 1920s Vauxhall appeared to be trapped between the reputation it had created by its high performance vehicles, the desirability of the Board to keep that reputation in tact and the changing nature of the market. It attempted to resolve this problem by reorganising production on a 'semi flow assembly' basis. Until 1924 the hope of the Vauxhall Board was that the old market conditions would return, a

[39] Derbyshire, op. cit., ch. V.
[40] The Luton News, 27 February 1919, p. 7.
[41] Ibid.

theme frequently reiterated by the Board in its annual reports. Reality was fully faced in 1925 when on the verge of bankruptcy it was forced to sell to General Motors.

The indecision as what to do with their newly acquired British company continued this air of uncertainty, and Vauxhall plodded along with its rather pedestrian sales and marketing techniques. In some respects it was forced to continue in this vein due to the hostility and controversy engendered over the GM purchase. Consequently, the American ownership of the company was kept in low profile.

In 1928 GM decided to make available to Vauxhall the full resources and expertise of marketing and distribution of not only Hendon, but GM world-wide. In 1928 the Hendon Branch began to produce *The General Motors News*. Its first edition stated that:

> It is essential that constant and intimate touch with retailers should be ensured, and that they, in turn should have easy means of maintaining constant touch with the principal executives of the firm.[42]

Such promotional journals were not new in the British motor industry. Austin had pioneered this development with the *Austin Advocate* started in 1911.[43] Morris had founded *The Morris Owner* in the early 1920s.[44] Leading British car firms were fully aware of the importance of advertising and promotion and developing dealer and distribution networks. The main difference between them and their American rivals was in the advancement of these sales techniques; and in this respect GM was in advance of Ford. In the early 1920s Ford had seen his business as 'making cars not selling them.'[45] The lead which GM took over Ford in the 1920s was strongly based on its development of strong marketing policies created by Richard Grant, whose pioneering sales methods he brought from his work with the National Cash Register Company.[46] In 1928 Grant visited Britain and gave a lecture to 260 GM Hendon staff and dealers. He emphasised that the basis of all successful selling was 'the right model, in the right place, at the right time.'[47] 'The right model' was the first decision to be taken, and this resulted in the production of the Cadet which failed to make a large penetration into the British market and which Sloan described as 'disappointing.'[48] The Light Sixes had more success and the Ten enabled a peak in Vauxhall car sales by the end of the decade, but given the resources available to Vauxhall from GM its overall performance did not match that of Morris, Austin and, its American rival on the British market, Ford. There were two major reasons for this. Firstly, Vauxhall could not market a full range of cars in each price and horse power bracket as GM had done in the USA, because the British car market had enough ranges of models already to fill adequately these areas. In addition the late entry into the

[42] Walter Boyle, 'Why a House Journal?' in *General Motor News* vol. 1, no. 1 (July 1928).
[43] R. Church, *Herbert Austin* (1979), p. 25.
[44] R.J. Overy, op. cit., p. 32.
[45] 'How to Sell Automobiles,' *Fortune Magazine* (February 1939), reprinted in A.D. Chandler, *Giant Enterprise* (New York, 1964).
[46] Ibid., p. 160.
[47] 'Grant the Great,' *GM News* vol. 1, no. 1 (July 1928).
[48] Sloan, *My Years with General Motors*, p. 328.

mass producer market by Vauxhall, with a new and smaller model, was more difficult to achieve in a mature market which many suspected had reached saturation by the late 1920s and the early 1930s.[49] In contrast GM with its much earlier start in the USA had all the advantages of being in at the beginning of market developments.

The 'right model (s)' proved to be the Chevrolet truck and more specifically the Bedford light truck which found a previously untapped market among small retailers and businessmen, and it was in this market that GM marketing techniques proved to be so successful. By the end of the 1920s British manufacturers had highly developed sales and distribution networks contained in a structure of distributors, agents and dealers both nationwide and abroad. For example, Morris had 1,750 dealers in 1927[50] whereas GM had only about 120 dealers in 1930[51] with about 300 to 400 dealers which sold GM and Vauxhall products, though not exclusively. This marked difference in size of dealerships clearly indicates the significant lead that the large British manufacturers had in this area.

In 1929 GM reorganised its sales department at Hendon (see Chart 1[52]) with A.F. Palmer-Phillips as Director of Sales, and under him were a staff of 11 sales managers and three teams of fieldmen numbering 22 employees, giving a total of 34 in this department.[53] A fieldman was 'the link between the motor manufacturer and motor dealer. He represents both parties, the manufacturer when he is with the dealer, and the dealer when he is with the manufacturer. His task was to explain the sales campaign, details of models, rebates, discounts and generally assist the dealer with all manner of sales weapons.'[54]

Grant, in his British talk, explained that the main problem of dealers was bad debts and 'this meant creating an accounting system from the evidence derived from thousands of dealers. There are 2,000 dealers (in the USA) conforming to the scheme with profit.'[55]

He believed in good commission for salesmen. 'Don't starve a good man – I'm the protector of the under-paid salesman.'[56]

Other slogans of advice poured forth. 'You can't cheat and have good will.'[57] He recommended 'Two minute talks for salesmen,' so the prospect (the potential car buyer) would be assured of at least two minutes sound product talk. Photographs, books and pamphlets he claimed as important to impress and convince the prospect. It was important to improve the salesman's small talk and initiate promotion schemes for high sales. Offers of prizes to top salesmen such as radios, cigarette lighters or fishing rods were recommended, as well as a 'Sales Speeder' – a fortnightly sheet of selling ideas.[58] None of these ideas were new and were practised by many British firms at the time. What was different was the

[49] Church, 'Marketing of Automobiles,' p. 66.
[50] Ibid., p. 70.
[51] GM News vol. 2, no. 10 (April 1930).
[52] Chart reproduced from 'The New Sales Set Up,' GM News vol. 2, no. 4 (October 1929).
[53] 'The New Sales Set Up,' ibid.
[54] Ibid.
[55] GM News (July 1928).
[56] Ibid.
[57] Ibid.
[58] Ibid.

Chart 1

Vauxhall's New Sales Organisation 1929

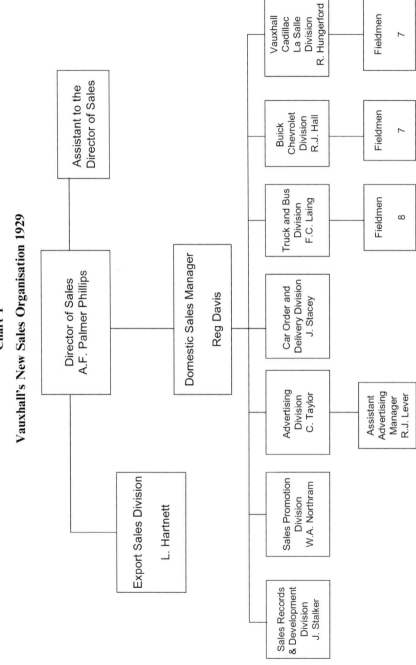

Chart 2
Potential Sales Prospects for Bedford Light Trucks – GM-Style Market Analysis

(taken from *General Motors News*, May 1929)

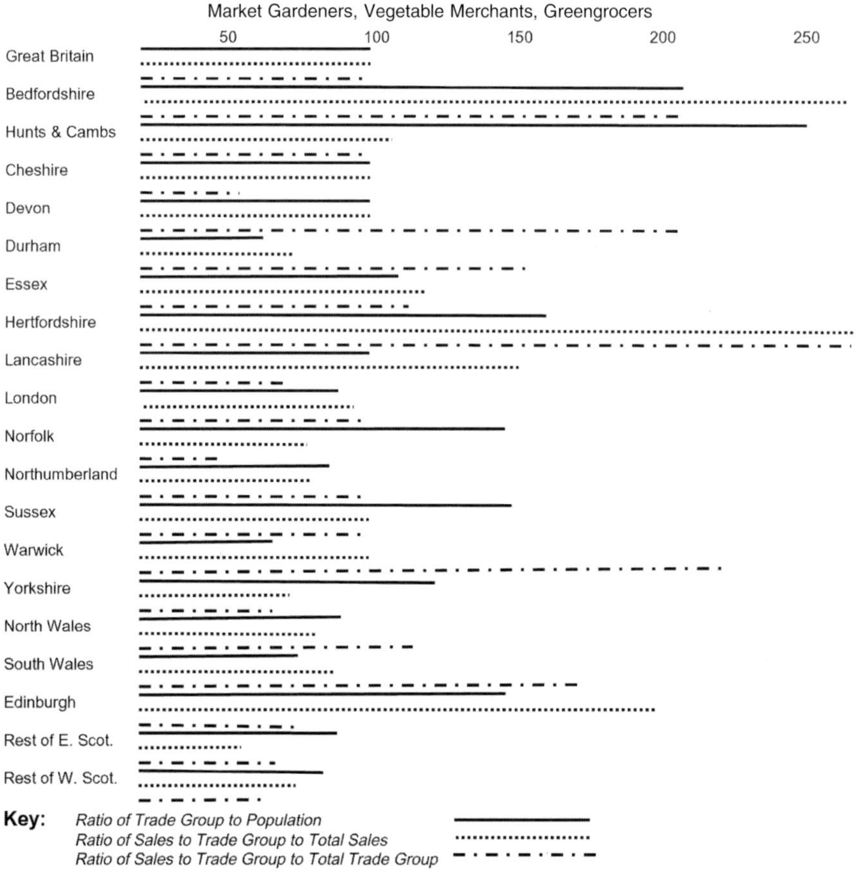

Market Gardeners, Vegetable Merchants, Greengrocers

	50	100	150	200	250

Great Britain

Bedfordshire

Hunts & Cambs

Cheshire

Devon

Durham

Essex

Hertfordshire

Lancashire

London

Norfolk

Northumberland

Sussex

Warwick

Yorkshire

North Wales

South Wales

Edinburgh

Rest of E. Scot.

Rest of W. Scot.

Key: Ratio of Trade Group to Population
Ratio of Sales to Trade Group to Total Sales
Ratio of Sales to Trade Group to Total Trade Group

collective intensity of this sales approach, and more importantly backed by a thorough research of market intelligence. It was in this latter area that GM played its most influential role particularly in the sale of the light truck. From the early 1920s Sloan had been especially interested in this side of the Corporation's organisation. 'We began to make economic studies of the market and its potential in terms of population, income, past performance, business cycle and the like.'[59] Pinpointing markets and their potential was an important marketing innovation, and the use of combined and accurate statistics were invaluable. This expertise was transposed to the British experience by GM and in 1929 a thorough examination of the light truck potential market was undertaken. A statistics department was set up at Hendon to carry out this work. A series of statistics sheets were produced and continually updated. A detailed example of one of these sheets was reproduced in a *GM News* article and related

[59] A.P. Sloan, *My Years with General Motors* (1965), p. 284.

to the sales potential of light trucks to greengrocers, fishmongers and related traders.[60] On the reproduced sheet on the previous page (Chart 2), the black line indicates, that on average there are approximately six greengrocers for every 10,000 of the population throughout the country. Obviously some counties have more greengrocers than others, and the longer the line the more greengrocers there are to the population proportion of 10,000. The black line opposite Britain represents that proportion of the total trucks bought by greengrocers throughout the country. For example, the black dotted line for Bedfordshire shows that Bedford bought more trucks than the rest of the country on average. The white dotted line indicates the proportion of greengrocers who bought GM trucks.

Similar charts were drawn up for other traders and small business categories. Then having identified the sales potential within each of these areas this was followed up by sending in fieldmen to help create a sales campaign with dealers and their salesmen. GM did stress that there must be as much decentralisation and delegation as possible.[61] In this way GM was not seen to control totally the operation, dealers and salesmen could use their own initiative, and valuable time could be saved by top management not doing lower level duties. A concept which Austin, Morris and, particularly, Ford found difficulty in coming to terms with.

The follow up campaigns were intensive and combined advertising and stunts, the latter included driving a Bedford truck up the steps of Alexandra Palace, driving through and along streams and negotiating hills with a 50 per cent overload. Shows and exhibitions were held in places with high sales potential and many other features. Dealers and sales men were bombarded with suggestions to improve their image and hence their sales, which included:

> Better letter paper with improved designs for headings; repainted fronts of a more dignified type; improved show room fitments; new methods of approach by means of more carefully conceived sales letters; better recording of prospect particulars by means of Kardex; more comprehensive stocking of parts to avoid delays; swifter service; closer acquaintance with newspaper editors and motoring correspondents to ensure easier and bigger flow of publicity; more carefully mapped out demonstration routes and the conversations to take place during trial runs; a greater use of advertisement columns by calling on our Advertising Department for steros and special layouts; more conferences with salesmen to learn all the difficulties and overcome them; more frequent rearrangement of show room models and decorative materials; better lighting equipment.[62]

Other potential selling points were the use of Bedford trucks as travelling shops with the traders name on the side advertisements of the goods sold. A.F. Palmer-Phillips identified in Leicester alone a potential market of 359 grocers, 209 greengrocers, 190 butchers, 84 fishmongers and poulterers, 71 bakers, 44 chemists and 38 milkmen and dairymen, a total of 995 potential buyers of travelling shops.[63]

Sales were also facilitated by the making available of deferred payment

[60] 'How Statistics are Developed at Hendon,' *GM News* vol. 2, no. 11 (May 1929).
[61] 'Decentralise and Delegate,' *GM News* vol. 1, no. 4 (October 1928).
[62] 'Improvement in New Models: Why Not in Selling Methods,' *GM News* vol. 2, no. 4 (October 1929).
[63] 'Reminiscences of a Salesman,' *The Vauxhall-Bedford News* vol. 7, no. 9 (March 1935).

purchase schemes. GM had established the General Motors Acceptance Corporation for this purpose in the USA in 1919, and the first GMAC office was opened in England in 1920.[64]

The practice was rapidly spread in Britain and Europe in the 1920s in the face of intensive price competition, and most large vehicle manufacturers had their own schemes in operation by the end of the decade.[65] By 1927 instalment buying 'accounted for 60 per cent. of car sales in Britain, compared with 75 per cent. of all sales of motor vehicles . . in the United States in 1925.'[66] This new form of purchasing had a considerable stigma attached to it in large sections of the public eye both in the USA and in Britain.

This social prejudice was just as prevalent among the business community and it was the newer industries like automobiles which spearheaded its diffusion. In 1927 the fruits of research by Professor Edwin Seligman was published in his work entitled *The Economics of Installment Selling*.[67] The research and writing of this work had been sponsored by GM at the behest of Sloan and did much 'in bringing about an acceptance of instalment selling among bankers, businessmen and the public.'[68] Social acceptance was longer delayed in the more conservative atmosphere of Britain and continual attempts were made to demonstrate the respectability of the 'never-never' in Vauxhall-GM advertising. In 1929 GM News gave much play to the fact that 'two eminent financiers,' Lord Beaverbrook and Philip Snowden, Chancellor of the Exchequer, approved of hire purchase.[69]

The availability of deferred payments schemes played a considerable role in the sales of Vauxhall vehicles, one must surmise, particularly in the depressed years of 1930 to 1934. This was despite a drop of nearly 7,000 in national CV figures from 1931 to 1932.[70]

Another pioneering feature of GM was the recognition of the value of the used car trade in its effects on new model sales. In 1925 the General Sales Committee of GM gave considerable attention to a policy of trade-ins and used cars. Whereas Ford wanted his dealers to show a profit on such deals, GM was more concerned in preventing overstocking and hindering turnover of car sales.[71] Grant claimed that second-hand car sales were,

> a blessing not a curse, but this depends on the ability of the second-hand operator. The more second-hand cars sold the more new cars sold, because people with last year's model want to get rid of it and buy this year's model. Second-hand customers will move the market.[72]

The growth of the used car market was an indicator of the maturation of the vehicle market[73] and enabled a wider income range to become car owners while

---

[64] F.G. Donner *The World-wide Industrial Enterprise* (New York: McGraw-Hill, 1967), p. 21.

[65] R. Church, 'The Marketing of Automobiles,' p. 67.

[66] Ibid.

[67] Mentioned in Sloan, op. cit., p. 306.

[68] Sloan, op. cit., p. 306.

[69] 'Two Eminent Financiers Approve of Hire Purchase,' *GM News* vol. 1, no. 8 (February 1929).

[70] See Table 14 above.

[71] Federal Trade Commission, *Report on the Motor Vehicle Industry* (Washington, 1939), extract in A.D. Chandler, *Giant Enterprise* (New York, 1964), pp. 171 and 172.

[72] 'Grant the Great,' *GM News* (July 1928).

[73] R. Church, 'The Marketing of Automobiles', p. 74.

previous owners moved on to a higher class of vehicle or a newer model – a factor in helping to create the price-model competition characteristic of the British car industry after 1934. The organisation of this market was not without problems, both in the USA and in Britain, and 'until agents learned to gauge the probable selling values of used cars money was lost and capital locked up in second-hand cars for which no profitable outlet could be found due to the excessive allowance given to the original owner.'[74]

In order to help solve such problems GM decided on a supportive policy towards dealers, and in 1925 the General Sales Committee issued its recommendations

> It was unanimously agreed that the future volume of sales on new cars would depend largely upon the efficient selling and servicing of used cars. It is, therefore, necessary for the manufacturers to take an interest in the sale of used cars.[75]

Men were employed (by each car division) specialising in used cars to give dealers help and advice in selling their stock. Firstly, reconditioning and after sales service were to be offered. Secondly, special used car show rooms and advertising were to be organised; and thirdly, financial advice and stock taking was to be undertaken.[76] This last point was characteristic of the GM approach. Dealers were encouraged to report the types and number of used cars in stock regularly, and as often as once a day. The division would then give advice on prices, offers and trade-in discounts. If a profit could be made then the dealer would obviously be advantaged. GM, however, was not too concerned about making a profit on a used car if ultimately the customer was to purchase a new model.[77]

Another idea to move second-hand car sales was an Automatic Dutch Auction.[78] By this method, 'a prospective buyer having the price he is willing to pay for one of the cars, will make a bid in writing and pay a deposit on that figure.'[79] If the selected car has not found a buyer on the previous day, the bidder gets the car, but if there has been a buyer, the bidder receives the return of his deposit. In this case the dealer will induce the buyer to transfer his bid to another car. The scheme was often labelled 'Buy at Your Own Price.'[80] According to Grant such selling techniques should be transferred to GM in Britain.[81]

The policy of the major motor manufacturers in the USA was to secure as many franchised dealers as possible which would be under their direct control. Ford's attempt to do this in Britain was not successful.[82] However, GM starting

[74] Ibid.
[75] Minutes of the General Motors Sales Committee October 1925, reprinted in Chandler, *Giant Enterprise* (New York, 1964), p. 172.
[76] 'Grant the Great,' *GM News* (July 1928); Chandler, op. cit., p. 172.
[77] 'Grant the Great,' op. cit.
[78] 'Automatic Dutch Auction – a Good scheme for selling second-hand cars,' *GM News* vol. 1, no. 2 (August 1928).
[79] Ibid.
[80] Ibid.
[81] 'Grant the Great,' op. cit.
[82] R. Church, 'The Marketing of Automobiles,' op. cit., p. 70.

from a lower base was able to build up franchises gradually. They no doubt profited from Ford's early 1920s British experience in which only 400 of its 1,200 dealers renewed their contracts, rather than become franchised.[83] Donner states that the GMOO policy was:

> Wholesale distributors, who had handled the distribution of General Motors products to retail dealers, were replaced in the large markets by a growing number of directly franchised dealers who sold and serviced General Motor products. During this period General Motors also assumed the responsibility for financing inventories all the way to the point of delivery to the retail dealers.[84]

Not only did GM franchise dealers have the full financial weight of the Corporation behind them, but also the skills of the staff of the Motors Accounting Company set up in 1927. This 'developed a standardised accounting system applicable to all dealers and sent a staff into the field to help install it and to establish an audit system.'[85] Such procedures were transposed to the British market with modifications for local conditions and attitudes.

One British feature of marketing campaigns in the 1920s and 1930s was the economic nationalism engendered in the 'buy British' campaigns, launched by Morris and Austin and often with tacit approval from the motoring press. There is little evidence that these were successful, but one influence which they did have on Vauxhall was to eliminate any reference to General Motors in its publicity, and emphasise the 'all Britishness' of Vauxhall products produced by British workmen. It also caused Vauxhall to completely take over the Hendon premises from GM so that all marketing and sales were carried out under the Vauxhall name from 1932. By that time GM imports had been completely run down and a small GM office was opened in London completely separate from the Vauxhall organisation.[86] The marketing strategies developed by GM were undoubtedly influential in up-dating Vauxhall performance in this area. Charles Bartlett after returning from a trip to inspect the GM organisation in the United States commented, 'there may be much for all of us to learn of the new methods for discovering prospects. The forward planning methods of the States are generally more detailed and scientific than ours.'[87]

James D. Mooney felt that the American methods were more advanced than the British marketing techniques. He saw the British salesman's approach as much more individualistic than the American 'and is superior in this respect,' whereas the American,

> as an individual is but a fair salesman. But he is an organiser, especially a sales organiser. He knows how to mass his forces . . . He defines the task to be done and then organises to it.[88]

---

[83] R. Church, 'The Marketing of Automobiles'.
[84] Dormer, op. cit., p. 20.
[85] Sloan, op. cit., p. 287.
[86] *The Vauxhall-Bedford News* vol. 4, no. 11 (May 1932).
[87] 'Mr. Bartlett on his Return From America,' *GM News* vol. 2, no. 2 (August 1929).
[88] James D. Mooney, 'Selling Must be Organised,' *GM News* vol. 1, no. 10 (April 1929).

He finishes his article by stating 'that all that is needed is for the English businessman to study the organised sales effort of a few successful American firms.'[89]

GM thus not only influenced Vauxhall but attitudes in the British motor vehicle market as a whole, and in 1931 Vauxhall proudly boasted

> We can say with pride, and without any tinge of annoyance, that our competitors are copying our sales promotion efforts. We know they take steps to obtain copies of this journal each month as soon as it is issued . . . This should be an inspiration to all of us to keep ahead with ideas and activities.[90]

Throughout the 1930s Vauxhall adopted the method of regular reporting of current stocks and sales by dealers in order to guide the factory in the scheduling of production to meet future dealer requirements. In 1947 the Vauxhall Motors Dealer Council was set up to provide regular programmes of dealer meetings with the top management of the company for an exchange of views on the business, policy and operations.[91]

Export strategies

The significance of exports in the development of Vauxhall Motors after 1930 cannot be over stressed. Up until that time Vauxhall had enjoyed some minor success in overseas sales on a limited scale before the First World War, but the 1920s was to see a considerable decline in terms of percentage of Vauxhall output – a reflection not only of its own internal financial difficulties, but also of the preoccupation of the British car industry as a whole with domestic sales, and intensive price competition.

The early Vauxhall and West Hydraulic Company was well established in the field of exports for its marine engines and other manufactures found overseas outlets through the Board of Trade, the India Office and Crown Agents for the Colonies. In 1905 the *Luton News* stated, 'A large amount of their trade is export to the colonies and abroad.'[92] The first recorded overseas Vauxhall car sale was in 1904 to a client in New Zealand.[93] The Empire and dominion markets were to prove important not only to Vauxhall, but to the British vehicle industry as a whole: and it was the sporting successes in the colonial countries that gave added impetus to sales in these markets. Indeed, in 1913, Vauxhall produced two 'special Colonial' 20hp models equipped with a two-seater body and a goods platform at the back. In consideration of the rougher roads they had larger wheels and different gear ratios from the home products.[94]

It would be interesting to know if Vauxhall made use of its contacts overseas in the marine engine market as channels for its car sales. This is not recorded.

[89] *GM News* (April 1929).
[90] 'Editorial' in *GM News* vol. 4, no. 3 (September 1931).
[91] Philip W. Copelin, 'Development and Organisation of Vauxhall Motors Limited' in R.S. Edwards and H. Townsend (eds.), *Studies in Business Organisation* (London, 1961).
[92] *Luton News*, 30 March 1905, p. 3.
[93] K. Ullyett, *The Vauxhall Companion*, p. 22.
[94] Ibid., p. 57.

By 1912, however, Vauxhall did have 'in many parts of the world special agents . . . not only in the British dominions, but in Russia, Sweden and other parts of Europe.'[95] It must be assumed that this overseas network did benefit from know-how and intelligence gained from Vauxhall's sister company, and despite the break in 1907 their locations were adjacent.

Apart from the colonies, Vauxhall's next biggest overseas market was Russia. A foothold had been gained there due to successes in reliability trials alluded to in the section on marketing. Kidner, who had driven in the 1,400 mile trial between St. Petersburg and Sebastopol, stated that the success in this race 'was calculated to leave its mark,'[96] indicating the awareness of the Vauxhall management of these overseas successes in securing orders. The Russian orders which followed these triumphs led to the establishment of an agency combined with a workshop staffed by British engineers, and there was even a lavish catalogue in Russian.[97] Catalogues were also produced in Spanish, French and Swedish[98] and a few cars were dispatched to South America.[99]

Despite these diverse markets Vauxhall exports probably did not exceed 50 cars per annum before the First World War, although by 1912 they accounted for nearly 15 per cent of Vauxhall sales, as the following table shows

Table 21. Vauxhall exports 1908–1912[100]

Year	Estimated exports	Exports as % of Vauxhall output
1908	15	15.9
1909	25	12.8
1910	30	12.3
1911	35	13.2
1912	45	14.9

Throughout the war years the total output was taken by the War Department as staff cars, in which duties they proved themselves as sturdy and reliable vehicles on the diverse roads to be found in Arabia, Palestine, Egypt, Greece, Albania, East Africa and Flanders. The war experience had proved fruitful in extending Vauxhall's name both at home and abroad, and in 1919 the Board announced some bold overseas initiatives.

> The reputation of the Vauxhall car has been very greatly enhanced by its performance in war service, and the fact that it has proved so successful has become very widely known through the medium of officers and others, and has occasioned enquiries of a significant nature from both the United States and Canada, as well as from many other parts of the world.[101]

[95] *Luton News*, 14 November 1912, p. 7.
[96] *Luton News*, 2 November 1911, p. 7.
[97] K. Ullyett, op. cit., p. 57.
[98] *Luton News*, 14 November 1912, p. 7.
[99] *Luton News*, 27 October 1910, p. 6.
[100] Source: 'Vauxhall Facts and Figures,' (Vauxhall Motors, 1966).
[101] *Luton News*, 27 February 1919, p. 7.

Recently resigned, L.H. Pomeroy was asked to make a report on the American and Canadian markets, as he was leaving to tour these countries. It can be assumed that one of the results of this investigation was the setting up of a Canadian branch in 1922.[102] In addition Vauxhall stated in 1919 'there are large and valuable markets abroad which were formerly chiefly served by the Germans, which with an energetic policy, we ought to be able to capture.'[103] Such was the optimism that Vauxhall even produced a film showing the making of Vauxhall cars, 'and there is no doubt it will serve a very useful purpose in informing foreign customers of the fine modern conditions under which the cars are made.'[104] Such expectations were to prove groundless in the following decade, and with the exception of 1927 and 1928 when exports reached 590 and 853 respectively, Vauxhall's export record was poor to say the least, especially when seen in terms of percentage Vauxhall output, as the following table indicates.

Table 22. Vauxhall exports 1919–1930[105]

Year	Exports	Exports as % of output	Exports as % of GB exports
1919	25 *	4.4	—
1920	97 *	14.0	1.3
1921	52 *	10.8	1.7
1922	66 *	10.3	—
1923	108 *	7.3	2.1
1924	88	6.4	0.8
1925	95	6.8	0.3
1926	112	7.3	0.3
1927	590	35.8	1.7
1928	853	32.9	3.2
1929	156	12.2	0.4
1930	223	2.4	0.9

* Estimated figures (no records).

Apart from 1920, 1927 and 1928 the percentage of exports in relation to Vauxhall output never exceeded the peak pre-war figures and thus most of Vauxhall sales were very much in the domestic market. There are a number of reasons for this declining trend in Vauxhall exports. They included the nature of the 1920s car market, the financial difficulties of Vauxhall and the nature of the Vauxhall product. Up to 1924–5 the British car export performance was not good generally.

This can be explained by the importance of the domestic market which was being tapped, the effects of the 1921 slump on world markets, and the smaller size of British engines occasioned by taxation, which rendered them less competitive in overseas markets where engine size was not a factor so much

[102] Report of 9th Ordinary General Meeting, *The Times*, 13 April 1923, p. 21 col. 1.
[103] *Luton News*, 23 January 1919, p. 4.
[104] *Luton News*, 4 December 1919, p. 8.
[105] Sources: 'Vauxhall Facts and Figures,' op. cit.; last column based on table 4 in Maxcy Appendix, op. cit., and table 7 in R.J. Overy, op. cit., appendix 1.

in sales. Vauxhall was hit doubly. The models were too large and expensive for the home market, and comparatively inefficient and costly in overseas markets. Vauxhall did not have the financial resources to develop a special overseas model and therefore had to rely on models for the home market for overseas sales. The 30/98, which had proved a good export model in the immediate years before and after the war, was too exclusive for the home market and did not warrant large production, as it was difficult to sell in the price-falling 1920s home market. It was discontinued in 1926 and replaced by smaller models more suitable for home markets but less suitable for overseas markets. Laurence Hartnett clearly illustrates the problem of Vauxhall's overseas sales, in the late 1920s, when he stocked them at a GM sale outlet in Stockholm.

> The creators [of the Vauxhall 14/40] had not made a single concession to public demand for style in cars. They had produced a plain, functional machine, and if the public didn't like it they could lump it.[106]

When Hartnett was put in charge of export sales at Luton in 1929 he reviewed the 14/40 once again.

> The Vauxhall 14/40 as a vehicle for sale overseas, was a hopeless proposition. A check of exports against actual sales showed that distributors in several parts of the world held large stock of them that wouldn't sell. They had poor reputations; the axles and other parts gave trouble and, of course, the Vauxhall was no beauty.[107]

The steep rise in exports in 1927 and 1928 can only be attributable to the use which Vauxhall was making of the availability of vast overseas GM outlets. The slump back to a figure of 156 in 1929 can be seen to reflect the inferiority of Vauxhall products mentioned by Hartnett as GM agents failed to shift them.

The success in the export field in the 1930s is clearly attributable to a complete change of product which could utilise the enormous potential of the GM overseas sales network. That was, of course, the Bedford truck which was to penetrate deeply dominion and colonial markets

On taking over Vauxhall, James D. Mooney had been perceptive enough to see the importance of the British Empire and having a British industrial base with which to feed it. In an address to the American Chamber of Commerce in London, he stated that

> The use of the motor car would have a remarkable growth in the British Empire, and during the next ten years the British Empire would move forward aggressively and rapidly in the development of its own economic coherence and strength (hear, hear).[108]

In 1928 Mooney was to reiterate this point when he presented his reasons for the retention and expansion of the Vauxhall Company.

---

[106] L. Hartnett, *Big Wheels and Little Wheels* (1965), p. 38.
[107] Hartnett, ibid.
[108] 'Address to American Chamber of Commerce in London,' *Luton News*, 19 November 1925, p. 15.

The fact that the British Empire covered 38 per cent of the world markets outside the United States and Canada was important in the consideration of England as a source for export markets.[109]

The decision to develop Vauxhall Motors was in effect a decision in GM overseas strategy and only clearly was viewed as such in the light of the 1930s experience. In retrospect Sloan wrote in his memoirs,

> We were fortunate in acquiring Vauxhall Motors and Opel during the late twenties. For then the great worldwide depression began in 1929, our export business went into a sudden steep decline – as did that of other American producers.[110]

The organisation of GM overseas sales had first been undertaken in 1911 with the formation of the General Motors Export Company. By 1920 GM overseas sales were 420,000 of which about half were sold in Britain, France, Germany and Italy.[111]

Whilst the rich European market was able to afford American cars, it had placed barriers against imports to protect their own vehicle industries. In Britain the McKenna Tariff, combined with engine tax and petrol tax made it increasingly difficult for GM to penetrate the market. This is clearly seen in the experience of the GM Hendon operation set up in 1919 which soon changed from importing vehicles complete, to importing CKDs for assembly with the body work made locally. The full effects of the growing trend toward economic nationalism became more apparent in the latter half of the 1920s. In the first half of the decade British car manufacturers were preoccupied with recovering from the war, shaking off the effects of the 1921 depression and satisfying their home demands. By 1929 British exports were over five times greater than the 1920 figure.[112]

It was not by accident that GM took over Vauxhall in 1925. Mooney could see that if GM was to retain an interest in the valuable European market it must establish more than an export/assembly operation. The brief reduction of the McKenna Tariffs in 1924 had inflamed British car manufacturers, including Vauxhall, and demands were loudly and stridently made for protection to return, and the campaign which was carried out to re-establish this added fuel to the flames of economic nationalism. Mooney also plainly saw that the major British overseas markets were in the British Empire, and thus by having a manufacturing base in Britain, GM could not only penetrate the British market more effectively but increase its overseas sales at the same time by exporting a British made GM product. This was not fully appreciated by all GM executives in the boom conditions of the 1920s particularly when GM exports reached an all time peak of 290,000 vehicles in 1928.[113] This was nearly six times the exports of the whole of the British vehicle industry and 340 times the overseas sales of Vauxhall, which also reached an export peak in

[109] A. Sloan, *My Years with General Motors* (London, 1965), p. 322.
[110] Ibid., p. 328.
[111] Ibid., p. 315.
[112] Maxcy and Silberston, op. cit., table 4, UK Exports, p. 226.
[113] Sloan, op. cit., p. 315.

that year.[114] There is little wonder that Mooney's ideas concerning Vauxhall met with considerable opposition within GM The experience of the depression after 1929 rapidly dispelled all opposition. American sales fell more dramatically than the British sales, and the pattern was repeated in the export field. By 1932 GM exports were at a nadir of 40,000, equivalent to the combined British export figure.[115] More importantly the intervening years had witnessed a growing dollar gap market in the world including a widening division between the pound and the dollar, which prevented purchase of the now relatively expensive American vehicles. The footholds in Britain and Germany enabled GM to stay in the valuable European market and 'the poor relation,' Vauxhall, gave an important opening in tbe British Empire market. So valuable to British exports was the British Empire that it has been calculated that between 1928 and 1939 the Empire absorbed 81 per cent of British overseas sales.[116] It was in this area that Vauxhall was to prove so invaluable to GM in the 1930s.

After the disappointing performance of the Cadet, the manufacture of the Bedford truck, on the advice of British management, proved to be 'a world beater.'[117] Its overseas sales, together with Vauxhall cars, accounted for nearly 40 per cent of Vauxhall output in 1932 and averaged about one third of Vauxhall sales throughout the rest of the decade, as is indicated below.

Table 23. Vauxhall vehicle exports 1930–1950[118]

Year	VM exports CVs + cars	GB exports CVs + cars	VM Exports as % of VM output	VM exports as % of GB exports
1930	223	30,000	2.4	0.7
1931	1,657	24,000	10.9	6.9
1932	6,309	40,000	37.3	15.7
1933	8,479	51,000	30.6	16.6
1934	14,263	58,000	35.2	24.5
1935	15,314	68,000	31.4	22.5
1936	14,636	83,000	28.8	17.6
1937	20,768	99,000	34.7	20.9
1938	20,271	84,000	33.7	24.1
1946	22,867	133,000	42.6	17.1
1947	28,690	193,000	46.6	14.8
1948	52,840	302,000	70.8	17.4
1949	57,831	351,000	68.7	16.4
1950	61,471	545,000	78.9	11.2

More striking was the fact that Vauxhall exports accounted for nearly a quarter of British exports in 1934 and 1938, and averaged about 20 per cent for the decade as a whole after 1931. From 1933 Vauxhall and Opel sales were

[114] Calculated from Sloan, and Maxcy and Silberston, and 'Vauxhall Facts and Figures,' op. cit.
[115] Sloan, op. cit., p. 328; Maxcy and Silberston, op. cit., table 4, p. 226.
[116] M. Miller and R. Church, 'Motor Manufacturing' in Buxton and Aldcroft (eds.), *British Industry between the Wars* (London, 1979), p. 196.
[117] Bartlett quote in *Luton News*, 30 March 1933, p. 11.
[118] Sources: 'Vauxhall Facts and Figures,' (Vauxhall Motors, 1966). Unfortunately CV sales are not separated from car sales. Maxcy and Silberston, op. cit., table 4, p. 226.

greater than the sales abroad of American made GM vehicles exported from USA and Canada.[119] This was a true vindication of Mooney's policies.

The Vauxhall commercial vehicle export performance was even more impressive if placed in the context of British commercial vehicles. Much of the credit for enhanced British exports rests with cars rather than commercial vehicles, and by comparison commercial vehicle exports accounted for less than a quarter of total British vehicle exports in 1930, and averaged about one fifth of total vehicle exports for the rest of the decade.[120] Although separate Vauxhall export figures for cars and commercial vehicles are not available, the fact that Bedford trucks continually outsold Vauxhall cars throughout the 1930s, with the exception of the years 1935 and 1938[121] and as much as 50 per cent of all Bedfords produced were for export[122] indicates the importance of the light truck to the firm in overall sales and hence in exports. Although there had been steady growth in British commercial vehicle export performance in the 1930s, it could only be described as of 'minor importance in the industry and the economy.'[123] In fact *Commercial Motor* was a consistent critic of the relatively poor export performance of British commercial vehicles compared with those from the USA. In a lengthy article in 1931 the journal blamed the British emphasis on production of heavy vehicles, those of 5 tons and above, whereas the demand was for sturdy light trucks which could stand up to considerable overloading, and could negotiate the rough roads usually found in colonial countries. The American 30cwt truck was cited as a prime product for such markets.[124] British models were criticised for lack of easy maintenance, and sales techniques and after sales service were noted as being particularly poor compared to that of the Americans. Spare parts were also quoted as being expensive and relatively difficult to obtain. British manufacturers were also criticised over their pricing methods. The export price was fixed in Britain without due regard to extra costs such as tariff charges, freight costs and selling expenses and 'the final price was left to the discretion of the overseas agent who adds as much as he can.'[125]

Finally, *Commercial Motor* took to task the inept and inadequate advertising which was seen as 'neither interesting nor effective,' largely because London agents did not know the markets.[126]

Not surprisingly British commercial vehicle exports remained relatively low. For example, exports to India totalled 398 in 1930 whilst the USA exported 12,000 commercial vehicles in that year.[127] While US sales slumped to 1,800 in 1933, British exports managed to increase only to 528 in the same period even with the aid of a preferential import tariff.[128] Even in a prime market such as

[119] Sloan, op. cit., p. 328.
[120] G. Maxcy and A. Silberston, *The Motor Industry* (1959), calculated from table 4, p. 226.
[121] See Table 9, above.
[122] Hartnett, op. cit., p. 42.
[123] Church and Miller, 'The Motor Industry,' op. cit., p. 209.
[124] *Commercial Motor*, 10 February 1931, p. 912.
[125] *Commercial Motor*, 10 February 1931, p. 912.
[126] *Commercial Motor*, 10 February 1931, p. 912.
[127] *Commercial Motor*, 16 December 1932, p. 602.
[128] *Commercial Motor*, 15 June 1934, p. 566.

New Zealand, British manufacturers of commercial vehicles were slow to seize opportunities, and although British cars accounted for 90 per cent of imports, commercial vehicles were considerably less predominantly British and were led by Ford US-made trucks in 1932.[129]

Although Britain managed to increase its percentage in many overseas markets it was more due to US decline as a result of the depression than an overall British export performance, and it was not until the middle of the decade that commercial vehicle exports began to make creditable progress rising from 5,000 units in 1931 to 18,000 by 1936.[130]

Much of the American advantage had been in its manufacturers' ability to make mass produced vehicles, which were cheap, easily maintained, with large engines for small trucks. British producers came to follow these trends by the mid 1930s but more due to domestic pressure of taxation and weight legislation rather than the need to respond to export markets.

A considerable part of the Vauxhall success lay in attempts to meet this potential market by the export of the 30cwt and 2-ton truck. The 30cwt was a direct descendant of the Chevrolet 30cwt vehicle which had already proved itself in these markets. The Bedford, with all the resources and sales expertise of the worldwide General Motors Corporation, had a ready made organisation to channel its overseas sales, which did not suffer the defects of its British rivals so vividly outlined by the *Commercial Motor*. As we have seen in the section on marketing much of these sales and after service techniques were taken on board by the Vauxhall organisation, and run by Englishmen like Charles Bartlett, Laurence Hartnett and A.F. Palmer-Phillips, trained by the General Motors organisation when it was an autonomous company in Britain, and naturally they transferred their knowledge and skills to the Vauxhall context.

The importance of exports to Vauxhall is also reflected in the importance of car exports to British car manufacturing as a whole in the 1930s. Between 1931 and 1933 exports absorbed one third of British production and therefore had a crucial role to play in the upturn following the slump.[131]

Again in 1937 and 1938 exports were to prove important in cushioning the British motor industry against a slump which hit it far more severely than the 1931 experience.[132] Whereas the home market shrank by 6 per cent in 1931, in 1938 this decrease was 10 per cent. In the export field, however, overseas sales fell by 44 per cent in 1929–31 and only 13 per cent in 1937–38.[133] Vauxhall followed this trend (Table 23 indicates), although the fall in Vauxhall exports was not as great as the national motor industry as a whole. Vauxhall also had the additional cushion of the Ten model which boosted its car sales considerably. An impressive feature of Vauxhall's exports was the sharp rise in figures. There was a tremendous rise of 743 per cent between 1930 and 1931, followed by a 380 per cent rise in the following year. These initial rises can be

[129] *Commercial Motor*, 16 December 1932, p. 603.
[130] Maxcy and Silberston, op. cit., table 4, p. 226.
[131] This case is put forward by M. Miller and R. Church in 'Motor Manufacturing' in N.K. Buxton and D.A. Aldcroft (eds.), *British Industry between the Wars* (1979, 1982), p. 186.
[132] Ibid., p. 187.
[133] Ibid., p. 187.

sensationalised when a low base figure for 1930 is used but the annual rises remained impressive from one year to another: 34 per cent 1932–3, 68 per cent 1933–4, and 42 per cent for 1936–7. There were small drops of 4.5 per cent and 2.4 per cent in 1935–6 and 1937–8 respectively, but the trend was one of rapid expansion of exports. Naturally, Vauxhall gave ample publicity in the annual reports for these years as impressive testimony of their growth.

The British Dominions provided the principal markets and in 1932 the Board stated that their main markets were to be found in Australia, New Zealand, South Africa, India, China, Japan, Norway, Denmark, Sweden, Belgium, Holland, Spain and Portugal. Next came the smaller and less wealthy Empire countries such as the West Indies, Malaya, Malta and Cyprus.[134]

Laurence Hartnett, who had been elevated to Director of Vauxhall overseas sales in 1929, embarked on a tour of the main potential markets of the world in that year, including most of the Empire and Dominion countries.

The technical data which I gathered, with two thousand feet of movie film dealing with road conditions and technical points, did contribute to the final specification details of the Bedford trucks and later Vauxhall cars.[135]

On his return to England Hartnett set about organising his department.

As production increased so did the work of the export department. Soon I had a dozen or more on my staff, and with these few working to a pattern I had evolved, we got Bedford trucks flowing out to General Motors assembly plants in Africa, Europe, Australia – all over the world. In some parts we still retained our own direct distributors.[136]

As early as 1925 Vauxhall had realised the full potential of the large overseas outlets which GM had built up in the 1920s, including assembly plants and agents and dealers. These now came into full use for Vauxhall along with the sales techniques adapted to the indigenous conditions.[137]

A thorough study of new markets was made including costs imposed by local tariffs, landing charges and local taxation. In this, Vauxhall made full use of the Board of Trade knowledge and expertise on overseas markets. Little was left to chance and such practical concerns as the size of boxes to export CKDs were examined so that size and shape could be reduced and designed to facilitate more economical shipping costs. The smallest details were taken into account before proceeding with a market offensive in each country.[138] By 1932 so great was the overseas demand for Vauxhall products that £20,000 was spent on a new boxing plant for the sole purpose of putting cars and trucks into cases and sending them abroad.[139]

---

[134] Report of 18th Ordinary General Meeting, *The Times*, 13 April 1932, p. 21.

[135] Hartnett, op. cit., p. 41.

[136] Ibid., p. 42.

[137] Acknowledgement of the importance which Vauxhall accredited to GM overseas outlets was recorded in 1927: 'Particularly important are the market facilities made available overseas. In every land where motor cars were used General Motors have a selling organisation that is going to be used to sell British cars': 'Yesterday's Declaration of Policy – Vauxhall Motors,' *Luton News*, 15 September 1927, p. 9.

[138] Hartnett, op. cit., pp. 46 and 47.

[139] *GM News* vol. 4, no. 8 (February 1932).

As high as 50 per cent of the factory output of Bedfords was allocated for export, and emphasis was given to the 'easy' markets of Australia and New Zealand before the company turned its attention to Europe.[140] A continual 'pleasant' complaint in the annual reports between 1932 and 1936 was the difficulty in fulfilling orders, despite working the plant to capacity. The result was continual extensions taking place in this period, culminating in the reorganisation in 1937/8 for the Ten production.

The 1930s picture was not a totally rosy one and, when exports declined slightly in 1936, Leslie Walton blamed rising costs for making export vehicle prices less competitive, particularly when preferential duties operated in some overseas markets.[141] High priced materials, particularly steel, were blamed. In addition, Charles Bartlett, the Managing Director, expressed considerable concern at the growing international tension which he felt could seriously affect overseas trade, 'and a large portion of our business is now export business.'[142]

These fears were, of course, justified with the outbreak of war in 1939. Very soon exports became negligible as the works was turned over to wartime production. A larger range of trucks was produced including a much bigger vehicle than had hitherto been produced. Over a quarter of a million trucks were produced for war service together with 5,640 Churchill tanks.[143]

After the war exports assumed an even greater significance in Vauxhall production, engendered by Labour Government policy which emphasised overseas trade in its attempts to rebuild war-torn Britain and achieve a trade equilibrium. By 1948 Vauxhall vehicle production was largely devoted to overseas trade, and exports accounted for 70 per cent of sales in that year and nearly 80 per cent in 1950. Despite the export of over half a million vehicles in 1950, Vauxhall's percentage of British total exports fell to just over 11 per cent (see Table 23). This reflected the export orientation of the vehicle market as a whole in this period.

Vauxhall's sales of nearly a quarter of British exports in 1938 was never to be achieved again but was a true indicator of the prodigious rise of Vauxhall to the 'Big Six' status. This success undoubtedly rested chiefly on its exports of commercial vehicles in Empire and Dominion markets.

---

[140] Hartnett, op. cit., p. 42.
[141] Report of 23rd Ordinary General Meeting, Luton News, 1 April 1937, p. 3.
[142] 'Vauxhall Plans for 1936,' Luton News, 2 January 1936, p. 11.
[143] A History of Vauxhall (Luton: Vauxhall Motors, 1980), p. 48.

Chapter Five

Management and Labour Relations to 1929

Vauxhall's labour relations policies between 1900 and 1950 have a natural division in 1929 from which date Charles Bartlett took the post of Managing Director. The earlier period was one in which Vauxhall was growing and before the First World War industrial relations were generally amicable. The firm was small and the close relationship between management, who were working engineers themselves, and the workforce was conducive to an atmosphere of co-operation. This was further stimulated by expectations of greater success.

The First World War gave the first indications of stress in management-labour relations. The loss of skilled men to the armed forces, the replacement by dilutees (unskilled or semi-skilled labour taking over skilled jobs) and women, and the enlargement of the workforce contrasted strongly with the relatively stable pre-war workforce. Vauxhall along with other engineering firms, both nationally and locally, was forced to give concessions in the form of higher wages, lower hours of work and the granting of premium bonus. It was willing to concede these demands in return for high productivity and profitability.

By the end of 1920 the economic climate was changing radically as the economy slid into depression which had heavy repercussions in the motor industry. Vauxhall began to make enormous losses and retrenchment was seen as the only solution. This meant cutting labour costs and increasing productivity which could only result in confrontation with the unions and a return to complete managerial control in the work place.

Pre-war developments
The basis of industrial relations at Vauxhall is in the development of Luton itself, which is discussed in detail in later chapters. Luton's population had grown from 2,986 in 1821[1] to 36,404 by the end of the century.[2] The chief occupation had been hat-making, which was based partly on the domestic system, and partly on small workshops in the centre of Luton and employed predominantly female labour.[3] The nature of the main Luton industry was a crucial factor in explaining the relative docility of the workforce in terms of union organisation. It was never an organised industry as far as trade unions were concerned, due mainly to the small size of units, the casual nature of the

---

[1] *Census of Population 1821*, quoted in J. Dyer and J. Dony, *The Story of Luton* (Luton 1964; 3rd edition 1975), p. XIV.
[2] *Census of Population 1901*, quoted in ibid., p. XIV.
[3] A major work on the Luton hat-trade is J.G. Dony *A History of the Straw Hat Trade* (Luton, 1942).

work, in terms of irregular hours, and the seasonal unemployment which affected the industry in the summer months, and more particularly in the period from November to January.

Equally important was the relatively isolated nature of Luton itself; 30 miles outside of the London metropolis, and 70 miles from the large engineering centres of Birmingham and Coventry. Not surprisingly such unionism that did exist was small and mainly confined to skilled workers.[4] This is confirmed by the Luton Chamber of Commerce which in its attempts to attract new industries to the town mentioned that 'few firms have cognisance of unionism so that it might be possible if deemed desirable, to aim in any new works at freedom from this influence.'[5] The meaning implied was that Luton was free of union influence, and this was an added attraction for companies thinking of moving to Luton.

In fact the major engineering union, the Amalgamated Society of Engineers (ASE), had only 19 members in Luton in January 1900[6] and the membership was only 37 by June 1904.[7] A branch of the Amalgamated Society of Joiners and Carpenters was set up in the 1890s by a journeyman carpenter, Millott-Severn. In his biography he records,

> Although so near to London, trade wages were only sixpence an hour, as compared with nine pence in London, and though we worked from six in the morning to six in the evening, and to four on Saturdays, the total wages were less than 30 shillings a week.[8]

Having organised a branch, successful agitation followed to gain an extra half pence an hour. Millott-Severn was, however, 'marked as a disturbing influence'[9] and so he moved on to London. When the Luton Trades Council was formed in January 1904 the Joiners and Carpenters are not mentioned, perhaps indicating the short life of the Luton branch.[10]

The major unions which formed the first trades council were: ASE, the Steam Engine Makers' Society, the United Builders' Labour Union, the Amalgamated Society of Railway Servants, the Central Moulders' Union, the Toolmakers' Society, the Scientific Instrument Makers' and the Workers' Union.[11] In 1906 the trades council had 11 unions affiliated which Chamberlain calculates as representing approximately 500 workers.[12] Thus of a total workforce in Luton of 29,100 in 1901, about 1.7 per cent of workers would have been unionised; of a total workforce of 39,000 in 1911, 1.2 per cent would have been unionised.[13] Assuming that most of the unionists were men this accounts for 4 per cent of

[4] John Chamberlain, 'The Development of the Trade Union Movement and Labour Movement in Luton from 1904 till the General Strike 1926' (unpublished paper, Luton 1972).
[5] Thomas Keens, 'Luton as an Industrial Centre,' *Engineering*, 13 April 1900, p. 10.
[6] *Amalgamated Society of Engineers Monthly Journal* (January 1900).
[7] *Amalgamated Society of Engineers Monthly Journal* (June 1904).
[8] J. Millott-Severn, *The Life Story of a Phrenologist* (Brighton, 1929), p. 86.
[9] Ibid.
[10] Chamberlain, op. cit., p. 4 – this paper is relatively short and no footnotes are given but the impression is that the author relied heavily on the *Luton News* and Trades Council Records.
[11] Ibid.
[12] Ibid., p. 5.
[13] *Census of Population* 1901, 1911.

the male workforce in 1901, and 2.7 per cent of the total male workforce in 1911, and indicates the small degree of unionisation.

The first recorded dispute in Luton after 1900 involved the recently moved Vauxhall Iron Works in May 1905, although the main concern seems to have centred on the West Hydraulic sister company.[14] It involved the ASE and Steam Engine Makers' Society who objected to Vauxhall and West Hydraulic Company paying only one and an eighth extra time for night shift work. The unions made the case that time and a quarter was normally paid for the night shift, and Mr. Barnes, the ASE spokesman[15] stated that when West Hydraulic had moved from Bradford they had 'somewhat altered the conditions.' Barnes also stated that the company had introduced a longer working night shift and had not consulted the workforce, some of whom had come from Bradford, about the new conditions. The dispute involved 200 to 300 men but given ASE Luton returns most must have been either in the Steam Makers' or in no union at all.[16]

The employer's case rested on the fact that the foreman, who was also an ASE member, had proposed the one and an eighth night shift rate, but the unions stated that this was done only after the workers realised that the company was not going to pay any extra for a 13 hour night shift. The dispute throws interesting light on local conditions as the employers strongly state that another firm in the district paid no extra for night shift work. This other firm was Hayward-Tyler, an engineering firm and Federation member (the only other Federation employer in Luton), who backed Vauxhall and West Hydraulic at the national and local conferences by stating that they paid no extra at all for night shift work. The unions claimed that Hayward-Tyler did not work night shifts and had only done so once after a fire in the 1890s when the men worked throughout the night at no extra pay in order to help the works become operable as quickly as possible.[17] No agreement was reached, but the employers stated that union members did not have to work night shifts, and as there was no agreed district rate the situation would remain the same. This dispute would seem to suggest that the West Hydraulic Company had found the lack of unionism in Luton a strong incentive to move there as the District rate was claimed by Barnes to be one and a quarter in Bradford.[18]

The relative weakness of organised labour and its lack of militancy in Luton is shown by the fact that there were only two strikes in the town before the First World War, during a period of great industrial unrest in many parts of the country. One involved the Diamond Foundry in 1910 and the other was part of a national dispute involving the National Amalgamated

---

[14] Microfilm reference N (2) 7, EEF Archives.

[15] The case sent to central conference at York in September 1905. Barnes went on to become General Secretary of the Union and a Labour Minister in later years. See J.B. Jeffreys, *The Story of the Engineers* (London, 1945).

[16] 'Vauxhall Facts and Figures' (Vauxhall Motors, 1966) estimates that less than 200 men worked for Vauxhall at this time. In addition the EEF claim that West Hydraulic only employed 30 men in Bradford. The only explanation is that the West Hydraulic side of the business must have taken on a lot more workers.

[17] Letter dated 26 October 1905 issued by Hayward-Tyler to reconstituted local conference after failure of central conference: EEF archives, N (2) 7.

[18] Ibid., EEF file N (2) 7.

Society of Operative House and Ship Painters and Decorators.[19] Equally on the employers' side four firms had become affiliated to the Engineering Employers Federation (EEF) – Hayward-Tyler in 1903, West Hydraulic in Bradford in 1899, Commer Cars in 1911 and Clarks Machine Tool Company in 1914.[20] When Vauxhall separated itself from the marine side of the business in 1907 to concentrate on car production it too joined the EEF in April 1907.[21] According to its application form its estimated wages bill was £10,000 and its workforce consisted of smiths, machine fitters, toolmakers, painters, trimmers and labourers.

There were no agreements with trade unions and no disputes pending. The number of hours worked per week was 54, which was the district rate, and overtime was 1¼ for the first two hours and 1½ after this, up to 6am.[22] This last point indicates that Vauxhall was paying the night shift rate above that originally demanded by the men in the 1905 dispute. This may have part explanation in the fact that Mr. Ash, the works manager of the West Hydraulic–Vauxhall company, did not join the Vauxhall motor company formed in 1907. The new works manager was A.H. Hancock.

Little is known of Vauxhall managerial policies in the years before the First World War. It was a comparatively small firm employing approximately 180 workmen in 1905, rising to 575 in 1913.[23] It had two foremen in 1905[24] and, if the same proportion of men to foremen were applied to the 1913 workforce, there would be about seven foremen.[25]

It is a pity that such information is not available as debate concerning aspects of managerial control hinge upon such data. In all probability little consideration was given to questions of overall strategy in terms of management in this period as the firm was small, allowing a much closer personal relationship between management and men. The firm was gradually expanding and was meeting international and national success and building a reputation in the car world.

The first mention of a managerial strategy appears in an article by L.H. Pomeroy in 1914.[26] His address concerns car production in general but he is clearly using his Vauxhall experience as a solid example. In that year Vauxhall had reorganised and registered the reconstituted company Vauxhall (1914) Limited, after having gone into the hands of the receiver. Its profitability had been in question and the Pomeroy article in many respects represented his thoughts on how to create greater efficiency in the workforce by increasing productivity. This he saw being done mainly by more efficient organisation of production and improvements in machine technology. E.W. Hancock

[19] Chamberlain, op. cit., pp. 5 and 6.
[20] EEF Membership Files for Hayward-Tyler, West Hydraulic, Commer Cars and Clarks Machine Tools.
[21] Vauxhall Membership Application Form, Membership Files, EEF Achives.
[22] Ibid.
[23] *Vauxhall Facts and Figures*, op. cit.
[24] *Luton News*, 30 March 1905, p. 3.
[25] This is pure speculation. On the 1905 figures it works out at one foreman for every 90 workers. Of course, other departments had been added and the number of foremen could have been much higher.
[26] L.H. Pomeroy, 'Automobile Engineering and the War,' *PIAE* IX (1914).

Plate 21. The Vauxhall and West Hydraulic Engineering Company works, Luton 1905.

described his apprentice experience in 1911 at Vauxhall in his reminiscences published in 1960.[27] At this time car production at Vauxhall was reliant upon skilled workers to a great degree.

From the beginning to the end – that is from the fitter to the final tester – there was a gradual increase in the application of individual skills. Hancock states that the breaking down of skills had already begun to change job titles and descriptions.

> This change started before 1914, when the marker off had moved back into the tool-room, . . . by this time, the advent of planning engineers and the issue of process operation sheets led to the establishment of a logical sequence of operations, although for some years the operation sheets were used only as a general guide.[28]

Pomeroy saw the drawing office as the nerve centre of operations.

> If the . . . functions of the drawing office be given full scope the duties of the works officials become purely as they should be, and they can give their attention to the business of production. These steps are all necessary if we are to maintain maximum output for man and machine.[29]

Pomeroy also felt that the 'old style of foreman and mechanic was rapidly disappearing and work was being done by men not so intimately in touch with the practical difficulties.'[30]

This process was hastened by the war and the introduction of dilutees (unskilled or semi-skilled workers, often women, replacing skilled workers), which became an important subject in disputes between unions and management and indeed between skilled and unskilled unions themselves.

Definitions of skilled jobs became increasingly difficult and job demarcation disputes were often used by both management and unions for their own advantage. Unionism in Luton had steadily increased by 1914 and in that year the ASE membership numbered just over 200[31] and an estimate of all skilled engineering workers in unions would be approximately 600.[32] The war years enhanced this trend and in 1916 two Luton ASE branches had been established and the membership was over 500 by February 1917.[33] The war also increased the importance of the engineering industry in the town as the war effort required vehicles and munitions. Vauxhall itself had its total car production taken by the Army, and it had gained war contracts for the manufacture of munitions. It is not surprising therefore, that Luton began to

[27] E.W. Hancock, 'A Lifetime in Automobile Production,' *Automobile Engineer* vol. 50, no. 6 (June 1960).

[28] Ibid.

[29] Pomeroy, op. cit.

[30] Ibid.

[31] *ASE Monthly Journals* for 1914. A peak of 208 was reached in October.

[32] On amalgamation of most engineering unions in 1920 the *Amalgamated Engineering Union Monthly Journal* shows an increase of three times the ASE figure.

[33] *ASE Monthly Journal* (January 1916 and February 1917). This would give a figure of 1,500 for all engineering unions based on 1920 calculations, and a figure of between 4,000 and 5,000 for trade unions as a whole in Luton based upon 1906 trades council figures. This may of course be an overestimation, considering the growing importance of the engineering trade in the First World War.

Plates 22–28 show the batch production process of early motor manufacturing. The photographs indicate how sections of the car are produced in separate workshops, and are then assembled and tested: a long way from the assembly line pioneered by Henry Ford. **Plate 22** shows the forge shop in Luton 1910.

Plate 23. Engine assembly shop, Vauxhall Motors, Luton 1910.

Plate 24. Erecting shop 1910.

Plate 25. Paint shop 1910.

Plate 26. Running shop 1911.

Plate 27. Erecting shop highway 1913.

Plate 28. Mounting shop 1914.

join the main stream of unionism and echo the growing militancy in these years. The engineering employers' members also responded by establishing a Luton Association in 1916 with L.H. Pomeroy as its secretary and Chairman.[34] It consisted of only five firms: Vauxhall, Commer Cars, Hayward-Tyler, Clark Machine Tool and Skefko Ball Bearing Company, a Swedish owned company which joined in 1915.[35] Government involvement was reluctantly agreed to on both sides of industry in the first year of the war and this process increased as the war continued. Patriotic duty was becoming increasingly outweighed by growing industrial tension by 1917. In essence it was a four way conflict between employers, union officials, the union rank and file and the government. Employers resented the emasculation of their managerial rights; union officials the putting into abeyance of hard fought agreements shelved for the duration; and the rank and file felt an increasing sense of exploitation as inflation increased. The government's primary concern was to win the war and that meant increased military production, and it would use the strength of the Defence of the Realm Act and the Munitions Act to do this.[36]

The shortage of labour, particularly skilled labour, which became acute in the later war years, hit Vauxhall almost immediately as 'about 150 men . . . joined the colours and consequently the rate of production was seriously affected.'[37] The lack of skilled workers became a constant complaint. In 1918 Vauxhall calculated that in June 1914 it had about 400 men in the machine shop of whom 308 were skilled and 92 unskilled or 23 per cent unskilled. By 1917 the machine shop number was reduced to 330 men and women, of which 120 were skilled and 210 unskilled, i.e. 64 per cent unskilled. In 1918, 125 more hands were employed which made a total dilution of the workforce in the machine shop of 73 per cent unskilled.[38]

Serious disputes began to emerge in Luton in 1916 when a spontaneous strike by women workers at the Chaul End munitions factory took place in May.[39] The women were mainly non-unionised and although presenting no coherent demands the strike stemmed from poor working conditions and low pay, the highest rate being about 18 shillings and 10 pence for a 54 hour week. The management response was to lock out the workers and bring the 17 'ring-leaders' before an industrial tribunal at Westminster for contravening government regulations about war work. The Tribunal Judge, while recognising that the women's strike was illegal, strongly criticised the management and only fined the girls one shilling instead of a possible £5 a day he was capable of imposing.[40]

In February 1917 a dispute arose at Vauxhall involving women dilutee workers who were not being paid the same rates as skilled and semi-skilled men

---

[34] Minute Book 1916–1918, Luton Engineering Employers Association, Mid Anglia EEF Archives.
[35] Ibid. (no pagination).
[36] See ch. VIII in J.B. Jeffreys, *The Story of the Engineers* (1945) and ch. 5 in Eric Wigham, *The Power to Manage: A History of the Engineering Employers Federation* (Macmillan, 1973).
[37] Report of the First Ordinary General Meeting, *The Times*, 9 April 1915, p. 6. col. 4.
[38] Report of the 4th Ordinary General Meeting, *The Times*, 20 April 1918, p. 11 col. 2.
[39] Chamberlain, op. cit., p. 11.
[40] Chamberlain, op. cit., p. 11.

who were doing the same jobs.[41] The National Federation of Women Workers were using Vauxhall as a test case because all the women were in the union and the men supported their demand for equal pay, and they wanted to see that the Treasury agreement between the ASE and other unions was carried out. Vauxhall refused the application on the grounds that the women's representative, Miss Sloan, 'be more specific in her definition of skilled jobs.'[42]

In a confidential letter to the EEF headquarters in London Pomeroy wrote:

> The point at issue is that we have been employing men on capstan lathes, milling machines and grinding machines, largely due to local trade union influence. At the same time we believe that this class of work has been done very largely by semi-skilled and under-rated men in the Coventry and Birmingham Districts.[43]

The union stated that they rested their case 'on Luton, Vauxhall Motors being typical of the district.'[44] No agreement was reached at the local conference and the matter was to be looked into by a tribunal of the Board of Trade. The outcome seems to have been favourable to the women for it is recorded in the Luton Association minutes of 1918 that anomalies had arisen regarding women's wages at Vauxhall 'arising from the rates granted last year, being so much higher than those at which women can be properly started at this.'[45]

The first big industrial dispute to affect the town was the engineers' strike of May 1917, which was part of a nation wide campaign by the unofficial Joint Engineering Shop Stewards' Committee, and centred around the dilution of labour and the withdrawal of the 'trade card.'[46] On withdrawal of the trade card, at the discretion of the management, men could be drafted into the armed forces. There was a strong feeling that this was used by employers, often with official union collusion, to get rid of 'troublemakers,' and in areas like Sheffield skilled men were conscripted while dilutees remained exempt.[47] The Luton strikers numbering over a thousand held a meeting in the football ground on 14 May. Attempts by the mayor and union officials to get the men to return to work failed.[48] The following day another mass meeting was held and the men voted by 787 to 150 to stay out. At national level after fierce criticism by the press, official union opposition and even the arrest of eight shop steward movement leaders by the government matters came to a head. The government, now fully aware of the strength of feeling, promised no victimisation and the release of the union leaders if they would return to work.[49] In Luton the men

[41] EEF Archives Document D (8) 2.
[42] Local Conference Report 6 June 1917. EEF Archives Document D (8) 2.
[43] Letter from L.H. Pomeroy to EEF HQ, 7 February 1917. EEF Archives Document D (8) 2.
[44] Reported in Luton Association Minutes for 6 June 1917. Special Meeting, EEF Archives.
[45] Luton Association Minutes 6 June 1918. Mid-Anglian EEF Archives.
[46] *Luton News*, 17 May 1917, p. 6 col. 3.
[47] Jeffreys, op. cit., pp. 181 and 182. The national strike was precipitated at Rochdale when the government decision to extend dilution to private work was applied in a provocative way 'by putting women on grinding machines to grind cotton spindles and dismissed the men who refused to instruct them.' On 3 May the Rochdale engineers went on strike in protest and this was followed by large sympathetic strikes in many engineering centres, including Luton.
[48] *Luton News*, 17 May 1917, p. 6 col. 3.
[49] Jeffreys, op. cit., p. 184.

agreed to do this unanimously at a meeting on 20 May.[50] The strike would appear to have been a failure, but in the long term it shook the government sufficiently to drop the extension of dilution to private (non-war) work in the Munitions Bill of August 1917. The leaving certificates, 'perhaps the most hated section of the 1915 Act,' were withdrawn in October, leaving the men free to change their employment at will.[51] The abolition of leaving certificates immediately gave concern to the Luton Engineering Employers' Association because non-federated firms began to attract away skilled labour with higher wage rates. In October, the Association minutes record that Kents, a Luton non-federated engineering firm, was attracting away Vauxhall workers.[52] The Association approached Kents to not pay higher than the district rate but with little success. The result was that wage demands by workers became more strident with threats of moving to more amenable firms if their wishes were not granted.

Pomeroy stated that in the Vauxhall tool room, men were applying for increases 'and after discussion it was agreed that this should be met by the introduction of a Premium Bonus System in the tool room into which the 1½d per hour bonus now paid should merge.'[53] The basic week was also reduced from 54 to 50 hours with one instead of a two break system. The Premium Bonus System, which was a form of payment by results, was heavily influenced by American practices and generally introduced by EEF federated firms from the turn of the century. It had many variations, of which the best known were the Rowan and Halsey systems, but all were based on establishing a fixed time for a worker, or group of workers, to do a job. 'However long he took, he would get the time rate for the hours worked, but if he did the job in less than the fixed time, the saving would be divided between the worker and the employer.'[54]

The Vauxhall management was never happy with this system and in the mid-1920s they devised a peculiar system of bonus payment of their own having by then left the EEF.

The problems of shortage of skilled labour, dilutees and the advancement of machine technology continued to affect the engineering industry and also Vauxhall in the immediate post-war years. The boom was to last until late 1920, and in this optimistic atmosphere of expansion Vauxhall wished to remain on good terms with its workforce as far as possible without sacrificing too much in terms of managerial control, high wages and shorter hours. In addition, union strength was in the ascendancy and by October 1920 the recently formed Amalgamated Engineering Union gave a total Luton membership of over 2,000.[55] At a conservative estimate this was approximately a 25 per cent increase on the 1917 figure.

[50] *Luton News*, 24 May 1917, p. 6 col. 2.
[51] Jeffreys, op. cit., p. 184.
[52] Luton Association Minutes 4 October 1917. Mid-Anglian EEF Archives.
[53] Luton Association Minutes 18 October 1914. Mid-Anglian EEF Archives.
[54] Eric Wigham, *The Power to Manage: A History of Engineering Employers Federation* (London: Macmillan, 1973), p. 72.
[55] *Amalgamated Engineering Union Monthly Journal* (October 1920) exact figure was 2,072; the peak reached was 2,111 in January 1921.

In July 1919 Luton Town Hall was burnt down by outraged ex-soldiers denied the opportunity to celebrate the victory of war at Wardown Park by the town council.[56] This was not a direct result of socialist revolutionary militancy or union agitation but was reflective of the militant atmosphere which engendered 'Red Clydeside' and the general unrest of the period.[57] However, such an event was unlikely to take place at any other time than 1919 in Luton's history, and was uncharacteristic of a town far less militant than other industrial strongholds.

Nevertheless, for Luton employers these were worrying times. The Trades Council claimed over 7,000 members[58] and in January 1918 the largest strike in Luton had taken place over the role of the Local Food Committee, which many workers felt had been unfair in its allocations.[59] The Food Committee gave way almost immediately and allowed three labour representatives to become members in order to appease the protesting workers.[60]

Appeasement became the main policy of the Luton firms, including Vauxhall, in dealing with the continuing demands by the workforce, both by national and local union bodies. Attempts were made to counteract union pressure by uniting the Bedford Engineering Employers' Association with the Luton Association in May 1919.[61] The Bedford association had seven member firms which tended to be smaller than those of Luton. Luton had five members and managed to persuade Kents Limited which was one of the largest firms in Luton at this time to join in January 1920.[62] The formation of the Bedfordshire Engineering Employers' Association had little immediate impact in attempting to improve the bargaining position of the employers. Luton was sufficiently different in character as a district from Bedford to create difficulties in co-ordination of policies, and attempts to establish a district rate for skilled and other workers proved impossible 'owing to the variations in rates of different firms.'[63] In eagerness to attract workers, fulfil orders and expand capacity any attempts at agreements between local firms were undermined by enticement away of labour by higher rates of pay and the offer of better conditions and hours. By the end of 1918, for example, Vauxhall had agreed to a basic 47 hour week which was part of the national agreement between the engineering unions and the Employers' Federation. In July 1919 Vauxhall was forced to reduce the night shift to 47 hours 'as some firms in Luton already worked a 47 hour per week night shift.'[64]

[56] *Luton News*, 24 July 1919, p. 3.
[57] One school text book, W. Robson, *20th Century Britain* (Oxford, 1973), p. 103 gives the impression that the Luton incident was part of the demobilisation mutinies that occurred in that year. There is not a shred of evidence to support this view, as is shown in the detailed account of events in J.G. Dony, *The 1919 Peace Riots in Luton* Bedfordshire Historical Records Society Vol. 57 (1978).
[58] *Luton News*, 31 January 1918, p. 5.
[59] Ibid.
[60] Ibid. and Chamberlain, op. cit., p. 15.
[61] Bedfordshire Engineering Employers' Association (BEEA) Minute Book 1919–1921. Inaugural Meeting 15 May 1919 at 96 Midland Road, Bedford. Mid-Anglian EEF Archives.
[62] Luton Engineering Employers' Association Minute Book 1918–1920, 18 January 1920. Luton Association kept their own minutes until June 1920. Mid-Anglian EEF Archives.
[63] Luton Engineering Employers' Association Minute Book, 4 December 1919. Mid-Anglian EEF Archives.
[64] Ibid. 8 July 1919.

In early 1920 Hancock complained that trimmers at Vauxhall were being enticed away by Hewlitt and Blondeau, a Luton aircraft firm 'by offering rates higher than the District rates i.e. one shilling per hour.'[65] Vauxhall management was therefore forced to raise their own trimmers rates in order to retain them.

The anxiety of Vauxhall to avoid disputes is clearly illustrated by two cases, one of which reached the central conference at York. One of these disputes predictably involved the machine rating question, which the skilled unions regarded as fundamental in maintaining differentials in pay and status which they correctly saw as having been eroded in the war years of acute labour shortage. The first case reached central conference on 15 October 1919 and was brought forward by the Workers' Union.[66] This involved a dilutee who had joined Vauxhall in 1915 and eventually became a full setter. The ASE objected to this at the end of the war and the man was put on semi-skilled work and his rate was reduced from 11d to 8d per hour. The Workers' Union claimed that ASE members did exactly the same work as their member and were paid considerably more – as much as is 3d per hour. Vauxhall management immediately tried to wash its hands of the whole affair claiming that it was really a dispute between the Workers' Union and the ASE. A satisfactory solution was arrived at after a local conference held in November 1919.[67] It was decided that the man in question should 'remain off the machine until given sufficient training.'[68] In no way did it affect the Workers' Union designation of skilled work.

The second involved the question of overtime which the engineering unions had banned until the settlement of the 44 hour week demand by the unions at national level. In May 1920 the Vauxhall workforce wanted to hold a mass meeting on the question of overtime, at 4 pm on the Vauxhall premises. The management refused and so the workers decided to hold the meeting in spite of this refusal. Faced with this intransigence the management decided to accede and agreed 'for the time being not to work overtime, save on breakdowns etc as agreed by the unions.'[69]

In the latter part of 1920 the passive nature of Vauxhall management towards the unions began to change. This was mainly caused by the difficulties which the firm began to experience from this time, and exacerbated at the end of the year by the slide into depression of the economy as a whole. In essence their resentment of union militancy was not substantially different from most employers of the time, and the Engineering Employers' Association nationally, led by the formidable Sir Allan Smith who viewed with alarm and distaste the union militancy and erosion of managerial control in the war years and its immediate aftermath. The main difference was the over-reaction by Vauxhall management to events and, more importantly, the short-sighted break with the EEF in 1921 because the Vauxhall management felt it had not had the back up

[65] Luton Association Minutes 4 March 1920.
[66] 'Manning of Machines and Removal of Men.' Minutes of Central Conference held at York 15 October 1919. Microfilm reference M (9) 45. EEF Archives.
[67] 'Manning of Machines and Removal of Men.' Minutes of Local Conference held at Midland Road, Bedford, 18 November 1919. Microfilm reference M (9) 45. EEF Archives.
[68] Local Conference 19 November 1919. Microfilm reference M (9) 45. EEF Archives.
[69] BEEA Minute Book 1919–1921, 6 May 1920. Mid-Anglian EEF Archives.

it deserved in some of its disputes. Attempts were made as early as 1919 to root out 'trouble makers' at Vauxhall. A letter in the local press from 'a humble workman' accused the Vauxhall management of hypocrisy in that the firm claimed it could take on 200 skilled men but in that very same week a number of 'old skilled hands' were discharged.[70]

The origins of Vauxhall disillusionment with the EEF concerned a dispute which began in September 1920 and involved payment of an operation known as crank grinding.[71] The AEU claimed that Vauxhall had paid one penny in excess of the district rate, 'but recently they had altered that practice by starting a man on the bare district rate on night shift.'[72] This was, the union claimed, contrary to the shop stewards' agreement and also to the Wages Temporary Regulation Act. After being referred back from central conference at York, another local conference decided that 'the claim of the union be conceded on the condition that the agreement refers solely to Messrs.Vauxhall Limited.'[73] Hancock was furious with the decision and vociferously explained that the reason for Vauxhall's action was 'a period of acute crisis' and there was urgent need for Vauxhall to reduce costs. He further stated that Vauxhall would not put the local conference decision into operation, but after a long discussion he withdrew his remarks.[74]

Further evidence of the hardening of attitudes is clearly shown in two disputes which took place in the last quarter of 1920 while the crank grinding dispute was pending. The first involved the sacking by Vauxhall of eight men in November 1920, following which the employees' union threatened action. Vauxhall was accused of being anti-union and had victimised these men because of their union activities.[75] The sacking of the men was not so much the cause of the dispute as the employment of 'men outside the district.'[76] At a works conference the management were persuaded to reinstate the men.

A week later 150 men were discharged; the reason given was lack of work. This was approximately 15 per cent of the total workforce. The unions stated that at least 40 per cent of the workforce could be made redundant according to their information from the management.[77] The *Luton News* reported that:

> The men cannot reconcile these dismissals with the position only a week before when it contended the firm were seeking men from outside the district. Many of the dismissed men, it is stated, are shop stewards.[78]

The *Luton News* not a noted pro-union newspaper, evidenced by its printing of 'black leg' editions of the *Daily Mail* during the General strike, questioned Vauxhall's harsh attitude in its redundancy policy. It suggested to the Vauxhall management the policy pursued by Commer Cars during the coal strike of

[70] *Luton News*, Letter entitled 'From War to Peace,' 30 January 1919, p. 6.
[71] 'Machine Rating Question.' Minutes of Local Conference held at Midland Road, Bedford, 17 September 1920. Microfilm reference M (14) 10. EEF Archives.
[72] Ibid.
[73] BEEA Minute Book 1919–1921, 6 January 1921. Mid-Anglian EEF Archives.
[74] Ibid.
[75] 'Another Vauxhall Grievance,' *Luton News*, 25 November 1920, p. 6.
[76] Ibid.
[77] Ibid.
[78] Ibid.

putting men on short time rather than carrying out wholesale sackings.[79] The management's reply was that they were not anti-union and indeed 99 per cent of their works was unionised.[80] However, it was to become increasingly clear that the management's intention was to break the stronghold of the union within the firm.

In December the blacksmith strikers asked for an increase in their hourly rate but Hancock bluntly refused although there was no objection to an increase by the National Federation.[81] In the same month the Workers' Union enquired of the local association as to the rates for a man working on a Gridley capstan lathe. Vauxhall management claimed that the setting up of such a machine was a semi-skilled job, despite the claims by the union that another Luton firm (unnamed) paid the skilled rate.[82] This was another example of Vauxhall management's efforts to reduce costs.

In the new year the management offensive against the unions began in earnest. The onset of the depression and the failure to sell enough models put the company under increasing financial pressure. Hancock saw that the immediate solution was to reduce the workforce and in uncompromising language he announced to the local association that Vauxhall management was to lay off between 500 and 600 workers and suspend the premium bonus scheme and reduce lieu rates of payments.[83] This dictatorial approach led to protests from the AEU district secretary, Mr. Mullins, that the management was in breach of the York Memorandum of 1914 and the Shop Stewards' and Works' Committee agreement of 20 May 1919.[84] A local conference was convened on 28 February but, as no agreement was reached, the dispute was taken to a central conference in April.[85] The Employers' Federation both nationally and locally loyally backed Vauxhall at these conferences in front of the unions, and a failure to agree was recorded in both cases. Privately, however, there were strong reservations by the national and local associations as to how the Vauxhall management had handled the situation. In a confidential letter from Mr. Brown, the national secretary, to Mr. Allen the local secretary, it is stated that,

> employers are entitled to stop a system of payments by results without consulting the work people . . . I feel it extremely desirable that the work people should be taken into the confidence of the firm and the whole of the circumstances of the case explained to them.[86]

[79] *Luton News*, 25 November 1920, p. 6.
[80] Ibid.
[81] BEEA Minute Book 1919–1921, 18 December 1920. Mid-Anglian EEF Archives.
[82] Ibid.
[83] BEEA Minute Book 1919–1921, 6 January 1921. Mid-Anglian EEF Archives.
[84] The York Memorandum was a national agreement between the Federation and the engineering union agreed in 1914 but shelved for the duration of the war. The Vauxhall Agreement of 1919 obviously applied to practice within the firm but there are no records available concerning its details. See Wigham, op. cit., p. 85 for details of the York Memorandum.
[85] 'Suspension of Premium Bonus System: Affects on Earnings.' Local Conference held at Midland Road, Bedford, 28 February 1921. National Conference at York 8 April 1921. Microfilm reference W (3) 48. EEF Archives.
[86] Letter from Mr. Brown, EEF, to Mr. Allen, BEEA, 6 March 1921. Microfilm reference W (3) 48. EEF Archives.

At the same central conference the AEU had brought another complaint against the Vauxhall management that men were being induced to leave the union particularly on being offered promotion to the level of foreman.[87] The union claimed it was clearly in contravention of the Shop Stewards' Agreement of 1919 which had been drawn up with the firm. Once again the EEF and the local association gave full backing to the Vauxhall position and 'it was agreed that the question be allowed to drop.'[88]

Despite the loyalty which the EEF and the local association had shown to Vauxhall, Percy Kidner wrote a letter of resignation from the organisation in July 1921.[89] Although the local association had been aware of the growing dissatisfaction of Vauxhall with the employers' association it was still a great shock to the local committee, who consequently begged Vauxhall to reconsider their decision. The Vauxhall Board regretted that they could not. This was indeed the climax of the discontented rumblings which had been felt since early 1920. Kidner, on behalf of the Board, gave as its main reason for withdrawal because

> we feel that we cannot administer agreements stewards' entered into between the Employers' Federation and the various trade unions, and therefore we feel that during the continuance of such agreements our only course is resignation from the Federation.[90]

This entrenched anti-union position of the Vauxhall Board contrasted starkly even with the EEF, not known at this time for its soft approach to the unions. This was a time of growing unemployment which began to undermine the union position and as early as February 1921 the local association was talking in terms of a lock out over the question of the unions ban on overtime.[91] This was the beginnings of the employers' offensive against the unions which was to lead to the engineering lock out in 1922. Vauxhall had clearly jumped the gun; driven to do this by its enormous losses.

The Vauxhall managerial offensive continued throughout the rest of 1921 with vociferous, but ineffective, protests by the unions. In October the AEU presented a number of complaints to the Luton Employment Committee concerning Vauxhall.[92] They accused the firm of importing labour from outside the district while there were unemployed men available in the district for such work.

The reason why Vauxhall refused to take on the local men was because they were unionists the AEU claimed. It was suggested that the Employment Committee were helping Vauxhall procure these outside workmen. This was denied by the Employment Committee who were concerned enough to ask Vauxhall to give an account of these accusations. The union also accused Vauxhall of working excessive overtime while unemployment prevailed.

---

[87] 'Vauxhall Inducing Men to Leave Trade Unions.' Central Conference 8 April 1921. Microfilm reference W (3) 48. EEF Archives.
[88] Ibid.
[89] Letter from Percy Kidner, Vauxhall Motors Limited, to J. Brown, EEF Secretary, 15 July 1921. Vauxhall Membership file, Broadway House. EEF Archives.
[90] Ibid.
[91] BEEA Minute Book 1919–1921, 24 February 1921.
[92] 'Engineer's Complaints,' *Beds. and Herts. Saturday Telegraph*, 1 October 1921, p. 6.

In the following week the Vauxhall management replied to these accusations through the columns of the *Luton News* and the lengthy article gives some interesting, if not unexpected, insights into the managerial motivations of the firm.[93] It claimed that due to the failure to sell its product in adequate numbers it had to reduce the price of its cars and this meant a drastic reduction in cost. This was rationalised by closing the works for a six week period earlier in the year and completely reviewing its manufacturing processes to achieve this end. Jobs were re-graded and times made more 'realistic.' 'The result showed that our labour costs reduced by one third and our output increased by approximately one third.'[94] In this way the price of Vauxhall cars could be reduced. It was obvious that Vauxhall could not carry out this process in the ruthlessly effective way it wished if it was hampered by agreements between the EEF and the unions, which thus led to its resignation from that body. Though this last point is not stated in the article it is the logical concomitant for such a decision. In addition the close down could be used not to re-employ union agitators; a charge often levelled against the firm by the engineering union which saw this as gross victimisation.

Regarding the point concerning importation of labour, Vauxhall said this had been overly exaggerated by the unions and that only 2 per cent of the workforce or 25 men were engaged from outside the district on jobs which local workers may have applied for in skilled areas of work. The unions put the figure at over 100, and claimed that men were denied employment if they refused to undertake to do overtime.[95] This was union policy at this time. Hancock, as spokesman for the firm, replied that they had the right to draw on labour from throughout the whole world if they so wished.[96] He did not deny that they refused to employ men who did not wish to do overtime. Little favourable for the union emerged from this public exchange with the exception that the Employment Committee agreed not to help procure outside workers for local firms if workers were available in the district. Of course, Vauxhall's merely undertook to do work itself by placing its own advertisements in other areas, a point clearly stated by the unions at the original hearing with the Employment Committee.[97]

It is clear that by the end of 1921 union activity within Vauxhall had been considerably subdued and the management felt that it was once again in control of its affairs. The Luton branches of the AEU, which now numbered ten, still remained active in the district although by June 1921 its membership had fallen from a peak 2,111 in December 1920[98] to 1,759.[99] This downward trend was to continue, hastened by the 1922 engineering employers lock-out, until an interwar nadir of 338 was reached in June 1927, as the following table indicates:

[93] 'Vauxhall Motor's Reply,' *Luton News*, 6 October 1921, p. 7.
[94] Ibid.
[95] *Luton News*, 6 October 1921, p. 7.
[96] Ibid.
[97] *Beds. and Herts. Saturday Telegraph*, 1 October 1921, p. 6.
[98] *The Amalgamated Engineering Union Monthly Journal* membership figures for Luton District no. 10 Division, December 1920.
[99] *The AEU Monthly Journal* membership figures for Luton District no. 10 Division, June 1921.

Table 24. AEU membership figures for Luton
1920–1934[100]

Year	Total membership	Number of branches
1920	1895	10
1920	2111	10
1921	1759	10
1922	1166	8
1923	760	7
1923	491	4
1924	526	4
1925	426	4
1926	426	3
1927	338	3
1928	391	3
1929	403	3
1930	428	3
1931	409	3
1932	386	3
1933	402	3
1934	591	3
1934	788	3

This downward trend in the AEU membership was also heavily influenced by rising unemployment which peaked in April 1921, remaining above one thousand until 1924 and rising once more with the onset of the great Depression of the early 1930s. (See Table 25 overleaf.)

In 1921 and 1922 the main issue concerning local labour was high unemployment which was more severe in these years for Luton than it was to be in the depression of the 1930s, clearly indicated in Table 23. The resentment against Vauxhall smouldered into 1922 and in March a demonstration took place outside the works by unemployed men protesting against the firm continuing to work overtime while men in the district were out of work.[101] However, for the remainder of 1922 the engineering industry became consumed by the struggle involved in the lock-out, a campaign with which Vauxhall was not directly involved which had the effect of further reducing AEU membership in the firm. The lock-out was particularly effective in Luton. Federated firms reported little more than verbal protests from the unions and the conditions laid down by the employers were reluctantly accepted.[102] By 1923 the engineering unions' strength had effectively ebbed and membership was only one third of the early 1922 figure by the end of that year.[103] Throughout the 1920s, however, Vauxhall's reputation as an employer in the locality was not high. Instant dismissal, lay-offs with little or no notice and virulent anti-trade unionism are criticisms levelled against the management in this period.

---

[100] Source: *AEU Monthly Journals* 1920 June 1921, and *AEU Quarterly Reports* 1921–1934.
[101] 'Overtime: Unemployed Demonstration at Vauxhall Works,' *Luton News*, 30 March 1922, p. 7.
[102] BEEA Minute Book 1921–1923, 14 March 1922.
[103] Source: *AEU Quarterly Reports* figures as quoted in Table 22, p. 000 above.

Table 25. Unemployment in Luton 1920–1934[104]

Year	Month	Number unemployed	Percentage of unemployed insured Luton workforce
1920	January	880	3.8
1920	October	740	3.0
1921	January	3,210	14.0
1921	April	4,140	18.0
1921	October	3,730	16.0
1922	April	2,960	12.8
1923	September	1,908	n/a
1924	April	993	n/a
1925	April	560	n/a
1925	May	362	n/a
1926	March	339	n/a
1926	December	1,046	n/a
1927	April	724	n/a
1928	April	420	n/a
1929	May	515	n/a
1930	August	1,392	n/a
1931	August	2,509	n/a
1932	November	3,765	11.4
1933	January	3,717	11.0
1933	August	1,320	3.7
1933	September	976	2.7
1934	January	2,276	6.8

It was hell in those days. I've seen men sacked for washing their hands as the hooter blew. I came in 1929 and it was just a good old sweat shop in those days – they'd sack you just like that.[105]

Harold Horne, a long serving Vauxhall employee and AEU shop steward, recalls,

---

[104] Source: Periodic reports from the Luton Employment Office printed in the *Luton News*. Unemployment figures for Luton alone were not published in the *Labour Gazette* until after the Second World War. The Ministry of Employment office could not or would not furnish the figures for the interwar years. This source therefore had to be used and gives a fairly accurate picture of unemployment as measured by government departments at the time.

The 1920s figures are fairly uniform and are straight reports of the Luton employment office figures. However, in the 1930s the editor wished to show how low the Luton unemployment figures were in comparison to the rest of the country, and that the percentage unemployment figure on what was known to be a more accurate figure than that used by the Luton Employment Office. Thus the figures are lower than the official figures although loses the element of comparison with the rest of the country as these percentages were also calculated on the old figures. It must also be noted that sharp variations within one year, as for example 1933, are partially explained by the seasonal nature of the Luton hat trade. In the 1920s the hat trade was hit less severely than the engineering trade, particularly at the beginning of the decade, but the 1930s Luton experience was the reverse with the hat trade beginning a sharp decline which emphasised its seasonal nature more acutely than in previous decades. The engineering industry fared much better in the 1930s depression than that of the early 1920s. This is clearly shown by the actual lower peak of unemployment in the 1930s and more clearly by the much lower percentage unemployment for Luton as a whole.

[105] Quoted from Graham Turner, *The Car Makers* (Penguin, 1964), p. 123.

The stories that are told by early Vauxhall employees . . . it was said that to hold a trade union card, to have it known meant instant dismissal. It was impossible to declare your union membership, and like most firms at the time, in slacker periods you were laid off. Stories are told of how, at any time of the day they'd come to the end of a run. There was a shortage of material or whatever. The foreman would come round with a board saying 3 o'clock. That meant at 3 o'clock everybody clocked out and went home.[106]

Peter Vigor another long serving Vauxhall employee and one time editor of the *Vauxhall Mirror* confirms a similar picture of uncertainty of employment,

My father started at Vauxhall Motors in 1916. He went into the machine maintenance division. In 1922 he became a foreman, but when work slackened at Vauxhall – it was boom and slump, boom and slump – he was demoted to a super grade . . . but he wanted to be foreman and get back on the 'staff.' (This meant greater security and no 'layoffs' in slack periods.) My father started me at Vauxhall as an office boy in 1927. His idea was that I should stay on at Vauxhall until I was 16 to get an apprenticeship. Then he said there was no future in the industry. First of all I'm foreman. Then down graded. Then made up again. So he took me away.[107]

Vauxhall and the movement towards direct control

A recent piece of research on Vauxhall managerial policy in the period previously reviewed attempts to demonstrate that 'Vauxhall showed a greater tendency than most British firms to move in the direction of direct control and Fordism.'[108] It is the intention of this section to examine the validity of this viewpoint.

The starting point must be an explanation of what is meant by direct control, Fordism and related managerial strategies. It has been argued that the antagonistic relationship between labour and capital forced capital (management) to adopt new production methods to increase its control over the intensity of work.[109] Braverman emphasises the importance of the use of machine technology. By introducing new machinery management can build into it a control function which enables direct control over the workforce.[110] The move towards a theory of scientific management evolved by F.W. Taylor and his disciples, who developed methods of timing operations, was part of this attempt to refine direct control strategies. Such strategies can ultimately lead to Fordism whereby the productivity and output of the worker is controlled by the pace of automatic conveyors on flow assembly lines.

Criticism has been levelled at the Braverman model for overemphasis on machine pacing and Friedman argues that capital has not been limited to methods of direct control through machine pacing, but has also adopted alternatives which he calls 'responsible autonomy.'[111] This means that the

---

[106] Interview with Harold Horne (taped) July 1978.
[107] Interview with Peter Vigor (taped) October 1978.
[108] Wayne Lewchuk, 'Technology, Pay Systems and Motor Companies,' a paper presented to the SSRC Conference on Business and Labour History, The Business History Unit, London School of Economics, 23 March 1981 (part of unpublished Ph.D. thesis), p. 18.
[109] H. Braverman, *Labour and Monopoly Capital* (New York, 1974).
[110] Ibid., pp. 98 and 99.
[111] A.L. Friedman, *Industry and Labour* (Macmillan, 1977), p. 78.

worker retains a greater degree of control over the production decisions. Others have criticised Braverman for ignoring the human element in the social relations of the workplace and that welfarism and paternalism were significant strategies by which management aimed to shift labour's perception of capital.[112] Attempts in the interwar years to implement the classic forms of control, as advocated by Taylor, were made through the application of the Bedaux system. This was a modified version which gained some popularity in Britain, and which was applied to much larger concerns than the relatively small Vauxhall firm. Taylorite views were widely discussed in the industry but there is little evidence that any factory put them into practice in the wholesale and specific ways advanced by advocates of such systems. The Bedaux system for example was only put into operation in one car firm in Britain – that of Rover.[113] Generally such systems of direct control did not find wholesale acceptance in British industry and tended to be unpopular by the 1930s.[114] In Luton, for example, Messrs. George Kent wrote to the Bedfordshire Engineering Employers' Association about the 'desirability of introducing the Bedaux system' into their works. In a reply the local association stated its views in a question and answer form:

Q1.   Whether the Federation looks kindly on the 'Bedaux' system of payments by results as compared with direct piece work?
A.   No, definitely, no.

Q2.   Whether there is any objection to changing over to any system of that type?
A.   Desperate resistance may be expected from Trade Unions.

Q3.   Their considered opinion as to whether it would be desirable to adopt this system as an alternative to direct piecework?
A.   The unions will not have the system at any price. Nothing annoys them more than Bedaux. There have been half a dozen strikes against it.

Q4.   Can they give us the name or names of any Federated firms who are working the Bedaux system?
A.   Hoffman's of Chelmsford. They only managed to adopt it in a very slack period, when the unions were not strong enough to resist.[115]

In actual fact Lewchuk states that: 'In its final state, the Vauxhall system closely resembled the Ford system.'[116]

---

[112] B. Palmer, 'Class, Conception and Conflict – The Thrust for Efficiency: Managerial Views of Labour,' *Review of Radical Political Economy* (1975).

[113] Craig R. Littler, 'Rationalisation and Worker Resistance in Britain between the Wars,' background paper seminar at King's College Research Centre, 23 February 1981.

[114] Littler, op. cit. Revealed in discussion following the presentation of the paper.

[115] Private and confidential letter from BEEA to Messrs. George Kent Limited, 6 September 1937. Box file for Kent Limited. Mid-Anglian EEF Archives.

[116] W. Lewchuk, 'Vauxhall: The Move towards Direct Control,' part of a paper entitled 'Technology and Managerial Practice in the Car Industry to the Early 1920s,' presented to The Working Group of the Social History of Car Workers in Britain at the London School of Economics, April 1981, p. 47.

His starting point for this assertion is based on the views of the pre-war Vauxhall manager, L.H. Pomeroy, who in an article published in 1914 stated that the drawing room should be made the nerve centre of all managerial organisation from which all instructions should be issued and all information collected 'and is then responsible for work planning, sequence of operations and times therefore.'[117] To interpret this as a move towards direct control can be misleading. There is no evidence that Vauxhall eventually reorganised along these lines. A description of the Vauxhall Works in 1920 does not indicate that this was the case.[118] In fact Vauxhall came into line with the general practice within the engineering industry by being reluctantly forced to adopt the Premium Bonus System in 1917.[119] This was a system which Lewchuk admits was used in Britain as a viable alternative, together with the cultivation of common interests between capital and labour, because it was seen 'to be potentially more profitable than direct control through mechanisation' as proposed by Braverman.[120] In addition Pomeroy's article must be viewed as general comments directed to the industry as a whole. While new ideas on management were often discussed particularly after the war, there was little opportunity to put into practice tighter methods of direct control up to 1922 without the full consent of the workforce – such was the power of the unions at this time. Lewchuk sees the decisive move towards direct control in Vauxhall occurring in 1921 when the market for motor vehicles collapsed and the firm was forced to take drastic action.[121] The factory was closed for six weeks during which each of the 6,000 jobs were studied, timed and assigned to a specific grade of labour. Premium bonus was dropped and the firm withdrew from the Engineering Employers' Federation over the question of works committees.[122]

After this time Lewchuk states that Vauxhall adopted 'what appears to have been straight day work.'[123] Such a statement strongly suggests that this is pure speculation and no evidence is cited to support this view. Indeed one feature of the straight day work system, eventually adopted at Vauxhall in the late 1950s, is the increase in the number of foremen. This is because when bonus incentive schemes are abandoned there is much more of a need for direct overseeing by staff to induce workers to maintain levels of output. There is no evidence that the number of foremen substantially increased in this period.

In 1925 Vauxhall management claimed that it operated an 'efficiency system.'[124] The workers were paid a base rate plus a supplement stated as a percentage of their base rate. This percentage reflected the firm's calculation of the value of the worker to the firm. *Automobile Engineer* remarks on the uniqueness of this payments system and states the 'system of efficiency pay has been adopted which takes into account both quantity and quality of work.'[125]

[117] L.H. Pomeroy, 'Automobile Engineering after the War,' *PIAE* IX (1914), p. 22.
[118] 'The Works of Vauxhall Motors,' *The Automobile Engineer* (June 1920).
[119] Luton Association Minutes 18 October 1917. Mid-Anglian EEF Archives.
[120] Lewchuk, 'Technology, Pay Systems and Motor Companies,' op. cit., p. 3.
[121] Ibid., p. 18.
[122] Vauxhall Membership File, EEF Archives. Letter, Vauxhall to EEF 15 July 1921.
[123] Lewchuk, 'Vauxhall: The Move Toward Direct Control,' op. cit. in n. 116, p. 46.
[124] 'The Works of Vauxhall Motors Limited,' *Automobile Engineer* vol. XV, no. 207 (October 1925).
[125] Ibid.

This phrase is particularly revealing and when juxtaposed with the comment that 'Vauxhall have achieved the happy mean between the two extremes of quality regardless of price, on the one hand, and cheap standardisation without individuality on the other,'[126] it is clear that this efficiency system was an adaptation of a semi-flow production line rather than a conscious policy by the management to directly control the workforce. In other words it was reacting to a system that had evolved rather than planning one with specific labour control elements. This system was therefore to enhance greater efficiency as its title suggests rather than purely control the workforce as an end in itself. After all Vauxhall clearly had complete control of its workers from the confrontations of 1921. Indeed the comparatively small Vauxhall concern which employed less than two thousand workers and produced less than fifteen hundred vehicles per annum in 1925 could hardly implement the classic systems of control through production processes which used the speeds of the mass flow conveyers to dictate the work rates of employees.

Lewchuk identifies skilled workers as being the main concern for which the Vauxhall management were motivated towards direct control. In 1921 Hancock complained that production costs were too high due to the excessive amount of skilled labour.[127] Lewchuk contends that the machine grading disputes before and just after this time was an attempt by Vauxhall management to cut costs by reducing some skilled jobs to a semi-skilled status and thus be much more on a par with Midland manufacturers. While this is undoubtedly true it must be remembered that the most vociferous and numerous cases took place before 1921. Even accepting this view it must surely be the case that skilled labour was heavily relied upon in a manufacturing process that used a semi-flow assembly line and produced quality cars in comparatively low numbers. It is also known that Vauxhall did not pay its workforce below district rates during the 1920s but cut costs when necessary by layoffs.[128] In this way non-militant skilled workers maintained a reasonable wage and at the same time union activists could be excluded. There was thus little necessity to implement rigid controls over the workforce as Lewchuk suggests.

Finally, in 1928 Vauxhall introduced the Group Bonus System, which paid workers bonuses on their contribution to a group within a department.[129] Lewchuk ends his piece on Vauxhall by stating confidently that 'it was realised that individual piece work was not compatible with flow production.'[130] By that time a crude type of line had been implemented.[131] However, one of the main characteristics of group bonus is that it has less direct control elements than measured day work. Fewer foremen are required as the men discipline themselves within the group because if an individual slackens his effort the group will berate him for jeopardising the bonus of the group as a whole.[132]

[126] 'Works', *Automobile Engineer*.
[127] 'Vauxhall Motors Reply,' *Luton News*, 6 October 1921, p. 7.
[128] *Luton News*, 6 October 1921, p. 7.
[129] E.W. Hancock, 'The Trend of Modern Production Methods,' *PIPE* vol. VII, no. 2 (1927–28).
[130] Lewchuk, 'Vauxhall: The Move Towards Direct Control,' op. cit. in n. 116, pp. 47 and 48.
[131] 'The Works of Vauxhall Motors Limited,' *Automobile Engineer* vol XX, no. 270 (August 1930).
[132] A detailed account of the group bonus system is given in chapter six.

Such a bonus system tends to conform much more with what Friedman describes as 'responsible autonomy' rather than 'direct control.' As Les Cowell recalls 'if you got someone on the line who didn't want to work, you didn't have to see the foreman to take him away. The men on the line would make sure he got moved.'[133]

Sir Reginald Pearson, in an article which gives reasons for the change over to measured day work in 1956, explains that the major reasons were the fact that the times had become disjointed and earnings had become disproportionate to output. Glyn Morgan recalls 'we used to knock hell out of those times.'[134] Pearson also revealed the Group Bonus System was incompatible with progress in mechanisation.

> In such circumstances efficiency would be determined less and less by the physical endeavours of the operatives and more and more by technical planning, appropriate equipment and improved methods.[135]

He later states:

> Put shortly and bluntly, management today is committed to pre-production planning and cannot delegate its responsibilities for co-ordinated output to any system other than that controlled by the management.[136]

It would seem that Wayne Lewchuk had predated the move towards direct control at Vauxhall by some 30 years.

It is clear, however, that the Vauxhall management did use the workforce as a scapegoat for its financial failures. The view taken was that if the union militancy within the firm could be broken, then cost reduction could follow which would enable the concern to become more profitable. That this did not happen is part testimony of the failure by the Vauxhall management to identify the real weaknesses of the company. Graham Turner excuses the management by explaining that 'in the 1920s Vauxhall was not noticeably different from the hire-and-fire employer typical of the motor trade.'[137] There is a great deal of truth in such a statement if one takes into account the dictatorial attitudes and paternalistic nature of Ford, Austin and Morris but such companies could sugar their authoritarian pill by paying wages high above their respective district rates.[138] In 1927 earnings in motor manufacturing were 28 per cent higher than in general engineering.[139] Vauxhall could not afford to pay higher than the Luton district rate, and its isolated position in Luton, far from the engineering centres ensured that no intense competition for skilled and other labour need be so acute. Morris, although in a similar situation to Vauxhall in

---

[133] Interview with Les Cowell (taped) March 1980.
[134] Interview with Glyn Morgan (taped) December 1979. He means here that the men found little difficulty in achieving the set times and earned huge bonuses.
[135] Sir Reginald Pearson, 'From Group Bonus to Straight Time Pay,' *Journal of Industrial Economics* (October 1960), p. 116.
[136] Ibid., p. 117.
[137] G. Turner, *The Car Makers* (Penguin, 1964), p. 123.
[138] See for example Austin quoted in Wigham, op. cit., p. 198.
[139] Ibid.

terms of location, was very profitable in this period and combined a policy of high wages in return for dictatorial control.

Additionally, the Vauxhall layoffs must have been far harsher given the uncertain future of the company as is adequately described by the experience of Peter Vigor and his father.[140]

Vauxhall had shared in the increasing intensity of national management-labour relations in the engineering industry between 1916 and 1920. Management's desire to regrade work resulting from technical advances in machinery had to be approached cautiously, as the engineering unions increased in power. Pomeroy saw the Vauxhall position as being worse than the Midlands where he complained semi-skilled and under-rated men carried out work on capstan, milling and grinding machines, where fully rated men were used at Vauxhall.[141] Anxious to sustain output in the optimistic post-war years, the Vauxhall management did not press its demands for regrading what had once been skilled jobs to a semi-skilled status. The Bedfordshire Engineering Employers' Association was unable to establish a district rate, and attempts at co-ordination between Bedford and Luton firms signally failed.

The situation rapidly changed towards the end of 1920 as Vauxhall came under increasing pressure as a result of financial losses. A.J. Hancock, the works manager, identified the problem as being due to an excessive amount of skilled labour which had the effect of keeping Vauxhall labour costs artificially high.[142] It therefore became the objective of the management to carry out what it had been unable to do before 1920 – regrading and re-rating machine operations. Hancock believed that this could only be carried out by management, and realising that this would be in contravention of the Shop Stewards' Agreement drawn up between the engineering unions and the EEF, he decided that the only recourse was to resign from the EEF to give management a totally free hand. The factory was therefore closed for a six week period and jobs were retimed and regraded. Premium bonus was dropped and an Efficiency System eventually came into being – a system peculiar to Vauxhall. This was undoubtedly a sharp move in the direction of greater managerial control, but it would be misleading to interpret this as a move in the direction of a Fordist system of direct control. Even in 1925 when the Vauxhall works was expanded and reorganised, the system of production and organisation was not advanced, nor was the output of vehicles large enough to conform to the Fordist system.

The adoption of the Group Bonus System in 1928 was a move away from the classic forms of direct control and could be described as conforming to a greater degree to what Friedman describes as 'responsible autonomy.' Even in the 1930s, when Vauxhall reorganised in accordance with classic forms of assembly line production using automatic conveyors, Group bonus remained, and was to continue to do so until its abandonment was necessitated by the installation of advanced mechanisation.

---

[140] Peter Vigor interview quoted on p. 111 above.
[141] Letter from L.H. Pomeroy to the EEF, 7 February 1917. Document D (8) 2, EEF Archives.
[142] *Luton News*, 6 October 1921, p. 7.

Chapter Six

The Bartlett Years: Industrial Relations Policies 1929–1950

We have seen how in the 1920s under pressure of its heavy financial losses Vauxhall management dealt harshly with the unions and eventually created an uncompromising regime in its dealings with the workforce.

By contrast the Bartlett period of managerial control under General Motors does appear to have been one of stability and enlightenment. However, the period 1929–1953 was very much one of expansion and huge profitability and few of the problems which beset Hancock, Walton and Kidner occurred under Bartlett's 'golden reign.' How then did Bartlett achieve this peaceful state; peaceful enough for Vauxhall to be dubbed 'the turnip patch.' Is this view totally true? Outwardly it would appear so. There were no major strikes in the period and such disputes that did exist, mainly in the Second World War, were described by Sir Reginald Pearson as stoppages and lasted for a few hours at the most.[1]

Bartlett achieved these ends in a number of ways. Firstly, he aimed at creating a more stable workforce which was not prone to the uncertainties of lay-offs in short times. Harold Horne, a militant communist AEU shop steward (and later Convenor), states:

> He [Bartlett] began to introduce schemes, where in bad times, where other companies like Ford, would lay off workers – Bartlett would try to keep them on by doing jobs like cleaning up, painting machinery, repairing windows, things like this. Bartlett acquired the reputation of being a good humanistic progressive employer for these reasons.[2]

Secondly, in the 1930s Vauxhall began to pay good wages compared with other industries in the town and compared with other car companies in Britain. Glyn Davies, a public relations officer, who began work at Vauxhall in 1935 in the body shop recalls that 'Vauxhall were paying good wages. Up to £3 a week. This meant a long waiting list to get a job. Kent Instruments (another Luton firm) paid £1.18s a week, which was poor by comparison.'[3] Harold Horne concedes that Vauxhall had 'a reputation for paying comparatively high wages, in excess of the general standard of wages in the motor industry.'[4]

The high local wage rates of Vauxhall are given documentary backing by the Bedfordshire Engineering Employers' Association, which recorded in its minutes continual complaints from its members concerning the 'excessive

---

[1] Interview with Sir Reginald Pearson (taped) February 1979.
[2] Harold Horne interview (taped) July 1978.
[3] Glyn Davies interview (taped) July 1978.
[4] Harold Horne interview.

Plate 29. Sir Charles Bartlett, Managing Director Vauxhall Motors 1929–1953, Chairman 1953–54. He was the driving force in taking Vauxhall from a low production unprofitable firm into the ranks of the 'Big Six' vehicle producers by the end of the 1930s.

Vauxhall wage rates.' As early as 1934 Skefko and Kent were very concerned about 'the high rates being paid by Messrs. Vauxhall Motors to toolmakers and millwrights as compared with those paid by members of the Association.'[5]

[5] BEEA Minute Book 1934, January 1934. Mid-Anglian EEF Archives.

These complaints appear periodically in the Association minutes right into the 1950s.

Thirdly, it can be argued that the Group Bonus System was one which gave workers some degree of control over his work situation and relied less on direct means such as the use of foremen as in measured day work. Although this was introduced in 1928, a year before Bartlett became Managing Director, it was refined and improved under his control.

Under the Group Bonus System workers were formed into groups which differed in size, in accordance with plant and production features. All machining, assembly and other group work was subject to a time study, and each group had a time standard by which its daily and weekly output could be judged. Each member of the group was ensured a basic hourly rate of pay but when group efficiency exceeded 75 per cent every group member was entitled to group bonus in accordance with a published table.

Bonus increments were set at 0.6 per cent for each 1 per cent rise in efficiency between 75 and 90 per cent; and at 1 per cent bonus between 91 and 100 per cent. This bonus rose to 10 per cent for 90 per cent efficiency, and 20 per cent for 100 per cent efficiency. Group efficiencies were calculated and published daily and cumulatively for all the days in the week. As a further incentive 1.2 per cent bonus was paid for every 1 per cent efficiency above 100 per cent efficiency achieved. Up to the outbreak of the war in 1939, overall efficiency of the factory was around 102 per cent, but with variations between groups.[6]

According to shop floor workers the money earned under such a system was good. Les Cowell, a capstan operator, who started at Vauxhall in 1937 recalls with nostalgia,

> As far as I was concerned it was a marvellous way of earning money . . . the line I worked on was very good bonus. We averaged 124 per cent per week. We took 130 per cent on odd occasions.[7]

The system is also recalled as having produced more of a group atmosphere,

> You would get help from your mates then . . . if I had a bit of trouble during the day or during the night, my mate, who had got his quota off to earn say 124 per cent bonus would say 'What's up Les?' I'd say 'I'm in a bit of a mess here.' 'Right oh mate I'll give you a bit of a hand.' And he'd change his capstan over and get stuck in to help out with my work, which was beneficial to us all.[8]

The Group Bonus System also ensured that men disciplined themselves within the group. Glyn Morgan remembered:

> If a chap went to the toilet. You see at the end of each section was a board. If someone was in the toilet longer than his mates thought they

---

[6] Sir Reginald Pearson, 'From Group Bonus to Straight Time Pay,' *Journal of Industrial Economics* (October 1960), pp. 113 and 114.
[7] Les Cowell interview (taped) March 1980. Also quoted in Len Holden, 'Think of Me Simply as the Skipper: Industrial Relations at Vauxhall 1920–1950,' *Oral History Journal* vol. 9, no. 2 (Autumn 1981), p. 24.
[8] Les Cowell interview; Holden, op. cit., p. 24.

ought to be, they would shout 'Board, board,' and point to the board where the bonuses were written up.[9]

Similarly Peter Vigor, who spent some time as a capstan operator, relates:

If someone talked or distracted another worker the others in the group would shout 'cuckoo, cuckoo,' because they thought he was fouling the nest. Also lateness was disapproved of by banging the chuck key so that all the group knew that you were late.[10]

Despite his comments in the *Journal of Industrial Economics* there is little doubt that Sir Reginald Pearson thought that the system worked well. In a taped interview he praises the system:

The men knew what to do in order to earn more. They knew their STINT as it was called on the shop floor. The time study was fair. It was a comfortable working time and if they wanted to do a bit extra work, they could. There were never any quarrels. Men on the line knew most jobs around them so if a man wanted to go to the toilet he could be replaced by a fellow worker.[11]

Staunch unionists took a different view. Glyn Morgan, an AEUW convenor, saw the system as 'an utterly carrot and donkey syndrome. From the trade union point of view it was iniquitous. It had its own discipline, but it was self discipline for the wrong motive.'[12] Harold Horne, another AEUW convenor, who actually worked on group bonus although against the system in principle was less scathing in his criticism.

It became a matter of debate later about whether it was a bad move to abolish the Group Bonus System, or, like myself, think it was the best thing we ever did. We reached an agreement to end the Group Bonus System. Ford had always been on measured day work. Employers throughout the industry were pushing for measured day work [in the late 1950s] to end the constant disruptions on the shop floor because a group would stop work because it was fixed at a lower rate. The only way to stop this was to go to a system irrespective of work done, where a basic rate of pay was guaranteed.[13]

In 1955 Vauxhall management began a reassessment of the desirability of the retention of the Group Bonus System, and it came to the conclusion that its replacement by Measured Day Work was necessary. The main reasons were cost and increased mechanisation. Firstly, group bonus earnings were becoming too high and factory efficiency was substantially above 100 per cent and the average bonus was just under 60 per cent on the base rates. Secondly, a large expansion programme was being embarked upon which markedly accelerated the introduction of mechanisation. 'In such circumstances, efficiency would be determined less and less by the physical endeavours of the operatives, and more

[9] Glyn Morgan interview (taped) December 1979; Holden, op. cit., p. 24.
[10] Peter Vigor interview, October 1978; Holden, op. cit., p. 211.
[11] Interview with Sir Reginald Pearson (February 1979).
[12] Interview with Glyn Morgan (December 1979).
[13] Interview with Harold Horne (July 1978).

and more by technical planning, appropriate equipment and improved methods.'[14] In other words increasing mechanisation could create a situation whereby workers could earn enormous sums under the old group bonus rates.

The AEU at Vauxhall was generally amenable to the proposed changes because after 1949 the union nationally preferred Measured Day Work because it guaranteed higher basic earnings. In addition resentment had been created because production workers had often earned as much and sometimes more than skilled workers. The National Union of Vehicle Builders (NUVB), which had a smaller membership than the AEU in Vauxhall, objected to the introduction of Measured Day Work. Therefore, added to the attractive conditions of high stable earnings, a higher night shift premium and higher overtime rates was the caveat that the system would be reviewed after six to eight months of implementation at the end of 1956.[15] Whatever the merits and demerits of group bonus there is little doubt that many workers and Sir Reginald Pearson viewed the system with a great deal of nostalgia, particularly in contrast to the 1960s which became a time of considerable industrial unrest, and Vauxhall's reputation of tranquillity was besmirched. Such nostalgic memories only heightened the reputation of Bartlett as an ideal employer.

Another of Bartlett's innovations was the introduction of a profit sharing scheme. At the 21st Ordinary General Meeting Leslie Walton announced 'that 10 per cent of the net profits of the company, after deduction of 6 per cent on the capital employed in the business, will be divided among our employees in proportion to the wages and salaries they earn.'[16] Only those employed at Vauxhall for more than one year could participate in the scheme and allowances were made in recognition of long service.

There is little doubt that it was a popular scheme. Peter Vigor remembers: 'It was the most eagerly awaited notice of the whole year. My brother bought a bicycle under this scheme.'[17] Fred Smith, a worker in the heat treatment department, adds, 'There was some good profit sharings. Very good. I know there was one which was £80 odd.'[18]

Harold Horne generally agrees but also offers a reason for its demise:

> In the first two years in which I participated it was fairly good. This was in the early 1940s. Everybody looked forward to this handout in profit sharing. Then it began to decline in sum of money year after year . . . to the point where the unions reached an agreement with the company that on annual wage increases, on say 4 pence an hour, which established the profit sharing scheme worked out at, they would abolish the profit sharing scheme.[19]

The general impression given by the workers who talked about the scheme was that really large annual bonuses were the exception rather than the rule,

[14] Sir Reginald Pearson, 'From Group Bonus to Straight Time Pay,' *Journal of Industrial Economics* (October 1960), p. 116.
[15] Ibid., pp. 119 and 120.
[16] Report of 21st Ordinary General Meeting, *The Times*, 1 April 1935, p. 23 col. 4.
[17] Peter Vigor interview.
[18] Fred Smith Interview (taped) March 1980. Began at Vauxhall 1935.
[19] Harold Horne interview.

particularly in the late 1940s and early 1950s. In the 1950s the scheme appears to have laid virtually dormant, until it was finally replaced by the union-management negotiated agreement referred to by Harold Horne above. Peter Vigor tends to endorse this view:

> In later years the company wanted to get rid of it but the workers did not, and it was a bone of contention, but there were no strikes over it. But unless it paid well it was self defeating. It only came up to expectations on a few occasions.[20]

It is worth noting, however, that this scheme was phased out after Bartlett's retirement in 1953.

One particular idea instituted under Bartlett's control was the Management Advisory Committee (MAC). This body was the lynch pin of management-labour relations at Vauxhall. In a 1945 Vauxhall publication the MAC is given pride of place and extolled as the prime example of how industrial relations should be conducted.[21] Turner comments: 'He [Bartlett] left behind him a monument which more than any other has kept the firm free of strife.'[22]

The MAC was set up in 1941. The factory was split up into over 20 areas and a secret ballot enabled a representative from each to be elected. The members nominated from the workforce sat for three years, and there were six nominees from the management. The chairman was the Managing Director. Meetings were held monthly unless there were emergencies to deal with sudden disputes. Seymour describes the aim of the MAC as helping 'the management settle problems of policy and then go out and explain that policy to their constituents.'[23] All minutes were published and posted throughout the factory. The MAC had a wide brief and discussed not only disputes and their avoidance, but grading schemes in relation to rates of pay, pensions schemes, and holidays. In addition a number of sub-committees were formed to deal with the problems of absenteeism in the war years: a Transport Committee to facilitate easier travel to work and a Suggestions Committee to test ideas from the workforce to improve production.[24] At a time when both management and unions were suspicious of proposed production committees in the early years of the war, this Vauxhall initiative appeared to be an advanced experiment in industrial democracy.

Richard Croucher referring to production committees at the time when Vauxhall set up the MAC states that 'most managers were not in favour of any such schemes . . . they only came to accept them as a "fact of life" because of the pressures brought to bear on them by government on the one hand and the shop stewards on the other.'[25] Croucher continues by emphasising that only 6 per cent of Joint Production Committees were set up by the end of 1941. The majority were set up in 1942 and appeared to have met only once 'and

[20] Peter Vigor interview.
[21] W.J. Seymour, *An Account of Our Stewardship* (Luton: Vauxhall Motors, 1945).
[22] G. Turner, *The Car Makers* (Penguin, 1964), p. 123.
[23] Seymour, op. cit., pp. 6, 7 and 8.
[24] Seymour, op. cit., pp. 7 and 8.
[25] Richard Croucher, *Engineers at War 1939–1945* (London, 1982), p. 149.

effectively ceased to operate.'[26] In Coventry, for example, 'only 15 out of 44 met regularly.'[27]

It would appear that Vauxhall management were far ahead in progressive methods of labour consultation. However, non-cooperation in other areas was not entirely attributable to management and some trade unionists in two Coventry factories dubbed them 'Gaffers' Committees.'[28] In this respect it could be seen that Vauxhall was effectively emasculating the rights of the workforce by creating a facade of democracy in the workplace. The evidence does not seem to generally support this view. Unionism, as is described below, began to expand within Vauxhall in the war years and does not seem to have been hampered by the presence of the MAC. Indeed such shop floor militants as Harold Horne were soon to be elected to the Committee and to serve on it until the late 1950s.[29] Horne claims that the MAC was initially an idea emanating from the Luton Communist Party.

> During the war a campaign was organised by the trade union movement largely initiated by the Communist Party to set up a production committee for the war effort. At one of our meetings leaflets were given out about these, and Bartlett came along with Reg Pearson. He said to Reg 'Look at this leaflet. There you are Reg, that's what we want.' He was astute enough to see the trend, and very soon after that established the Management Advisory Committee.[30]

It seems that Bartlett's attitude towards the unions was not vociferous opposition, as had been the experience in Vauxhall in the 1920s. He did not, however, encourage them and probably took an attitude of 'letting sleeping dogs lie.' Unionism within Vauxhall and in Luton in general lay dormant for much of the 1930s and only began to gain footholds in the war years.

In the car industry as a whole unionism remained generally weak and Patrick Fridenson states:

> In post 1926 Britain, the motor car industry 'drew on its vast supplies of destitute people in the depressed regions' . . . this heterogeneous recruitment outgrew existing divisions of labour. It also weakened the already declining trade unions. Being based on skilled workers, they did not easily accept or incorporate semi-skilled workers.[31]

The assembly line workers and other unskilled and semi-skilled workers in the interwar years thus remained largely non-unionised. The employers did not encourage the unions (and were often vociferously against them as in the case of Ford, Austin and Morris), the skilled unions did not want to encourage dilution of skills by allowing the assembly line workers to join. In the Luton

[26] Ibid., p. 155.
[27] Ibid.
[28] Ibid.
[29] Harold Horne interview.
[30] Harold Horne interview.
[31] Patrick Fridenson ,'The Coming of the Assembly Line to Europe' in Krohn, Laytons and Weingart (eds.), *The Dynamics of Science and Technology, Sociology of the Sciences* vol. 11 (Dortrecht, Holland, 1928). He quotes from R.D. Sealy, 'From Carriages to Cars' (unpublished Diploma thesis, Ruskin College, Oxford, 1976).

area the militancy, never as great as in other areas, which took place in the latter part of the First World War and the immediate post-war years proved to be an exceptional time and petered out as quickly as it had emerged. As Huw Beynon puts it, describing the unskilled and semi-skilled car workers in this period, 'mostly these men were on their own.'[32]

Before examining the growth of unionism within Vauxhall it would be of interest to examine the influence of migrants on the labour situation. Did the influx of migrants into Luton have the effect, as Fridensen seems to indicate, of stunting unions growth; or did the workers from depressed regions bring with them their union consciousness, and help engender an upsurge which began to take place after 1934?

The evidence seems to suggest that Fridenson's view is somewhat mistaken, particularly regarding the Luton-Vauxhall experience. The union protests relating to the importation of labour in the early 1920s concerned mainly labour brought in from Bedfordshire and surrounding regions and London. Though there was immigration into the area in the 1920s the vast bulk from the depressed regions did not begin to arrive until the 1930s. Titmus and Grundy estimate that by 1945 41,760 immigrants had entered the town, who accounted for 46 per cent of the total population.[33] Although this would seem to be a large figure, they stress that 'the bulk of Luton's new population came from Bedfordshire and the South-East.' In fact, they calculate that 13,526 immigrants had come from the depressed areas of Scotland, Wales and Northern England, and accounted for 13 per cent of the total population.[34]

This evidence is clearly backed by the fact that the principal source of attraction was the growing Vauxhall works, which did not experience large scale expansion until the 1930s. Initial post-1926 union weakness in the Vauxhall car industry was therefore not a result of mass immigration from the depressed areas helping to create a pool of labour.

In fact workers moving to the town from the depressed areas found a feeble union structure as Table 26 indicates. It would be reasonable to suggest that the immigrants brought a union consciousness with them from areas with stronger union traditions than Luton. Glyn Morgan for example began work in Luton in 1934 and became a strong unionist influenced by his father who had left Wales in the 1920s.[35] Fred Smith, who came from Swindon, claims, 'I was a union man because I had to be on the railway. But there was not a lot of union then, not till after the war.'[36] Though some of the immigrant workers were strong unionists the evidence suggests the depressed state of the economy as a whole generally held back militancy in the 1930s and the work of militants only became effective during the war when labour shortages of an acute nature began to occur. Arthur Excell tends to endorse this view in the experience of Morris Motors in Oxford. When ex-railwaymen were introduced into the tool room they brought with them trade union practices. Significantly, this took

---

[32] Huw Beynon, *Working for Ford* (London: Penguin, 1973), p. 44.
[33] Richard Titmus and F. Grundy, *Report on Luton* (Luton, 1945), p. 118.
[34] Ibid., p. 119.
[35] Glyn Morgan interview.
[36] Fred Smith interview.

place in the 1940s when the labour supply situation had radically changed.[37] Glyn Morgan dates the influence from 1940 in Vauxhall.

> The shop stewards committee had just started in 1940. In the skilled areas you had a lot of people from the traditionally skilled areas like Coventry and Birmingham, and even British who had worked in Detroit. They came in with their union cards in their pockets. They formed the nucleus of the trade union in the skilled areas.[38]

The main unions at Vauxhall from the earliest days were the engineering unions, mainly the AEU, and the NUVB. British car workers had traditionally been organised in craft unions like the AEU and the NUVB. While the engineers kept some small presence throughout, it appears that by the mid-1930s the NUVB had little or no members at all in Vauxhall, and it was only in the 1940s that they began to build up again among the mass production workers, including women. The Transport and General Workers Union (TGWU) did not attempt systematic recruitment of assembly line workers in the 1930s and 1940s and according to Harold Horne, whose brother became the TGWU District Organiser, they were not able to gain footholds and recognition in Vauxhall until the 1950s.[39]

Unfortunately, there are no specific union membership figures relating to Vauxhall alone, although accurate and regular figures are available for the Luton AEU branches and the NUVB to give a clear indication of union strength in the district. AEU membership began to steadily rise after 1934 as the Table 26 indicates.

Unionisation within the engineering industry in Luton was comparatively slow. In July 1935, the AEU district organiser, F.E. Chappell, reports 'we have not made the progress in this district we are entitled to expect . . . there is a drive on for 2,000 members for Luton.'[40]

The membership did in fact triple between 1935 and 1938 and the number of branches increased from three to six, and Chappell records in June 1938 that 'a special, effort is being made to organise the people employed at Vauxhall Motors Ltd., and considerable attention has been given to this task.'[41] However, it is clear from the membership figures, that immediate numbers fell below the 1938 peak until 1940, no doubt set back by the recession in the car industry in that year.

In fact the 1920 interwar peak was not equalled again until 1940, and even then the percentage of the workforce engaged in engineering which was unionised was much lower in 1940 than it had been in 1920. Approximately 47 per cent of the engineering workforce were unionised in 1920[42] but in 1939 this percentage was only 11.2, and was still only 14 per cent in 1945.[43] Comparing the rise of Luton's AEU membership with the major engineering

---

[37] Arthur Excell, 'Morris Motors in the 1940s,' *History Workshop Journal* no. 9 (Spring 1980), pp. 92 and 93.

[38] Glyn Morgan interview.

[39] Harold Horne interview.

[40] Report of District Organiser, Division 17, Luton, *AEU Monthly Journal* (December 1935).

[41] Report of District Organiser, Division 17, *AEU Monthly Journal* (June 1938).

[42] The 1921 Census enumerates 4,496 men engaged in making metals, machines and implements. No figures for women are given. Vehicle manufacture in Luton is not given a separate category.

[43] Titmus and Grundy calculate that 17,325 were engaged in general engineering and motor engineering in1939, and 26,634 in 1945: *Report on Luton*, table 18, p. 101.

Table 26. AEU membership figures for Luton 1933–1950[44]

Year	Month	Total membership	Branches
1933	December	402	3
1934	June	591	3
1934	December	788	3
1935	June	643	3
1935	December	723	3
1936	June	806	3
1936	December	1,159	4
1937	June	1,792	5
1938	January	1,952	6
1938	June	2,048	6
1938	December	1,924	6
1939	January	1,845	6
1939	June	1,938	6
1940	January	2,278	6
1940	June	2,734	6
1941	January	2,612	6
1941	June	2,773	6
1942	January	3,225	6
1942	June	3,507	6
1943	January	3,806	6
1943	June	3,709	6
1944	January	3,896	6
1944	June	3,876	6
1945	January	3,592	6
1945	June	3,472	6
1946	February	4,242	9
1946	July	4,777	9
1947	January	5,751	9
1947	June	5,897	9
1948	January	5,604	10
1948	June	5,967	10
1949	January	5,946	10
1949	June	5,961	10
1950	January	5,647	10

centre of Coventry, a poor performance is clearly seen in Luton after 1937 as shown in Table 27.

The rate of recruitment in Coventry was almost double that of Luton after 1937; and within the Luton context the indication of union recruitment in Vauxhall was much worse than the district generally. In 1938 the Joint Organiser for the South of England Economic League reported that 'with the exception of the motor industry, the works of Messrs. G. Kent Limited are regarded by the trade unions as the most difficult in the district.'[45]

---

[44] Source: *AEU Quarterly Reports*, 1933–1945, and *AEU Monthly Journals*, 1946–1950.
[45] Letter and Report from L.R. Stanford, Joint Organiser of The South of England Economic League, to W.F.T. Trunchion, Secretary of BEEA, 29 July 1938. Mid-Anglian EEF Archives.

Table 27. Comparison of numerical and percentage rise of AEU membership in Luton and Coventry 1934–1940[46]

Year	Month	Members Coventry	% rise	Branches	Members Luton	% rise	Branches
1934	Oct.	2,622	—	10	788	—	3
1937	June	6,145	234% on 1934	15	1,792	227% on 1934	5
1940	June	9,402	53% on 1937	21	2,278	27% on 1937	6

Attempts to recruit within Vauxhall by the Transport and General Workers met with even less success and Stanford reports that:

> On March 22nd, 1938, Twort (a local TGWU organiser and labour activist) received a letter from the TGWU reprimanding him for having distributed trade union recruiting literature at the Vauxhall factory. It stated that as this firm was not affiliated to the Employers Federation it might cause trouble if he got many members there, as there would be no method whereby any conversations could take place with the firm.[47]

The NUVB performance in recruitment was also slow and its membership was tiny compared with the AEU. Sid Dalley, a vehicle builder who moved to Luton in 1933, recalls that there were only 28 members in the Luton branch, and of these only 12 worked in Vauxhall, and the management there did not know they were members.[48] The Luton NUVB members were controlled from London at this time.[49] Even by the time of the outbreak of the war the NUVB membership had only increased to 40 in the Luton area.(4) The *NUVB Quarterly Reports* in its journal record only 12 members in the Luton branch in 1933, rising to 29 by 1935.[50]

NUVB membership followed a closely similar pattern to that of the AEU in the Luton area from the First World War until the 1950s, although at a much lower level in terms of numbers as shown in Table 28.

Table 28 reveals, that like the AEU, the NUVB membership did not equal the 1920 figure until 1940. It would seem therefore that union presence in the Luton engineering industry and in Vauxhall began to grow in the Second World War. Zeitlin points to a time between the late 1930s and the early 1950s when an upsurge in unionism was significant enough to enable what might be described as job control by the unions.[51] Superficially this appears to be true but

---

[46] Source: *AEU Quarterly Reports* (1934, October 1937, June 1940, June 1941).

[47] Letter and Report Stanford to Trunchion, 22 April 1938, p. 2. Mid-Anglian EEF Archives.

[48] Interview with Sid Dalley (taped and typed by Steve Tolliday, King's College, Cambridge), 15 June 1981, p. 15.

[49] Information from Tim Claydon from a paper given to the Car Workers Group, the London School of Economics, entitled 'Trade Union Recruiting Strategies in the Inter-War Car Industry,' October 1981.

[50] *NUVB Quarterly Journal* (April 1934 and April 1936). These are membership returns for the end of 1933 and end of 1934.

[51] Jonathan Zeitlin, 'The Emergence of Shop Steward Organisation and Job Control in the British Car Industry: A Review Essay,' *History Workshop Journal* issue 10 (Autumn 1980), p. 121. Job control is seen as the autonomy from central union control enjoyed by shop stewards. The concrete embodiment of constraints which shop stewards impose on management's attempts at

Table 28. NUVB membership in Luton 1916–1958[52]

Year	Membership	Year (July)	Membership
1916	53	1940	174
1917	61	1941	210
1918	73	1942	425
1919	119	1943	416
1920	151	1944	349
1921	86	1945	367
1922	72	1946	638
1923	89	1947	748
1924	81	1948	703
1925	78	1949	688
1926	53	1950	634
1927	37	1951	665
1928	31	1952	666
1929	29	1953	758
1930	30	1954	843
1931	24	1955	938
1932	13	1956 (Oct.)	1,098
1933	12	1958 (July)	1,826
1934	22	1958 (Dec.)	2,108
1935	29		
1936	38		
1937	46		
1938	45		
1939	132		

closer examination of the period from 1940 to the late 1950s clearly shows that this was not the case. Steve Tolliday challenges this and he sees the late 1950s as the time when mass unionism made large incursions into the major motor firms, such as Morris, Austin, Ford and BMC.[53] The Vauxhall experience tends to concur with this view. There is considerable evidence of increased union activity in Vauxhall in the war years. However, as late as 1942 the NUVB organiser for the area (which included Luton) only mentions Vauxhall for the first time in his report, and none too encouragingly. 'Trade union membership is not up to the standard we would like to see' in this firm.[54] Nevertheless, the NUVB had established a firm foothold in Vauxhall by the end of the war. For example, by

---

technical and organisational innovation are seen to be 'informal' work roles and restrictive practices, such as demarcation lines, seniority systems, over-manning and limitations on the speed and output of machine, p. 119.

[52] Source: *NUVB Quarterly Journal* for April of each year, except for the October 1956 figure which is in the January 1957 issue, and July 1958 which is in the October 1958 issue. The April journal gives the end-of-year membership for the previous year.

[53] Steve Tolliday, 'Management Strategy and Shop Floor Organisation: Standard and Austin Motors, 1920–1950,' paper presented to a seminar on 'Shop Floor Bargaining, Job Control and National Economic Performance: The British Experience in Comparative Perspective, 1870 – The Present,' Kings College, Cambridge, 16 November 1981. Unionism clearly did make some inroads in the smaller firms, especially Standard, Humber, Jaguar and Daimler, from the time of the Second World War.

[54] *NUVB Quarterly Journal* (January 1942). District Organiser's Report.

July 1943 the NUVB have a representative on MAC[55] and in December the local NUVB minutes record how their representatives were 'now able to meet the Vauxhall Management' concerning grading and rates of pay, a position which A. Penn, the Area Organiser, describes as being a considerable move forward on the pre-war situation.[56] In fact the Luton NUVB branch seems to have had the strongest presence in Vauxhall Motors and Percival Aircraft as much of their minutes up to 1950 and beyond are taken up with questions in these two firms.[57]

From late 1944 and throughout 1945 lengthy and protracted negotiations took place between the NUVB and Vauxhall over the question of grades and rates of pay between body builders and body assemblers, and towards the end Bartlett himself became involved in these discussions.[58] By mid-1946 the NUVB had shop stewards in the paint shop, trim shop, finishing shop and body shop.[59] In July of that year a strike by NUVB members is recorded in the paint shop but no details given as to its cause.[60] In September the body shop received an upgrading of all its members, a sign that the NUVB were having some effect.[61] In November it was proposed that a shop stewards' committee be set up and the minutes for this particular meeting close with the words: 'all the above stewards reports were acceptable with thanks to them for their efforts in building up a strong NUVB presence at Vauxhall Motors.'[62] Likewise the AEU also witnessed an expansion of its membership within Vauxhall in the war years, and for the first time widespread recruitment of semi-skilled and unskilled workers, began to take place.

According to most of the Vauxhall workers interviewed, the unions were not recognised as such, except in the skilled areas, which even then were very weak until the early years of the war. According to Tom Adair and Don Smith, two AEU semi-skilled shop floor workers and union activists, the starting point for unionisation was in the Tank Shop.[63] Adair was elected the shop steward and when the MAC began in 1941 was one of the first AEU men to be elected on to that body. In 1941 and 1942 these men attest to a number of incidents with the management which had the effect of improving union presence in Vauxhall and enabling union recognition. The first was in 1941 and revolved around the nature of the proposed MAC. Bartlett wanted it to be selected by him but, according to Adair, the AEU members wanted it to be elected. 'He wanted to hold control.'[64] Finally, after a meeting Bartlett agreed to a 12 month experiment of elected representatives, after which it continued in this form.

[55] NUVB Minute Book, Luton no. 1 Branch, 2 July 1943.
[56] NUVB Minute Book, Luton no. 1 Branch, 7 December 1943.
[57] Ibid., Minutes for the Period 1942–1955.
[58] Ibid., Minutes late 1944 to mid-1945.
[59] Ibid., 5 July 1946.
[60] Ibid., 14 July 1946.
[61] Ibid., 6 September 1946.
[62] Ibid., 8 November 1946.
[63] Tom Adair estimates that less than 3 per cent of the unskilled were unionised, and in the skilled areas unionisation was not higher than 40 to 50 per cent by the late 1930s: taped interview with Tom (Jock) Adair, 1 April 1981 – started at Vauxhall in 1938. Interview with Don (Jock) Smith, 11 March 1981 – started at Vauxhall in 1938. Both worked in the Tank Shop during the war, so named because of the Churchill tank engines produced there.
[64] Tom Adair interview.

The second incident involved an increase in wage rates after it was discovered that men working on Churchill tanks in factories in the Midlands and High Wycombe were being paid a higher rate. The increase resulted in a rise from 1s 10d per hour, top rate, to 2s 10d per hour. Immediately the skilled men wanted comparative adjustments, 'and this started them off.'[65]

The third dispute centred around production for war work. Adair, Horne and Smith were all Communists and wanted to see improved production in the effort to help the Soviet Union. In early 1942 they felt that production was too slow due mainly to shortages of materials, and so after repeated requests to the management to get the government to hasten raw material supplies, with little result, they sent a telegram to Lord Beaverbrook, the Minister of Supply, outlining the Vauxhall needs. The materials came through rapidly after this piece of direct action but the Vauxhall management were furious that the men had gone over their heads. Adair was summoned to Bartlett's office and threatened with the sack but the men, on hearing this, pledged full support to Adair to the point of using strike action if necessary. Bartlett climbed down and Adair recalls 'after that the attitude of the management changed – instead of being tough, antagonistic and nasty, they swung round the other way, and we got on famously. We never had any trouble in the Tank Shop after that.'[66]

Smith states that it was from the Tank Shop that unionisation of the semi-skilled and unskilled workers spread throughout Vauxhall, and from Vauxhall to the rest of Luton.[67]

From 1942 until the end of the war there were no major incidents at Vauxhall but there was a strike by AEU members in September 1945 concerning bonus payments.[68] Harold Horne gives an account of the strike in which he recalls Bartlett coming down to the strike meeting to address the men.

> We allowed him to get up on the box to talk to the workers, and he believed that just by talking to them he could get them to go back to work, but he got a bit of a shock when somebody called out from the back of the meeting, 'We don't want management here. This is a workers meeting.' And he had to retreat. A big meeting was held in the canteen after the strike had been on for a few days. A settlement was arrived at whereby payments of bonus were improved.[69]

These incidents would seem to support Zeitlin's thesis of a strong move toward workers job control. However, put in the wider context of the development of unionisation within Vauxhall, and indeed Luton, stretching up to the 1970s, a balanced and accurate picture emerges. For example, in 1948 the total insured workforce in Luton is put at 71,860[70] of which 14,000 are unionised.[71] This works out at less than 20 per cent of the insured workforce. Of

---

[65] Tom Adair interview.
[66] Tom Adair interview.
[67] Don Smith interview.
[68] The only documentary evidence is a reference in the NUVB.Minutes no. 1 Branch, 5 October 1945.
[69] Harold Horne interview.
[70] E. Sterne, *Bedfordshire County Development Plan 1952* (Bedford, 1952), table VII 'Industrial Structure Luton 1948,' p. 37.
[71] *Trade Union Membership Drive* (Luton: Luton and District Trades Council, 1949), p. 7.

the insured workforce, 27,730 were engaged in vehicle and aircraft manufacture and other types of engineering, whilst the combined NUVB and AEU membership in 1949 of 6,649 represented 24 per cent unionisation, of those engaged in engineering in Luton.

This would be hardly sufficient union power to exercise union control of jobs. Turner, Clack and Roberts state that up until the early 1960s only half the workforce in Vauxhall were in the unions.[72] Keith Burns, a Vauxhall employee from 1942 to 1976 and AEU member, fully backs this view.

> The unions never had power in Vauxhall. They have gone from strength to strength, but they have never had the power. It wasn't until 1958–59 that the unions started to get more membership in a big way . . . there was always more non-union members than union members up until that time . . . In fact Vauxhall did not become a closed shop until the 1970s.[73]

The Vauxhall experience would thus clearly repudiate the Zeitlin view, which contends that from the war unions began to exert control over jobs, and far from the process being complete by the late 1950s the evidence suggests that this was the time at which it started. Having rejected Lewchuk's view that the management had exercised full control through the production processes, and Zeitlin's view that the workers, i.e. unions exercised control over their jobs, what would be an accurate picture of the relationship between management and labour at Vauxhall?

The picture which emerges is one where management dominance was maintained in the interwar years as unions in the car industry generally were affected by the depression. The union recovery began in the 1930s particularly from 1934 when the car industry began to expand rapidly. This expansion, however, was set against a backcloth of continuing depression in the economy as a whole and, while areas like Luton and the Vauxhall works acted like magnets to the unemployed, lack of union militancy was ensured. The pool of labour was always ready to be boosted in areas like Luton by the influx of workers from other areas desperately searching for work; but these workers brought with them a strong sense of unionism which remained dormant until the demands of war production reawakened activism. Set against this labour supply backcloth was the changing character of the Vauxhall management. The older hard managers of the struggling 1920s firm, with their virulent anti-union attitudes, were replaced by a more enlightened group of men, led by Charles Bartlett. Bartlett was not only an initiator of ideas but was astute enough to see trends and adapt to them. Thus while attempts at unionisation within Vauxhall were not encouraged in the 1930s, policies were introduced and developed which encouraged the workforce to feel part of the organisation. Such an idea Bartlett plainly expressed in 1948 when he called on industry in Britain for better leadership. He wished to see 'leadership that understands the social demands of the men and women with whom we work. "With whom we work."

---

[72] H.A. Turner, G. Clack and G. Roberts, *Labour Relations in the Motor Industry* (London: Allen and Unwin, 1967), p. 195.

[73] Interview with Keith Burns (taped) 21 January 1982 – began work at Vauxhall in 1942 and retired in 1976.

It is a great shift from "those we employ."[74] This quotation reveals the essential dichotomy of Bartlett's approach. While he also clearly sees that it needs strong and enlightened leadership.

Harold Horne held the view that 'he had ideas of the Corporate State, as in Mussolini's Italy.'[75] Indeed in an article he wrote in 1929 he invokes Mussolini's example as one which GM/Vauxhall salesmen should emulate. 'In a general way there are spheres where all can do things more in the Mussolini manner. This lead must come from the boss or businessman, he must be ready to take the initiative, for it is he who sets the work ethic.'[76]

Such words are hardly likely to come from one who would allow workers to control their jobs. Bartlett's radical right wing leanings were less overt once it became clear that war with Germany was a possibility, but the essential ideas in terms of management-labour relations remains beneath the surface – a popular and strong management leading a cooperative and contented workforce.

In the 1930s this could easily be achieved by adopting policies of high wages, a Group Bonus System, where it appeared that the men were in control of their work situation, and a profit sharing scheme. In addition Bartlett followed a policy of promoting men to positions of responsibility from off the shop floor. Sir Reginald Pearson is a prime example of a man who left Derbyshire in search of work and began at Vauxhall on the shop floor in 1919. On his retirement he was on the Board of Directors and had been knighted for his services to industry. Asked why Bartlett had singled him out for promotion Pearson replied, 'probably because I got on well with the men and was able to do the jobs of the men.'[77] Such managers as Pearson were respected by the men, not only because they could do many of the shop floor jobs, but because it was clear to them that underneath the blunt, truthful approach was a real interest in their welfare, and a genuine concern to see fair play. In his interview Pearson recounts a couple of instances when he had foremen removed as a result of their overbearing and dictatorial attitudes to the men.[78]

This feeling of concern was engendered by shop floor presence. Les Cowell comments:

> I think Charlie Bartlett and Reginald Pearson are the two greatest chaps that ever worked there. Charlie Bartlett when he came round the section, he wouldn't look at a chap and say, 'I don't know him.' He would come and talk to everyone.[79]

Bartlett saw social and sporting activities outside working hours as an important way of cementing the social fabric of the firm. It was also viewed by Bartlett as a testing ground for potential promotees. Peter Vigor recalls,

> If you wanted to get on with Bartlett you had to take an interest in the recreation club. For example you might take up tennis and sit on the

[74] Sir Charles Bartlett, 'Management and Productivity: The Results to be Achieved and the Penalties of Failure,' *British Management Review* (1948), p. 74.
[75] Harold Horne interview.
[76] Charles Bartlett, 'Mussolini Says,' *General Motors News* (October 1929).
[77] Sir Reginald Pearson interview.
[78] Sir Reginald Pearson interview.
[79] Les Cowell interview.

Plate 30. Sir Reginald Pearson. He worked his way from the shop floor after joining the company as a tool maker in 1919. He retired in 1963 with a knighthood and a place on the Board.

Tennis Club Committee and become chairman. This showed Bartlett that you could organise.[80]

In the 1930s the canteen facilities and recreation facilities were expanded along with the works. Bartlett's intelligent adaptability is clearly evidenced by the structural changes he initiated in the labour relations machinery. In the 1940s he sensed the change in the industrial atmosphere engendered by the war, and Harold Horne states:

> Bartlett delivered lectures to employers organisations in which his ideas came out very clearly. The concept that came out at the end of the Second World War, that the workers are more knowledgeable and articulate. They will want a greater share in what goes on in the company, and you resist there will be confrontation in which everybody will lose. [He claimed that management] must go along with the legitimate demands of the workforce, and not let it develop so that it will fall into the hands of extremists.[81]

One major result of this shift was the setting up of the MAC which was to remain the cornerstone of industrial relations at Vauxhall until the late 1950s, and in 1948 Bartlett writes,

> Joint consultation, in its best and fullest form, is in my view, one of the inevitables: and we should be wise to see that it is really and truly

[80] Peter Vigor interview.
[81] Harold Horne interview.

consultation, not just a form of ceremony which will propitiate the new gods which seem to have arisen amongst us.[82]

This stronger element of industrial democracy must not, however, be confused with workers' control or even job control. The ultimate power still rested with the Board, and such reforms were partly aimed at forestalling the fundamental shift of power to the shop floor.

Peter Vigor, writing as editor of the *Vauxhall Mirror*, and therefore mouthpiece of Vauxhall, states that if

> employees can be welded into one team, fully aware of the aim and purpose of the company, the ups and downs of industrial life can be weathered with fewer disputes and less wastage.[83]

In essence this was the Bartlett view.

The influence of General Motors

The influence of General Motors on the development of Vauxhall has been seen to have been fundamental in terms of finance, production, marketing and overseas sales. How far did this influence extend to industrial relations? In essence the answer must be very little. It seems that this side of the business was left very much in the hands of the British management. This was probably due to the desire of Vauxhall to tone down the American aspects of Vauxhall, and industrial relations problems could bring the full glare of publicity on to the firm in a most undesirable way. Secondly, in all probability the GM Overseas Operations men felt that British managers would understand British workers far better, and thus such sensitive problems would be better left to them. The GM Board were no doubt encouraged in this view by the profitable expansion of Vauxhall and its peaceful relations with the workforce, which was in contrast to GM's own experience in the USA in the 1930s.[84]

Thirdly, Bartlett was noted for his independence and Maurice Platt recalls:

> The sturdy independence natural to our Sir Charles had undoubtedly become more marked in the war years, although I remember being surprised at the off hand manner in which he treated J.D. Mooney, when J.D. visited Vauxhall in 1938.[85]

In fact it was the wresting back of this control by Mooney's successor, Ed Riley, which led to Bartlett's demise and the running down of the Bartlett institutions in the 1950s. Initially, the disagreements centred around post-war production policies concerning car models but this was the beginning of 'a prolonged and unhappy tug-of-war . . . during which neither side would give way.'[86] Riley's own determination with the weight of GMOO behind him

[82] Bartlett, 'Management and Productivity,' op. cit., p. 79.
[83] P. Vigor, 'Putting the Worker in the Picture: The House Magazine,' in Blayney Thomas (ed.), *Welfare in Industry* (London, 1949), p. 211.
[84] A.D. Chandler, *Giant Enterprise* (New York, 1964), p. 197. The United Automobile Workers held sit down strikes in GM's Detroit plants, which successfully gained union recognition, but not without a great deal of bitterness and violence in 1936.
[85] M. Platt, *An Addiction to Automobiles* (Warne, 1980), p. 148.
[86] Ibid.

eventually led to Bartlett being 'kicked upstairs' to the post of Chairman in 1953.[87] From that time, on the American influence significantly increased in Vauxhall.

As Vauxhall developed against a background of a reviving economy during the war years and after, so too did the relations which Bartlett had nurtured. The growth in size of the Vauxhall plant militated against intimate cordial relations on a personal level and the MAC proved inadequate to cope with the changes. In the supply scare economy of post-war Britain the shortage of labour ensured a less docile workforce, and this too was in a period in which workers had learnt much from their experiences of the war time economy. The gradual growth of unions, particularly by the late 1950s, meant the step by step replacement of the Bartlett institutions. The men looked to the example of Ford's for Measured Day Work, a system whereby workers were paid a flat rate of pay without the inclusion of bonus rates. These, if any, were added after the basic rate had been calculated. The advantage was that men did not have to look to the group bonus to ensure a decent wage. The Measured Day Work rates were annually renegotiated by the unions.

An important final factor was that the American controlling company began to see the necessity of more direct involvement. The number of Americans on the Board increased significantly and began to exercise tighter job control. 'They demanded the arbitrary right to speed up the production line at will.'[88] In addition the company was at 'liberty to transfer men from one job to another, and even from the Luton factory to the Dunstable factory[89] and there is no resistance from the union side to such transfers.'[90] In return for these controls Vauxhall continued to pay relatively high wages, with shorter hours than the engineering industry in general, and had a guaranteed working week.[91] Such a bargain could only be maintained in an expanding market and, once that expansion began to slow significantly, trouble was predictable. In 1966 with the Luton factory on short time a strike occurred and workers besieged the Directors' Offices and 'cries of bloody Americans were heard.'[92] It would appear that by this time the 'turnip patch' mentality no longer existed in Vauxhall.

In concluding this chapter an attempt will be made to answer the question why was Vauxhall so tranquil in its industrial relations for so long. Firstly, the Luton economy itself was significant. Its reliance on the hat trade up to the First World War ensured little union activity and militancy. The experiences of the period from 1916 to 1921 were exceptional for Luton, apart from the burning of the town hall which was not directly caused by labour problems. Militancy died as quickly as it arose. Secondly, the general state of depression which existed in the interwar years was a general dampener on unionism in the country, particularly after the disappointments of the General Strike.

---

[87] *Who Was Who 1951–60*, entry on Sir Charles Bartlett.
[88] Ken Weller, 'The Truth about Vauxhall,' *Solidarity* Pamphlet no. 12 (undated but from mid-1960s), pp. 4 and 5.
[89] A Dunstable factory was built in the early 1950s.
[90] Ferdynand Zweig, *The Worker in an Affluent Society* (Heinemann, 1961), p. 238.
[91] Ken Weller, op. cit., p. 4.
[92] 'Office Siege as Vauxhall Men Strike,' *Daily Mail*, 18 October 1966, front page, lead story.

Thirdly, the rapid expansion of the town due to the attraction of workers to its growing engineering and new industries ensured a constant pool of labour from which employers could draw up until the early 1940s. Fourthly, the paternalistic policies pursued by the Bartlett regime continued to ensure a compliant workforce, whose growing demands were intelligently met and catered for by reforms to the industrial relations structure. This included high pay, relative job security, group bonus, profit sharing, union recognition and the setting up of the MAC, as well as better welfare, sporting, social and canteen facilities. In addition, channels of communications were considerably improved and attempts were made to deal with potential problems as soon as they were recognised. The workers were made to feel part of the company and not mere productive adjuncts to machines. Many managers were chosen not only for their technical abilities but also for their concern and understanding of the workers on the shop floor. Promotion was open to all and based upon ability.

One must also not forget the relatively isolated nature of Luton, which ensured that Vauxhall was insulated much more from the general influences of the engineering and motor industries, both in managerial and union terms. Vauxhall was always regarded as something on its own by other car firms.

In addition Bartlett's reign was in a period of expansion and, while an upsurge of unionism did take place at Vauxhall from the 1940s, trouble inevitably begins when contraction or lack of growth thwarts the expectations of the workforce. This process did not begin until the 1960s. Finally, the close cordiality of the Bartlett approach to industrial relations could work effectively in a relatively small workforce on one site: there were about 12,000 at Luton by the time he left. By the mid-1960s that figure had jumped to over 33,000 on three different sites (Luton, Dunstable and Ellesmere Port). Such institutions as the MAC were bound to prove less effective in such a large and geographically spread organisation.

In addition to these fortuitous circumstances, which coincided with his period as Managing Director, he was intelligent, adaptable and had considerable foresight and there is little doubt that under his paternalistic tutelage Vauxhall industrial relations were exceptionally good, due in large measure to his policies. As one of his old Communist protagonists Harold Horne states, 'Among British industrialists I would say he was one of the leaders in this field. He was astute and far seeing.'[93]

---

[93] Harold Horne interview.

Chapter Seven

The Growth of Luton: From Hats to Cars

The intention of this chapter is to show how the engineering industry super-seded the hat trade as the staple industry of Luton and how, because of this, the momentum of growth begun by the hat trade increased. We shall consider how employment was affected and specifically draw attention to the transition in which a predominantly female workforce was replaced by a largely male one.

The rise of the 'new industries' and their cushioning effect on the population from the Great Depression will be seen to explain Luton's prosperous local economy from the mid-1930s. Within this general structure we shall examine the role and importance of the New Industries Committee and the extent of diversification in Luton's economy after the influx of new industries.

The growth of Luton to 1921: the hat economy
The growth of Luton's population between 1851 and 1951 was rapid. Luton's growth was always well above the national average, and in some decades surpassed it by over 30 per cent, as can be seen in Table 29 overleaf.

There are three periods of exceptional growth, and they all coincide with periods of increased industrial activity. The 1850s and 1860s saw the rise of the hat industry; the decade from 1901 to 1911 saw the establishment of many new industries in Luton; and the 1930s witnessed the expansion of these new industries, particularly that of Vauxhall. This growth was comparable to such towns as Middlesborough, Crewe and Barrow-in-Furness in the 19th century. Whilst the development of these three towns rested heavily on the railways, Luton's expansion rested on the growth of the hat industry in the latter half of the 19th century, and on the arrival of engineering concerns in the 20th century.[1] Thus while the hat industry declined in the interwar years the population growth was not adversely affected, as the predominance of engin-eering, particularly that of vehicle building, attained supremacy. This change in Luton's industrial structure was to have profound effects, not only on the prosperity of the town but on the balance of the labour force.

---

[1] The similarities are closer between Luton's population growth and Coventry's (another rapidly growing engineering town), which after experiencing a decrease in 1871, due to the decline of the textile industries, rose rapidly from the end of the 19th century with the establishment and growth of the bicycle industry and motor car industry. In fact Coventry's growth was double that of Luton in the decade before 1914, though Luton's growth was comparable in the interwar years.

Table 29. Population of Luton in relation to national growth 1821–1951

Year	Luton pop.	% increase	Nat. % inc. England and Wales	% inc. Coventry
1821	2,986	—	—	—
1831	3,961	32	16	—
1841	5,827	47	14	—
1951	10,648	82	12	—
1861	15,329	43	12	—
1871	17,317	13	13	-4.7
1881	23,960	38	14	—
1891	30,053	25	11	—
1901	36,404	21	12	—
1911	49,978	37	10	74.0
1921	57,075	14	5	4.9
1931	68,523	20	5	30.0
1939	92,062	34	3	34.0
1947	106,500	15	—	—
1951	109,600	3	6	—
		(19% on 1939)	(on 1939)	

Sources: J. Dyer and J. Dony, *The Story of Luton* (Luton, 1964); *Population Censuses for the County of Bedfordshire* 1901, 1911, 1921, 1931, 1951 (HMS0); E. Sterne, *The County Development Plan 1952*, Beds. County Council (Bedford, 1952); A.L. Friedman, *Industry and Labour* (Macmillan, 1977), pp. 158 and 247.

The growth of the hat industry

The main stimulus to the growth of the hat industry had been the imposition of tariffs during the Napoleonic Wars, which severely restricted Italian imports and encouraged the home trade.[2] Initially, the plait was mainly locally grown and made and Luton emerged as a manufacturing centre of the final product, predominantly women's bonnets. The characteristics of production were small units, most of which were housed in small workshops and were heavily reliant on female labour. By 1851 women accounted for 85 per cent of the workforce. Of the total workforce engaged in straw manufacture in Luton, 2,990 were female and 521 were male.[3] By the end of the century this imbalance between male and female employees was less marked. The 1901 census showed that the percentage of female labour had fallen to 67 per cent, whereas the number of workers who were engaged in the hat trade had risen to over 10,000.[4] One of the main reasons for rapid expansion in the trade was the arrival of the railway. A branch line had been opened in 1858 and by 1860 connected Luton with Dunstable to the West, and Welwyn to the East. By 1868 a direct route of the Midland Railway constructed to London passing through Luton and eventually extending to Leicester.[5] The railway facilitated access to large markets and enabled cheaper imported plait to be used bringing cost reductions. This

[2] James Dyer and John Dony, *The Story of Luton* (Luton 1964; 3rd edition 1975), pp. 103 and 104.
[3] C.M. Law, 'Luton and the Hat Industry,' *The East Midland Geographer* vol. 4, no. 30 (December 1968), table 1, p. 340.
[4] *Census 1901* (HMSO, 1903), County of Bedford Occupation Tables, table 35A, p. 40.
[5] F.G. Cockman, *The Railway Age in Bedfordshire* (Bedford, 1974), pp. 32 and 42.

had the effect of curtailing plait making in rural Bedfordshire and concentrating the industry much more in Luton.

Equally influential to the development of the industry was the introduction of the sewing machine, and a concealed stitch machine invented by Edmund Wiseman in 1878 which enabled high quality hat making to be mechanised. Despite the introduction of machinery powered first by steam and then by electricity, the basic structure of the trade changed little. Dony states that 'machinery, which in so many industries had forced the small manufacturers out of business and concentrated production into the hands of a few larger firms, had no such effect on the Luton hat industry.'[6] The reason was that homeworkers could use the machines just as easily as the factory workers, and thus the change from hand to machine sewing only had the effect of increasing productivity. The large number of production units continued to be the feature of the industry, and they varied in size from factories employing 200 to 300 people to semi-domestic units employing a family and one or two hired workers. In fact, the number of firms increased from about 40 in 1850 to over 400 by 1910.[7]

According to Dony, in the years up to the First World War 'Luton . . . impressed visitors with its large surplus of women and had the reputation of being a place where men were kept by the women.'[8] The population censuses between 1901 and 1921 clearly show this imbalance.

Table 30. Population and workforce of Luton 1901, 1911 and 1921[9]

Year	Total pop.	Male pop.	Female pop.	Male workforce	Female workforce
1901	36,404	16,424	19,980	12,492 +	16,008 +
1911	49,978	23,522	26,456	18,481 +	21,320 +
1921	60,257	28,279	31,978	26,734 +	30,341 +

+ This includes unoccupied and retired.

What occupations employed the male labour force? According to the census return, before the First World War the largest single male occupation was that of hat making. In 1911 a total of 4,125 males are given as working in the hat and dress trade and allied occupations.[10] The men tended to be owners of the firms, and all the blockmakers were men.[11] Bleaching and dyeing was also a solely male area of employment. Other hat trade employment for men was in the general fetching and carrying of materials and finished products, as well as boxing and packing. The next three largest occupations were general engineering 1,839,

[6] Dyer and Dony, op. cit., p. 127. Dony was responsible for the chapters on Luton in the period from the 17th century.
[7] C.M. Law, 'Luton and the Hat Industry,' op. cit., p. 338.
[8] Ibid., p. 128.
[9] Sources: *1901 Census, Bedford Part 1* (HMSO, 1903), Population Tables, table 35, p. 40; *1911 Census*, County of Bedford Occupation Tables, table 25, p. 80; *1921 Census*, County of Bedford Occupation Tables, table 16, pp. 21, and 28.
[10] *1911 Census*, Occupation Tables, table 24, p. 79.
[11] Blockmakers made the wooden moulds which formed the basic shape of the hats.

buildings and construction 1,565 and 'conveyance of men, goods and messages' 1,121.[12] Probably the railways took the majority of this last section. The rest were absorbed in retailing, performing work in public houses and fulfilling a variety of service and maintenance functions in sundry trades. It is interesting to note that 'motor car' makers appears as a separate category for the first time in the 1911 census, and they number 666; those were almost entirely workers at Vauxhall and Commer Cars.[13] In the areas surrounding Luton males tended to work in agriculture and the growing brick industry.[14] By the late 19th century two basic problems afflicted the hat trade, excessive productive capacity caused by mechanisation and the effect of seasonality in the trade which led to high unemployment at certain times of the year. The effects of seasonality was lessened, to some degree, by the production of men's boaters, which were less liable to fashion fluctuations than women's headwear.[15] However, seasonal unemployment remained a worrying feature of the trade. The competitive structure of small units also prevented attempts at control by the employers, and ensured that the trade was incapable of solving the underlying difficulties.[16]

The New Industries Committee

The responsibility of attempting a solution to these problems, therefore, fell to bodies outside the hat trade. In 1876 Luton had been granted municipal borough status[17] and in the following year a Chamber of Commerce was founded.[18]

Both the Chamber and the Borough Council were well aware of Luton's reliance on one trade, and the problems that it would bring to the town if that industry were to suffer a decline or a depression. These bodies felt that they could not solve the problems of the hat industry but could offer an external solution in attracting industries to the town. In 1889 a New Industries Committee was set up consisting of an equal number of representatives from the Town Council and the Chamber of Commerce, and serviced by the Town Clerk and the Secretary of the Chamber of Commerce.[19]

The civic leaders took a conscious decision to reduce the town's reliance on one trade, by attracting new industries to the town, particularly those which would employ male labour. Thomas Keens, who had been associated with the committee from its earliest days, wrote of the aims in the *Luton Chamber of Commerce Journal*:

> The Luton Chamber of Commerce was the first Chamber in the country to consider the question of systematically bringing before firms who were

---

[12] *1911 Census*, Occupation Tables, table 24, p. 79.

[13] *1911 Census*, Occupation Tables.

[14] Dyer and Dony, op. cit., p. 128.

[15] D.A. Pinder, 'The Luton Hat Industry: Aspects of the Development of a Localised Trade' (unpublished Ph.D. thesis, University of Southampton, 1970), p. 77.

[16] For a detailed recent survey of the hat trade in Luton see S. Bunker, *Strawopolis: Luton Transformed 1840–1876*, Bedfordshire Historical Records Society vol. 78 (Bedford, 1999).

[17] Dyer and Dony, op. cit., p. 141.

[18] Ibid., p. 143.

[19] *Luton Chamber of Commerce Journal* vol. 1, no. 1 (December 1919), p. 4. The Luton New Industries Committee was the first of its kind in Britain.

compelled to move out of London, or other large centres, the advantages of Luton as an industrial centre. The reasons were twofold. The hat industry by its nature, must employ a far larger proportion of women than men, therefore employment of men was required, and at the same time experience has proved that the finest class of workers come from families of the highly skilled artisan.[20]

The last phrase meant that by attracting skilled male labour the town would attract skilled female labour as well to supply the hat trade. In 1926 Keens re-stated:

> We have had many opportunities of getting industries which might have absorbed female labour, but the idea guiding our work was that in Luton industry absorbed very much more female than male labour . . . [we] therefore endeavoured to secure such industries as would provide employment for males locally.[21]

This policy was very successful and before the First World War Luton attracted a number of new industries unrelated to the staple trade. The most important were engineering based and employed predominantly male labour. Before this wave of new industries hit Luton the number of firms outside the hat trade were few. Hayward-Tyler established a brass and iron foundry in Luton in 1871, and produced soda-syphon machinery.[22] By far the biggest firm in Luton, it employed over 500 men towards the end of the 19th century. There was also Balmforth and Company which produced boilers and was much smaller.[23]

The first of the 'new' industries to arrive was Laporte Chemicals which transferred its concern from Shipley in Yorkshire.[24] In Luton the company manufactured hydrogen peroxide which was used in the bleaching process in the hat trade and it seems possible that this may have provided the incentive for the operation to be removed to Luton. However, the Luton plant was never reliant solely on the hat trade for orders and despite the rising tariff barriers expanded on the basis of a growing export trade to Europe.[25]

In 1895 a small branch of the Davis Gas Stove Company was formed in Luton and in 1907 the main part of the firm moved from Scotland. At the time of the move 450 men were employed, many coming from Scotland to become known as the 'Scotch Colony.'[26] As its name suggests, Davis mainly produced gas stoves, but it also made heating and laundry apparatus, as well as radiators and general castings. Although most of its employees were male, some women were also employed.[27]

In 1902 the English and Scottish Joint CWS cocoa and chocolate factory was

---

[20] Thomas Keens, 'The New Industries Committee,' *Luton Chamber of Commerce Journal* vol. 3, no. 33 (August 1922), p. 89. See also Thomas Keens, 'The Commercial Development of Luton,' *Luton News*, 14 November 1912, p. 3 col. 3.

[21] *Luton Chamber of Commerce Journal* vol. 7, no. 75 (February 1926), p. 41.

[22] Keens, 'The Commercial Development of Luton,' op. cit.

[23] Dyer and Dony, op. cit., p. 131.

[24] *Progressive Luton* (Luton: The Empire Trade League, 1933), p. 13.

[25] Ibid.

[26] *Luton News*, 11 July 1907, p. 5. col. 4.

[27] *Luton News*, 8 June 1911, p. 7 cols. 3 and 4.

opened, and in the following year the British Gelatine Company arrived.[28] It was not until 1905 that the new engineering firms, at which the New Industries Committee's location policy was aimed, began to arrive. First was the West Hydraulic Company which moved from Bradford and, of course, Vauxhall Motors from London. In 1906 a potential rival to Vauxhall, Commercial Cars Limited arrived. Although the new company did produce a few passenger vehicles, production was soon concentrated on commercial vehicles.[29] Although Vauxhall was to outgrow Commercial Cars in the long run, until the First World War and immediately thereafter the companies employed similar numbers of employees as Table 31 indicates.

Table 31. Size of major non-hat firms in Luton to 1914[32]

Year	Davis	SKF	Kents	Laporte	Commer	Hayward-Tyler	Vauxhall
1907	450			(1898 c. 25)	208	500	200
1911	700	150			500		500
1912	900	200	350				560
1913	1,000	250		(1924–274)		600	575

In 1906 another engineering firm George Kent Limited established itself in Luton after having removed from London. Specialising in the production of water meters and air, gas and steam meters, the workforce comprised mainly skilled men, such as instrument makers.[30]

In 1910 Skefko Limited, later to be SKF, was the last of major new industries to arrive before 1914. Part of the Svenska Kullager Fabriken Organisation (Swedish Ball-bearing Factory based in Sweden), Skefko specialised in the production of ball-bearings.[31] Significantly, it was the first foreign-owned company to establish itself in Luton. There were a few smaller engineering concerns but they were not to assume much importance to the growth of the Luton economy.

A testament to the importance of the railway as an attraction to these industries was the fact that most of them acquired sidings adjacent to the main lines. By 1914 the stirrings of change to the structure of the Luton economy had begun. When measured by the number of people employed, a pattern emerges of a number of relatively small, but rapidly growing concerns.

Dony's rankings places Hayward-Tyler as the largest non-hat firm[33] but the

---

[28] Keens, 'The Commercial Development of Luton,' op. cit.

[29] *Progressive Luton*, op. cit., p. 19; H.G. Castle, *Britain's Motor Industry* (1950), p. 189; *Luton News*, 11 August 1911, p. 7. col. 4.

[30] *The George Kent Centenary* (Luton: George Kent Limited, 1938), pp. 114 and 115; 'The George Kent Group 1838 to Today' (Typescript, Kents, 1978), p. 1.

[31] *Progressive Luton*, op. cit., p. 25; 'The History of SKF Limited' (typescript, SKF PR Dept., 1979), p. 1.

[32] Sources: **Davis**: *Luton News*, 11 July 1907, p. 5 col. 4; 'Luton's Biggest Industrial Concern,' *Luton News*, 8 June 1911, p. 7 cols. 3 and 4; *Luton News*, 29 January 1914, p. 6 col. 3. **SKF**: 'History of SKF (U.K.) Ltd,' op. cit., p. 1; review of the company, *Luton News*, 28 April 1932, p. 8 col. 3. **Kents**: *The George Kent Centenary*, op. cit., p. 16. **Laporte**: *Laporte Quarterly* (Spring 1976), p. 3; *Luton News*, 14 August 1924, p. 7 col. 1. **Commercial Cars**: *Luton News*, 11 July 1907, p. 5 col. 4; *Luton News*, 17 August 1911, p. 7 cols. 4 and 5. **Hayward-Tyler**: Dyer and Dony, op. cit., pp. 130 and 154. **Vauxhall**: 'Vauxhall Facts and Figures' (Vauxhall Motors, 1966).

[33] Dyer and Dony, op. cit., p. 154.

evidence in Table 31 clearly shows that Davis was already larger than Hayward-Tyler by 1911, and the two vehicle producers were close behind.

In order of size of workforce, the six main firms were Davis, Hayward-Tyler, Commer and Vauxhall, Kents and Skefko. Each was larger than the largest single hat firm, which Law estimated as employing 300 to 400 workers.[34]

However, the hat trade as an industry was to remain important in Luton until the Second World War. In 1911 nearly 44 per cent of the total workforce and 72 per cent of all employed women were engaged in the hat trade.[35] By contrast the seven largest non-hat trade firms shown in Table 31 employed no more than 3,500 workers which accounted for less than 14 per cent of the total occupied workforce and, even including the few women which were employed by these firms, only accounted for 22 per cent of the total male occupied population.[36]

The First World War gave a huge impetus to the engineering trade, and Skefko, Kents, Commer and Vauxhall received war contracts which necessitated considerable expansion. Skefko was employing nearly 7,000 workers at the height of the war[37] and Kents over 8,000.[38] A large shell filling factory was also built at Chaul End and the town witnessed the arrival of the first aircraft factory in the shape of Hewlitt and Blondeau.[39] The effect was to strengthen the position of the female workforce as they were required in the labour short economy, and many were attracted away from the hat trade by higher wages and regular employment. The hat trade, although not hampered by government restrictions was often short of materials and always short of labour and lost many of its overseas markets.[40] It never regained its previous position. Although the engineering industry declined from its war time output high, at no time was it reduced to its pre-war level.

The predominance of women is also clearly reflected in the arrival of union militancy when in 1916 the women munitions workers at Chaul End struck for better pay and conditions.[41] This was an indication of their awareness of their importance to the war effort.

At the end of the war there was a sharp decline in female labour as the men returned from the war and sought employment. The trend was a national one but Luton shared this experience, particularly the resentment by some men who accused women of preventing them from gaining employment in the traditional male occupational preserves such as engineering. In 1919 and 1920 the *Luton News* had regular references in its editorial and letters columns to this ill feeling.[42] The decline of the wartime peaks in female

---

[34] Law, *Luton and the Hat Industry*, op. cit., p. 338.
[35] *Census 1911* (HMSO 1914), County of Bedford Occupation Tables, table 25, p. 80.
[36] Calculated from ibid., Occupation Table 25, and table 28, p. 187.
[37] *Luton News*, 15 January 1920, p. 4 col. 5.
[38] *The George Kent Centenary*, op. cit., p. 16.
[39] 'Aeromania,' *Flight*, 11 June 1915, p. 419.
[40] Dony and Dyer, op. cit., p. 169.
[41] See Chapter 5 above.
[42] 'Industrial Report,' *Luton News*, p. 14 col. 5, for example on 30 January 1919. Also letters from disgruntled unemployed men in *Luton News*, 8, 15 and 22 April 1920, in the Letters columns.

employment in Luton are evidenced by the 1921 census returns. Though the potential female workforce actually had increased from 20,629 in 1911 to 24,417 in 1921, the numbers actually engaged in occupation had slightly declined from 10,286 in 1911 to 10,057 in 1921.[43] Even female employment in the hat trade seems to have declined in these ten years from 7,411 in 1911 to 5,992 in 1921.[44] The picture is complicated, however, by the depression in 1921 and the census of that year shows almost 14,500 women in Luton either retired or unoccupied.[45] Dony's description of Luton at the end of the First World War as an engineering centre[46] might be taken as implying the concomitant decline in female employment in the local economy, but this would be an erroneous interpretation of the effect of engineering expansion in Luton during the war.

By comparison with the Midlands Luton was still a small centre of engineering in 1920 when the hat trade continued to predominate in terms of employment. In 1911 2,505 workers were employed in general engineering and machine making (including cars).[47] By 1921 that number had risen to 4,496[48] but the 1921 figure still only represented 16 per cent of the total occupied Luton workforce and 24 per cent of the total male occupied workforce.[49] In fact, the 1921 depression and its after effects hit the engineering industry very severely in Luton and for the first few years of the 1920s contraction occurred when firms such as Vauxhall, Commercial Cars, and Hewlitt and Blondeau struggled for survival.[50]

The hat industry, by contrast, seems to have succeeded in weathering the depression for in 1921 the *Luton News* reported that the 'Straw Trade was having a good time.'[51] Unemployment tended to be less on average than in engineering and women's unemployment was always well below that of the men. Nevertheless, some caution should be used in making bold statements based on such information. Seasonal unemployment still remained in the trade, adding to the overall register from June to August and to a greater degree from November to the beginning of January, periods when the trade was traditionally dull. In addition, some women would not register as unemployed and therefore accurate statistics for comparison are lacking. Nevertheless, the following returns from the Luton Employment Office (shown in Table 32) give some indication of the relative effects of the depression on the hat and engineering trades.

[43] Sources: *Census 1911*, Occupation Tables, table 25, p. 80; *Census 1921*, County of Bedford Occupation Tables, table 16, pp. 21–28.
[44] Ibid.
[45] *Census 1921*, County of Bedford Occupation Tables, table 16, pp. 21–28.
[46] Dyer and Dony, op. cit., p. 169.
[47] *Census 1911*, Occupation Table, op. cit.
[48] *Census 1921*, Occupation Table, op. cit.
[49] Calculated from *Census 1921*, Occupation Table, op. cit.
[50] Hewlitt and Blondeau went into liquidation in 1919: see 'Aeromania', *Flight*, op. cit. Commercial Cars was in financial difficulties from 1920 and went into the hands of the receiver in 1924. Until 1926 it continued production in a small way run by the receiver when it was purchased by Humber, and later absorbed by the Rootes Group. See *Luton News*, 10 July 1924, p. 13 col. 1, and *Progressive Luton*, op. cit., p. 19.
[51] *Luton News*, 12 May 1921, p. 2.

Table 32. Unemployment in Luton 1920–1924

Month	Year	Men	Women	Total	Engineering	Hats	Total % unemployed
Sept.	1920	474	60	534	150	100	3.0[52]
Jan.	1921	2,761	394	3,155	n/a	n/a	14.0[53]
May*	1921	3,029	637	3,666	n/a	n/a	(18.0)*[54]
Nov.	1921	2,610	570	3,180	1,456	530	16.0[55]
Feb.	1922	2,909	309	3,218	1,500	n/a	14.2[56]
Sept	1923	1,109	801	1,910	n/a	n/a	8.2[57]
May	1924	814	179	993	225	242	4.3[58]

* The highest figure was recorded in April 1921 and was 4,140. This was 18.0 per cent of the workforce.

It can be seen that unemployment among women was always much lower than that of men, and in the hat trade was much lower than that in engineering. It was not until 1924 that unemployment in both trades was roughly equal and by that time engineering was fully emerging from the depression. The hat industry cushioned the effects of the depression to some extent. Had engineering been less prominent in the post-war years Luton would have suffered far less severely from the effects of the depression. As it was, the peak of 1921 accounted for 18 per cent of the insured Luton workforce, whereas the national peak never reached 17 per cent in that year.[59]

The Luton economy 1921–1950: the rise to predominance of engineering
In the first section of this chapter we have seen how the hat industry grew in the 19th century, and at the same time gave rise to concern over Luton's total reliance on one trade. The New Industries Committee which was formed in 1889 to absorb male employment and to diversify the town's industrial base, succeeded in attracting a considerable number of new industries before the First World War. The interwar years continued to witness their considerable growth and the far sighted policies of Thomas Keens and others were to see engineering rise to pre-eminence. While the hat trade returned to pre First World War levels in the 1920s, it was to experience a relative decline in the 1930s as Table 33, on the following page, reveals.

By the mid 1920s Luton and the country in general were experiencing a spurt of industrial growth as the worst excesses of the post-war depression were left behind. New industries began to arrive in Luton once again. In 1926 the Swedish firm Electrolux established its main British base in Luton.[60] In 1925 the Cundall Folding Machine Company set up a factory[61] and in 1929

---

[52] 'Luton Unemployment,' *Luton News*, 30 September 1920, p. 5 col. 6.
[53] 'Unemployment Figures,' *Luton News*, 27 January 1921, p. 5.
[54] 'Luton Unemployment Figures,' *Luton News*, 26 May 1921, p. 6.
[55] 'Luton and District Unemployment Committee,' *Luton News*, 17 November 1921, p. 7.
[56] 'Unemployment Figures,' *Luton News*, 9 February 1922, p. 6.
[57] 'Unemployment in Luton,' *Luton News*, 20 September 1923, p. 9.
[58] 'Unemployment on the Downward Path,' *Luton News*, 15 May 1924.
[59] Stephen Constantine, *Unemployment between the Wars* (1980), p. 3.
[60] *Luton Chamber of Commerce Journal* (February 1926), p. 42.
[61] *Progressive Luton*, op. cit., p. 13.

Table 33. Insured and occupied workforce in Luton 1901–1951

Year	Hats	% of total w/f	Engineering	% of w/f	Vehicles	% of w/f	Total eng/vehicle	Vauxhall % of w/f
1901	10,080	53	1,111 a	5.8	—	—		
1911	11,536	44	2,505 a	9.5	—	—	—	1.9
1921	8,717	30	4,496 a	16.0	—	—	—	4.2
1931	11,515	32	4,259 b	11.9	2,500	7.0	19	6.8
1939	11,700	24	6,883 b	14.0	10,442	21.0	35	18.5
1945	2,111	5	12,089 b	28.0	13,545	31.0	59	27.2
1951	5,763	9	13,575 c	21.6	13,993	22.3	44	19.2

a = vehicles included; b = separate from vehicles; c = separate from vehicles but includes aircraft.
Sources: *Census 1901*, Bedfordshire Occupation Tables, table 35A, p. 40; *Census 1911*, Bedfordshire Occupation Tables, table 24, p. 79; *Census 1921*, Bedfordshire Occupation Tables, table 16, pp. 21–28; *Census of England and Wales 1931*, Industries and Classification Tables vol. 111, table 2, pp. 13–19; 'Vauxhall Facts and Figures' (Vauxhall Motors, 1966).

the chemical firm of Alcock (Peroxide) Limited established itself in Luton.[62] Cundall and Alcock were not large concerns but Electrolux was to witness considerable expansion, particularly in the 1930s, when the growth of the consumer goods market induced rising sales of products such as refrigerators and vacuum cleaners, including those produced by the Luton companies.

The production of motor vehicles, ball bearings, domestic consumer durables and chemicals all enjoyed a considerable expansion, particularly after 1934 when the worst of the depression had passed. Towns such as Luton, Coventry, Oxford and Birmingham, together with suburban London areas which contained new industrial estates near main arterial roads, participated in this prosperity and were in stark contrast to the depressed regions in the North, South Wales, and Scotland, which languished in depression until the onset of war. Luton exemplified this new growth and the depression was in many senses an unfortunate interlude in its rapid growth. The one drag on the prosperity of Luton was the hat trade which began to experience serious difficulties in the 1930s. In terms of its workforce it experienced only a slight decline in numbers and it appeared to be static but this hid a multitude of structural faults, which were to ensure that it never re-emerged as the largest single industry in Luton after the Second World War.

The largest single concern in Luton was Vauxhall Motors which had enjoyed that status since the early 1920s. After it was acquired by General Motors in 1925, and re-organisation and expansion had taken place after 1929, that lead was to grow significantly as Table 34 reveals.

In 1933 the Luton Town Clerk declared that 'Vauxhall Motors was a very great asset to the town and 10,000 people or 12 per cent of the population, were dependent on them.'[63] By 1938 Vauxhall had a larger workforce than the next five largest firms in Luton combined. If Commer Cars is added (unfortunately there are no records of their workforce in this period), it can

[62] *Progressive Luton*, op. cit., p. 32.
[63] *Luton News*, 21 September 1933, p. 5 col. 1.

Table 34. Size of Luton firms 1919–1950

Year	Davis	Skefko	Kents	Laporte	Electrolux	Vauxhall
1919	—	775	1,114	—	—	1,023
1921	—	1,000	—	—	—	1,210
1924	—	1,000	—	271	—	1,750
1926	—	—	—	—	300	1,934
1933	—	—	—	400	700	5,200
1934	—	1,700	—	—	—	6,352
1935	2,000	—	—	—	—	6,726
1936	—	2,000	—	—	1,500	7,660
1938	—	—	1,750	—	—	8,589
1950	1,800	3,000	3,000	—	2,000	12,659

Sources:
Davis: *Luton News* 3 March 1935, p. 7; Beds. Engineering Employers' Association Minute Book, 16 November 1950.
Skefko: *Luton News* 15 January 1920, p. 4. For 1921 and 1924, 'History of SKF (UK) Ltd' (typescript, PR Dept., 1979), pp. 2 and 4. For 1934, *Luton News* 3 December 1936, p. 10.
Kents: *The George Kent Centenary, 1838–1938* (Luton: Kent Ltd, 1938), p. 23; *Luton News* 22 September 1949, p. 2.
Laporte: *Luton News* 14 August 1924, p. 7; *Progressive Luton* (Luton: Empire Trade League, 1933), p. 31.
Electrolux: 'Electrolux Limited: Historical Notes' (typescript, PR Dept., 1977), p. 2.
Vauxhall: 'Vauxhall Facts and Figures' (Vauxhall Motors, 1966), pp. 1 and 2.

be seen that Luton was becoming reliant on engineering and particularly upon vehicle production. Indeed, concern was felt that Luton was moving from the original concept of the New Industries Committee as a town with diversified industry to one reliant on two industries – hat making and vehicle building. It is not surprising that such worries were aired during the motor vehicle slump of 1938 which temporarily raised unemployment levels in Luton.[64]

Vauxhall's central position in the Luton economy tends to overshadow the impressive performance of the other new industries. Skefko's workforce doubled between 1924 and 1936.[65] Electrolux expanded similarly and its workforce grew from 300 people in 1926 to 700 in 1933 and 1,500 in 1936 – a fivefold increase. Much of the growth occurred after 1933.[66]

George Kent also witnessed expansion in the interwar years, though on a more modest scale than the above firms. This was partly due to the fact that it was the largest single concern in Luton at the end of the First World War, and that its products – water, gas and steam meters – would never achieve the mass market demand of consumer durables such as motor vehicles and vacuum cleaners. Nevertheless, its workforce increased by 57 per cent between 1919 and 1938.[67] Laporte, the chemical firm, had been less severely affected by the depression in the early 1920s, but also experienced an upsurge in this period. Its workforce increased by 47 per cent to 400 between 1924 and 1933.[68] Although small compared with the major Luton engineering firms it was a less labour

[64] *Luton News*, 3 February 1938, p. 10 col. 4.
[65] See Table 33, p. 146
[66] See Table 34, p. 147.
[67] See Table 34, p. 147
[68] See Table 34, p. 147.

intensive industry and its annual net profits increased impressively from £18,000 in 1928 to £107,000 by 1939.[69] The relative importance, as employer of the Davis Gas Stove Company, Luton's largest single concern on the eve of the First World War gradually declined.

Table 35. The five largest firms in Luton 1900–1950 (listed in order of size)

Year	1st	2nd	3rd	4th	5th
1900–1914	Davis	Commer/ Vauxhall	—	Kent	Skefko
1920s	Vauxhall	Skefko	Davis/Kent	—	Commer
1930s	Vauxhall	Skefko	Davis	Kent	Electrolux
1940s	Vauxhall	Skefko	Kent	Electrolux	Davis

Source: Based on the statistics in Table 30 above.

Aircraft manufacture was to re-establish itself in Luton with the arrival of Percival Aircraft in 1936 which specialised in the production of light aircraft.[70] The factory was based at Luton Airport and initially employed 250 workers, rising to 400 in 1939, and 1,500 by 1950.[71]

The expansion of the new industries, and particularly that of Vauxhall was to turn Luton into a predominantly engineering town. The trend was accelerated by the drastic decline of the hat trade in the Second World War. It was not regarded as essential war work, and it emerged from the war with only a fifth of its 1939 workforce. Though its workforce almost trebled between 1945 and 1948, the old staple was never again to assume the important position it had enjoyed in previous decades.

Vauxhall's importance in the post-war economy cannot be over stressed. It accounted for over a quarter of the insured workforce and, indirectly, many engineering and other concerns were reliant upon the firm for business. In 1945 engineering reached a war peak of 59 per cent of all Luton employment, and after the drop in war time activities, still accounted for 44 per cent of the Luton workforce. In drawing up the County Development Plan in 1952, Stern, the author, noted that 'Luton depends on the prosperity of engineering and motor vehicle building.'[72]

The influence of the 'new industries': migration
One consequence of the radical change in Luton was a rapid growth in population during the 1930s, a considerable proportion of which was attributable to migration. The phenomenon was shared with other towns where new industries were located, for example, Oxford, Coventry and the London region.

Nationally two trends were taking place: one was a marked shift of population away from town centres towards the suburbs; the second was from the depressed regions, where the old staple industries of the 'Industrial

[69] *Luton News*, 16 May 1929, p. 4 col. 5; ibid., 6 June 1940, p. 2 col. 6.
[70] *The History of Percival Aircraft Limited* (Aylesbury: Hunting Group, 1951), p. 8.
[71] Ibid., pp. 1, 2, 3 and 4.
[72] E. Stern, *The County Development Plan 1952 Beds.* (Bedford: Bedford County Council, 1952), p. 31.

Revolution' were located, to the South, where superior employment opportunities in the 'new industries' attracted migrants. London experienced the convergence of these two flows on the outer edge of the region[73] and Luton was also in the mainstream of these influences. Between 1931 and 1937 the population of Britain rose by 7½ per cent, but London and the Home Counties experienced an increase of 18 per cent.[74] Despite these marked trends in population distribution closer examination reveals that internal migration was not particularly high by comparison with the 19th century, and exercised less of an effect in evening out the incidence of unemployment than might have been expected.[75] Oxford, for example, attracted far more workers from the surrounding areas than it did from the depressed regions. Forty-three per cent of all insured male adults in Oxford in 1936 came from other parts of the country and of these less than a quarter came from Wales and the North.[76] Statistics for Luton confirm a similar picture. In 1945 it was calculated that 54 per cent of the population was born outside the town and, as the following table indicates, only 13 per cent came from the depressed regions.

Table 36. Birth-place of total Luton population 1945

Place of origin	Number	% of total
Scotland	3,140	3*
Wales	3,170	3*
North	7,216	7*
Midlands	4,901	5
East Anglia	2,611	3
South West and others	3,470	3
London	12,108	12
Remainder of South East	11,448	11
Bedfordshire	7,500	7
Luton	47,881	46
Total	103,445	100

* Depressed areas, total 13 per cent.
Source: F. Grundy and R. Titmus, *Report on Luton* (Luton, 1945), table VIII, p. 119.

By far the largest number of migrants originated from London, the South East, and Bedfordshire and collectively accounted for 30 per cent of Luton's total population.

Grundy and Titmus refer to a feeling held by contemporaries that most newcomers to the town were of Scottish, Welsh and North Country origin, and explain that 'the popular misconception has probably arisen because these men and women are conspicuous by reason of their alien accents, whereas newcomers

---

[73] D.H. Aldcroft, *The Inter-War Economy: Britain 1919–1939* (Batsford, 1973), pp. 98 and 99.
[74] Ibid., p. 102.
[75] S. Glynn and J. Oxborrow, *Inter-War Britain: A Social and Economic History* (Allen & Unwin, 1976), pp. 208 and 209.
[76] Aldcroft, op. cit., pp. 97 and 98.

from the county and the South East pass unnoticed.'[77] An additional factor was that many more migrants entered the town than actually stayed, and it is known from studies of other areas that many migrants either moved on or returned to their place of origin, unable to adopt or adapt to the new area.[78]

The *Luton News* noted this trend by the end of the 1930s, and stated that the town had 'now largely become a port of call instead of the main objective.'[79]

In towns such as Oxford, Coventry and Luton migrants found work primarily in the motor trade and in the industries connected with it. This was because it was the fastest growing sector of industry in these towns. Much of the migration was through individual or collective efforts, although state schemes existed to help people, particularly the young, to settle in growth areas.[80] Hearsay, letters home, and word-of-mouth were more import- ant than official channels. Fred Smith, for example, who came to Luton from Swindon in 1935, had heard through friends and contacts in Swindon that work was to be had at Vauxhall, and many people who came from his own street in Swindon found work in Luton.[81] By 1938 the Welsh in Luton were numerous enough to establish a Welsh Society, part of whose proceedings were conducted in their native language.[82] The preference of Vauxhall in employing migrant labour highlighted the fundamental differences in struc- ture between the 'new industries' and the hat trade. Vauxhall preferred migrant labour because it was more reliable as a workforce needing employ- ment all the year, and having no attraction to work in the hat trade during the busy seasons. The 'new industries' had never really settled amicably within Luton next to the hat trade. The unorganised nature of the hat trade, its small units of production, its seasonal nature and lack of regimentation in the work place did not suit the new industries whose modern forms of production needed greater control of their workforce towards large scale organised machine production. The hat trade in Luton had some similarities with the early textile industries of the 18th century, using partly domestic production and partly small factory units. Work was taken up or stopped at will, and it was common for hat trade workers to cease production for an hour to read the local paper when it arrived. Women home workers organised their work around family activities when children were at school or after the evening meal was finished.[83]

The factory work of the new industries required much more regimentation and control. Clocking-in and clocking-out, set times for breaks, control of output on an hourly basis, and discipline all had the effect of making work in the new industries less attractive to many hat trade workers. In addition

[77] F. Grundy and R. Titmus, *Report on Luton* (Luton, 1945), p. 118.
[78] G. Daniel, 'Some Factors Affecting the Movement of Labour,' *Oxford Economic Papers* (1940), pp. 165 and 171. Those returned tended to be older men, beyond the age of 30 and usually married.
[79] *Luton News*, 11 May 1939, p. 11 col. 4.
[80] Aldcroft, op. cit., p. 101.
[81] Interview with Fred Smith (taped and typed), 17 March 1980.
[82] *Luton News*, 3 March 1938, p. 10 col. 4.
[83] I am grateful to Dr. Dony for this information on hat workers' conditions. He was the acknowledged authority on the Luton hat trade. The information was given in a taped interview.

Vauxhall had unfortunate experiences with hat trade workers who took up employment, only to leave when the hat trade season resumed.[84] Thus although hat trade workers were not excluded, Vauxhall preferred migrant labour, and hat trade workers generally preferred their own trade, although each made use of the other when necessary. In addition there were comparatively few openings at Vauxhall for women until the Second World War. Therefore these conditions largely affected male hat workers who were in a minority of 1 to 3 in the interwar years.

The flow of migrants into the motor car industry has given rise to debate concerning their influence on unionisation. It has been suggested that workers particularly from the depressed regions brought with them strong union traditions which played a significant role in unionising the industry.[85] This has been denied as a main motivating factor.[86] The debate has particularly centred on Oxford and Coventry, and it is intended to examine whether the Luton experience conforms with either of these views.

The Pressed Steel strike at Oxford in 1934 has been presented as the result of organisation chiefly by workers from the depressed areas; the two main strike leaders had been members of the South Wales Mining Federation.[87] However, Lyddon has argued that the role of the Communist Party and its organisers from London were more significant in directing and expanding the strike than in initiating it.[88] Of the Welsh who migrated to Oxford only 60 to 70 per cent came from the South Wales coalfield area, and only 20 per cent of those came specifically from the Rhondda Valley which were a stronghold of militant trade unionism.[89] The Welsh in Coventry represented only 3 per cent of the adult males in the aircraft and motor industries of whom a quarter were migrants.[90] Lyddon emphasises the youth of the migrants many of whom 'had never, or only briefly worked in the mines, because of the chronic unemployment in the South Wales coalfield,' and he further states that 'lodge officials, unemployed activists and communists stayed and fought in their own communities.'[91]

The Luton experience would seem to corroborate Lyddon's view. The Welsh represented only 3 per cent of the entire population of the town by the end of the 1930s[92] and, as we have seen, the arrival of considerably more from other depressed regions (13 per cent in total) had little effect on the 'turnip patch' mentality of the Vauxhall workforce. One Vauxhall militant has estimated the extent of unionisation among the semi-skilled as having been less than 3 per

---

[84] F.A. Acres, the Production Manager of Vauxhall, wrote to the local paper stating 'that the experience of Vauxhall Motors Limited in employing out-of-work hat trade operatives is very unfortunate in as much as the hat trade busy season commences at about their busiest time, so that any such operatives they may have engaged earlier in the season and trained to their work, leave them when they have most need of their services': *Luton News*, 14 November 1929, p. 6 col. 5.

[85] J. Zeitlin, 'The Emergence of Shop Steward Organisation and Job Control in the British Car Industry: A Review Essay,' *History Workshop Journal* 10 (Autumn 1980), p. 126.

[86] D. Lyddon, 'Workplace Organisation in the British Car Industry: A Critique of Jonathan Zeitlin,' *History Workshop Journal* 15 (Spring 1983), pp. 133 and 136.

[87] Zeitlin, op. cit., p. 127.

[88] Lyddon, op. cit., p. 135.

[89] Lyddon, op. cit., p. 134.

[90] Lyddon, op. cit., p. 135.

[91] Lyddon, op. cit., p. 134.

[92] See Table 35, p. 148.

cent, and about 40 to 50 per cent in the skilled areas, when he began work there in 1938.[93] Zeitlin admits that 'it should not be thought that Welsh immigration automatically led to industrial militancy,' and mentions Slough 'where Welsh migrants were overwhelmingly single men working in Government Training Centres and no stable community developed.'[94] He also cites Luton and Vauxhall Motors as another example. Richard Whiting believes that militancy and unionisation may have varied because of different conditions prevailing in the car factories themselves.[95] There is much evidence to support this view in the Vauxhall case, and, as we saw in Chapter 6, Charles Bartlett pursued a policy of enlightened paternalism whereby lay-offs were kept to a minimum and opportunities to earn relatively high wages under group bonus were increased, which contrasted vividly with the Morris factories in Oxford. The Lyddon-Zeitlin argument centres on the influence of migrants in the interwar years, but in Vauxhall the beginnings of growth of unionisation began in the Second World War, and the leaders of this movement in the semi-skilled areas were all immigrants to Luton. Tom 'Jock' Adair was born in Glasgow, worked there as painter and decorator in the building trade, arrived in Luton in 1937 and began at Vauxhall in 1938.[96] Don 'Jock' Smith was born in Kerry Muir in Scotland, moved to Bedford in 1936 and also worked in the building trade before taking up employment at Vauxhall after moving to Luton in 1938.[97] Russell 'Taffy' Jones originated from Mountain Ash in South Wales.[98] Alec Tuckwell came from a strong trade union background on the railways in Swindon, as had Fred Smith, mentioned earlier[99] and Harold Horne originated from London, having worked for London Transport, then at Hemel Hempstead, before joining Vauxhall in 1940.[100] These five militants thus shared the common experience of movement to Luton in search of work, and Communist Party affiliations. None came from mining backgrounds and four had been engaged in trades noted for their lack of unionisation. While the evidence would seem to substantiate Lyddon's argument there is obviously some connection with migrants and unionisation in Vauxhall. Three of the five came from depressed regions noted for large scale unemployment, and Tom Adair and Don Smith both attest that this had a fundamental impact on their political leanings.[101] Alec Tuckwell moved from Swindon, a town suffering from the decline of the railways, and where depression was undermining the strong union presence within the railway workshops there. Their socialist conscience was created out of the resentment of the humiliation that unemployment brought, as Tom Adair states: 'the unemployed were regarded as industrial scrap.'[102] That no Lutonian is mentioned as having played a key role in Vauxhall unionisation is

[93] Interview with Tom 'Jock' Adair (taped and typed), 1 April 1981, p. 10.
[94] Zeitlin, op. cit., p. 128.
[95] R.C. Whiting, 'The Working Class in the "New Industry" Towns between the Wars: The Case of Oxford' (unpublished Oxford Ph.D. thesis, Oxford University, 1977), pp. 292–295.
[96] Interview with Tom Adair.
[97] Interview with Don Smith.
[98] Mentioned in interview with Don Smith as one of the militants in the AEU.
[99] Mentioned as one of the main leaders in the AEU by Tom Adair.
[100] Interview with Harold Horne.
[101] Interview with Don Smith and Tom Adair.
[102] Interview with Tom Adair.

scarcely surprising as Luton was a town where unionisation had always been weaker than in the areas whence these men originated.

The main problem of the Zeitlin-Lyddon argument is one of periodisation. By emphasising unionisation in the 1930s only, the important subsequent developments in the war years are ignored. Thus while the Luton evidence would suggest that migrants had little impact on unionisation in the 1930s, the growth of unionism in the 1940s is seen to be stemming from the efforts of the migrants. The onset of war radically altered the labour market to one where by 1941 there was a shortage of workers and this, combined with government encouragement of worker participation through works committees, created the pre-conditions favourable for men such as Harold Horne, Alec Tuckwell, Tom Adair and Don Smith to recruit into the unions. The Luton evidence would seem to suggest that by concentrating the debate in the 1930s a full picture cannot emerge. It is indisputable that migrants played key roles in Vauxhall unions, but only in the labour short economy of the 1940s which was conducive to greater union activity.

The decline of female labour: the New Industries Committee's aims achieved?

This chapter began with an examination of the role of women labour in the Luton economy, and it demonstrated how their predominance in the staple industry caused sufficient anxiety to stimulate the setting up of a New Industries Committee to attract firms which would employ mostly male labour. It is the intention of this concluding section to examine how women were affected by the rise of new industries and the decline of the hat trade, and whether the aims of the New Industries Committee were achieved in the long term. Reference has already been made to the structural weaknesses which the hat trade began to experience in the 1930s and, while the employment levels declined only slightly, beneath this were concealed real difficulties. The major symptom was the increase in seasonal unemployment for, while the number of workers engaged in the trade fell from 13,550 in 1933 to 11,717 in 1939,[103] unemployment peaked at 4,109, of which nearly 3,500 were women; this gave a 34 per cent unemployment rate for the trade as a whole, and 29 per cent for women. It was thus the hat trade that was a restriction on the prosperity of Luton at a time when the new industries were enjoying a considerable expansion.

The pattern of the Luton economy had thus changed significantly by the 1930s and, while the hat trade had cushioned the effects of the early 1920s depression, the new industries, and Vauxhall in particular, enabled Luton to weather the 1930s depression. A declining hat trade inevitably worsened employment opportunities for women, evidenced by a significant rise in female unemployment from 1935.

Winter rises continued in the succeeding three years, reaching a peak in the winter of 1938/39. However, these rises cannot be fully blamed on the hat trade because additional male unemployment was caused by the annual falling off of

[103] J.G. Dony, *A History of the Straw Hat Trade* (Luton, 1942), appendix table showing unemployed in the hat trade, p. 198.

car sales after the Olympia Motor Show in October, and also the inclement weather which always affected the building trade. Further more, in 1938 a slump in the motor trade nationally affected the unemployment figures in Luton in the winter of 1938/39. This is part explanation for the large rise at that time, but the graph indicates that in November 1939 female unemployment had reached a pinnacle for the decade. Another indication of the problems facing the hat trade was the increased female unemployment in the other dull season, in late June, July and early August. From 1935 female unemployment in this season outstripped male unemployment in every year from 1935.[104]

In the early 1930s female unemployment in the season was non-existent. By the end of the 1930s it was 2 or 3 per cent.[105] High unemployment in the trade, particularly that of women, was hidden by seasonality, and the 'seasonality was rapidly intensified.'[106]

The accelerator in the decline of the hat trade was the onset of war in 1939. Strong government interference led to a rapid and intense contraction and 47 per cent of hat manufacturing units ceased trading between 1939 and 1943.[107] The Essential Works Order also had the effect of directing labour into engineering and other firms engaged in war work. Vauxhall, for example, engaged a considerable number of women in production work for the first time.[108]

By 1945 the hat trade had reached a low of 2,111 workers accounting for 5 per cent of the Luton workforce.[109] There was some expansion in the post-war years as the trade was able to take advantage of international markets while war torn countries such as Germany were recovering from military defeat. Once that phase was passed the trade settled down to a capacity of 50 per cent of the pre-1939 years, and by 1948 5,980 workers are recorded as working in the industry, accounting for 8.3 per cent of the Luton workforce.[110]

By contrast employment in engineering and vehicles accounted for over 44 per cent of the insured workforce by the end of the 1940s.[111] The percentage total workforce in hats shows a steady decline whilst engineering and vehicles combined, show a considerable growth. Vauxhall alone accounted for over a quarter of Luton's insured workforce in the late 1940s. Hence, far from the diversified economy which the New Industries Committee desired, a picture of the Luton economy emerges in which engineering, and motor engineering in particular, were predominant. As early as 1935 the Mayor of Luton stated: 'It is an engineering town on the automobile mechanical side, and what we want to do is to endeavour to attract the other sides.'[112] In 1938 the editor of the *Luton News* wrote: 'The fortunes of Luton are too closely bound up with those of only

[104] *Luton News*, quarterly reports on unemployment figures 1935–1940.
[105] D.A. Pinder, 'The Luton Hat Industry: Aspects of the Development of a Localised Trade' (unpublished Ph.D. thesis, University of Southampton, 1970), p. 126.
[106] Ibid., p. 126.
[107] Ibid., p. 131.
[108] W.J. Seymour, *An Account of our Stewardship* (Luton: Vauxhall Motors, 1945), p. 6.
[109] Grundy and Titmus, op. cit., p. 101, table 18.
[110] E. Sterne, *County Development Plan 1952* (Bedford: Bedfordshire County Council, 1952), table Vii, p. 37.
[111] See Table 34, p. 147.
[112] *Luton News*, 12 December 1935, p. 6 col. 3.

two industries – hats and motor engineering. And motor engineering is very largely represented by one company.'[113] Little was done or could be done to alter this situation, as the Second World War emphasised Luton's dependence on such industries.

Planning for the post-war reconstruction was a concern in the latter years of the war, and Professor Abercrombie in surveying the Greater London Area commented that 'the present population and size of Luton is such that further expansion is not desireable – it is clearly over industrialised.'[114] He opposed the settlement of new industries and the expansion of those already in existence, with one exception: that 'of a limited number of clothing firms to supplement female labour in the hat trade if the industry shows any marked tendency to post-war decline.'[115] Not surprisingly there was much hostility to the plan in Luton, particularly from the Chamber of Commerce and the Borough Council, which saw this as a limitation to the growth and therefore the prosperity of the town.[116]

The recommendations of the Barlow Commission on the post-war planning of industry, and the findings of the Abercrombie Plan, were given some legislative force in the Town and Country Planning Act of 1947[117] but, although this may have had the effect of preventing some new industries coming to Luton,[118] it did not stop the growth of Vauxhall which in 1949 breached Abercrombie's proposals on Luton. The Vauxhall victory, which resulted in the £14 million extension completed in the early 1950s, attested to the strength of the firm's economic influence. It also revealed the conflicts between planning for the interests of the community as a whole and the post-war drive for exports and greater production. The Vauxhall management exploited this conflict of interests by claiming that prevention of their plans would hinder their future production performance.[119]

The Vauxhall victory did not please all Lutonians. The editor of the *Luton News* commented: 'Luton is fast reaching the point where it will depend too much on light engineering.'[120] The 1950s boom period swayed concerned Lutonians away from any serious thoughts of tackling the imbalance, but it was only in the 1960s that some people began to reassert that the place occupied by the motor industry was dangerously large.[121] Had the New Industries Committee therefore failed? The answer must be a qualified one. In terms of economic diversification, in the short run the policy was successful. Many new industries had been attracted, particularly before the First World War, and at that time it was difficult to see which of these industries would be successful. Indeed, in the early 1920s the most optimistic growth among Luton firms would appear to have been Skefko and Laporte, followed in the latter part of that decade by Electrolux. Had not General Motors decided to purchase

[113] *Luton News*, 3 February 1938, p. 10 col. 3.
[114] Patrick Abercrombie, *The Greater London Plan 1944* (HMSO, 1945), p. 127.
[115] Abercrombie, op. cit., p. 127.
[116] *Luton News*, 21 December 1944, p. 5 cols. 2 and 3.
[117] Harry Hopkins, *The New Look: A Social History of the Forties* (1963), p. 474.
[118] *Luton News*, 25 July 1946, p. 5 cols. 2 and 3.
[119] *Luton News*, 13 January 1949, p. 5 col. 6.
[120] *Luton News*, 10 February 1949, p. 4 col. 1.
[121] *Luton Year Book 1962–63*, p. 91.

and develop Vauxhall, that concern may not have been in existence today, and Luton would have been smaller but more diversified. Such developments were impossible to predict.

In the long term, the rapid expansion of Vauxhall in the 1930s ensured its central position up to the 1960s in the Luton economy and its subsequent growth ensured its predominance. In the long term, therefore, the New Industries Committee seems to have failed, outflanked by unforeseen developments. Nevertheless Luton was more diversified than it had been in the 19th century. In the 1920s and 1930s there could be said to have been two staple trades, and it was not until the years after the Second World War that the traditional trade was truly eclipsed. These trades helped Luton through two depressions.

In terms of providing more occupations for men and lessening Luton's reliance on female labour, the Committee had a much more successful record. The decline of the hat trade ensured the decline of the female workforce in relative terms to men. This process was delayed by the two world wars at which times female labour was in demand for the war effort. However, female presence in the engineering trade does not seem to have survived long after the First World War and a similar experience took place after the Second World War. Where women did gain a foothold in the new industries was in firms such as Electrolux and Skefko engaged in unskilled assembly work. Their labour was cheap and thus far less costly than the men. The average weekly wage in the hat trade in the mid-1930s was between £1 12s and £2 per week.[122] Men by contrast could earn between £3 and £4 a week and with overtime in the car trade even higher sums.[123]

The cheapness of female labour always ensured a demand. In the mid-1920s this became a regular complaint amongst employers. For example, Skefko complained to the Engineering Employers' Federation (local branch) of the 'difficulty experienced by Luton firms in obtaining and keeping girls . . . owing to the high wages paid in the straw [hat] trade.'[124] Kent's agreed with this view. Despite the depressed state of the hat trade from the mid-1930s it still provided sufficient attraction. Instead of the women remaining in the hat trade all year as seemed to be the case in the 1920s, a decade later the pattern seemed to be that the 'girls leave to take seasonal work in the hat trade and return to Electrolux at the end of the season.'[125] This also applied to Skefko and to Kents and some other firms to a lesser degree. Besides the high seasonal wages, the hat trade proved attractive to women because of the flexibility of working hours and conditions. They could work at home if they so wished on many operations thus enabling women with small children and other dependants to work. In addition, they were not subjected to the regimentation of work which was the

---

[122] E.D. Smithies, 'The Contrast between North and South in England 1918–1939: A study of economic, social and political problems with particular reference to the experience of Burnley, Halifax, Ipswich and Luton' (unpublished Ph.D. thesis, University of Leeds, 1974), table 3.11, p. 142.

[123] Ibid., p. 137.

[124] BEEA Minute Book 1927, 15 September 1927, 15 December 1927.

[125] 'Report on the Industrial Position of Luton,' South of England Economic League (April 1938), p. 3. Mid-Anglian EEF Archives.

norm on assembly lines in the new industry factories. When the war interrupted this interchange of female labour between the hat trade and the new industries, the women became more aggressive in the demands for higher pay. The safety valve of the hat trade had been removed as they were drafted into engineering and other types of factory work, often against their will. In Skefko there was a very militant strike involving some violence in 1940. They were demanding more money. 'The girl shop stewards alleged that they were unable to control their members . . . there had been some scrapping.'[126] The 80 per cent women workers who were on strike were fully supported by the men.[127] At Davis Gas Stove Company women welders requested and received higher rates in August 1940.[128] Despite some gains by women factory workers there was still great resistance by women to enter the factories. In December 1940 over 1,000 women are recorded as being unemployed and 'awaiting hat work.'[129] The Bedfordshire Association of the EEF were anxious to know why women did not want to work in their concerns. The delegate from Skefko suggested three reasons: 'that the work was dirty, they did not like machine shops and they objected to shift working.'[130] No mention is made of low pay and regimentation. It was only firm government redirection of labour, that significantly enabled the new industries to obtain sufficient female labour. Of the disputes which reached works conference and local conference level in the war many involved women workers, and as late as 1943 some women were complaining that their wage levels were not much higher than in pre-war years, and that the differentials with the men were very noticeable.[131]

In most respects the Second World War was the last time in which women could assert some influence on the Luton economy. When the war ended the need for women workers was greatly reduced. Vauxhall, for example, had taken on women workers in the production areas for the first time, and female employees increased considerably on the non-production and staff side. In 1943 women accounted for over 25 per cent of the total Vauxhall workforce,[132] and towards the end of the war some 20,000 women were engaged in various kinds of work in Luton.[133] By 1946 the total female workforce in Vauxhall had fallen to just over 6 per cent of the total Vauxhall workforce, and on the production side it had fallen from just over 25 per cent of the total in 1943 to 1.6 per cent.[134]

Combining this fall with the decline in the fortunes of the hat trade, female employment had become very much secondary to male employment. By 1951, the male workforce was more than twice that of the female.[135]

Female labour tended to be disadvantaged in the long run as a result of the

---

[126] Skefko File, three-page management report of the strike, 25 April 1940. Mid-Anglian EEF Archives.

[127] *Luton Saturday Telegraph*, 27 April 1940, p. 6 col. 2.

[128] BEEA Minute Book 1940, 18 August 1940.

[129] BEEA Minute Book 1940, 12 December 1940.

[130] Ibid.

[131] BEEA Minute Book 1942–1945, 19 August 1943.

[132] Vauxhall Motors Personnel and Employment Sheets 1939–1978, Vauxhall Motors Archives.

[133] Dyer and Dony, op. cit., p. 184.

[134] Vauxhall Motors Personnel and Employment Sheets 1939–1978, Vauxhall Motors Archives, p. 1.

[135] *Census 1951*, County of Bedfordshire Occupation Tables, table 251, p. 41. Occupied males = 34,948; occupied females = 16,473.

economic changes in Luton. The decline of hat trade employment during the period was not sufficiently offset by the increase in the number of jobs made available in the new industries. The picture is distorted by the experience of the two world wars during both of which demand for their labour was high. However, at the end of the First World War the hat trade was sufficiently large to reabsorb the women who had gone into engineering and munitions work, and its relatively large, though declining size, enabled women to choose between new industry assembly jobs and the seasonal hat trade. But the pattern of unemployment in hats in the 1930s made less stable employment prospects for women.

The true picture of female employment did not fully emerge until after the Second World War. The war had greatly damaged the hat industry, and the engineering and motor vehicle industries, particularly Vauxhall, had prospered. The absorption of women into the hat industry could apparently not be repeated after the Second World War and therefore unemployment among women in percentage terms increased.

In fact the hat trade still held a great appeal for women after the Second World War, because of the more relaxed industrial relations than those in the engineering industries. We have seen the comparatively greater freedom offered. One example Dony cites is that in one hat workshop a person was hired by the women to read to them while they worked.[136] By contrast female hat workers were reluctant to enter factories during the early years of the Second World War. This evidence would suggest that women, who could have found work in many of the new industries, chose to stay at home rather than be subjected to factory drudgery. Women wanted to start and raise families after six years of domestic upheaval caused by the war. In effect women voted with their feet against entering the new industries, and it was not until the 1950s that they began once again to show significant numbers in the Luton workforce.[137]

---

[136] Interview with Dr. Dony.
[137] *1961 Census*, for Luton workforce.

Chapter Eight

Vauxhall and the Luton Economy to the 1950s

Introduction

Up to 1930 Vauxhall was as vulnerable to the influences within the town as the other new industries and, far from creating initiatives within the Luton economy, was often adversely affected by local pressures. Although Vauxhall had emerged from the First World War as one of the largest single Luton concerns, its size was insufficient to offset the problems which it faced within the local labour market, those of a shortage of skilled workers and high rates of pay. In addition its problems were compounded by the changing state of the national economy from one of boom to slump between 1919 and 1921, and its relative performance in the car market in the 1920s. Its posture was in essence a defensive one in this period.

By contrast after 1930 Vauxhall's growth and profitability gave it the strength to exert considerable influence on the competitive bidding for labour between Luton firms. In order to attract sufficient skilled labour, Vauxhall continually raised its level of pay so that in 1950 the local association of the Engineering Employers' Federation complained that it was unable to counteract its influence.

Luton and Vauxhall to 1930

The period between 1916 and 1920 was a time of labour shortage due to the war and the post-war boom. Workers were able to make progress in organising themselves and as we have seen in Chapter 5, not only did unionism in Luton reach new peaks, but for the first time even female labour was unionised, though not that employed in the hat trade.

After the abolition of leaving certificates (which prevented employees moving from one firm to another) in 1917, there was considerable enticement between firms by bidding up wages in order to attract labour. Thus inter-firm competition for labour was intense. It was a time of worker offence and employer defence. During this period Vauxhall was continually forced to follow wage rises given by other companies to retain workers.

Attempts were made to control the bidding up of wages by inducing firms to join the local EEF association. In May 1919 Bedford and Luton associations had amalgamated to form a Bedfordshire association, the BEEA.

This had little short term influence due to the differing natures of the two towns. In October 1920 this was acknowledged by the fact that Bedford increased its piecework rates by 2½ per cent and Luton by 4 to 5 per cent.[1]

---

[1] BEEA Minute Book 1919–1920, 14 October 1920.

Bedford, the smaller and less industrialised of the two towns, had greater and more effective control by the EEF over the local engineering workforce. In 1919, for example, of the 13 firms which were members of the BEEA only five were from Luton, and it was calculated that there were 12 possible firms that could be recruited in the Luton area but had refused to join.[2] Nevertheless, of the five Luton firms, Vauxhall, Kent, Skefko and Davis were the largest with an approximate combined workforce of between 3,000 and 4,000. The post-war boom and shortage of labour, however, meant that there was little hope of controlling wage bidding, and a defensive policy was the only one that the Association could adopt at this time.

The wresting back of managerial ascendancy had to wait until the onset of depression from the latter half of 1920. This process began in 1921 with Vauxhall leading the assault. But even the EEF could not work hard or vigorously enough and Vauxhall resigned from the BEEA in July 1921.[3] Unimpeded by EEF agreements, Vauxhall was able to break the union presence and power within the firm and introduce its own form of bonus system based upon time and motion studies worked out by the management alone.

The local association waited until 1922 when the Federation coordinated a national lockout. In Bedfordshire 591 engineering trade unionists were sacked and only taken back when they acquiesced to Federation demands.[4] By the time the dispute had finished a thorough demolition job had been carried out on the unions as shown by the dramatic decline in engineering unions membership from a peak of over 2,000 in 1920 to 760 by early 1923.[5] Though the local association members had regained 'the power to manage'[6] by cooperating with the national efforts of the Federation, their victory in many respects was a hollow one.

By 1923 four firms had left the local association and only one had joined.[7] Membership had thus declined from 13 to 10, and of these only four were Luton firms. The decline in trade union membership was thus paralleled by a decline in employers' association membership. Both sides had been badly affected by the depression, but the employers had decided to use the unions as a scapegoat. Earlier in 1926 the decline of the association was minuted when 'it was noted that due to the smallness of the executive committee it was virtually the same as the general committee, and that efforts should be made to recruit members.'[8] There was no successful recruitment campaign and association membership did not return to its 1921 level until 1940.[9] In many respects the association had made a rod for its own back. Its policy of weakening the unions had enabled the non-federated firms to reap the benefits. While

[2] BEEA Minute Book Luton Committee 1916–18, 7 March 1918.
[3] BEEA Minute Book 1921–1924, 20 July 1921.
[4] BEEA Minute Book 1921–24, 14 March 1922. 'Mr Carmichael (of Commers) stated . . . that a written statement was made by the men in each department stating that they had ceased to be members of AEU, and those who did not sign were automatically paid off at noon Saturday.'
[5] See Table 24, above.
[6] Eric Wigham's book on the EEF is entitled *The Power to Manage: A History of the Engineering Employers' Federation* (1973); ch. 6 is entitled 'Power Regained, 1920–34.'
[7] The Bedford Engineering Company joined in 1921.
[8] BEEA Minute Book 1926, 4 January 1926.
[9] Annual Report of BEEA for 1940, dated January 1941.

federated firms were held in check by national guide lines on pay, local non-federated firms had no such impediments and could raise wage levels to attract skilled labour when required. There was thus little incentive for these firms to join the Federation. They were better off outside it. After a dismal failure in recruiting local firms, Mr. Kent (of George Kent Ltd.) bitterly remarked 'that if it had not been for the Federation they [non-federated engineering firms] would have had to pay very much higher wages.'[10]

In the latter half of the 1920s trade picked up considerably among Luton engineering firms and the local press began to run optimistic surveys in which the potential for industrial growth within Luton was painted in glowing terms. The two motor concerns did not share in this prosperity. Vauxhall was still ailing and unsure of its future under General Motors control; Commer was put into the hands of the receiver in 1924 with accumulated losses of £280,000.[11] Its affairs were controlled by the receiver until it was purchased by Humber Ltd. of Coventry in 1926, which in turn amalgamated with Hillman Cars and the Rootes Group in 1928.[12] Skefko was seen much more as the glittering jewel in the Luton industrial crown, to be followed by another Swedish-owned subsidiary, Electrolux, which was established in Luton in 1926.

It can be said that Electrolux, and particularly Skefko, set an example to other firms in the locality in terms of plant layout, and provision of welfare services. As early as 1921 the *Luton Chamber of Commerce Journal* reported that 'visitors were much struck with the excellent manner in which the factory is planned . . . [and] light and air space is plentiful.'[13] Skefko also provided a spacious canteen and a sports and social club for its employees.[14] This expansion at the end of the decade led to increasing demands for workers in two areas: skilled and cheap unskilled. Very cheap unskilled labour was often drawn from the ranks of women workers in the hat trade but they proved difficult to recruit in the 1920s because in relative terms the hat trade was more prosperous than the engineering trade and the seasonal slump in the car/engineering trade and the hat trade coincided at the end of the year. It was possible, however, to recruit some women in the summer months when the hat trade was traditionally slack.

Skilled workers, realising they were greatly sought after, began to demand increased wages. At Kents, for example, the tool room workers were given a compensatory bonus which enabled them to be paid 'higher than the district

---

[10]   BEEA Minute Book 1926, 23 September 1926.
[11]   *Luton News*, 10 July 1924, p. 13 col. 1.
[12]   *Progressive Luton* (Luton: Empire Trade League, 1933), p. 19.
[13]   *Luton Chamber of Commerce Journal*, 21 May 1921, p. 86.
[14]   It may be noted that a contradiction exists in the fact that Skefko appeared to be an enlightened employer and yet belonged to the EEF which had virulently crushed engineering unionism in many areas, including Luton, in 1922. It is generally accepted practice in Sweden for employers to belong to associations, the national one being the SAF (Svenska Arbetsgivare Foreningen – a more powerful equivalent of the British CBI). Centralised bargaining procedures had been established in Sweden before the First World War. The SAF had used the lock-out to institute centralised control in 1906 and 1909. See P. Jackson and K. Sisson, 'Employers Federations in Sweden and the U.K. and the Significance of Industrial Infrastructure,' *British Journal of Industrial Relations* XIV (3) (1976). There was thus no contradiction in Skefko belonging to the EEF, which employed similar procedures. A policy of firm but enlightened paternalism was aimed at in industrial relations.

rate.' At Commer a compensatory bonus was also paid plus a cost of living bonus.[15] The extra cost of living bonus alarmed Sir Walter Kent who 'was anxious that Commer not upset the district rate and ought to come into line with Kent and Skefko practice. They [Kents] had a large tool room and did not want to upset an arrangement which was working perfectly satisfactorily.'[16] This situation, where the skilled workers envisaged regaining the lost ground from 1922, was to be thwarted by the onset of the Great Depression. By November 1930 the draughtsmen at Allens Engineering Company in Bedford were forced to take a reduction in wages, and at Commer in Luton they worked an extra half hour for the same pay.[17] In 1931 Kents introduced a piecework system whereby 'if a man made a loss on a job then he had to bear that loss; in other words the day work rate would not be guaranteed.'[18] The depression was not to affect the engineering trade as badly as it did the old staple industries.

Vauxhall and Luton 1930–1950
Unemployment peaked for the decade in Luton in 1932 at 8 per cent.[19] After 1934 Luton was to experience a rapid expansion in its new industries. That expansion was very much spearheaded by Vauxhall. The influence of Vauxhall on Luton up to 1930 was limited and its presence could not be called predominant. The policies of General Motors to turn Vauxhall into a mass producer of cars and commercial vehicles was to cause Luton to become gradually more reliant on the firm and its success for continued prosperity.

Even in the planning stages of its growth in the late 1920s, the economic and political strength of Vauxhall in influencing local government policy was decisive throughout most of 1930s. The Luton Town Council agonised over whether to allow Vauxhall to add 500,000 square feet of floor space, which included a covered bridge over the main road leading to the works. The General Motors owned subsidiary helped the Council come to a speedy decision by threatening to build a huge alternative plant 'in some other part of the country.'[20] At a time of worsening unemployment the Council realised that other areas would not be so particular about planning.

Permission was duly given for the Vauxhall extension. For the rest of the decade no such embarrassing hold ups were to occur for Vauxhall expansion plans, and a mutual cooperation sprang up between the firm and the Town Council. In November, 1931 Charles Bartlett gave the Mayor and members of the Luton Corporation a guided tour of the reorganised works.[21] A half million pound expansion scheme in early 1933 received no opposition at all from the Council and this was followed by a further £250,000 expansion in the last quarter of that year, with similar results.[22] With over 5,000 workers employed

[15] BEEA Minute Book 1921, 24 October 1929.
[16] Ibid.
[17] BEEA Minute Book 1930, 13 November 1930.
[18] BEEA Minute Book 1931, 26 November 1931.
[19] 'Average Unemployment for Years 1923–1939 (Burnley, Halifax, Ipswich and Luton),' table in E.D. Smithies, 'The Contrast between North and South in England, 1918–1939' (unpublished Ph.D. thesis, University of Leeds, 1974), p. 114.
[20] *Luton News*, 4 September 1930, p. 8 col. 4.
[21] *Luton News*, 12 November 1931, p. 6 cols. 2 and 3.
[22] *Luton News*, 9 February 1933, p. 6 col. 3; ibid., 21 September 1933, p. 11 cols. 4 and 5.

at Vauxhall, and a net profit declared at £170,000, Leslie Walton could justly boast of Vauxhall's growing importance to the prosperity of the town at the 1934 Annual General Meeting.

> We have naturally been able to contribute in no small measure to the prosperity of our country, and particularly to Luton and district, for not only is there practically no unemployment in the district, but believing as we do that good work entitles a man to good wages, it means a substantial circulation of money locally every week.[23]

In the following year, after the announcement of 75 per cent dividend to shareholders, the *Luton News* hailed Vauxhall as 'a Luton Goldmine.'[24] The million pound investment expansion to produce the Vauxhall Ten received not so much as a murmur of protest from the Council in 1937. The only time that worry of Luton becoming increasingly reliant on Vauxhall was publicly aired during the motor trade slump in 1938.[25] Any doubts were soon dispelled when trade picked up, and later in the year when Vauxhall announced plans to develop a 26 acre site in nearby Dunstable, the main concern in the press was whether this would detract from Luton's prosperity.[26] As it was, the Dunstable plant was not developed until the Second World War and the large scale expansion did not take place until 1954.[27]

From the early 1930s Vauxhall had also begun to exert an enormous influence on the labour market. The need for a greater workforce caused Vauxhall to act like a magnet to the unemployed not only in the locale, but also in London and the Home Counties and depressed areas farther afield. The attraction of unskilled and semi-skilled labour was relatively easy. Competition between local firms was particularly keen for skilled labour and from the early 1930s Vauxhall began to use the enticement of high wages to obtain sufficient men. The first recorded instance was in the dispute between the Skefko management and their tool room workers in 1933. The dispute is an interesting one as it shows two contrary pressures operating on the Skefko management, which were to be applied in turn to other firms in the Luton district. Firstly, the men began to demand wage increases and pointed to the example of Vauxhall. It was made clear by the men that if these demands were not forthcoming then they would leave and go to Vauxhall.[28]

Secondly, Skefko's membership of the Engineering Employers' Association would not allow the management to increase the tool room workers' rates as this would be contrary to national agreement negotiated by the EEF. The only winners would be the workforce and in the long run the unions. In such a situation any thoughts of free collective bargaining were anathema to the local association.[29] It suggested two courses of action which would prevent Skefko

---

[23] *Luton News*, 22 March 1934, p. 13 col. 3.
[24] *Luton News*, 3 January 1935, p. 11 cols. 3 and 4.
[25] Editorial, *Luton News*, 3 February 1938, p. 10 col. 4.
[26] *Luton News*, 14 July 1938, pp. 6 and 10.
[27] *A History of Vauxhall* (Luton: Vauxhall Motors Limited, 1981), p. 52.
[28] 'Rates of Pay – Skefko Tool Room,' Works Conference, 15 December 1933. The Skefko Papers, Mid-Anglian EEF Archives.
[29] Ibid., pp. 5, 6 and 7.

contravening EEF agreements. They were: to approach Vauxhall as a non-federated firm and appeal to them to keep in line with local federation practice; and/or 'to approach the Ministry of Labour with a view to a transference of labour from distressed areas to meet the present labour demand in Luton.'[30] Even before these measures were taken Skefko had given in to the Vauxhall pressure and had granted higher wage rates to their tool room men. This pattern of Vauxhall setting the wage norms, which the other local firms were forced to follow, became fully established in the 1930s. The local association minutes record numerous similar occurrences and these complaints by local federation members continued throughout the 1940s.[31]

In December 1933 Kents complained of dissatisfaction among their pattern makers, which had sprung from such comparisons.[32] Even the production workers at Skefko began to demand the restoration of the pre-1931 bonuses and piece rates.[33] The scene was set by 1934 for a membership drive and a wages assault by the small but growing AEU. The policy pursued was to use Vauxhall as a stick with which to beat other firms in order to gain wage advances. The Federation viewed with alarm the successes gained by the Skefko workforce, particularly the fact that the management had reported a rise in the firm's union membership.[34]

The high rates paid to skilled workers by Vauxhall began to have a wider influence which reinforced the upward trend. For example, Kent's management accused Commer of having excessive rates – on average £3 16s 1d per week for tool room workers, whereas Kents paid £3 13s 8d. Commer Federation delegates explained that they were forced to pay these rates to retain workers in the face of Vauxhall competition.[35]

The AEU tactics were then to switch their attention to non-federated firms. Vauxhall was out of the question for two reasons: the first and most obvious being that Vauxhall was the trendsetter in the district in terms of wages and conditions; and, secondly, the fact that union presence in Vauxhall was limited and by no means active. A Mr. Gillies was sent by the Communist Party 'to organise this works . . . and then to make it a union shop.'[36] That he signally failed to do this is evidenced by the fact that he eventually became employed at the Park End Clothing Company as a canvasser.[37]

The AEU therefore concentrated their efforts on three other non-federated firms: Adamant, Davis Gas Stove and Electrolux. In September 1934 a strike took place at Adamant Engineering. The AEU were able to apply a three-way pressure on the firm: within the firm by means of the striking workforce; by getting AEU members in other firms to pledge support for the strike; and by

---

[30] Ibid., 'Rates of Pay', p. 7.
[31] Vauxhall predominance in this respect continued into the 1970s.
[32] BEEA Minute Book 1934, 4 January 1934.
[33] Ibid.
[34] BEEA Minute Book 1934, 1 February 1934.
[35] Ibid., 12 April 1931.
[36] Letter and Report from L.R. Stanford, Joint Organiser of The South of England Economic League, to W.F.T. Trunchion, Secretary of BEEA, 29 July 1938, p. 11. Mid-Anglian EEF Archives.
[37] Ibid., pp. 2 and 3. AEU workers interviewed by the author all confirm a small union presence in Vauxhall in the 1930s.

gaining the cooperation of AEU members in other firms in other parts of the country to black Adamant goods. This in turn caused anxiety within the EEF as it would adversely affect some of their member firms. Pressure was thus put on Adamant to join the local Association, but they refused.[38] The Federation then informed Adamant that 'if any Federated firms are inconvenienced by any action of theirs the whole Federation resources would be used to support the union. It would be wise to meet the union half way.'[39]

Finally, the union was able to have pressure applied by the Ministry of Labour. Adamant was a government contractor and threats were made to withdraw that privilege 'due to the fact that the firm were not paying trade union wages.'[40] Inevitably Adamant acquiesced and sought advice as to the district rate but the local association refused to furnish them with this information. Adamant therefore decided to seek advice in this respect from Vauxhall. Alarmed by this move the association hurriedly sent Adamant the district rates.

By early 1935 the local association had come to realise that such was the shortage of skilled labour

> that they could not attract men to their works because of the district rate fixed by the federation. The men preferred employment with non-federated firms or operative work on production jobs where they could earn considerably more than they could in the tool room.[41]

This problem was not only a Luton one. The Federation found that associations north of Leicester were against raising rates nationally and those south were in favour.[42] This was indicative that the engineering and new industries centres of the South and Midlands were experiencing an upswing in trade, whereas the North and other depressed areas were still very much experiencing slump conditions. Indeed in 1934 there were still 140,000 engineering workers unemployed.[43] Luton's place in the national context was complex. Nationally, the Federation had allowed a two shillings a week rise to the engineers on the grounds that general claims for the district must always be rejected.[44] Almost immediately after this national agreement Luton and three other areas had submissions by the AEU for an increase in the District rate.[45] Luton was unique in the sense that it was a town whose engineering workforce was largely outside of the control of the Federation, and that was due to the phenomenal rise of Vauxhall. Therefore, although the local association rejected the claim and 'a failure to agree' was recorded at the central conference, the federated firms in Luton knew that they were fully under

---

[38] BEEA Minute Book 1934, 13 September 1934.
[39] Ibid. 25 October 1934.
[40] Ibid., 13 September 1934.
[41] BEEA Minute Book 1935, 7 February 1935. Mr. Kent was probably referring to Vauxhall. In fact there are many recorded instances of migrant skilled workers taking production jobs if they could not get skilled work in Vauxhall. Several skilled body builders interviewed took jobs in the heat treatment and chassis departments although they had been fully skilled men in the Swindon railway works.
[42] Ibid. National Report presented to the meeting.
[43] E. Wigham, *The Power to Manage* (Macmillan, 1973), p. 145.
[44] Ibid., pp. 142 and 143.
[45] Ibid., p. 143.

the influence of Vauxhall. Within the local association a lengthy debate ensued. The representative from Hayward-Tyler was against granting any increase on the grounds that the rates for fitters and turners in Oxford were one shilling lower than in Luton.[46] Kents, on the other hand, referred to the difficult position in regard to the shortage of labour and that 'they could not attract labour even from the outside at the Federation rates as the non-federated firms were willing to pay higher rates.'[47] Nevertheless, the local association refused to grant the increase 'as there were few unionists in the federated firms today and they would not risk their jobs and wages for the sake of a three shillings per week increase. The earnings by payment by results workers were high.'[48] The Association seemed correct in its analysis as no strike or dispute is recorded. It would seem that the AEU in Luton had over played its hand but this victory was a pyrrhic one for in denying the increase they consistently denied themselves skilled labour. In early 1937 the AEU once more put in an advance for the Luton district, 1½d for unskilled grades and 1d per hour for skilled workers. Kents noted the increase in union membership in the AEU from 800 to 2,000 in the District, and that the union had regarded the growth of Luton as an engineering centre as so important that the area headquarters was moved from Essex to Luton, with Chappell, the area organiser permanently in residence.[49]

The local association resisted any increases and therefore the union pressurised non-federation firms Davis, Electrolux and Adamant. Adamant applied to join the EEF in an attempt to avoid being isolated by the union, but they preferred to keep their five day a week practice which federation firms were not allowed to do, and so they never reached the stage of actually subscribing.[50] Towards the end of 1937 all three non-federated firms had acceded to the union demands. At Davis the tool fitters had refused to work overtime until the situation was 'clarified.'[51] Under such local pressure the local association granted a small increase: fitters and turners from 45s to 46s per week, and labourers from 28s 1½d to 30s.[52]

The unions did not have enough collective strength in this period to gain overall advances by themselves, but there were enough pockets of unionism in non-federated firms like Adamant, Davis and Electrolux to apply adequate pressure.

In 1938 trade union activity was much less, due mainly to the slump in the motoring and engineering industries. During this lull the Davis Gas Stove Company applied to join the BEEA because 'the AEU were attacking non-federated concerns,'[53] and they did not wish to fight alone when the next demands were made. In this way the attacks on non-federated firms gave cause for local firms to join the federation – a state of affairs to which the local association did not readily object. In fact the relationship between the local

---

[46] BEEA Minute Book 1935, 25 August 1935. Morris Motors was at Oxford.
[47] Ibid.
[48] Ibid., 19 September 1935.
[49] BEEA Minute Book 1937, 11 February 1937.
[50] Ibid., 6 April 1937.
[51] Ibid., 9 December 1937.
[52] Ibid.
[53] Letter from Secretary of BEEA to EEF, 11 January 1938. Davis Gas Stove Company Ltd Membership Files, EEF Archives.

association and the AEU was good throughout most of the 1930s particularly after 1937.[54] A particular example of this was the amicable way that the nationally negotiated Relaxation Agreement[55] concerning dilution, was smoothly worked between the two bodies.

The war years were to hasten the trend towards organised collective bargaining. Union membership noticeably increased, and local firms began to join employer associations. BEEA membership jumped from 12 in 1940 to 23 by 1943 and by the end of the war 30 firms had affiliated.[56] Two notable new members from Luton were Electrolux and Percival Aircraft. The main reason for this was increased government involvement in production as a vital part of the war effort. This had the effect of creating an atmosphere of industrial cooperation through such bodies as production committees, and the need to cooperate over the operation of the Essential Works Order, industrial training, reserved occupations and dilutions. Unions and employers' associations could much more easily represent individual firms and their workers in the increased bureaucratic wartime economy. Another reason for the growth in membership of the BEEA was that in a labour short economy the bargaining strength of workers had considerably increased. Individual firms began to seek sanctuary within the ranks of an experienced belligerent organisation which could take on both the government and the unions more effectively than a firm on its own. Luton's own special ingredient to this recipe for industrial conflict was the policy of high wages paid at Vauxhall, which continued to create problems for the local association throughout the war. W.T.F. Trunchion, the BEEA Secretary, calculated the following index of wages, which shows a remarkable increase of wages between 1939 and 1942.

Table 37. Bedfordshire District index of wages in BEEA firms[57]

Year	Wages index
1939	100
1940	—
1941	—
1942	322
1943	363
1944	348
1945	295
1946	281
1947	300
1948	355
1949	372
1950	382

Base year 1939 = 100.

[54] Annual Reports of the BEEA 1938, 1939 and 1940. Mid-Anglian EEF Archives.
[55] Wigham, op. cit., p. 146. Because of the acute shortage of skilled labour the union and employers finally agreed to some dilution from 1939. This was at the prompting of government, anxious to have war contracts fulfilled.
[56] Annual Reports of BEEA 1940–45. Mid-Anglian EEF Archives.
[57] Annual Report of BEEA 1950. Mid-Anglian EEF Archives.

The leap in wages was greatest between 1939 and 1942/43 when war production had reached fever pitch. This high peak was to be sustained throughout most of 1944 but by the end of the war there was a decrease in earnings as demand wound down and with it overtime and extra bonuses. The flooding of the labour market with demobbed servicemen, and fuel, iron and steel shortages, had the effect of lowering wages and output levels. In addition much plant which had been worked unceasingly and to full capacity throughout the war needed replacing, and the new capital investment programmes were as yet incomplete. By 1948 wage levels had reached a wartime high as industries, especially motor vehicles, worked hard to fulfil rocketing overseas demand. By 1949 a new wage peak had been reached.

The pattern of local negotiations parallels this picture quite closely. The number of local negotiations increased dramatically in 1942 and tailed off suddenly in 1946, although the number of works conferences remained at a much higher level than in the pre-war years

Table 38. Local Negotiations of the BEEA 1937–1949

Year	Works Conf.	Local Conf	Central	Special	Total
1937	6	3	1	—	10
1938	1	3	3	—	7
1939	1	1	2	—	4
1940	5	3	3	—	11
1941	8	3	—	—	11
1942	33	8	2	—	43
1943	29	5	3	3	40
1944	22	4	3	—	29
1945	25	3	2	—	30
1946	14	7	2	—	23
1947	16	6	—	1	23
1948	15	5	2	—	22
1949	18	5	1	—	24

Source: The Annual Reports of the BEEA 1937–1950; the BEEA Minute Books 1937–1950; Mid-Anglian EEF Archives.

The number of works conferences, which remained high after the war, must not be only interpreted as an increase in the bargaining power of organised labour. It was more indicative of the greater acceptance of collective bargaining procedures of management and labour, and in fact the number of disputes reaching central conference actually decreased after the war even though the number of firms which were BEEA members had tripled since before the war.

The growth of unionism must not be exaggerated nor its influence over-emphasised. While AEU membership increased elevenfold between 1933 and 1950,[58] it was starting from a very low base. As we have seen in Chapter 6, even by 1949 only 20 per cent of the Luton insured workforce was unionised.[59] It was

[58] See Table 26, above.
[59] *Trade Union Membership Drive* (Luton: Luton and District Trades Council, 1949), p. 7.

the growth of Vauxhall and its demand for workers which had added considerable strength to the ranks of the local unions. Interestingly, this process was deflected away from Vauxhall and towards non-federation firms in the 1930s. In the 1940s, as many more local firms began to join, pressure was brought to bear on the Federation itself. It could be argued that Luton was experiencing the general increase in trade in new industry and that this factor was more pertinent to its growth, and in turn acted as a catalyst for changes in industrial relations. Vauxhall could then be seen to have been just one part of this general growth. Vauxhall was very much a leader in the growing motor vehicle industry in the 1930s and 1940s. Nevertheless, it is also true that it introduced local factors which had a profound and unique effect on Luton. It acted as a wage leader, in the sense that it not only paid the highest wages in Luton but also within the engineering and motor industries.

It has already been shown that this process began in the 1930s. In the Second World War it was to continue. In 1942 Electrolux, as a newly recruited member of the Federation, wanted to know the local rates for skilled workers. The information supplied by the BEEA clearly shows that Vauxhall was at the head of the wages table.

For the highest paid workers in the tool room Electrolux paid 29.34d per hour, Skefko paid 30.42d and Davis Gas Stove Company 26.75d. By contrast Vauxhall rates were as follows: all skilled workers started at 28d per hour plus 8s 6d per week bonus. This would add just over 2d per hour. Middle grade were paid 31d per hour, plus an extra penny after two years' service. Merit awards up to 35d per hour could be earned, and if made a group leader could earn 37d per hour.[60] It was clear that even the lowest grade and least experienced skilled workers in Vauxhall began on a level with the highest paid workers in these three firms. When additional payments such as bonuses and profit sharing are added the difference between Vauxhall and other local firms widened even further.

In the national context Vauxhall was also noted for its high wage payments. Its wages for all categories of workers were higher than the highest paid, for example, in Ipswich, Halifax and Burnley, towns representative of the depressed North and rural East Anglia.[61] Even within the car industry Vauxhall was considered to be a good firm to work for. Fred Smith, who had moved to Luton in the late 1930s from the railway works at Swindon, considered Vauxhall to be 'one of the best paying firms in the country.'[62] Harold Horne, an AEU convenor at Vauxhall who began work there in 1940, was of the opinion that high wages and good conditions at Vauxhall had the effect of attracting away Ford workers, as both firms drew on the London catchment area for labour.[63] Further, it has already been noted that the Luton district rate

---

[60] 'Conference with Mr. Trunchion of the Employers Federation on Outstanding Labour Matters Affecting Electrolux Limited,' 20 July 1942. Electrolux Box File, Mid-Anglian EEF Archives.

[61] E.D. Smithies, 'The Contrast between North and South in England 1918–1939: Study of Economic, Social and Political Problems with Particular Reference to the Experience of Burnley, Halifax, Ipswich and Luton' (unpublished Ph.D. thesis, University of Leeds, 1974), see pp. 130, 131, 132, 136 and 137, tables 3.8, 3.9, 3.10. Smithies points out that this was not true for all other workers in Luton, particularly those in the hat trade.

[62] Interview with Fred Smith (taped), March 1980.

[63] Interview with Harold Horne (taped), July 1978.

for fitters and turners was a shilling per week higher than that of Oxford.[64] The only area where pay rates per hour were higher was in Coventry, particularly at Standard Motors[65] and not until 1940.

By 1943 the BEEA identified the unions' policy as 'to get what they can nationally and afterwards, to go farther, by attacking individual firms and playing off one against the other.'[66] The result was that districts which had a powerful influence on local rates of pay would tend to have average wages for their district higher than the national average. Vauxhall acted as a catalyst for Luton in this respect. The result was that in the years between 1942 and 1950 the idea of a district rate, which the EEF was keen to maintain, became something of a myth. Thus in 1946 the BEEA complained that 'while the majority of firms have similar rates as agreed for the district lieu bonuses and piece bonuses have caused a considerable difference in inclusive earnings.'[67] Such additions to basic rates had been carried by local firms in order to prevent enticement by Vauxhall. Such was the concern that once again the BEEA wrote to Sir Charles Bartlett to ask for a meeting to discuss the problem. On 1 November the BEEA met with Sir Charles with a six point document of complaint.[68]

That the meeting little affected Bartlett's attitude is evidenced by the fact that the local association was forced once again to write a strongly worded letter to Vauxhall in the following year.[69] The reply was considered 'unsatisfactory' by BEEA members, but they could do little about the situation. This was clearly shown when in the following year Kents and, more surprisingly, Percival Aircraft, one of the highest wage payers in the district, lost workers to Vauxhall. The BEEA 'agreed that no useful purpose would be served by making further contact with them, and the matter was left for Luton members to take up individually if they desired to do so.'[70] In 1950 Vauxhall was accused of enticing workers away from Bedford firms (20 miles to the north of Luton).[71] The upshot was for the local association to renew an enticement agreement that they had composed in 1947. It had stated three conditions to be observed by federated firms: that a person employed in one federated firm should not be employed in another, unless unemployed and had his cards with him; that the telephone be used to enquire whether the man is employed or not; and that if the new position offered promotion then the firm should not stand in the person's way.[72]

The amended agreement added that 'if an applicant is unemployed and is not in possession of his cards, then it is desirable that the interviewing employer

[64] BEEA Minute Book 1935, 25 August 1935.
[65] R. Croucher, *Engineers at War, 1939–1945* (1982), p. 158. Standard was paying even higher than the district rate, which had been raised due to the erection of five shadow factories, run by the government. In order to attract labour they paid higher than the district rate and Federation firms were forced to follow suit. See Wigham, op. cit., p. 147.
[66] BEEA Minute Book 1943, 11 February 1943.
[67] BEEA Minute Book 1946, 26 September 1946.
[68] BEEA Minute Book 1946, 24 October 1946.
[69] BEEA Minute Book 1947, 12 March 1947.
[70] BEEA Minute Book 1948, 21 October 1948.
[71] BEEA Minute Book 1950, 18 May 1950.
[72] BEEA Minute Book 1947, 10 September 1947.

should telephone the previous employer to ensure that the applicant is, in fact, unemployed.'[73] Some members argued that this amendment was almost the same as before and a tighter agreement was needed. The realists in BEEA recognised that the control of the movements of the local and migrant labour force was but a pipe dream, and employers would have to 'put a steel fence round their employees with an Essential Works Orders of medieval severity,' in order to do this.[74] The local association had come to accept the predominance of Vauxhall as a fact of life, and they attempted to retain their workforce by other methods.

Skefko and Electrolux, for example, allowed 100 per cent unionisation in their skilled shops and their semi-skilled and unskilled workers were largely unionised.[75] Davis Gas Stove paid measured day work long before Vauxhall, and this seemed to be popular with the workforce there.[76] Percival Aircraft was a good wage payer, and if not up to Vauxhall level certainly above the district rate.[77] In addition there must have been attraction in the fact that the type of work there was not as monotonous as the assembly work so much prevalent at Vauxhall. George Kent Ltd., on the other hand, emphasised loyalty, length of service and security of job as attractive factors to keep their workforce.[78]

Nevertheless, the lure of high wages at Vauxhall was an important factor in enticing workers from the above firms and others in the Luton and Bedfordshire District. The 'cash nexus' was to remain as strong in the 1950s and 1960s as it was in the 1940s and 1930s in influencing the supply and distribution of the labour force.[79] Another Vauxhall policy which had the effect of causing friction between the firm and the BEEA was that of paid holidays. In 1937 Vauxhall was the first Luton firm to give a full week's pay for the workers' summer holiday. The whole factory was to close in the first week in August 'to make it as complete a closure as possible.'[80] This was not a particularly radical move as the EEF had negotiated a holiday with pay in their 1937 agreement with the unions but Vauxhall was the first to do so in Luton.[81] Of greater concern to the local association was the proposal by Vauxhall to give their workforce two weeks' paid summer holiday. This was introduced in 1946, five years before the Federation agreed to such a policy with the unions at national level.[82] Such a policy was looked upon with envy by workers in other Luton firms and by 1948 the BEEA noted that the workers in their own firms had voted with their feet in favour of two weeks. Most Luton workers decided to

[73] BEEA Minute Book 1951, 21 April 1951.
[74] BEEA Minute Book 1951, 20 September 1951.
[75] Goldthorpe, Lockwood et al., *The Affluent Worker: Industrial Attitudes and Behaviour* (Cambridge, 1968), p. 94. See also 'Skefko Co Ltd: Women Workers Strike,' document describing women's dispute over a few women who did not wish to join the union. Skefko Box File, Mid-Anglian EEF Archives.
[76] 'Davis Gas Stove Co. Ltd., Membership Application Form to EEF.' Davis Membership File, 1938, Broadway House EEF Archives.
[77] 'Percival Aircraft Co., Ltd., Application Form to EEF.' Percival Membership File, 1941. Broadway House EEF Archives.
[78] *The George Kent Centenary, 1838–1938* (Luton: G. Kent Ltd., 1938), p. 24.
[79] Goldthorpe et al., op. cit., p. 27.
[80] *Luton News*, 25 March 1937, p. 11, cols. 6 and 7.
[81] Wigham, op. cit., 143 and 144.
[82] *Luton News*, 18 April 1946, p. 14 col. 5.

take a fortnight's holiday, unpaid or not. The local association recorded that 'this action must be resisted as long as possible.'[83] The *Luton News* recorded that 60 per cent of Luton workers followed the Vauxhall holiday 'exodus.'[84] By the end of the 1940s the Vauxhall two week closure virtually reduced Luton to a 'ghost town.' Smaller establishments, which relied on Vauxhall for contracts, were also strongly influenced to follow suit, and shops and services were similarly affected.

Each time Vauxhall expanded it impinged itself on the life of the Luton community. Housing needs increased, adding to the post-war shortages. Bus routeing became centred around Vauxhall Works entrances and exits at rush hour times.[85] In many senses Vauxhall became Luton. In politics many of its workers and staff became local councillors. Voluntary and church organisations received considerable direct help from Vauxhall employees in terms of money and support. The whole social fabric and economic structure became Vauxhall influenced. The firm acted as a barometer to the prosperity of the local and national economy as represented by the motor vehicle industry.

Conclusion to Part One

Chapter 1 concluded that Vauxhall's initial success in motor manufacturing before the First World War was due to its steady, but not over extended, rate of capital formation and expansion of productive capacity. A balanced managerial board which ensured the cooperation of engineering skill and commercial expertise was important, and a solid engineering background provided by a skilled workforce enabled Vauxhall to design vehicles for a changing market at a time when many firms were merely assembly plants. Also, the vehicle designs of Laurence Pomeroy, culminating in the legendary 30/98, were to raise Vauxhall's reputation to considerable heights.

However, the post-war era was to witness the beginnings of the transition of motor vehicle manufacturing into realms of mass production, and inability and unwillingness by Vauxhall management to adapt and change sufficiently led to continuing financial problems. Over extension of capital and plant in the boom of the immediate post-war years was in retrospect for many firms, including Vauxhall, a serious mistake. The depression which began in late 1920 thus caught many firms with enormous debts and falling profits and, in the case of Vauxhall, large losses. The situation was not helped by the resumption of competitive racing, an expensive sideline which Vauxhall finally abandoned in 1923. Though Vauxhall began production of a smaller 14hp model which had the effect of increasing sales, the onset of falling prices, caused initially by the slump and later in the decade by mass production of smaller vehicles by Austin and Morris, ensured that Vauxhall's profitability remained marginal. In essence Vauxhall, Sunbeam and similar firms were caught three ways: by the financial inability to move into manufacture on a large enough scale to compete with

[83] BEEA Minute Book 1948, 16 September 1948.
[84] *Luton News*, 22 August 1946, p. 4 col. 3.
[85] *Luton News*, 27 August 1946, p. 4.

Austin and Morris, the unwillingness to compromise engineering prowess, upon which the reputation of Vauxhall rested, and the inability to compete in the narrowing luxury end of the market epitomised by Rolls-Royce.

The acquisition of Vauxhall by General Motors was eventually to lead the company into the realms of mass production, but not without conflict within both Vauxhall and General Motors. Chapter 2 saw that considerable doubt was expressed by Alfred Sloan and other GM executives about the future worth of Vauxhall. James Mooney convinced the GM Board that Vauxhall should be made a base for British and Empire markets, which he correctly envisaged were of great importance. Thus the small British subsidiary began an important innovation in GM policies, followed shortly by Adam Opel in Germany, which was to have a far less impressive record than Vauxhall.

Controversy over the sale of Vauxhall engendered by the motoring press, and the atmosphere of economic nationalism fostered by William Morris amongst others, led GM to keep a low profile. Anxious to promote an all British image, American presence was kept to the minimum, with the effect that Vauxhall was allowed considerable autonomy within the GM structure.

In Chapters 3 and 4 the rise of Vauxhall to Big Six status was explored. Of enormous importance were the initial injections of capital to enable Vauxhall to survive the 1920s and begin to expand and reorganise for mass production. In addition Vauxhall freely used GM expertise in matters concerning technical developments, such as synchromesh gears and all-metal body shell production. Of inestimable importance was the adoption of American marketing methods which contrasted to the pedestrian British approach. Distribution networks were built up in which the Vauxhall sales department was in constant and intimate contact with retailers, agents and dealers. The *General Motors News*, later retitled the *Vauxhall–Bedford News*, was established to promote a constant stream of new ideas. Economic studies of the market potential for each area were accrued for the use of fieldmen. Hire purchase and deferred payments schemes were generated through the General Motors Acceptance Corporation, and the promotion and turnover of used cars and trucks was seen as enhancing sales of new models in the long run.

As important as the advantages bestowed by the American parent company was the skill of Vauxhall's British managers. They introduced these innovations into the British context which was a principal factor in Vauxhall's success. We have seen that both Ford and General Motors failed to perceive the divergences and dissimilarities between the British and American markets and that Ford's large Model A and Vauxhall's Cadet failed to make the expected inroads into the British market. Percival Perry of the British Ford Motor Company and Charles Bartlett of Vauxhall insisted on the production of the smaller Ford Model Y and Eight and the Vauxhall Light Six and later the Ten.

The most successful Vauxhall vehicle of the 1930s was the Bedford 30cwt truck which found large markets both at home and abroad. Indeed, Vauxhall trucks accounted for over a quarter of British commercial vehicle exports by 1938. The General Motors worldwide sales outlets and back up services played a crucial role in channelling Vauxhall models into export markets, where the

Commercial Motor revealed the inefficient and anachronistic marketing methods used by British commercial vehicle manufacturers.

Chapters 5 and 6 considered the labour relations of Vauxhall Motors. The long term view shows how expansion of the firm combined with changes in production techniques shifted the relationship between management and men. This was considerably affected by the changing economic climate. In the First World War and the immediate post-war years management was willing to make concessions to the workforce due to labour shortages and the need to quickly fulfil demand. The onset of depression created a sharp change in management policies. What could be conceded to workers in 1919 was vigorously resisted by management in 1921 under the burden of large financial losses. Essentially, the Vauxhall management changed from a defensive to an offensive position, compelled into this prematurely by its needs to cut costs in a market where vehicle prices were rapidly falling. The Board perceived that it could not continue with the Premium Bonus System reluctantly adopted in 1917, as the bonus payments were in excess of what could be afforded.

The abandonment of premium bonus, the breaking of the union presence in the firm and Hancock and Kidner's feeling that Vauxhall was not receiving sufficient support from the EEF, led to the resignation of the company from that body in 1921, because the Vauxhall Board stated it could no longer adhere to the national agreements of 1914 and 1920. Freed from the constrictions of the EEF, Vauxhall management proceeded to reduce its workforce, resisted attempts to restrict overtime and re-graded and re-timed jobs in accordance with what was to be called an 'efficiency system.' To interpret this as a move towards 'direct control' and, in particular, towards a Fordist system, as Wayne Lewchuk has proposed, can be considerably misleading. Even when the works were expanded and reorganised in 1925 the system of production and organisation was not advanced, nor was the output of vehicles large enough to conform to the Fordist system.

The adoption of the Group Bonus System in 1928 was a move away from the classic forms of direct control and could be seen as conforming more to what Friedman describes as 'self-autonomy.' Group bonus was to remain until 1956, when its abandonment was necessitated by the installation of advanced mechanisation. Lewchuk seems to have pre-dated the move towards direct control under the Fordist model by 30 years.

In Chapter 6 an attempt is made to explain the tranquil industrial relations which pertained under the managing directorship of Charles Bartlett. The 'turnip patch' mentality of the Vauxhall workforce has its roots in the development of the Luton economy. The hat industry ensured no tradition of unionism and the engineering firms established in Luton before the First World War were too small to create a large union presence. Despite the militancy of the First World War, the history of trade union organisation in Luton was limited in force and militancy by comparison to more industrialised areas, the burning of Luton Town Hall in 1919 originating from causes other than militancy. Equally important was the isolated position of Luton, which ensured that Vauxhall was insulated much more from the influences of the engineering and motor industries in general.

When Bartlett assumed the managing directorship in 1929 the economy was about to enter the Great Depression, and although the vehicle industry emerged more quickly than the staple industries, the effect of the depression was to create a permanent pool of readily available unskilled and semi-skilled labour until the Second World War – an effect that was a general dampener on rapid union growth in the motor vehicle industry.

Within Vauxhall Bartlett promoted paternalistic policies calculated to create a contented workforce, whose growing demands were intelligently met and catered for by reforms to the industrial relations structure. These included high pay and relative job security. A group bonus scheme existed which enabled good reward for collective effort, unions were eventually recognised and were shortly followed by the setting up of the MAC. At the same time this period saw the introduction of improved welfare, sporting, social and canteen facilities. Channels of communication between management and the workforce were considerably improved and attempts were made to deal with potential problems as soon as they were recognised. Efforts were made to engender in the workforce a feeling of belonging, by fostering a cooperative atmosphere; promotion, which was based on organisational talent and ability to get on with the men, was open to all and based on merit. Another important consideration was that the Bartlett era was one of expansion and, while an upsurge of unionism did take place at Vauxhall from the 1940s, trouble inevitably began when contraction or lack of growth thwarted the expectations of an organised workforce. Finally, the close cordiality of the Bartlett approach to industrial relations could work effectively until the 1950s when a relatively small workforce was located on a single site, but by the 1960s the workforce had grown threefold scattered among three sites. Institutions, such as the MAC, were bound to prove less effective in such a large and geographically spread organisation.

Bartlett was, nevertheless, intelligent, adaptable and had considerable foresight, and there is little doubt that under his policies Vauxhall industrial relations were exceptionally good.

In the final chapters of this section, Vauxhall was placed in the context of the growth of the Luton economy. In Chapter 7 we saw how the Luton Chamber of Commerce and the town council became worried by the predominance of the hat trade which in the late 19th century employed mainly female labour and was prone to seasonal unemployment. A New Industries Committee was created with the intention of attracting businesses which would mainly employ male labour. This object was successfully achieved in that new industries settled in Luton in the period before the First World War, and witnessed considerable expansion in the interwar years. The aims of providing work for men and attracting industries less susceptible than the hat trade to seasonal fluctuations appeared to have been achieved. During the interwar years the combination of the hat trade and engineering industries helped Luton survive two depressions. In the early 1920s, it was the hat trade that recovered quickly and maintained employment in Luton, whereas in the 1930s it was engineering and particularly that of motor vehicles which ensured Luton's prosperity in the face of a structurally weak hat trade.

In the long term the rapid expansion of Vauxhall ensured its central position in the Luton economy but fears were expressed that Luton was becoming largely reliant on two trades: hat making which was to undergo a severe decline in popularity during the Second World War, and motor vehicle manufacturing, largely represented by Vauxhall. As Glyn Morgan, an AUEW convenor at Vauxhall, put it, 'When Vauxhall sneezes Luton catches a cold.'[86] It would seem that in the long run the aims of the New Industries Committee had not been achieved in these years, outflanked by unforeseen circumstances. Nevertheless, compared to 19th century Luton the town's industrial structure was far more diversified. Certainly attempts at creating more male employment succeeded to a point where the percentage of female labour to that of men declined sharply.

The strength of influence of a rapidly expanding Vauxhall quickly became evident in the 1930s and Chapter 8 reveals how Vauxhall acted as a leader in the competitive bidding for labour between Luton firms. Vauxhall paid above the district rate in order to attract skilled workers in particular. The effect was to increase the general wage level within the district, as firms attempted to check the movement of labour to Vauxhall. In addition the engineering unions were able to use the example of Vauxhall to extract better wages and conditions for their members in other Luton firms. The BEEA's attempts at controlling this process proved fruitless, and that body was forced to accept the situation. At the same time, Vauxhall's expansion contributed to the growth of unionism in Luton, and the AEU's policy of using Vauxhall as a stalking horse to put pressure on other firms, one by one, led to an increase in BEEA membership as firms began to seek greater security within its organisation. This trend intensified during the Second World War when an overheated labour market rendered greater cohesion among employers as imperative to ensuring orderly collective bargaining. The rapid expansion of Vauxhall in the post-war years, however, increased its dominance over the Luton economy and, in efforts to retain their workers, Luton firms adopted alternative strategies to Vauxhall. By 1950 the BEEA readily admitted, that it was unable to prevent Vauxhall's enticement of labour. In many senses Vauxhall had become the barometer of Luton's prosperity.

The next section will show how that predominance was gradually undermined over the next fifty years by events outside the control not only of Vauxhall and the local economy, but also the national economy. In a word – globalisation.

---

[86] Interview with Glyn Morgan, December 1979.

PART TWO

Chapter Nine

Vauxhall and Luton 1950–1970: Boom and Affluence

At the end of the Second World War there was considerable fear that the recession of the 1930s could possibly return. The commitment to the creation of the welfare state and huge spending to repair a war-torn economy stimulated government spending that, along with Marshall Aid (from the USA), gave enormous impetus to the economy. Once the hardships of the years of 'austerity' in the 1940s were left behind, the 1950s witnessed a boom that was to spread gradually over the country in the following two decades. Luton was to become one of the foremost symbols of this boom with considerable media and academic attention focused on the effects on the working population.

The growth of Vauxhall 1950–1970
As we have already seen, the seeds of this growth had been sown in the 1930s and before with the arrival in Luton of 'new industries.' Vauxhall was the most prominent of these and was to continue to lead the upswing in the local economy. Indeed, the motor vehicle industry in general came to symbolise the new consumerism, heralding the age of mass consumption, and Luton in that sense became a boom town.[1]

In the immediate post-war years and in the early 1950s the motor vehicle industry was heavily bound up with the government drive for exports to rebuild the economy. As a result Britain became the leading car exporter in the world for a brief period and in 1950 75 per cent of all cars and 60 per cent of all commercial vehicles were exported.[2] This age of austerity witnessed the continuation of rationing and home markets were starved of consumer goods in the drive for exports to balance trade and pay war debts. British industry was in a prime position to take advantage of this situation as the USA was very much concerned with providing for its huge home market, and later rivals, such as Germany and Japan, had yet to rebuild their post-war economies. Car production rose from 219,000 in 1946 to a million in 1958. This was a period when Britain enjoyed a brief ascendancy in the world car industry that, unfortunately, provided false hopes for its continuation and reinforced pre-vious poor managerial and industrial practices.

[1] Indeed a *Luton News* Supplement of 1964 (26 March) celebrating 60 years of Vauxhall is headlined 'Motor Industry Boom Town.'
[2] Roy Church, *The Rise and Decline of the British Motor Industry* (Basingstoke: MacMillan, 1994), p. 44.

By the mid-1950s most rationing had been removed, the country began to throw off the immediate post-war gloom and enjoy the beginnings of what later became called 'the age of mass consumption.' The increasing popularity of hire purchase (or the 'never-never') enabled buying by credit to lose some of its stigma and this gave an enormous stimulus to vehicle sales as they became available to a wider section of the population. The motor car was becoming something that all but the poorest sections of the population could afford.

Vauxhall was very much part of this boom in car as well as commercial vehicle sales, with rising popularity of the Bedford van for commercial and indeed family use. Vauxhall car sales increased from 19,772 in 1946, well below its highest pre-war figure, to 75, 634 in 1955, well above it. Though commercial vehicle (CV) output was initially greater than car sales in the immediate post-war years, by 1948 car output had superseded that of CVs. CV output and sales continued at a steady pace rising by over 300 per cent between 1946 and 1960 whereas cars' rose by over 750 per cent in the same period. This reflects the continually changing position of cars and CV sales within Vauxhall. In the early 1930s it was CVs that laid the foundations for Vauxhall success. By the 1950s the car side had become the more successful, although truck sales were rising and remained an important element in Vauxhall profitability until the 1970s.

Table 39. Vauxhall production, exports, employees and site acreage 1950–1970

Year	Total output	Cars	CVs	Exports	Employees	Floor area
1950	87,454	47,025	40,429	61,471	12,659	80
1951	77,877	35,374	42,503	53,271	12,059	82
1952	79,162	35,640	43,522	56,275	12,435	84
1953	110,141	61,606	48,535	66,435	13,836	85
1954	130,951	70,115	60,836	70,769	14,850	85
1955	143,156	75,634	67,933	76,071	16,487	85
1956	123,643	61,463	62,180	64,051	16,151	93
1957	150,227	91,444	58,783	84,422	22,084	155
1958	174,616	119,177	55,439	103,411	21,878	155
1959	246,085	157,365	88,720	134,912	26,251	159
1960	252,026	145,742	106,284	130,938	24,470	168
1961	186,388	90,549	95,839	105,275	23,584	168
1962	220,805	144,144	76,661	111,930	24,879	197
1963	249,785	164,287	84,798	112,537	30,843	212
1964	342,872	236,226	106,646	154,531	33,500	212
1965	333,167	220,807	112,360	141,660	33,022	268
1966	275,383	174,878	100,505	100,223	33,476	268
1967	290,706	198,946	91,760	94,853	34,179	290
1968	329,047	231,563	97,484	120,636	36,914	290
1969	285,574	182,644	102,930	120,366	34,156	290
1970	269,797	169,525	100,272	111,631	37,413	290

Sources: 'Vauxhall Facts and Figures' (Vauxhall Motors, 1966); Vauxhall Information Handbook (1978)

Vauxhall car models 1948–1970

At the end of the war most car companies did not have new designs to offer the limited home market and most effort was being put into the change over from wartime to peacetime production. Vauxhall resumed production of the range it had ceased producing in 1939 – the H (10hp), I (12hp), and J (14hp) models. In the Autumn of 1947 the government brought in a flat rate of engine tax and it was decided to cease production of the H model as it was close in size to the I model. The J model was increased from a 4- to 6-cylinder engine although the body work remained resolutely 1930s in design.[3]

It was not until 1948 that the first hints of a change in style began with the new designs of the Velox and Wyvern (L-type). In body styling they were the forerunners of the Cresta and Victor of the late 1950s, confections inspired by the new American styling of Harley Earl, General Motors chief designer. It was felt that the British market would not stand the exotic excesses of their Cadillac, Buick and Chevrolet sisters across the Atlantic with their space age designs, large fin tails and exaggerated tail lights. The Wyvern and Velox acted as a styling bridge between the sombre 'sit up and beg' black designs of the 1930s and the more colourful and sleek designs of the late 1950s. The L-types were the first Vauxhall cars to have a steering column gear change, and the new elongated smoother look with cream wheels which proved to be very popular in export markets. From 1951 the designs were updated ushering in the E-type Wyvern and Velox which were to remain in production until 1957 when they were replaced by the Cresta and Victor, although the Velox PA remained in production in a larger 2¼ litre 6-cylinder version. These car designs (along with their Ford rivals – the Consul and Zephyr Six) were symbolic of an era that was throwing off the dullness and drudgery of the 'age of austerity' and ushering in the era where 'you never had it so good.' The cars were colourful in their two tones, whitewall tyres and increased amounts of chrome. As if to shrug off the past designers got rid of the fluted bonnets that had previously made Vauxhall models so recognisable.

Maurice Platt[4] recalls that one innovation among many, that was imported from General Motors and put into the Victor and the PA Cresta, was the 'panoramic' or wrap around window. This piece of styling was very eye catching and modern looking but provided incredible technical problems as the windshield was bent round each side. This meant that the screen intruded into the door apertures and caused sealing problems that could lead to draughts blowing onto driver and passenger. Although these problems were successfully solved such new features became part of the annual model change to make last year's car appear 'out of date.' All this was the beginning of what later was called 'planned obsolescence.'

This was the age of 'modernity' and these designs indicated a bright new future. Car enthusiasts looking back to this time can be forgiven for thinking that these models were associated with the exciting new trends coming from America such as rock and roll, and there has been a heavy association of

---

[3] For more detailed descriptions of these and other Vauxhall vehicle models see Michael Sedgwick, *Vauxhall: A Pictorial Tribute* (London: Beaulieu Books, 1981) and Stuart Fergus Broatch, *Vauxhall* (Stroud: Sutton Publishing, 1997).

[4] Maurice Platt, *An Addiction to Automobiles* (London, 1980), pp. 167–68.

Plate 31. 1951–1957 E-type Cresta – the new look. The whitewall tyres and two-tone body were inspired by General Motors USA designs.

Plate 32. 1957–1961 F Victor. Note the wrap-around windscreen that gave Maurice Platt and his team production headaches.

Crestas and Victors with teddy boys and other youth cults. Yet it must be remembered that these cars were still relatively expensive and the owners of the new models were more likely to have been middle class people earning a relatively high salary such as bank managers. The rock and roll image was

Plate 33. The 'American Look' showing the influence of the General Motors designer Harley Earl.

Table 40. Main Vauxhall car models 1948–1970

Year	Type/Name	HP/capacity	Cyls.	Price
1948–51	L – Wyvern	12	4	£350–415
1948–51	L – Velox	18	6	£430–470
1951–57	E – Wyvern	1½ litres	4	£475–535
1951–57	E – Velox	2¼ litres	6	£515–580
1954–57	EIPC – Cresta	2¼ litres	6	£595–620
1954–57	FS & FD – Victor	1½ litres	4	£485–520
1954–57	PAS – Velox	2¼ litres	6	£655
1954–57	PAD – Cresta	2¼ litres	6	£715
1959	FD, FE – Victor	1½ litres	4	£505 & 565
1959	FS, FW – Victor	1½ litres	4	£505 & 605
1960–62	PASX – Velox	2.6 litres	6	£655
1960–62	PADX – Cresta	2.6 litres	6	££715
1961–63	FB Victor	1½ litres	4	£510
1962–63	VX 4/90	1½ litres	4	£510
1963–64	PB – Velox/Cresta	2.7 litres	6	£680 & 760
1964–66	HA Viva	1.1 litres	4	£436
1964	FB Victor	1.6 litres	4	£525
1964–67	VX 4/90	1.6 litres	4	£695
1965–67	FC Victor	1.6 litres	4	£560–710
1965	PB Velox/Cresta	3.3 litres	6	£695 & 780
1966–72	PC Cresta/Viscount	3.3 litres	6	£810–875
1967–70	HB Viva	1.2 litres	4	£470
1968–72	FD Victor	1.6 & 2 litres	4	c. £500–700
1968–75	Ventora/Victor	3.3 litres	6	£1,769 (1975)
1968–70	HB Viva	1.6 & 2 litres	4	c. £550–730

Plate 34. 1961–1964 FB Victor.

associated with the second hand trade in these vehicles once they had lost their initial value a few years later in the late 1950s and 1960s.

By the 1960s with the entry into production of the Viva (HA-type) the Vauxhall car range was now complete and covered vehicles from 1.1 to 3.3 litres. These included large expensive models such as the PB Velox and Cresta and later the Ventora and Victor (3.3 litre); medium sized models such as the FB Victor (1.6 litre), and the smaller model Viva (1.1 litre). Initially, the Viva did not endear itself to motoring enthusiasts and was described as 'ugly and less than fun to drive,'[5] but it was dependable, fuel economic and sold very well, becoming Vauxhall's first single model to sell over a million. While Vauxhall was not as innovative in vehicle design as some of its competitors in the 1960s, the constant face lifts and re-designs kept the public buying. This, of course, was one of the major strategies of its parent company General Motors, which Ford and others began to copy.

Commercial Vehicle production
While the new car designs caught the public attention in the 1950s the more mundane world of truck design and production was also undergoing a 'revolution.' As already noted trucks were, in Sir Reginald Pearson's words, 'a life saver' in the 1930s.[6] Under the commercial title 'Bedford,' Vauxhall had

[5] Michael Sedgwick, op. cit., p. 82.
[6] Interview with Sir Reginald Pearson, 1979.

Plate 35. 1963–1966 HA Viva – the 1960s best selling Vauxhall car, made at Ellesmere Port.

produced a variety of trucks that were adaptable for all kinds of working environments. They were lighter and cheaper than their rivals and they ranged from a 5cwt van through to a 2-ton truck. The body work could be adapted for a variety of purposes to meet the needs of small traders, farmers, builders and a whole host of businesses.

During the war much of Vauxhall production had switched to trucks to supply the armed forces, producing over 250,000 by 1945. In addition, 5,640 Churchill tanks were produced in the same period.[7] After 1945 the Luton factory switched to peacetime production and re-launched the 1939 K, M and O models. These trucks were heavier than their predecessors and Bedford produced a 5-ton model for the first time. Thus by the end of the 1940s Bedford commercial vehicles ranged from 5cwt vans to 5-ton trucks. The K and O models remained in production until 1953.[8]

By 1950 the Luton plant had reached capacity with 39,000 Bedford trucks and 45,000 cars being produced in the one factory, so a £10 million expansion programme was embarked upon which was to see commercial vehicles produced entirely at the new Dunstable plant from 1955.

In 1950 there was another major development with the introduction of the S-type truck raising the largest Bedford to 7 tons. Equally important was the

[7] L.C. Derbyshire, *The Story of Vauxhall 1857–1946* (Luton, 1946).
[8] Vauxhall Motors Ltd, *You See Them Everywhere: Bedford Commercial Vehicles since 1931* (Luton, 1978), pp. 17–20.

Plate 36. The AC paint shop in 1961. This is a long way from the 1910 paint shop with its dubious health and safety environment. No workers were directly involved in the deep dip approach.

introduction of new features such as a four-speed synchromesh gearbox and hypoid rear axle. The high bulbous one-piece cab, recognisable in army Bedfords, remained a familiar part of the design.

The CA van

One enormous success story in the commercial vehicle market for Bedford was the arrival of the CA van. It was the first Bedford light commercial vehicle designed as a van and not based on a Vauxhall car. It was first produced in 1952 but became an outstandingly successful vehicle throughout its production run to 1969. Initially it was produced and sold in one format – a 10/12cwt with sliding doors, an all-steel body and a 1500cc 'square engine.'[9] It retailed at about £480. Very soon it was being customised and adapted for a wide range of commercial and leisure activities including ambulances, works' buses, ice-cream vans and mobile shops. One of its adaptations was also reflective of the times. The new found prosperity of the masses combined with shorter working hours meant the desire for more holidays and leisure time. The CA van helped to provide that need by acting as camper vans for itinerant holiday makers in both Britain, and increasingly, on the continent of Europe as the picture of one being used for this purpose in Czechoslovakia in 1957 shows. It thus scored highly in two markets, that of light commercial use and private use by individuals and families.

[9] *You See Them Everywhere*, p. 21.

Plate 37. Bedford CA camper van in Prague 1957. This proved very popular in the early days of mass motor touring in Britain and on the continent.

In 1957 Bedford revamped its range of trucks incorporating new technological advances. The policy was diversification, and up to 50 models were offered, many of which incorporated Bedford's first home built diesel engine. The engine was placed outside the cab helping reduce noise and creating more space for the driver. Four and five speed gearboxes were introduced and there was a choice of petrol or diesel engines.

Expansion

To keep abreast of demand the Vauxhall plant at Luton underwent a major expansion in 1948 with an increase in floor area from 64 to 80 acres costing £14 million. Between 1947 and 1954 both car and commercial vehicle production more than doubled, and this led to the decision to separate CV production at a new purpose built plant in Dunstable costing £36 million. The 1950s boom continued and between 1954 and 1959 car production more than doubled again rising from an annual output of 70,000 to over 157,000. As soon as the Dunstable plant was completed in 1959 plans were already in progress to build another plant at Ellesmere Port, on the south side of the River Mersey, which finally opened in 1963, with the production of components.[10] The plant was built away from the Luton Dunstable area as many parts of Britain were not enjoying the same degree of prosperity as the South and Midlands. The government offered inducements to companies to relocate or expand in 'economic development areas.' An added advantage was that the Mersey area had good road, rail, sea and air connections.[11] The Viva was the first car to be produced there in 1964. Back at Luton a new engineering and styling

[10] Vauxhall Motors Ltd, *A History of Vauxhall Motors* (Luton, 1980), p. 57.
[11] Vauxhall Education Service, *The Vauxhall Story* (Luton, 2001), p. 13.

Plate 38. Vauxhall Motors Luton planned expansion in the early 1950s.

centre was opened in 1962 and in 1967 a large parts centre was opened near Toddington and can still be plainly viewed from the M1 motorway today. A test and proving ground was started near Amptill in Mid-Bedfordshire at Millbrook in 1968. These were the heady days of expansion before the oil crisis of the early 1970s was to have a devastating effect on the car industry as a whole. While the British owned car companies were the ultimate losers, Vauxhall also had a period of hardship and uncertainty until the 1980s.

General Motors influence on Vauxhall 1950–1970
When General Motors (GM) first bought Vauxhall in 1925 it was very much in the teeth of a patriotic and hostile motoring press. Consequently the policy adopted by GM towards the Luton subsidiary had been very much to allow British management to control the operational side of the business. GM provided the expertise and technical know-how as well as capital investment for the various expansions that Vauxhall undertook to enable it to become one of the Big Six car manufacturers in Britain. This polycentric policy[12] of international management had led to the promotion of Charles Bartlett to the position of Managing Director throughout the 1930s and 1940s. Sir

---

[12] A polycentric policy allows foreign subsidiaries to control their operations by employing host country management teams.

Charles, as he later became, undoubtedly did all that the Americans required and helped turn an ailing but respected car company into a viable and successful mass vehicle manufacturer.

This process was not always straightforward and there were differences of opinion between the Americans (in the Detroit HQ), who often felt that GM was pouring money into a bottomless pit for very little return, and the British management that felt the Americans did not really understand the needs of the British, Empire and European markets. The American champion of the British cause was J.D. Mooney, head of General Motors Overseas Operations (GMOO). He had played a main part in the purchase of Vauxhall and tended to regard the British subsidiary as 'his baby.' His advocacy of the Vauxhall cause had led the GM Board to undertake several large injections of capital in the Luton works. Bartlett had ensured that the Vauxhall story was one of outstanding success and this turn around of an ailing enterprise into a success story had mollified the powers that be at GM, including the CEO himself, Alfred Sloan.[13]

While Vauxhall was very successful under Bartlett not all GM executives were happy with the degree of control that he had in running the subsidiary and some felt that he managed it as his own personal fiefdom. This feeling was reinforced during the war years when Bartlett had virtual control of the

[13] Alfred P. Sloan, *My Years with General Motors* (New York, 1965).

Plate 39. Sir Charles Bartlett and his replacement as Managing Director, Walter Hill, in 1953. Bartlett never really got over his removal and retired a year later, also dying in that year.

operations, due largely to the difficulties of international travel and communications between the USA and Britain, and the requirements of the British War Department, which directed production away from civilian markets. In 1941 the GM Board appointed Ed Riley, a forceful American, as head of GMOO, and at the cessation of hostilities he was determined to wrest back control from Bartlett. This aim, together with the fact that both Bartlett and Riley had strong personalities, meant friction did not lie far beneath the surface. Maurice Platt (Director and Chief Engineer 1937–1963) describes several clashes between them. In the post-war years Bartlett became sold on the idea of updating the Vauxhall Twelve. As Platt recalls:

> Apprised of this intention, Ed Riley refused to authorise the 'face lift' and a prolonged and unhappy tug of war ensued during which neither party would give way . . . Riley was determined that ambitious plans for Vauxhall's expansion should be firmly based on a product programme of his own choosing.[14]

---

[14] M. Platt, *An Addiction to Automobiles* (London, 1980), p. 148.

Plate 40. Philip W. Copelin replaced Walter Hill as Managing Director of Vauxhall in 1955. An American then aged 51 who had extensive experience of General Motors Overseas Operations in Europe. Chosen by Ed Riley, head of GMOO, and according to Platt 'he always remained staunchly American in outlook'.

This fractious relationship eventually came to a head when Bartlett reluctantly resigned as Managing Director one year before his retirement in 1954. He served as Chairman, for a year – a role he did not relish – as it carried little real authority. He was replaced by Walter E. Hill. Although Hill was British by birth his family had emigrated to the USA in 1905 and had become US citizens.[15] He was very much a GM man and had worked in plants in Detroit, Australia and New

---

[15] *Pensioners Mirror*, supplement in *Vauxhall Mirror* (March 1988), p. 3.

Plate 41. Left to right: Daniel Jones (designer who joined Vauxhall in 1937), Maurice Platt (Chief Engineer and director who joined Vauxhall in 1937 and remained until he retired in 1963), John Alden (joined Vauxhall in 1938 and took over as Chief Engineer after Platt's retirement) and William Swallow (Managing Director 1961–1966). The photo was taken in 1963 and they are posing with the new Viva with the Vauxhall Corporate headquarters known as Griffin House being constructed in the background.

Zealand before joining the Vauxhall Board. He thus kept very much to the GM blueprint and ably handled the change over from a polycentric style to a more ethnocentric approach.[16] He retired due to ill health two years later in 1955 and was replaced by Philip Copelin, a 51-year-old American, who had a long experience of working for GMOO in Europe. Gradually Hill, Copelin, and from 1961, William Swallow (Managing Director and Chairman from 1961 to 1966) dismantled many of the managerial institutions and policies initiated by Bartlett. Although Swallow was a Yorkshireman by birth, by the early 1960s there were noticeably more Americans on the Board and Maurice Platt and Sir Reginald Pearson both expressed the view that the GM influence increased considerably in these years. Platt became particularly perturbed by the drive from Detroit to make styling changes in line with the GM policy of annual facelifts to various models. Often this was carried out with too much haste putting pressure on design and production teams, but Vauxhall management was forced to comply, despite the occasional strong protest. Platt felt that Copelin's deficiency in manufacturing experiencing did not help matters combined with the fact that 'he always remained staunchly American in outlook.'[17]

---

[16] With an ethnocentric policy the parent company takes more direct control in running subsidiary affairs.

[17] M. Platt, op. cit., p. 171.

Vauxhall and competition

Despite these grumbles General Motors were the paymasters and their views tended to prevail. They had injected a considerable amount of capital into the Luton plant and were building a massive plant in nearby Dunstable. It is hardly surprising that they wanted to ensure that their investments would be protected. Wresting back control was important in this respect. By the late 1950s and early 1960s the car market had changed considerably from the post-war years. A mass market was emerging but along with that was greater competition not only from other British manufacturers and Ford but also the beginnings of the rise of the German, French, Italian and, in the late 1960s, Japanese competition. Life in the motor manufacturing world remained profitable but manufacturers were increasingly having to fight, not only to gain new markets, but retain their old ones. Thus Vauxhall's share of the market in the 1950s and 1960s remained between 10 and 12 per cent. When it could have benefitted from the narrowing of British owned companies manufacturing base in the 1960s, this was off set by the increase of imports from Europe and later Japan.

Finance and Productivity 1952–1970

Vauxhall gradually increased profitability and productivity throughout the 1950s and 1960s. As it has already been noted General Motors underwrote considerable capital expansion and Vauxhall pursued a policy of ploughing back as much of its profits as possible. Profits increased eightfold between 1952 and 1965, and sales increased four and half times in the same period (Table 41 overleaf).

Despite these impressive increases in profitability and sales in Vauxhall and the rest of British motor vehicle manufacturers, British productivity rates never measured up to those of American and later German as Table 42, on the following page, indicates.

It might be regarded as misleading to lump Vauxhall and Ford in with all British vehicle productivity rates since American subsidiaries had higher productivity rates than their British owned rivals. Nevertheless, productivity was always below the German rates and this would be become a factor in restructuring considerations in later decades for both Ford and Vauxhall.

Industrial relations

After Bartlett retired there were considerable changes made in industrial relations policies. Some of these were as a result of changing circumstances, not only in Vauxhall and GM, but in the car industry as a whole. Group bonus was abandoned in favour of measured day work. This change of policy was not opposed by the unions[18] as they felt measured day work put less pressure on workers to perform. Union representatives had always compared themselves unfavourably to Ford, which had introduced the scheme some time before. Ford had given a higher basic wage than Vauxhall which workers received regardless of performance. Vauxhall workers always felt that they had to work notably harder via group bonus to reach these levels. The management also

[18] Philip Copelin, *'Consolidation of Group Bonus' Notice*, 13 April 1956.

Table 41. Net profit (after tax) and total
sales figures 1952–1970 (£000s)

	Profit after tax	Total sales
1952	1,651	44,532
1953	3,426	58,620
1954	6,861	66,631
1955	6,542	75,112
1956	4,634	71,293
1957	(1,135)*	76,000
1958	756	95,070
1959	6,428	130,115
1960	7,159	135,981
1961	4,329	117,903
1962	5,976	125,986
1963	8,267	147,782
1964	8,433	188,328
1965	13,477	195,009
1966	4,435	178,000
1967	3,351	190,580
1968	5,310	216,361
1969	(2,057)*	204,100
1970	(9,438)*	209,912

Sources: *This is Vauxhall* (Luton, 1966), p. 48;
Vauxhall Annual Reports to the Board.

Table 42. 'Equivalent' motor vehicles produced per
employee per annum 1955–1976

	Britain	Germany	United States
1955	4.1	3.9	19.8
1965	5.8	6.4	25.0
1970	5.6	7.5	19.6
1973	5.8	7.7	26.1
1976	5.5	7.9	26.1

Source: Jones and Prais (1978) in Church (1994), p. 49.

agreed because of changing technology on the production line. This made
group payment systems more costly. As technology improved so too did
individual productivity and this would have meant more costly wage bills,
and therefore constant annual renegotiations of the bonus system. This
phenomenon was particularly so with British owned car manufacturers,
whose wage bills were far higher than both Ford and Vauxhall and became
one of the main focuses of industrial relations disputes in the 1960s and 1970s.
Equally, Vauxhall workers pursued a parity of pay policy with the British
owned Midland companies throughout the 1960s and 1970s.

Another reason why Vauxhall abandoned group bonus was the question of
control. Group bonus gave the workforce some degree of 'responsible autonomy' and in a rapidly changing technological environment this could create

problems. What if the workforce did not want change, or wanted the same bonus rates? If the management changed the rates by lowering them, the workforce could impede production or find ways to bypass 'normal' procedures as they exercised a degree of control over their immediate work process. To some degree measured day work solved this problem and gave much greater control to management, although it meant increases in basic pay and an increase in day to day surveillance by supervisory and managerial staff.

Another significant change was the dismantling of the Management Advisory Committee (MAC) in the mid-1960s. Again this was not greeted with hostility by the unions. In fact quite the reverse. Some of the more militant shop stewards had always regarded it as a 'talking shop' with little real teeth, and a management device to throw a sop to the workforce. Views amongst shop stewards and indeed Communist and Labour Party members differed on this issue. Some, like Harold Horne[19] (a Communist shop steward), thought that the MAC was a useful forum through which the workforce could express their views. Others like 'Jock' Adair[20] (another Communist shop steward) felt that it had had its day and the true representatives of the workforce were the unions and their elected representatives. The evidence furnished by the 'Affluent Worker'[21] studies reveals the instrumentalist attitude of most of the workforce. They did not mind what system was in operation so long as it delivered the money. The boom times of the late 1950s and early 1960s ensured that this was the case.

The boom in cars and the growth in affluence of the Vauxhall workforce meant that until the mid-1960s Vauxhall experienced little disruption from industrial action. For this reason it was dubbed the 'Turnip Patch' by other unions. A major study of industrial relations in the motor industry showed clearly that Vauxhall had the least strikes and industrial disputes of all the car firms in this period and in the post-war period had no strikes until 1962, and only one major strike in that year.

Table 43. Strikes and man hours lost 1962–1964

	Strikes	Man hours (000s)
Vauxhall	29	41
BMC	952	6,571
Ford	87	904
Rootes	178	358
Rover	170	670

Source: Turner et al.[22] (1967), p. 73.

Because Ford and particularly Vauxhall were integrated companies (that is they had most of their requirements within the company), if disputes occurred

[19] Interview with Harold Horne, 1978. Harold was a convenor and shop steward for the AUEW from 1940 to 1968 when he retired.

[20] Interview with Tom 'Jock' Adair, 1981. He was an assembly line worker and shop steward for the AUEW from 1938 to 1960.

[21] J. Goldthorpe et al., *The Affluent Worker: Industrial Attitudes and Behaviour* (Cambridge, 1968).

[22] H.A. Turner, G. Clack and G. Roberts, *Labour Relations in the Motor Industry* (London, 1967).

they had less overall impact than in other British companies that drew on a wide variety of suppliers with varied industrial relation systems. After 1962 the number of strikes did increase in Vauxhall but they were never as severe as in other companies.

What were the reasons for Vauxhall's excellent record in industrial relations in this period? They are many and complex. The 1960s certainly witnessed an increase in militant activity in the car trade. The press, particularly the more sensationalist newspapers, were quick to point the finger at 'left wing agitators' and the 'boredom of the assembly line.' This latter theme was also particularly favoured by industrial sociologists as part of an alienation from work theory. The exhaustive study by Turner et al. found them either to be totally untrue or grossly exaggerated. There were generally deeper underlying causes. One suggestion was that Vauxhall was less unionised than other companies but, while this was true, a large majority of Vauxhall workers were union members – 85 per cent, compared with 99 per cent at Ford and 100 per cent unionisation at Rootes, Rover and Jaguar.[23]

Both Vauxhall, and its parent company, General Motors, had resisted recognising unions until the Second World War. In 1942 Vauxhall signed recognition and negotiation agreements with the AEU and the NUVB. By the 1960s there was only one other union to negotiate with (the electricians) and there have been some claims that the restricted number of unions made bargaining easier. By contrast Ford had to deal with 21 unions! While this may have had some effect on the number of disputes, it is not the sole reason for Vauxhall's relative industrial tranquility.

The good managerial qualities of Charles Bartlett and his team, and their philosophy, have already been alluded to as important factors in explaining the absence of strikes and major disputes. But Bartlett had retired in the early 1950s and subsequently, Bartlett institutions such as the MAC and group bonus, had been dismantled. Admittedly the welfare institutions and facilities, initially set up in Bartlett's period, had been expanded and improved, as the annual Vauxhall reports often proudly testified. There is little doubt however, that the managerial approach adopted by Bartlett, a concerned paternalism, was important in establishing the basis for personnel and industrial relations policies in later decades. Sir Reginald Pearson, for example, claimed to spend between 60 per cent and 75 per cent of his time on labour matters.[24] R.R. Hopkins, the Personnel Director, was affectionately referred to as 'Hoppy' by many MAC shop floor and union members, and operated an 'open door' policy.

The Americans rarely ventured directly into this area of policy and left much of the bargaining to their British counterparts. Indeed all personnel directors up to the present day have been British. As Turner et al. state[25]

> General Motors seems . . . to have been content to work within and gradually modify the existing organisation, rather than – like American Ford – set up satellite companies in its own image.

---

[23] Turner *et al.*, *Labour Relations in the Motor Industry*, p. 195.
[24] Graham Turner, *The Car Makers* (Penguin: Harmondsworth, 1963), p. 124.
[25] Turner, Clack and Roberts, op. cit., p. 348.

Turner et al. also point out that an indication that Vauxhall management took personnel/industrial relations issues seriously is reflected by the fact that the personnel director was elected to the Board in the 1950s, long before many of their competitors followed such a policy. This initiative gave a clear message to the workforce, unions and middle management of the importance of these issues, and in this way anticipated problems. By contrast many of their British counterparts dealt with labour relations issues in a reactive way when incidents blew up. This proactiveness was clearly indicated with the negotiation committees set up with unions. These eventually replaced the MAC with full union approval and 'Vauxhall met the sharp increase in union activity in 1962–63 by a grievance procedure operating through the shop stewards' hierarchy at several stages up to top management, and providing for their participation with union officials in discussions at that level.'[26]

Turner et al. allude to the geographical isolation of Luton and its predominance in the Luton economy as reasons for a good industrial relations record. Vauxhall was distanced from militant centres such as London and Coventry and the influence of a history of industrial action was lacking in the Luton area. The domination by Vauxhall of the Luton economy strongly influenced most area and other full time union officials to concentrate most of their efforts on solving problems in Vauxhall. It also, no doubt, created a much closer relationship between unions and management, often criticised by left wing workers as 'cosying up' to the management. Vauxhall also provided its works committee with an office and clerk that was quite uncharacteristic for the time.

The dominance of Vauxhall in the Luton area had caused much concern to the EEF. Workers could clearly see that Vauxhall was the best-paying firm in the district and this must have given them considerable status within the town. For this reason alone they would want to retain their position within the company and this would probably make then less likely to 'rock the boat.' Non-membership of the EEF also meant that Vauxhall was free from the national annual wage negotiations into which other vehicle producers were tied. The abandonment of a production bonus payment was another shrewd move that allowed Vauxhall to avoid the annual, often protracted, wrangling other firms experienced over such concerns.

The occupation and grading system has also been proposed as a contribution towards more harmonious industrial relations in Vauxhall. Six occupational groups were directly engaged in production and ten indirectly. Within each group there were five grades and a person's hourly rate of pay depended on their occupational group and grade. An employee's occupational group depended on their previous industrial experience and whether vacancies existed. A new employee would start at the lowest grade and after six months of satisfactory probation was promoted to the next grade. Further promotion depended on the recommendation of the departmental manager. To ensure fairness in the system there was a grading appeals committee that consisted of three workmen, one of whom was a shop steward. The group

[26] Ibid.

Plate 42. Velox E-type assembly line 1952. Fordist production techniques, i.e. the continuous assembly line, had begun to be implemented in the Luton plant in the 1930s. This is a more sophisticated version but nevertheless was often boring repetitive work for the workers on the line. Industrial sociologists had a field day analysing the effects of such work.

grading system acted as a disincentive to casual transfers of labour between jobs and departments, and thus avoided unnecessary disturbances within work groups. This was instrumental in avoiding disputes, particularly localised ones, which could cause chaos to the whole factory. In addition downgrading was rare and this also avoided potential disputes concerning deskilling as new automated machinery was introduced. The deskilling issue within the car industry was less and less of an issue by the 1960s. Vauxhall had reduced the number of skilled craftsmen by the outbreak of the Second World War and it never really featured in later disputes. In fact many skilled workers sought work at Vauxhall on the production lines in semi-skilled jobs as they could earn more than their trade could give them.

Vauxhall was also seen to be 'fair' in its employment dealings generally. Stress was laid on security of work (another Bartlett initiative) – a policy not widely adhered to in the rest of the car industry where lay-offs were common. Dismissals were also rare, particularly after the probationary period was over. If redundancy was inevitable then 'the principle of "last in, first out" was strictly adhered to, so that men with longer service . . . enjoyed a high measure of security.'[27] This security was also reflected in the relatively low absenteeism rates and low turnover compared with other vehicle companies.

[27] Ferdynand Zweig, *The Worker in an Affluent Society* (London, 1961), p. 236.

Welfare benefits and social life

There is no doubt that the generous welfare and fringe benefits played a considerable role in engendering firm loyalty among the workforce. There was a group accident and health insurance scheme and a life insurance scheme, providing cash payments in the event of disablement or death. There was also a generous pension scheme, and all were generous in their pay outs.

The social life of the company centred around the canteen, licensed bar and sports clubs. As was the custom of the time, these reflected the status of one's occupation within the company and the four canteen levels were exclusive to senior executive, middle and junior levels of staff, weekly paid staff and, finally, hourly paid staff.

There were numerous sports activities including football, cricket, rugby, fishing and tennis clubs. There was also a dramatic society, choirs and even a 35-strong orchestra. However, active participation was small, estimated by Zweig at between 5 and 6 per cent of the total workforce.[28] This was due to the long hours worked by employees, especially if a great deal of overtime was available and in this period that was more likely to be the case.

Pay and overtime

By far the most contentious issue was pay. Issues concerned either directly or indirectly with remuneration were the major cause of disputes in the industry as a whole and in Vauxhall in particular. This was closely linked to sales cycles within the industry. While the annual sales cycle of lay-offs in the winter months was avoided in Vauxhall by maintaining men in work through this period (another of Bartlett's innovations in the 1930s) there were nevertheless periods, sometimes lasting months, when sales and therefore earnings were down. In car companies where pay was closely linked to an elaborate bonus system the likelihood of disputes was greater than in those like Vauxhall where measured day work existed. However, Vauxhall workers relied heavily on overtime to make up their pay, and when this was not available this could cause tension. This was fuelled by the growth in consumerism with car workers buying their own houses, cars and other goods. Along with mortgage payments, much of this consumption rested on credit and was paid for in weekly and monthly instalments. When income fell this threatened some workers ability to maintain payments. The solution was to demand more pay. This was often expressed in the issue of parity in hourly rates of pay with Midland car workers.

The disputes in Vauxhall in 1967 clearly indicate this when there was a large slump in sales. Interestingly there were only disputes at Luton and not at Ellesmere Port. This was mainly because the Viva was produced at Ellesmere Port and its sales had not been affected by the slump. The less popular models were produced at Luton and were heavily affected by falling sales. As a result overtime was reduced, and at times eliminated, with considerable negative effects on pay. Graham Turner's journalistic account of Vauxhall in the early 1960s attests to this:

---

[28] Ibid., p. 246.

A flat week for the top skilled men brings in £18 10 shillings, minus the usual deductions. Hence a feverish scramble for extra earnings of all kinds; most take all the overtime they can get, and an extra hour three nights a week and all Saturday morning is normal. "The majority at Vauxhall get belly-ache grabbing it," said one union official. "It's a disease," said an elderly MAC man. "When there is no overtime, they turn pale. The new type of worker is only interested in how much overtime he can pile up."[29]

The demand of the unions was a basic weekly wage of £20 per week and the dispute was eventually settled with an improved basic wage offer from Vauxhall.

The development of Luton – boom town 1950–1970
A major concern that preoccupied Luton worthies at the turn of the century had been the reliance on one trade – the hat industry. Previous chapters have explored the policy of the New Industries Committee, set up at the turn of the 20th century, whose aims were to attract a wider diversity of employment organisations to the Luton area. In this it was very successful and it has been noted how the arrival of a number of industries in vehicles, chemicals, engineering and others prevented the reliance on one trade. The hat trade reached its zenith in employment terms in the late 1920s and from then on declined, although employment remained reasonably high in this trade until the Second World War, and even after continued to employ relatively high numbers. The decline in the hat trade did not mean the decline of Luton. In fact quite the reverse. The enormous success of the new industries in terms of growth and expansion was reflected in the growth of the town as the census of 1951 testifies.

Table 44. Luton population 1951

	Males	%	Females	%	Total
Total Pop.	53, 823	48.7%	56,558	51.3%	110,381
Occupied	37,795	68.1%	17,733	31.9%	55,528
Retired/unoccupied	3,398	11.3%	26,608	88.7%	30,006

Source: *Census Report England and Wales, 1951* (HMSO, 1954), table 2, p. 1.

By 1951 the town population had grown by 56 per cent from 1931, when the last census had been carried out. Even allowing for the missed census of 1941 due to the war, a growth rate of this magnitude is very impressive. It can also be clearly seen that the other concern of the New Industries Committee, the large number of women employed in relation to men compared with other areas of the UK economy, had also reversed in favour of male dominance in employment, despite the offsetting factor of female employment for the war effort. Table 44 indicates that notwithstanding the fact that women constituted a higher percentage of the population, over two-thirds of the working

[29] Turner, *The Car Makers*, p. 110.

population was male. In 1931 nearly 40 per cent of the working population was female, a drop of nearly 10 per cent. This declining trend in percentage employment for women as opposed to men was to continue, although actual numbers of females in employment rose considerably between 1951 and 1971. This was clearly a move from a 'matriarchal' to a 'patriarchal' economy, driven by the changes in the industrial make-up of Luton. The rise to predominance of vehicle production and engineering in Table 45 graphically indicates this sea change.

Table 45. Luton profile by sector and occupation 1951 and 1961

Sector	Male		Female		Total	
	1951	*1961*	*1951*	*1961*	*1951*	*1961*
Vehicles*	14,759	24,375	1,348	2,550	16,107	26,975
Engineering	5,492	9,604	2,291	4,236	7,783	13,840
Hats**	2,082	1,511	3,681	4,102	5,763	5,613
Building	2,399	4,088	48	270	2,447	4,358
Chemicals	1,133	1,157	169	318	1,302	1,475

*   Includes aircraft manufacture.
** Includes clothing in 1961.
Source: *Census Report England and Wales, 1951* (HMSO, 1954), table 2, pp. 13–15.

Vauxhall was the single largest employer in the town employing over a fifth of the workforce (19,000 and a further 6,000 at the Dunstable works) in 1964.[30] Its influence was therefore enormous. Skefko (later called SKF) was the second largest employer (6,000), followed by George Kent (2,700) and Electrolux (2,500). Well over half the workforce was engaged in occupations directly or indirectly associated with engineering. It must also be remembered that there was the beginning of a rise in service sector occupations that included retail distribution (accounting for 8 per cent of the workforce in 1961),[31] professional classes (6 per cent) and public administration (2 per cent). This last category was to grow considerably along with other public sector occupations in education, social work and health.

The affluent worker
Vauxhall wages were still the highest in the district, as they had been in the 1930s and 1940s, and in the boom time of the 1950s and 1960s that trend continued. It drew workers from a wide catchment area, including the adjacent counties stretching to London and to the Midlands. Zweig estimated that 60 per cent of the Vauxhall workforce lived locally and the rest travelled into Luton.[32]

As we have already noted in the 1930s Vauxhall also attracted a considerable number of workers from depressed areas and this trend continued in the post-war years. As one observer noted:

---

[30] James Dyer, Frank Stygall and John Dony, *The Story of Luton* (Luton, 1964).
[31] *Census England and Wales, 1961*.
[32] Zweig, *The Worker in an Affluent Society*, p. 236.

The boys from Glasgow and Greenock who arrive here . . . think that the streets of Luton are literally paved with gold.[33]

Vauxhall workers were very well paid by the standards of the time and earned on average about £18 per week, and some earned as much as £24 with over time. It is not surprising therefore that in this period the car industry had been associated with the new age of mass consumption. Not only were cars being mass produced at comparatively low prices, they were now becoming affordable to the workers who built them. These high paid workers became mass consumers using more easily available credit to purchase goods. As one Vauxhall worker commented in the early 1960s

Perhaps 45% of Vauxhall folk are buying their own houses, and they want fitted carpets, TV, fridge, all at once of course . . . the younger element spend their lives keeping up with the Joneses – cars, cocktail cabinets, tape recorders, the lot. And they want a de luxe Victor, not an ordinary one![34]

This phenomenon did not go unnoticed at the time, and a number of studies were undertaken to examine the trend more closely. Three in particular centred on Luton: *The Car Makers* by Graham Turner, a journalistic vox pop account reflected in the title of one chapter about Luton called 'Gadgetsville, U.K.' Two more academic studies examined the effects of affluence on the Luton population. Each of these studies, in their separate ways, examined the phenomenon of the high paid jobs in the car industry and the effect on the workers.

Turner, and Zweig in his more academically oriented study, posed the view that British workers of this 'new' type were increasingly becoming 'American-ised.' Turner speaking of Luton stated 'a transatlantic pattern of compulsive spending is everywhere evident.'[35] Zweig similarly describes Luton as 'rapidly expanding, prosperous, its people running after jobs and money more or less in the American fashion.' Luton is 'a slice of America in Britain, self assured, beaming with vitality and go-aheadness.'[36]

Goldthorpe et al.[37] were more interested in finding out whether this new affluent life style actually affected worker attitudes towards class, politics, work and a range of other issues. This became known as the 'embourgeoisification' thesis. In other words was this new-found wealth of Luton workers making them more bourgeois, i.e. middle class? The exhaustive study carried out on workers at Vauxhall, Skefko and Laporte found that while conspicuous consumption rose dramatically in Luton in the late 1950s and early 1960s, there was no evidence that this unduly affected their previously held positions in relation to voting intentions, attitudes towards class and other social issues. As Goldthorpe et al. stated:

---

[33] Zweig, *The Worker in an Affluent Society*, p. 235.
[34] Turner, *The Car Makers*, p. 113.
[35] Ibid.
[36] Zweig, *The Worker in an Affluent Society*, pp. 234–35.
[37] J. Goldthorpe et al., *The Affluent Worker: Industrial Attitudes and Behaviour* (Cambridge, 1968); idem, *The Affluent Worker: Political Attitudes and Behaviour* (Cambridge, 1968); idem, *The Affluent Worker in the Class Structure* (Cambridge, 1969).

Little qualitative change at all may have occurred in the class situation of the affluent worker – in the sense, that is, of the position that he holds within the social organisation of production and the constraints and life chances that he consequently experiences.[38]

At the time the issues thrown up by these studies, particularly Goldthorpe et al.'s work, created a considerable heated debate, as this had implications for voting behaviour; would better off workers defect from Labour, their previous 'natural' political home and become Tories? By 1964 Labour had lost the previous three elections and 13 years of Tory rule was seeming to have an air of permanency about it. However, in 1964 Labour was returned to power with a small majority, and in 1966 Harold Wilson, the Prime Minister, called another election that increased the Labour majority to a more comfortable margin. In both these elections Luton followed the general pattern of the country and returned a Labour MP. It would seem that the Luton electorate was in many senses reflective of the whole country, particularly in Labour – Conservative marginal areas such as the Midlands and London. Voters did respond to the 'pound in their pocket' and how it affected them and their families. They also responded to the need for a better quality of life that government and community could provide through increases in services, and this balance between taxation and individual income has become a feature of elections up to the present day.

The car workers and other 'affluent workers' were no different in their political responses than the electorate in other parts of the country. When the economic climate became less certain from the mid-1960s on, a change of government was seen to be essential to put things right. As with past politics, the ups and downs of the economy had a considerable influence on voting intentions. Lutonians wanted a government that could deliver for them as Vauxhall and other companies had done.

Conclusion

By the end of the 1960s the Luton economy had once again returned to a position whereby it was heavily reliant, not only on one sector, but one company – Vauxhall. Zweig in his study of Luton noted this as well:

> The preponderance of Vauxhall in the Luton labour market has meant that the population of Luton has grown mainly in response to Vauxhall labour requirements and the prospects of Vauxhall still control the fate of Luton to a large extent.[39]

As some people said, 'Vauxhall is Luton.' Others declared that 'when Vauxhall sneezes Luton catches cold.'

The worries about the reliance on one company for stability within the local economy had been widely expressed in the early 1950s. Even Sir Charles Bartlett aired such a view. But when things were going well these warnings were ignored, and the 1950s and 1960s witnessed greater expansion of Vauxhall

---

[38] Goldthorpe et al., *The Affluent Worker in the Class Structure*, p. 82.
[39] Zweig, *The Worker in an Affluent Society*, p. 236.

and thus a greater hold over the Luton economy. By the 1970s these warnings could no longer be ignored, and concerns about diversification within the local economy began to be aired once more, just as they had been at the turn of the century.

By the end of the decade Vauxhall was beginning to make a loss for the first time since the 1920s. Its effect would have repercussions for Luton.

Chapter Ten

Acme to Nadir: The Decline of Vauxhall
in Luton 1970–2003

The car industry national and international trends: the 1970s
The period between the Second World War and the late 1960s witnessed unparalleled growth in the car industry and in the Luton economy. The 1970s saw a considerable change in the fortunes of the British-owned car industry in particular, and the American-owned companies generally, as international and national events caused a grimmer situation to emerge. By the end of the 1960s four major producers were dominant in the British car market: Ford, Vauxhall, Chrysler and British Leyland Motor Corporation (BLMC). Most of the large British-owned companies, notably Austin, Morris, and Rover, had begun to merge in the 1960s into the BLMC. By 1976 BLMC had become known simply as BL. British manufacturers were aware that survival in an expanding, but increasingly competitive market, placed a considerable emphasis on being able to produce lower-priced cars. This in turn required higher production to bring down unit costs. It was perceived at the time, by those in the industry and in the government, that this could only be achieved by merger. A more long-term view has put the difficulties of the industry down to a combination of factors, including uninspired model design, poor productivity, the relatively low quality of vehicles, lack of investment, poor industrial relations and poor management. None of the major car companies were totally exempt from these influences.

Marsden et al.[1] divide the 1970s into three fundamental phases:

1. 1972/3, when imports had little impact and, apart from Vauxhall, major car companies continued to be profitable.
2. 1973 to 1978, a period which begins to reveal the full impact of the oil crisis and its effects on reducing the size of the market and thus sales, although employment levels in the industry remained relatively high.
3. 1978 to 1980s, a period in which demand had recovered from the oil crisis but UK production fell and imports from Japan and Europe increased. Employment levels came in line with market demands.

The period was marked by a high degree of turbulence reflected in the conflictual industrial relations at the time and bound up with, what the popular press dubbed, 'the British Disease' – continual strikes and industrial

---

[1] D. Marsden, T. Morris, P. Willman and S. Wood, *The Car Industry: Labour Relations and Industrial Adjustment* (London: Tavistock, 1985), p. 5.

disturbance.[2] Subsequent more sober accounts have tended to correct this picture and sought deeper causes.

The oil crisis
The oil crisis was to have a devastating effect on the industry. Oil-producing countries in the Organisation of Petroleum Exporting Countries (OPEC), mainly as a result of Arabian influence, decided to raise the price of oil for a number of economic and political reasons. These price rises were passed on in terms of the cost of petroleum and other oil products. Car demand slumped as the cost of motoring rose and few areas of the economy were not affected. This worsened an already inflationary situation as prices began to rise steeply. The government even ordered petrol rationing coupons to be printed and distributed, although in the end this scheme was never instituted. The decline in car markets was not helped by the attempts of various governments to cure the situation by a series of stop-go policies in the late 1960s, and attempts to control prices and wages through a series of freezes in the 1970s. From a peak of car sales of 1.68 million in 1973 demand fell to 1.27 million in 1974 – a fall of nearly a quarter. Equally, car production dropped from 1.7 million in 1973 to 1.26 million in 1975.[3]

Inflation rose from over 9 per cent in 1973 to 16 per cent in 1974, reaching a height of over 24 per cent in 1975. BL and Chrysler seemed to be heading for bankruptcy and tried to borrow to keep going and it was only government intervention that avoided this catastrophe. BL was virtually nationalised and Chrysler's arguments as to the consequences for regional unemployment persuaded the Department of Trade and Industry to give large injections of cash. Vauxhall was propped up by their GM parent company, and only Ford seemed to weather the crisis fairly much unscathed financially.

The second phase of the 1970s was marked by a number of virulent strikes across the industry and in individual companies. All vehicle companies experienced this trend, including Vauxhall whose impeccable industrial relations record was marred at this time. This was the period that was to lead to the infamous 'Winter of Discontent' in 1978–79, but the causes of these strikes were partly influenced by national trends, industry specific factors and conditions often only relevant to an individual firm. The combination made for a period of turbulence in the industry and economy as a whole.

Industrial relations
Despite the industrial turbulence of the period Vauxhall remained relatively less prone to disruptions as Table 46 indicates. Vauxhall lost no days to strike action in 1974 and 1975 while its rivals Ford and particularly BL experienced considerable unrest. Vauxhall strike activity reached a peak in 1977 and again in 1979, outdoing Ford in the number of days lost in those years.

---

[2] See for example T. Claydon's attack on this popular perception in T. Claydon, 'Images of Disorder: Car Workers' Militancy and the Representation of Industrial Relations in Britain, 1950–1979,' in D. Thoms, L. Holden and T. Claydon (eds.), *The Motor Car and Popular Culture in the 20th Century* (Aldershot: Ashgate, 1998).
[3] M. Adeney, *The Motor Makers: The Turbulent History of Britain's Car Industry* (London: Collins, 1988), p. 276.

Table 46. Days lost (000s) in car manufacturing 1974–1983

	Vauxhall	BL	Ford
1974	—	—	485
1975	—	7,987	231
1976	13	—	185
1977	414	3,375	371
1978	52	1,313	2,726
1979	637	1,850	71
1980	14	438	56
1981	15	380	371
1982	22	275	157
1983	41	188	207

Source: Marsden et al. (1985), p. 131.[4]

BL always remained a troubled and strike prone firm in this period, and even the Michael Edwardes administration and various government interventions could not ultimately, save the company from passing out of British ownership in the 1980s. The reason for BLs decline are complex and this is not the forum to go into the causes in detail. Whisler, Church, Marsden *et al.* put some of the blame on poor industrial relations but also stress poor management practices, lack of cohesion in the company, a lack of an international market base, poor product design and low productivity, among other factors.

Vauxhall's industrial relation record was much better than BL and Ford, its American rival. In only two years, 1977 and 1979, was the Vauxhall strike record worse than Ford, and yet Ford was profitable and Vauxhall was not! It could be argued therefore that poor industrial relations alone was not the sole reason for the industry's troubles. Each company had its own particular factors that influenced its production and financial performance.

The strike in October 1977 mainly concerned differentials in pay between Vauxhall workers and other car manufacturers, particularly BL, and differentials between skilled, semi-skilled and unskilled workers. Inflation had seen many workers' wages in relative decline and there was a move by unions to maintain pay levels and differentials between various groups. Vauxhall workers had come to expect high wages maintained by overtime, but overtime was severely cut in the 1970s for long periods as the flagging sales of the Victor and Ventora, made at the Luton plant, continued into the latter part of the decade. Another factor often mentioned at the time, though there is little evidence to support it, is that management almost welcomed strikes as this gave them a chance to reduce capacity of excess stocks.

While the large scale strikes of 1977 and 1979 were essentially concerned with money issues, an increasing number of smaller and more frequent strikes have been laid at the door of changing conditions in the national and international economy. While pay remained an important topic in the late 1970s, there was a considerable shift to issues concerned with redundancy, manning levels, lay-offs and related problems. In other words the car

[4] Marsden et al., *The Car Industry*, op. cit., p. 131.

Plate 43. 1970–1979 HC Viva, keeping Vauxhall afloat in the 1970s.

companies, including Vauxhall, were anxious to cut back on their workforce. The cost of labour is one of the largest single bills for a company and in time of trouble it is logical for management to reduce the size of the workforce or the hours employed by current workers in an attempt to save money. By the mid-1980s these issues had been resolved to some degree but at the cost of huge cut backs in employment levels in all areas of the car industry. Productivity had become the major issue and that meant high output with a smaller workforce. But that issue will be examined more thoroughly in a later section.

Vauxhall's poor performance
A more pertinent question was why did Vauxhall do so badly in this period? As Table 47 indicates, between 1970 and 1986 the company only had one profit-able year. The reasons are complex and a number of factors played their part in this poor performance. Adeney[5] is also perplexed about this but puts forward a number of points in explanation. One major cause was the decline in car sales in the early to mid-1970s. Vauxhall had relied strongly on the highly successful Viva series to maintain sales and it continued this policy throughout the 1970s until the Viva finally ceased production in 1979. However, the Viva's success

[5] Adeney, op. cit., p. 270.

Plate 44. 1972–1976 FE Victor – the last 'British' Vauxhall car.

was not enough to carry the rest of Vauxhall's poor car sales and the failure of the Victor, and to a lesser degree the Ventora, to sell in large quantities in the middle and upper middle range price bracket. This caused Vauxhall to be dragged into the red. As Broatch states:

> The FE range (Victor and Ventora) was not a sales success. In road reports there were complaints of the noisy gearbox (four speed), poor gear change and clutch pedals at different heights from the other pedals. The ohc engine had potential but was rather thirsty and the 3.3 litre engine was heavy and outdated . . .[6]

The fact that GM allowed Vauxhall to languish in this state is also a mystery. Adeney believes that this impassivity by its parent company was partly due to the poor performance of the car production side being disguised by the success of the Bedford truck and van operation which was highly profitable at this time. Once again part of the GM UK operation (Bedford trucks) had subsidised the other (Vauxhall cars).

The other factor was that GM's attention was much more concentrated on the German side of its European operations – that of Opel in Rüsselsheim, Germany. The plant there was far more productive than both the Luton and Ellesmere Port factories. In addition German design was superior and it is a

---

[6] Stuart Fergus Broatch, *Vauxhall* (Stroud: Sutton Publishing, 1997), p. 145.

sad reflection that the last fully designed British built Vauxhall car was the FE Victor. The cars that followed were gradually becoming German, and later all German, in design, and this trend was part of the emerging GM global strategy.

One of the major reasons for Ford's general profitability in the difficult times of the 1970s was that it had in the previous decade begun to create a global organisation. The Ford Company had realised that to sustain high sales of mass produced vehicles mass markets had to be accessed. Single home markets (outside the USA) were no longer viable. Thus Ford had reorganised globally and divided its operations into regions. Cars would be produced for a region not just a country. GM began to come round to the idea in the late 1970s and it was obvious that one important region was Europe. In 1973 Britain had joined the Common Market and it was becoming clear that more European states would join and that member states' economies would be increasingly integrated. In the light of these developments it was becoming evident that what was required was a European car. Car companies had long thought of a 'world car' – a car that would sell anywhere in world markets, but in previous times that had been impossible due to different taxation, customer demands and prevailing conditions in different national markets. By the 1980s both American companies were attempting to produce a car for all markets. In the light of these changing conditions and the strategies emerging to cope with them, GM began increasingly to favour Germany over Britain as the centre for its European operations. As this strategy emerged in the late 1970s Vauxhall was not so much ignored as seen increasingly as an unprofitable relatively small operation in the gigantic scheme of GM operations. As Marsden et al. put it '[Vauxhall's] poor performance meant that it became the junior partner in car production to its German sister company, Opel.'[7]

Table 47. Vauxhall vehicle sales, profits after tax and total employees 1970–1989

| | Profit after Tax (£m) | Vehicle sales (units) | | | Number of employees | Vehicle sales per employee |
		Home	Export	Total		
1970	(9.4)*	158,167	111,630	269,797	36,291	7.4
1971	(2.6)*	214,738	116,448	331,186	37,256	8.9
1972	(4.1)*	205,356	67,410	272,766	34,312	7.9
1973	(3.7)*	185,257	73,464	258,721	34,365	7.5
1974	(18.0)*	167,205	82,578	249,783	32,884	7.6
1975	(13.0)*	130,947	74,399	205,346	27,400	7.5
1976	(1.9)*	154,545	75,659	230,204	28,600	8.0
1977	(2.1)*	163,456	70,710	234,166	31,745	7.3
1978	2.0	185,847	75,636	261,483	33,344	7.8
1979	(31.3)*	171,392	59,028	230,420	32,732	7.0
1980	(83.3)*	137,224	57,921	195,145	30,670	6.3
1981	(57.4)*	151,490	34,926	186,416	23,770	7.8
1982	(38.7)*	227,620	16,914	244,534	20,527	11.9
1983	(1.1)*	249,645	551	250,196	11,519	21.7

[7] Marsden et al., *The Car Industry*, op. cit., p. 1.

Table 47 (*cont.*)

	Profit after Tax (£m)	Vehicle sales (units) Home	Export	Total	Number of employees	Vehicle sales per employee
1984	(9.4)*	299,355	546	299,901	11,931	25.1
1985	(47.4)*	333,369	3,457	336,826	12,467	27.0
1986	(61.7)*	298,724	6,605	305,329	12,638	24.1
1987	31.0	293,441	10,565	304,006	11,492	26.4
1988	151.9	345,345	8,201	353,546	10,943	32.3
1989	209.1	392,003	8,202	400,205	11,132	35.9

Source: Vauxhall Annual Reports.

As can be seen in Table 48, Vauxhall's share of the car market declined from 10 per cent in 1970 to a nadir of 7.4 per cent in 1974 and did not recover its market position until the early 1980s. Part of the reason for the Vauxhall recovery was the introduction of the Chevette which took over from the much revamped Viva. While it was mainly British in design a considerable portion was increasingly made in Germany including the floorspan, suspension, screen and doors.[8]

Table 48. Percentage share of the British car market of the main producers 1970–1989

Year	Vauxhall	BL	Ford	Chrysler/ Talbot/ Peugeot	Datsun Nissan/ Honda	Others	UK new car reg (000s)
1970	10.0	38.1	26.5	11.2	0.4	13.8	91.4
1971	10.8	40.2	18.7	12.4	1.0	16.9	108.5
1972	9.0	33.1	24.5	11.4	2.9	19.1	138.5
1973	8.0	31.9	22.6	11.5	5.1	20.9	137.1
1974	7.3	32.7	22.7	10.8	6.1	20.4	102.8
1975	7.4	30.9	21.7	8.4	7.9	24.1	98.4
1976	8.9	27.4	25.3	6.4	8.1	23.9	106.5
1977	9.1	24.3	25.7	6.0	9.1	25.8	109.5
1978	8.2	23.5	24.7	7.1	9.4	27.5	131.6
1979	8.2	19.6	28.3	7.0	8.9	28.0	142.0
1980	8.8	18.2	30.7	6.0	9.8	26.5	126.6
1981	8.6	19.2	30.9	4.6	8.6	28.1	124.5
1982	11.7	17.9	30.5	3.6	8.8	27.6	132.0
1983	14.6	18.2	28.9	4.4	8.7	25.2	148.9
1984	16.2	18.3	27.8	4.0	9.0	24.7	147.4
1985	16.6	17.9	26.5	4.0	(6.8)*	—	—
1986	15.1	15.8	27.4	4.6	(6.8)*	—	—
1987	13.5	14.9	28.8	5.0	(6.9)*	—	—
1988	13.7	15.0	26.4	5.7	(7.3)*	—	—
1989	15.2	13.6	26.5	6.0	(7.1)*	—	—

* Honda and Nissan only. Other Japanese car makers not included.
Sources: Marsden et al. (1985), table 1; Whisler (1999), table 48.

[8] M. Sedgwick, *Vauxhall: A Pictorial Tribute* (London: Beaulieu Books, 1981), p. 98.

Plate 45. The Chevette was the replacement for the Viva model in 1978. It was the first to have the popular hatchback design to become common on later Vauxhall models.

GM had also neglected investment in Vauxhall plant. Much of the capital equipment and plant expansion in the 1950s and 1960s was becoming worn and outdated. One capstan operator interviewed by the author stated that just before his retirement in 1978 he was working on US machines that came over with Lend Lease in the Second World War.[9]

By 1978 GMOO had carried out a ten year review and had come to the conclusion, as has already been noted, that the future lay in global operations based on integration of product and markets. In order to effect this it also became clear that extra production capacity was needed. An interesting postscript to this decade was the project code named 'Gemini.' Bob Price, the American Chairman and Managing Director of Vauxhall approached Michael Edwardes at BL and proposed that Vauxhall build cars in BL's underused factories. In return GM would provide the engineering that BL lacked and come to a mutual understanding about producing a range of cars and trucks between the two organisations.

Price remarked to Edwardes:

We think that your Austin Morris problem is bigger than you think it is, for we believe that you need not one, but two new models in the mid car sector. But you do not have the people resource or the cash resource to do it. And time is against you . . . We would build on our mutual strengths –

[9] Interview with Les Cowell, March 1980. He was a capstan operator and worked for Vauxhall from 1937 to 1978.

Plate 46. Mark I Astra Saloon, part of the 'mass Opelisation' of Vauxhall but, along with the Cavalier, a model that restored Vauxhall to profitability in the 1980s.

> we think that the mini can be developed and your new LC8 (Metro) would give us a ready made car in that sector. We can solve our mid-car problem quicker than you can.[10]

Edwardes was a great admirer and friend of Price (at one time he had tried to persuade him to join the Board of BL) and was therefore enthusiastic about the proposition. Unfortunately this was not to be as the General Motors Board in Detroit vetoed the proposal. It is interesting to speculate what the fate of BL and Vauxhall might have been had the Gemini project gone ahead.

Vauxhall from 1980 to the present
The 1980s were to see a considerable revival in the fortunes of the Company with the arrival of two highly successful vehicles – the Cavalier and the Astra, the latter still very much in production today, albeit in a fourth series design format. Both of these vehicles were fully German designed and built. This fact points to the restructuring that GM Europe undertook in the face of considerable losses in the UK in the 1970s and early 1980s. It was this ongoing crisis that stimulated reforms in the European arm of the company and when GM USA become embroiled in deep problems in the early 1980s and 1990s itself, it took a long time to take a leaf out of the books of lesser European subsidiaries.

---

[10] Quoted in M. Edwardes, *Back from the Brink* (London: Collins, 1983), pp. 190 and 191. The quote was edited and reproduced by Adeney, op. cit., p. 307.

Plate 47. The first UK-built Cavalier 1977, in reality a German Opel model which was to prove
to be a very popular seller throughout the 1980s and much of the 1990s.

The Europe GM headquarters, based in Zurich in Switzerland with a paired
down staff of 200 people, set about reorganising the European car plants in the
UK, Germany, Belgium and later Spain into one complementary organisation.
By the early 1980s in the UK market alone the writing was on the wall.
Japanese imports and their manufacturing bases in the UK began to seize a
greater share of the UK market. As Table 48 indicates the share of Japanese
cars grew from 0.4 per cent of the British market in 1970 to 9 per cent by 1984.
This was a prodigious rise and deeply worrying for established British and UK
based manufacturers. The Japanese produced high quality cars for relatively
low prices and the earlier resistance to these imports was gradually broken
down as Honda collaborated with Rover from 1979, Nissan opened a plant in
Sunderland in 1987 and Toyota opened a large plant near Derby in 1992. Other
Japanese plants were opened in South Wales and Swindon. Whilst there was a
core of BL customers that remained loyal to British cars built in British-owned
plants even that form of patriotism was being undermined by poor quality car

production. This combined with the fact that Honda took over a large share in BL nullified the patriotic market. People were increasingly buying on the economic principle of value for money. The days of nostalgia for the mythical great British car were over. That myth was only retained in the romantic perceptions of car collectors and museum curators for a past that never really existed.[11]

The impact of Japanese car manufacturing
The impact of the Japanese was worldwide, including America. As in the UK, inroads were being made into US markets. The initial reaction was to find the magic formula for success that Japanese companies had discovered and emulate it in American and British factories. By the mid-1980s such Japanese influenced management techniques as quality circles, total quality management (TQM), kaizen and kanban were hurriedly being implemented in car plants round the world. Few totally implemented such techniques and the success rate was disappointingly low. By the 1990s adaptations of these approaches were being applied to national and organisational contexts rather than attempting slavish imitations of the Japanese model.

GM suffered from Japanese competition in the USA and its market share declined by 10 per cent between 1977 and 1986 with a net loss of profits in 1980, its first since 1921. GM's response was to undertake a rather mistaken policy of automation in many of its plants in the USA in the belief that robotics could do what American workers could not – compete with the Japanese. Such early automation initiatives were often disastrous with malfunctioning robotic machines smashing windscreens on the floor, paint shop robots spraying everywhere but on the car body panels, and assembly lines breaking down so often that workers had to work alongside the robots.[12]

In 1983 GM reached an agreement with Toyota to produce a small car based on the Toyota Corolla and marketed it in the US as the Chevrolet Nova. The New United Motor Manufacturing, Inc., or NUMMI as it came to be known, was relatively successful but such was the poor quality of senior management in GM that it remained a fairly much 'one off' and relatively isolated project. Little of the knowledge, expertise and experience were transferred to other parts of the GM empire.

Vauxhall model range in the 1980s and 1990s
The inward looking GM Board also did not learn lessons from the 'turn around' in Europe. Nevertheless GM had financed the models that were to once again turn Vauxhall into a successful and profitable car manufacturer – namely the Cavalier and Astra. The J series Cavalier was designed by German engineers at Opel and was primarily aimed at the fleet company car market. This was the beginning of what Sedgwick called 'the mass Opelisation' of

---

[11] Adeney is particularly scathing about this romanticised perception of the British car industry perpetuated by an elite clique of motoring enthusiasts. See for example the concluding chapter of his book.
[12] M. Keller, *Collision: GM, Toyota, Volkswagen and the Race to Own the 21st Century* (New York: Doubleday, 1993), p. 170.

Vauxhall.[13] The first Cavalier, built in 1976, was in fact an Opel Ascona. It initially had a 1.6 litre engine although 1.9 and 2 litre versions were added later. This was to become a major challenger to Ford's dominance in the fleet car market. In 1988 the revamped Cavalier had incorporated a small engine version at 1.4 litre. This was partly in response to the market wanting fuel economic vehicles that were good performers.

The Cavalier could in many ways be classed as a world car in the sense that it sold in all parts of the world, including the US where GM companies had markets. It was a world car in another sense as Adeney describes:

> . . . in 1984, when the Mark II Cavalier was being assembled in Luton, one could watch parts coming together on the assembly line delivered from almost every country but Britain – the basic engine was made in Australia; if the gearbox was automatic it was American; if it was manual it was Japanese. The distributor and much of the pressings came from Germany; the carburettor by courtesy of the French, while the oil filter, some glass and the wheels, but little more was British.[14]

The Luton factory was becoming just an assembly plant for parts brought together from various parts of the GM empire.

The Cavalier's equally successful sister, the Astra, was another Opel design and was to be assembled in Ellesmere Port, where it continues in production today. The first Astras were produced in the UK in 1980 and were aimed at a smaller size market than the Cavalier, the first ones having only four cylinders and an engine capacity of 1.3 litres. To cover the luxury (executive) end of the market the Carlton and the Royale were produced in 1979 with capacities of 2.0 litres and 2.5 litres respectively, and in 1980 the Viceroy with a 2.5 litre engine.

The Astra was to prove equally as popular as its big sister, the Cavalier, and both were designed and redesigned with a 'sporty' feel in the 1980s, unusual in a fleet car and family saloon model at this time. The higher-range models were, compared with cars of the previous decades, high performance vehicles with relatively low energy consumption. The range also included the hatchback design, first put into the Chevette range, and proved to be increasingly popular. Both the Astra and Cavalier became strong rivals to the highly successful Ford Cortina and Sierra, and although they only outsold these two Ford models on a few occasions, they were always in the top ten and often the top five best-selling car lists.

The Vauxhall range was completed in 1983 with the introduction of the Nova, for the smaller end of the market. It offered a two-door saloon with the option of a 1.0, 1.2 or 1.3 litre engine.

These medium and small size cars were to put Vauxhall back in the black, and as Table 47 indicates, the Company showed its first profit since 1978 in 1987, and was to consistently do so over the next decade. Car sales increased threefold on the 1975 figures and Vauxhall increased its share of the market from 7.3 per cent in 1974 to 16.6 per cent in 1985 (Table 48). In 1989 Vauxhall

[13] Sedgwick, op. cit., p. 103.
[14] Adeney, *The Motor Makers: The Turbulent History of Britain's Car Industry* (London: Collins, 1988) p. 317.

output reached a peak of 400,205 units (Table 47). In the 1990s another recession hit car sales, including Vauxhall, and annual production slumped to 242,859 and has not reached the heights of the 1989 peak since (Table 50).

In the 1990s a number of new vehicles was introduced in line with contemporary trends. In 1991 the Frontera entered the increasingly popular recreational vehicle market. In 1993 the Corsa replaced the successful Nova and proved equally popular. In the following year the Omega replaced the Carlton and Senator in the executive luxury end of the market. The more sporty side was catered for by Tigra in 1993 and although small is, for its size, a high performance vehicle. Another growing specialist market also catered for was the multi-purpose vehicles (MPVs) with initially the Sintra in 1996, and later the Zafira in 1999. In 1995 the last Cavalier was produced at Luton and was replaced by the production of the Vectra, particularly the estate version, that has not sold so well as its predecessor. The Astra received a complete facelift and redesign in 1998 and remains a best-selling vehicle in its category.

The reasons for Vauxhall's improved performance
Undoubtedly the major reason for the improvement in Vauxhall's financial performance was the production of successful models – the Cavalier, Astra and Nova. In 1988 Vauxhall announced that it had sold over a million Cavaliers.[15] High car sales were also accompanied by investment plans in British plant. By the 1980s, due to Japanese competition in US markets, US car manufacturers, including GM, began to realise that an even greater integration of their global network was needed to meet this challenge. GM, Ford and Chrysler all increased investment in their overseas subsidiaries.[16] In 1984 GM announced a one million pound investment programme, £90 million of which went into a paint plant at Luton, and the rest to Ellesmere Port. In the next four years £85 million was invested in the Ellesmere Port plant with an added injection of £56.3 million in 1988.[17]

Other very important factors were vast improvements in output and productivity, combined with better quality workmanship. The number of workers employed by Vauxhall fell from a peak of 37,413 in 1970 to 10,943 in 1988 (Table 47). That figure had fallen to only 9,561 by 2000 (Table 50), but the decline in the Luton area is even more marked especially with the closure of the Bedford plant at Dunstable in the 1980s and the cessation of car production at Luton in 2002. Ironically, improvements in productivity are partly reflected in the declining workforce since more vehicles can be produced with fewer people. In 1970 the average number of cars sold per employee was 7.4, but by 1989 that was dramatically increased to 35.9 vehicles per employee (Table 47). Actual productivity, measured as output per employee, also showed enormous increases, rising from 11.2 vehicles per person in 1984 to a peak of 30.9 vehicles per person in 1999 (Table 49).

[15] Vauxhall Education Service, *The Vauxhall Story* (Luton: Vauxhall, 2001) p. 17.
[16] R. Church, *The Rise and Decline of the British Motor Industry* (Basingstoke: MacMillan, 1994) p. 108.
[17] Vauxhall Education Service, *The Vauxhall Story* (Luton: Vauxhall, 2001) pp. 16 &17.

Table 49. Vauxhall output of vehicles per employee 1984–2000

1984	11.2	1990	24.4	1996	28.8
1985	14.5	1991	23.3	1997	27.6
1986	14.6	1992	27.3	1998	26.5
1987	18.1	1993	23.2	1999	30.9
1988	18.8	1994	26.4	2000	29.4
1989	21.3	1995	25.1		

Plate 48. The 'marriage' of a Mark III Cavalier body with mechanical components in 1993. By this time automated plant and robots had replaced many workers and those that remained were trained in engineering and team working techniques.

Productivity was also considerably enhanced by the gradual introduction of automated machinery in the assembly process. Drawing on the experience (including the mistakes) of the GM parent company and benefiting from GM's investment in new plant, robotisation increased dramatically in the Luton and Ellesmere Port plants in the 1980s and 1990s. Investment in computerised technology combined with in-built quality control and 'just-in-time' management systems (or Material Production Control – MPC, as it is called at Vauxhall) have lead to enormous improvements in productivity and quality of vehicles. This has enabled Vauxhall and GM Europe to successfully compete with their Japanese, American and European rivals.

Another undoubted contribution to a more successful period after 1980 was the decline in militant union activity and wild cat strikes. Industrial relations gradually settled into a more peaceful mode by the end of the 1980s although there was still the occasional large strike. Generally all three unions cooperated with Vauxhall management in helping bring about improvements by not hindering policy and helping implement some of the initiatives. Unfortunately these acts of cooperation do not make news headlines in the same way as a strike. Agreements were reached on the contentious issue of downsizing the workforce. Although the unions did not like to see their members without work they were facing the realities of economic survival in an increasingly competitive global environment. In 1988 it was calculated that there was still over capacity within the industry in Europe alone of two million vehicles per year.[18] In the light of these facts it can be seen that the survival and success of Vauxhall was remarkable. As Whisler states:

> Of the Big Six firms that dominated the British motor industry in 1945, only the US multinationals, Ford and Vauxhall, survived into the late 1990s.[19]

In strong contrast to the 1970s the unions bent over backwards in the 1990s to cooperate with management.

Table 50. Vauxhall net profit, market share, employees and output 1990–2000

	Net profit before tax (£m)	Market Share %	Employees: weekly average	UK output (units)
1990	239.1	16.1	11,268	276,031
1991	132.6	15.6	11,248	261,896
1992	223.7	16.7	11,042	301,857
1993	185.1	17.2	10,554	245,313
1994	79.0	16.3	9,917	261,991
1995	2.5	15.1	9,641	242,859
1996	10.1	14.0	9,651	277,888
1997	24.4	13.6	10,022	277,442
1998	72.6	12.6	9,822	260,332
1999	127.7	13.3	10,178	315,205
2000		13.3	9,561	281,668

Source: 'Vauxhall Facts and Figures' (2000)

As Table 50 indicates Vauxhall has remained steadily in profit throughout the 1990s despite the recession in the early part of the decade and the East Asian financial crisis in the latter part.

The decline of the Bedford truck

In contrast to the car success story, the CV side of the business (trucks and vans) has fared less well. What had been a successful operation in the 1970s, helping keep Vauxhall's head above water financially, now had become a heavy loss-maker. Vauxhall (Bedford) were not alone in this predicament as Leyland sold out its truck division to the Dutch producer DAF. Times were hard in the CV market in the late 1970s and early 1980s as a world recession hit sales. A

[18] M. Adeney, op. cit., p. 338.
[19] T.R. Whisler, *The British Motor Industry, 1945–94: A Case Study in Industrial Decline* (Oxford: Oxford University Press, 1999), p. 401.

large number of engineering factories went into bankruptcy having disastrous effects on industries that supplied them. GM Europe had to make a serious decision concerning the haemorrhaging operations at Dunstable. The large size trucks did not have the advantage of economies of scale that vans based on car designs had. Much of the chassis and body work had to be specially adapted for different customers which increased its price and in a shrinking market this could not be maintained. By 1987 GM decided to withdraw Bedford from the market and sold the concern to AWD in 1988. AWD attempted to resuscitate the company by producing a range of five trucks based on the TL-type.[20] Although it made a small profit in the late 1980s, it succumbed to the recession in the early 1990s and closed completely in November 1992 with the loss of 720 jobs, thus ending truck production at Dunstable.

Vauxhall remained in the commercial vehicle sector by continuing its production of vans still under the Bedford badge. In 1987 IBC Vehicles was created as a joint venture with Isuzu and is a GM subsidiary located next to the Vauxhall plant in Luton. One of the first fruits of this cooperative venture was the Rascal truck later to be followed by the Frontera. In 1996 GM and Renault signed an agreement to develop a medium sized van. This stimulated a further investment of £130 million in the Luton plant. In 2001 production began on the new Vauxhall/Opel Vivaro and Renault Trafic vans.[21]

One interesting possibility in the CV story was the proposal by Leyland, Vauxhall and the British government to combine Bedford and Leyland in an attempt to reduce production capacity and thus save both companies. This time the talks were scuppered at the British end as the proposal met with a huge burst of patriotic outrage in the media, in that a great British institution – the Land Rover – would pass into the hands of an American company.[22] The patriotic ghost that accompanied the 1920s purchase of Vauxhall by GM had reared its ugly head again. The merger, of course, did not happen and within a decade Leyland was principally owned by a Dutch company and the Rover side was partly owned by a Japanese, then a German and now an American company!

The rationalisation of the CV side of Vauxhall had proved crucial to its survival and the IBC company has been moderately successful throughout the 1990s, with some considerable improvements in sales towards the end of the decade.

The end of the line for car production in Luton
In 2001 GM announced that it was to cease producing cars at the Vauxhall factory in Luton. This was greeted with a combination of disbelief and later anger as Vauxhall workers, their unions and the citizens of Luton felt betrayed by the company to which many British workers had given much loyalty and service. 'Stunned,' 'Shocked,' 'Sold Down the River' were some of the local and national newspaper headlines when the story broke concerning the closure on 13 December 2000. Even the British government expressed surprise and

[20] *Vauxhall–Bedford Mirror*, 22 September 1988, p. 4.
[21] Vauxhall Motors Ltd, *IBC Vehicles Home of the Vivaro and Frontera* (Luton, 2001).
[22] Adeney, op. cit., p. 327.

Plate 49. Nick Reilly, Managing Director of Vauxhall 1996–2001. It was he who had the painful duty of halting car production at the Luton plant after 99 years.

exasperation at the decision. Questions were asked in Parliament and local MPs expressed their anger and sorrow.

Within the week, protests by Vauxhall workers resulted in a mass demonstration outside Vauxhall's main office and when Nick Reilly, the Managing Director, attempted to address the crowd he was greeted with shouts of 'Judas' and 'liar' and calls for his resignation.[23] Others commented that they had only heard of the closure over the radio and that this was a blow just before

[23] *The Guardian*, 14 December 2000, p. 7.

Christmas. Vauxhall later announced that it was extending all workers' Christmas holidays from one to three weeks with full basic pay. This did little to placate the workforce.

In Government the Prime Minister, Tony Blair, and the then Trade and Industry Secretary, Stephen Byers, reeling from the shock news, announced 'We are not going to walk away from this. We are not going to just leave it to the market.'[24] Unfortunately, GM Europe had taken the decision and there was little that any government minister could do. The forces of globalisation and of multinational companies were proved to be beyond the control of national governments. Nick Reilly (the Vauxhall Managing Director) himself was only given 24 hours notice from the Zurich headquarters of GM Europe of the decision that approximately 2,000 workers at the Luton plant would no longer build cars and the assembly of the Vectra would cease there in March 2002.

The question that the media, the politicians and the workforce at Luton were asking was 'Why?' The truth of the matter is that the origin of the decision had its roots in events in Luton and the UK in the 1970s and some say even earlier. Of course there was no conscious policy expressed by GM that one day the Luton plant would be run down and eventually closed (in fact GM had pumped investment into the plant throughout the 1980s and 1990s) but all the signs were there that would lead inexorably to that decision.

The immediate causes for the GM decision

This was not the first time that the plant was threatened with closure. In April 1998 a series of crisis talks were held with management and unions in a bid to safeguard its future. It was agreed that if Vauxhall workers accepted a three year restraint on pay and conditions and increased productivity there would be a commitment to build Vectra's replacement model at Kimpton Road.[25] Unfortunately the conditions in the world car markets did not sufficiently recover to ensure this guarantee. GM in the United States was making losses and when this had happened in the past it had relied on the profitability of its European and other world operations to subsidise it. In the last quarter of 2000 GM Europe plunged from a profit of $32 million (£22 million) to a loss of $181 million.[26] The only immediate response that GM felt they could make was to reduce capacity in its European and American plant.

GM announced not only the loss of jobs in Luton on 13 December 2000 but also that 3,000 jobs were to be axed in its European plants, particularly in Germany and Spain. The Chief Executive of GM, Rick Wagonner, also announced that 10,000 jobs would disappear in the USA,[27] including the complete scrapping of the long-running GM car-make Oldsmobile.[28]

In examining why GM took the decision to cease car production at Luton four influences can be discerned: the crisis within the global car market and the

[24] *Daily Telegraph*, 14 December 2000, p. 18.
[25] *Dunstable Gazette*, 19 December 2000, front page.
[26] C. Buckley, 'UK Motors into an Uncertain Future,' *The Times*, 13 December 2000, p. 29.
[27] *Daily Telegraph*, 13 December 2001, p. 33.
[28] *The Economist*, 16 December 2000, p. 83.

globalisation of car making, the declining market for GM products, difficulties in the UK market and specific problems with the Luton operation.

By the end of the 1980s over capacity had been identified as a major worldwide problem in the car industry and it had long been speculated that two or more major motor manufacturers would have to go. This situation was also exacerbated by the severe recession in the early 1990s followed by the East Asian financial crisis in the second half of the decade. In the light of these events vehicle manufacturers were anxious to reduce capacity. For a brief period in the latter half of the 1990s there had been a buoyant car market and although sales had increased, profits had not improved due to heavy price competition. Ford had also found the European market growing especially competitive, which led to the decision to suspend car production at its large Dagenham plant. The tried and tested products of the two motoring giants were not really appealing to European buyers who were gradually turning to the more attractive designs of European manufacturers such as Peugeot – Citroen, Volkswagen, Mercedes and FIAT, as well as Japanese cars, that combined styling, quality, and competitive pricing.[29]

The lack of appeal of Vauxhall (GM) products was related to unimaginative design. The Vectra was condemned by many as the sort of car in which 'sales reps thrash up and down motorways.' Kennedy writing in *The Times* stated that the importance of style and beauty seems to have been forgotten at Vauxhall and GM. He quotes both Quentin Wilson's and Jeremy Clarkson's scathing criticisms of the Corsa, Vectra, Frontera and Tigra and continues:

> In today's market, when brands are king, Vauxhall became worthless . . . the reason why Vauxhall has zero affection and zero brand following is that the public intuits that they don't really make cars, they assemble cars designed in Germany. They're really Opels. There is no such thing as a Vauxhall researcher, designer or engineer any more. It's just an assembly plant for something else. It's a long time since Vauxhall had any design of any integrity.[30]

Another prime reason why Vauxhall Luton became a candidate for severe cut backs was that GM had identified Luton as the weakest of its 12 car factories in Europe. The Luton plant was described as 'old and cramped, and very cumbersome to operate,' whereas the main GM factories for Europe based in Russelsheim and Antwerp were more modern. A number of experts also believed 'that its [Luton's] productivity, though improved, lags behind Continental rivals.' The output of Vectra cars at Luton was 42 cars per person per year, while in mainland Europe it was 60 to 70 cars and the Nissan plant in Sunderland, a strong rival, was 100 cars per employee.[31]

Another important factor was that the British economic climate was seen by many large multinational manufacturers as unfavourable. A strong pound and Britain's refusal to join the Euro put many British producers at a disadvantage

---

[29] *Financial Times*, 13 December 2000, p. 34.
[30] Dominic Kennedy, 'Carmaker with Zero Brand Following or Affection,' *The Times*, 13 December 2000, p. 4.
[31] Tim Burt, 'Economic Arguments Sink Luton,' *Financial Times*, 14 December 2000, p. 2.

in terms of price competition in world car markets. There was also considerable criticism in the press of the UK market's inflated car prices compared to continental rivals. In 2000 a price war began to bring down the level of car prices in the UK, undermining profit margins. In the light of these factors American and Japanese car companies were no longer seeing Britain as a suitable place to manufacture, let alone a place for further injection of capital. Their interests were increasingly turning to the possibilities of producing in Eastern Europe where labour and general production costs are far cheaper than in Western Europe.

Trade unionists at the time also pointed to the fact that labour laws in the UK were far less regulatory than in the countries of their European partners, and for this reason it was easier and cheaper to make workers redundant than in Germany and Belgium. This may have been a factor in GM (and indeed Ford's) decision making but was unlikely to be a primary one.

The long term reasons for Vauxhall's decline

It could be argued that the roots of the closure lay in the events of the 1970s when Vauxhall ceased designing and producing their own cars and became an assembler of Opel vehicles badged under the Vauxhall name. Vauxhall had lost out to its sister subsidiary in Germany and when GM began to reshape its overseas operations and group European manufacturers together, the centre of it operations was too obviously going to Opel.

There were, however, a number of contemporary reasons for the decline. First and foremost there was the low productivity of the British workforce, both at Luton and Ellesmere Port, compared with their German and Belgian counterparts. This was not just a malaise of Vauxhall but infected the car industry and British industry as a whole. Secondly, there was the poor industrial relations record of the car industry and Vauxhall at a crucial decision-making time in GM's history, i.e. when they were deciding where to locate the centre of European car design and manufacture. Eric Fountain, a very experienced Vauxhall director in the 1970s and 1980s, saw the GM decision strongly influenced by events at the time.

> We lost out at the end of the road because of the strike situation that existed at the time. We would have had to make about 300,000 engines and about half would have gone for export – and that's the reason we lost; it would have been too much of a risk.[32]

While Fountain's explanation is partly true, the poor industrial relations situation was not the only reason.

Thirdly, the 1970s were times of poor government policy-making with stop-go policies and freezes which made for great uncertainties in an industry that had to rely on long term planning, involving intricate product design and manufacture. Britain in the 1970s could not provide that climate of certainty. By the time it could, in the 1980s, the decision in Detroit had already been made. The UK operations were to be secondary players.

---

[32] M. Adeney, *The Motor Makers: The Turbulent History of Britain's Car Industry* (London: Collins, 1988), p. 316.

Fourthly, the move towards a global and regional economy meant that national markets as entities in themselves were no longer viable. The UK was increasingly seen as part of the European market, and Marsden et al. state that 'European integration and international integration did not work to Britain's advantage.'[33]

Another question was why was Ellesmere Port not chosen for this treatment? Of course Ellesmere Port had not been immune from cutbacks and had suffered severely in the late 1970s with the delay in the change over from the Chevette to the Astra. But once the Astra was in production its success ensured Ellesmere Port's survival into the 1980s and 1990s. Luton's future remained certain with the production of the best-selling Cavalier. In switching production to the less popular Vectra, which had teething problems in its initial stages and was not received well by the motoring press, then the chances of survival of the Luton car plant declined as Vectra sales fell. Vectras were to be produced on the continent and shipped to Britain, but within the European Union free market context. Europe since 1992 was truly becoming a single market.

Who or what was to blame for the ceasing of car production in Luton after nearly a century? Were the unions, the less productive Luton workforce, successive British governments, Vauxhall managers past and present, GM executives past and present? The list could go on. All and yet no particular group were to blame. It was a conflux of events and changing circumstances beyond the control of individuals and groups.

By the 1990s the unions were generally cooperative and the Luton workforce had increased its productivity and output levels. GM had continued to inject capital to automate the plant. The workforce had gradually decreased in size but production of vehicles continued to increase. Governments had acted in the best interests of what they saw as the voter – and it was the voter that would return them to power. There had been bad management and good management in both Vauxhall and GM. Ultimately, events were outside one single group's control.

Executives of GM Europe operations had examined where cuts in production capacity needed to be made. In a fast changing world companies like GM have to make quick rational decisions. They can no longer keep an unproductive plant propped up until it 'might' become profitable again. All car companies and indeed all companies are making these decisions in the light of rapidly changing and highly competitive markets. This is the nature of globalisation in the 21st century.

The prospects for Luton with the decline of Vauxhall
Given the cessation of car production in 2002 and the subsequent decline of employment opportunities in Vauxhall it is interesting to ponder its impact on the town and its environs. Table 48 shows that at its height Vauxhall employed over 37,000 people in its three plants, the majority being employed in Luton and Dunstable at nearly 33,000. By 2000 that number had dropped to 9,500 employees. From the 1980s Vauxhall had ceased production at Dunstable and

---

[33] Marsden et al., *The Car Industry*, op. cit., p. 15.

about 5,000 employees have constantly been engaged at the Ellesmere Port plant. This left just over 4,000 employees working in Luton by the end of the 1990s. With the cessation of Vectra production only the IBC plant employing 1,870 remains. Another 500 jobs have been created in IBC to compensate for the loss of car production, but this is a monumental decline in employment terms of a once mighty organisation.

How has this decline in employment opportunities impacted on the town? From the 1930s to the 1970s Vauxhall's influence on the town was enormous. Even when it was announced that the Vectra would cease production with a loss of 2,000 jobs, people were trotting out old Luton cliches such as 'when Vauxhall sneezes Luton catches cold,' 'Luton is Vauxhall' or 'Vauxhall is Luton.' Vauxhall employees, local politicians, local traders, business people and other commentators bemoaned the fact that this would have an enormous negative impact on Luton employment and trading prospects. Not only would there be a direct loss of jobs but a loss of earnings from those who relied on contracts and trade from Vauxhall. At the time the town's Chamber of Commerce estimated 'that the closure could cost a total of around 6,000 jobs as well as affect tens of thousands of local people.'[34]

An initial reaction thus paints an alarming picture of a town brought to its economic knees by a mighty multinational corporation whose decision to cease car production was made without any thought of the men and women who might suffer from its effects. Whereas there is undoubtedly some truth in this view, this is not the whole the picture and, whilst the loss of 2,000 jobs is not a problem that any town would like to experience, in the cold light of hindsight its impact has been exaggerated.

A view directly in contrast to those above was expressed by Dai John, the Vice Chancellor of Luton University who stated:

> Luton hasn't really been a manufacturing town for years. And it hasn't been a Vauxhall town for decades. Quite frankly I couldn't see what all the fuss was about when the closure was announced. Yes, it was a shock for those who worked there. But I grew up in industrial South Wales. In the valleys you did have one-company towns. When they closed the steel works or coal mines in those places, the lights really did go out. Luton is nothing like that.[35]

This may be over egging the employment pudding too much in the opposite direction but there is much evidence to support this view. Whilst Vauxhall has always been influential in the town, there has been a marked decrease in its presence since the early 1980s when Vauxhall began to down size the work-force, along with other companies in the town, in the name of productivity and in response to growing global market pressures. The industrial presence in the town has declined considerably over the past decade with a loss of 500 jobs after the closure of Electrolux in 1998. Coulter Electronics also closed in that year with a loss of 300 jobs. Laporte closed its remaining administrative

---

[34] C. Gray, 'Vauxhall is Luton: What's Going to Happen Now?' *The Independent*, 13 December 2000, p. 6.
[35] R. Morrison, 'Those Bastards in Detroit,' *The Times* (T2 Section), 21 March 2002, pp. 2 and 3.

function in the 1990s with a loss of 150 jobs, and George Kent Ltd, which became part of the Brown Bouvri Group and then ABB, closed Kents Process Control in the 1990s, although ABB Kent Meters still operate in Luton. Most of these local firms were subsidiaries of large multinationals that have followed the economic trend of relocating production to cheaper environments such as third world or Eastern European countries. The one large company to remain, SKF, has also reduced its workforce considerably, restructuring operations, between 1990 and 1993 with the loss of 350 jobs. This paints a fairly grim picture of industrial decline in Luton and as Table 51 indicates there has been a steady decline in manufacturing for the past 20 years.

Table 51. Sectoral structure of Luton 1981–2000 (percentages)

	1981	1989	1991	1999	2000
Manufacturing	41.2	33.2	29.0	20.0	20.0
Construction	4.1	4.3	8.0	3.0	4.0
Services	51.4	61.0	61.0	72.0	78.0

Sources: *1991 Census, Employment in Bedfordshire* (Bedfordshire County Council Planning Department, 1995); *Luton 2000 – Succeeding with Enterprise* (Luton Borough Council, 1993), p. 15; *Quarterly Economic Bulletin* (Luton Borough Council Research & Intelligence Team, Dept. of Environment and Regeneration, March 2002).

In the face of the decline of manufacturing in the town, what occupies the working population in 2002? Unemployment in Luton is higher (just below 4 per cent) than the very low average for the South East (1.7 per cent), the national average of 3.1 per cent, and the average for Bedfordshire (2.4 per cent).[36] Industry was the traditional employment for a considerable number of immigrants who would take unskilled and semi-skilled jobs on the assembly lines. With the drying up of those occupations there is little alternative employment for this group and it is not surprising that unemployment is high among immigrant groups especially ethnic minorities which have grown considerably in the town over the past 30 years. However, of those in employment only 14 per cent are from black and Asian groups, which is a positive sign for the future.[37]

The single biggest employer now is Luton Airport which has grown considerably over the past 20 years with the increasing popularity of foreign travel, including package flights and individual flights in the much cheaper economy areas. The no frills travel to European and other close destinations has seen a marked increase in popularity. Easy Jet has its operational head-quarters at the airport and the number of airport service suppliers has increased employment prospects considerably in Luton. Another large employer is Luton University which has grown considerably in the 1990s at the urging of successive governments to expand higher education. Serving a large student population also stimulates many other employment prospects in the town,

[36] *Quarterly Economic Bulletin* (Luton Borough Council, Research and Intelligence Team, Dept. of Environment and Regeneration, June 2002).
[37] *1991 Census of Employment in Bedfordshire* (Bedfordshire County Council Planning Dept., 1995), p. 25.

including property renting, retailing, leisure activities and other services. A third large employer is obviously Luton Borough Council and other public sector local government agencies. These include local public administration, education, social services, health and social work and numerous other services provided by public and private organisations.

However, a noticeable trend in the private sector has been the decline of large bureaucratic organisations in favour of small business units. This type of organisation is particularly common in financial services and information technology which has witnessed considerable growth both locally and nationally over the past decade. Even manufacturing, which still remains above the national average in Luton in employment terms, has followed this trend. The high-tech new parks being developed, such as Capability Green on the southern edge of town, have contributed to employment prospects, and firms such as Interbrew, Astra Zeneca, Ernst & Young, Nacano, Barclays, Anritsu, Regus have opened operations there.

In these ways, Luton has followed the national trend with a decline in manufacturing and a rise in the service economy. Whether this can provide the employment needed by the local population, only time will tell. At the time of writing, however, there is great concern over the decline in population growth in Britain and the rest of Europe. Who will support our aging population when a considerable part of the workforce reaches retirement? The projected figures for the Luton labour force indicate a decline from 87,100 in 2001 to 86,100 in 2011.[38] If this is the case then we will need our unemployed to fill these employment gaps.

Another optimistic factor in Luton's favour is its geographical position. On a main railway line, near to the M1 motorway, close to London and the Midlands it is in a prime position to prosper, and, as at times in the past, it is coping with a phase of transition from which it will undoubtedly emerge well.

---

[38] *Quarterly Economic Bulletin* (Luton Borough Council, Research and Intelligence Team, Dept. of Environment and Regeneration, September 2001).

Appendix A

Managing Directors of Vauxhall

1857 Alexander Wilson founded Alexander Wilson and Co. at the Vauxhall Iron Works on Wandsworth Road. The company became known locally as the Vauxhall Iron Works.

1892 A limited liability Company was formed. Mr Gardener came in as Managing Director

1894 Alexander Wilson left the Company.

1895 Receiver appointed J.H. Chambers, subsequently joined the Board.

1896 Name of firm changed to Vauxhall Iron Works Company Limited.

1903 Chambers resigned and Percy Kidner became joint Managing Director with W. Gardener.

1905 Vauxhall Iron Works moved to Luton.

1906 Amalgamated with neighbour, West Hydraulic Engineering Company Limited. New firm called Vauxhall and West Hydraulic Engineering Company Limited.

1907 Vauxhall Motors Limited formed. Lesley Walton and Percy Kidner joint Managing Directors.

1914 Firm re-constituted and re-capitalised under the name Vauxhall Motors (1914) Limited. Walton and Kidner joint Managing Directors. Walton appointed Chairman after death of John Maitland.

1925 General Motors purchased ailing Vauxhall Motors.

1928 Kidner and A.J. Hancock resigned.

1929 Charles Bartlett became Managing Director.

1953 Walter Hill replaced Sir Charles Bartlett (June).

1955 Philip C. Copelin replaced Hill (July).

1961 William Swallow replaced Copelin (April).

1966 David L. Hegland replaced Swallow (January).

1970 Alexander D. Rhea replaced Hegland (October).

1974 Walter R. Price replaced Rhea (April).

1979 Ferdinand P. Beickler replaced Price (August).

1982 John M. Fleming replaced Beickler (February).

1986 John G. Bagshaw replaced Fleming (February).

1987 Paul J. Tosch replaced Bagshaw (November).

1991 William A. Ebbert replaced Tosch (September).

1992 Charles E. Golden replaced Ebbert (June).

1996 Nick Reilly replaced Golden (April).

2001 Kevin E. Wale replaced Reilly (July).

2002 Car production ends at Luton site (21 March).

Biographies of Sir Charles Bartlett and Sir Reginald Pearson appear in:
Len Holden, 'Bartlett, Sir Charles John,' *Dictionary of Business Biography* (London: Butterworths, 1985), vol. 1.
Len Holden 'Pearson, Sir James Reginald,' *Dictionary of Business Biography* (London: Butterworths, 1985) vol. 4.

Appendix B

Luton and Bedford Companies
referred to in the book

Vauxhall
Established in Luton in1905. Product: motor cars. Joined EEF 1907, left in 1921.

Adamant Engineering
Established in 1919. Product: steering gear for motor vehicles. Joined EEF in 1937.

W.H. Allen
Established in 1894. Products: pumps and electric generators. Joined EEF in 1913. Had been the largest Bedford firm.

Commer Cars
Established in 1906. Product: commercial motor vehicles. Joined EEF in 1911.

Davis Gas Stove Company
Established in 1895. Products: gas stoves, radiators and general castings. Joined EEF in 1941.

Electrolux
Established in Luton in 1926. Products: vacuum cleaners and refrigerators. Joined EEF in 1941.

George Kent
Established in 1906. Products: water, gas and steam meters. Joined EEF in 1920.

Hayward-Tyler
Established in 1871. Products: soda syphon machinery and general engineering. Joined EEF in 1903.

Laporte Chemicals
Established in 1898. Transferred from Shipley, Yorkshire. Manufactured hydrogen peroxide used in the bleaching process in the hat trade amongst other products.

Percival Aircraft
Established in 1936. Product: light aircraft. Joined EEF in 1941.

Skefko *(later SKF)*
Established 1910. Product: ball bearings. Joined EEF in 1915.

Appendix C

Explanation of Conference Terms

The following terms are used in relation to conferences between the Engineering Employers' Federation and trade unions

A **Works Conference** literally took place on the works premises and would usually involve the management, shop stewards, convenor and, on occasions, the union area full time official.

A **Local Conference** took place when the dispute could not be resolved at shopfloor level or factory level. This would involve BEEA officials and local union officials as well as the management and men of the firm involved. Evidence would be presented and usually recorded verbatim.

Central Conference was the final stage in the process when 'a failure to agree' had been recorded at the local conference. These meetings usually took place at York and to a lesser extent at London. National level officials of union and employers would conduct the proceedings and present evidence. The proceedings were recorded verbatim.

Bibliography

Primary Sources

Archival sources in Luton and Bedfordshire

Vauxhall Archives, Luton:
Reports to the Directors 1914–1950
'Vauxhall Facts and Figures' (Vauxhall Motors typescript, 1966)
Employment and Wage Grade Sheets 1938–50
Bound Volumes of *General Motors News*
Vauxhall–Bedford Mirror
Vauxhall–Bedford News

Bedfordshire County Record Office Archives – Local Collection
Luton Museum Archives – Local collection
Luton Reference Library – Local collection
NUVB Minute Book Luton no. 1 Branch 1942–55
Luton Trades Council Minute Book 1931–1933
Home Counties Federation Trades Union Minute Book 1927–1937
Luton Chamber of Commerce Minute Books 1877–1885

Mid-Anglian EEF Archives, Sandy, Beds.

Luton Engineering Employers' Association Minute Books 1916–1920
Bedfordshire Engineering Employers' Association Minute Books 1919–1951
Bedford Engineering Employers' Association Minute Books 1916–1920
BEEA Annual Reports 1938–1950
Membership Box Files 1915–1950 for Adamant, Commer, Davis, Electrolux, Kent, Percival, SKF etc.

In London and elsewhere

PRO, BT 31: file for Vauxhall
EEF Archives: Membership files Local and National disputes, Verbatim Records
Companies House Vauxhall File no. 135767
AUEW Archives: Monthly Journals and Quarterly Reports
TUC Archives: Luton Trades Council Annual Reports 1930, 1932, 1940, 1941; Luton Divisional Organisers Reports 1922–1923
Bartlett–Young Letters 1942–1943, The Young Papers, MSS 242: T:2
Modern Records Centre, University of Warwick
Vauxhall Collection, National Motor Museum Archives, Beaulieu
Veteran and Vintage Car Club, Library and Archives

Primary printed sources

Population Censuses for the County of Bedfordshire 1901, 1911, 1921, 1931, 1951, 1961, 1971, 1981, 1991 (HMSO)
National Register, Statistics of Population (HMSO, Sept. 1939)
Census of England and Wales 1931, Industries and Classification Tables, vol. III (HMSO, 1933)
Census of England and Wales 1951, Occupation and Classification Tables (HMSO, 1953)

Secondary Sources

Periodicals

Amalgamated Engineering Union Monthly Journal
Amalgamated Engineering Union Quarterly Reports
Amalgamated Society of Engineers' Monthly Journal
Autocar
Automobile Engineer
Beds and Herts Saturday Telegraph (cited as *Luton Saturday Telegraph*)
Beds and Herts Tuesday Telegraph (cited as *Luton Tuesday Telegraph*)
British Management Review
British Journal of Industrial Relations
Bus Fayre
Business History
Commercial Motor
Daily Mail
Daily Telegraph
Dunstable Gazette
East Midland Geographer
Economist
The Engineer
Engineering
Financial Times
Flight
George Kent News
General Motors News
Guardian
History Workshop Journal
Independent
Investors' Chronicle
Investors' Monthly Manual
Journal of Industrial Economics
Journal of Transport History
Labour Gazette
Laporte Quarterly
Luton Chamber of Commerce Journal 1919–1927, 1947–1955
Luton News
The Motor
National Union of Vehicle Builders' Quarterly Journal
Oral History Journal
Proceedings of the Institute of Automobile Engineers (*PIAE*)

Proceedings of the Institute of Production Engineers (*PIPE*)
Quarterly Economic Bulletin
Solidarity
The Times
Vauxhall–Bedford News
Vauxhall Mirror

Articles

Bartlett, Sir Charles, 'Management and Productivity', *British Management Review* (1948)

Bishop, G., 'Humber: Quality and Comfort before Performance' in I. Ward (ed.), *The World of Automobiles* (undated, late 1970s)

Bishop, G., 'Sunbeam: Milestones of Motoring History' in I. Ward (ed.), *The World of Automobiles: An Illustrated Encyclopaedia of the Motor Car* (undated, late 1970s)

Brown, Michael, ' "The Big Six", 3: Luton Spectacular – Vauxhall', *Autocar* 12 July 1957

Church, Roy, 'The Marketing of Automobiles in Britain and the United States before 1939' in Okochi and Shimokawa (eds.), *Proceedings of the 7th Conference on Business History* (Tokyo, 1980)

Church, Roy, 'Myths, Men and Motor Cars: A Review Article', *The Journal of Transport History* vol. IV, no. 2 (Sept. 1977)

Church, Roy, and Michael Miller, 'The Big Three: Competition, Management and Marketing in the British Motor Industry, 1922–39' in B. Supple (ed.), *Development of the Firm: Essays in Business History* (Oxford, 1977)

Claydon, T., 'Images of Disorder: Car Worker's Militancy and the Representation of Industrial Relations in Britain 1950–1979' in D. Thoms, L. Holden and T. Claydon (eds.), *The Motor Car and Popular Culture in the 20th Century* (Aldershot: Ashgate, 1998)

Copelin, P.W., 'Development and Organisation of Vauxhall Motors Limited' in Edwards & Townsend (eds.), *Studies in Business Organisation* (1961)

Daniel, G., 'Some Factors Affecting the Movement of Labour', *Oxford Economic Papers* (1940)

Dony, J.G., 'The 1919 Peace Riots in Luton', *Bedfordshire Historical Record Society* vol. 57 (Bedford, 1978)

Excell, Arthur, 'Morris Motors in the 1930s', *History Workshop Journal* issue 6 (Autumn 1978)

Excell, Arthur, 'Morris Motors in the 1930s Part Two', *History Workshop Journal* issue 7 (Spring 1979)

Excell, Arthur, 'Morris Motors in the 1940s', *History Workshop Journal* issue 9 (Spring 1980)

Fridenson, Patrick, 'The Coming of the Assembly Line to Europe' in Krohn, Layton and Weingart (eds.), *The Dynamics of Science and Technology*, Sociology of the Sciences vol. 11 (Dordrecht, 1978)

Hancock, A.J., 'Presidential Address', *Proceedings of the Institute of Automobile Engineers* vol. XXX (1935)

Hancock, E.W., 'A Lifetime in Automobile Production', *Automobile Engineer* vol. 50, no. 6 (June 1960)

Hancock, E.W., 'The Trend of Modern Production Methods', *PIPE* vol. VII, no. 2 (1927–28)

Holden, Len, ' "Think of Me Simply as the Skipper": Industrial Relations at Vauxhall 1900–1950', *Oral History* vol. 9, no. 2 (1981)

Holden, Len, 'Bartlett, Sir Charles John', *Dictionary of Business Biography*, Vol. 1 (London: Butterworths, 1985)

Holden, Len, 'Pearson, Sir James Reginald', *Dictionary of Business Biography*, Vol. 4 (London: Butterworths, 1985)

Holtom, T.W., 'Memories of Vauxhall', *Beds and Herts Saturday Telegraph* (23 November 1935; 3 April 1936)

Jackson, P., and K. Sisson, 'Employers Federations in Sweden and the U.K. and the Significance of the Industrial Infrastructure', *British Journal of Industrial Relations* vol. XIV, no. 3 (1976)

Jones, D.T., and S.J. Prais, 'Plant Size and Productivity in the Motor Industry: Some International Comparisons', *Oxford Bulletin of Economic Statistics* vol. 40, no. 2 (May 1978)

Keens, Thomas, 'Luton as an Industrial Centre', *Engineering* (April 1900)

Law, C.M., 'Luton and the Hat Industry', *East Midland Geographer* vol. 4, no. 30 (December 1968)

Lyddon, D., 'Workplace Organisation in the British Car Industry: A Critique of Jonathan Zeitlin', *History Workshop Journal* no. 15 (Spring 1983)

Maxcy, G., 'The Motor Industry' in Cook (ed.), *The Effects of Mergers* (1958)

Miller, M., and R.A. Church, 'Motor Manufacturing' in N.K. Buxton and D. Aldcroft (eds.), *British Industry between the Wars* (Scolar, 1979)

Palmer, B., 'Class, Conception and Conflict: The Thrust for Efficiency, A Managerial View of Labor', *Review of Radical Political Economy* (1975)

Pearson, Sir Reginald, 'From Group Bonus to Straight Time Pay', *Journal of Industrial Economics* (October 1960)

Pomeroy, L.H. (Snr), 'Automobile Engineering and the War', *PIAE* vol. IX (1914)

Rhys, D.G., 'Concentration in the Inter-War Motor Industry', *The Journal of Transport History* vol. 111, no. 4 (1976)

Saul, S.B., 'The Motor Industry in Britain to 1914', *Business History* vol. V (1962)

Silberston, A., 'The Motor Industry' in Burns (ed.), *The Structure of British Industry* (1958)

'Spartacus', 'The New Vauxhall Agreement', *Solidarity* vol. 4, no. 11 (January 1968)

'Spartacus', 'Vauxhall Follow Up', *Solidarity* vol. 5, no. 1 (May 1968)

Vigor, P.C., 'Putting the Worker in the Picture' in Blaney Thomas (ed.), *Welfare in Industry* (1949)

Weller, Ken, 'The Truth about Vauxhall', *Solidarity* no. 12 (1968)

Zeitlin, J., 'The Emergence of Shop Steward Organisation and Job Control in the British Car Industry: A Review Essay', *History Workshop Journal* issue 10 (Autumn 1980)

Books

Abercrombie, Patrick, *The Greater London Plan* (HMSO, 1945)

Adeney, M., *The Motor Makers: The Turbulent History of Britain's Car Industry* (London: Collins, 1988)

Aldcroft, D.H., *The Inter-War Economy: Britain 1919–1939* (London: Batsford, 1920)

Aldcroft, D.H., and H. Richardson, *The British Economy 1870–1939* (London: Macmillan, 1969)

Alford, B.W.E., *Depression and Recovery? British Economic Growth 1918–1939* (London: Macmillan, 1972)

Bannock, Graham, *The Juggernauts: The Age of the Big Corporation* (Harmondsworth: Pelican, 1971)

Beynon, Huw, *Working for Ford* (Harmondsworth: Allen Lane, 1973)

Bloomfield, Gerald, *The World Automotive Industry* (Newton Abbott: David and Charles, 1978)

Boyer, R.O., and H.M. Morris, *Labor's Untold Story* (New York, 1955)

Braverman, Harry, *Labor and Monopoly Capital* (New York: Monthly Review Press, 1974)

Broatch, Stuart Fergus, *Vauxhall* (Stroud, Glos.: Sutton Publishing Co., 1997)

Bunker, Stephen, *Strawopolis: Luton Transformed 1840–1876*, Bedfordshire Historical Record Society vol. 78 (Bedford, 1999)

Castle, H.G., *Britain's Motor Industry* (London: Clerke & Cocheran, 1950)

Chandler, Alfred D., *Giant Enterprise* (New York, 1974)

Chandler, Alfred D., *Strategy and Structure: Chapters in the History of American Industrial Enterprise* (Cambridge, Mass.: MIT Press, 1962)

Church, Roy, *Herbert Austin: The British Motor Car Industry to 1941* (London: Europa, 1979)

Church, Roy *The Rise and Decline of the British Motor Industry* (Basingstoke: Macmillan, 1994)

Clutton, C., and J. Stanford, *The Vintage Motor Car* (London: Batsford, 1961; paperback edition)

Cockman, F.G., *The Railway Age in Bedfordshire* (Bedford, 1974)

Constantine, Stephen, *Unemployment between the Wars* (London: Longman, 1980)

Cook, C., and J. Stevenson, *The Longman Handbook of Modern History, 1714–1918* (London: Longman, 1983)

Cook, P. Lesley, *The Effects of Mergers* (1958)

Croucher, Richard, *Engineers at War, 1939–1945* (London: Merlin, 1982)

Derbyshire, L.C., *The Story of Vauxhall 1837–1946* (Luton, 1946)

Donner, Frederic G., *The World Wide Industrial Enterprise: Its Challenge and Response* (New York: McGraw-Hill, 1967)

Dony, J.G., *A History of Education in Luton* (Luton, 1970)

Dony, J.G., *A History of the Straw Hat Trade* (Luton, 1942)

Dyer, J. and J.G. Dony, *The Story of Luton* (Luton, 1964; 3rd edition 1975)

Edwardes, Michael, *Back from the Brink* (London: Collins, 1983)

Empire Trade League, *Progressive Luton* (Luton, 1933)

Ensor, James, *The Motor Industry* (London: Longman, 1971)

Fletcher & Son Ltd., *The Motor Car Index 1918–1929* (Norwich, 1929)

Ford, Henry, with Samuel Crowther, *My Life and Work* (1922; 7th ed. London: Heinemann, 1924)

Friedman, A.L., *Industry and Labour* (London: Macmillan, 1977)

Garside, W.R., *The Measurement of Unemployment in Great Britain 1850–1979: Sources and Methods* (Oxford, 1980)

George Kent Limited, *The George Kent Centenary 1838–1939* (Luton, 1938)

Glynn, S., and J. Oxborrow, *Inter-War Britain: A Social and Economic History* (London: Allen and Unwin, 1976)

Goldthorpe, J.H., D. Lockwood, F. Bechhofer and J. Platt, *The Affluent Worker, Volume 1: Industrial Attitudes and Behaviour* (Cambridge: Cambridge University Press, 1968)

Goldthorpe, J.H., D. Lockwood, F. Bechhofer and J. Platt, *The Affluent Worker, Volume 2: Political Attitudes and Behaviour* (Cambridge: Cambridge University Press, 1968)

Goldthorpe, J.H., D. Lockwood, F. Bechhofer and J. Platt, *The Affluent Worker Volume 3 in the Class Structure* (Cambridge: Cambridge University Press, 1969)

Gray, Robert, *Rolls on the Docks: The History of Rolls Royce* (Salisbury, 1971)

Grundy, F., and B.M. Titmus, *Report on Luton* (Luton, 1945)

Hartnett, L.J., *Big Wheels and Little Wheels* (1965)

Hayward & Tyler Limited, *A Short History of the Company* (Luton, 1976)

Hopkins, Harry, *The New Look: A Social History of the Forties and Fifties* (1963)

Hunting Group, *The History of Percival Aircraft* (Aylesbury, 1951)

Jeffries, J.B., *The Story of the Engineers* (1945)

Karslake, K. and L. Pomeroy (Jnr), *From Veteran to Vintage* (1956)

Keller, Maryann, *Collision: GM, Toyota, Volkswagen and the Race to Own the 21st Century* (New York: Currency Doubleday, 1993)

Kennet, Pat, *The Foden Story* (Cambridge, 1978)

Kennett, David H., *Portrait of Bedfordshire* (Bedford, 1978)

Laporte Chemicals Ltd, *The House of Laporte 1888–1947* (Luton, 1947)

Laporte Chemicals Ltd, *The Laporte Apprenticeship Scheme* (Luton, 1953)

Lovell, John, *British Trade Unions 1875–1933* (London: Macmillan, 1977)

Luton & District Trades Council, *Trade Union Membership Drive* (Luton, 1949)

Luton Gas Company, *100 Years Service* (Luton, 1934)

Luton Water Company, *A History of the Luton Water Company 1865–1965* (Luton, 1965)

Marsden, D., T. Morris, P. Willman and S. Wood, *The Car Industry: Labour Relations and Industrial Adjustment* (London: Tavistock, 1985)

Marsh, Arthur, *Industrial Relations in Engineering* (Oxford, 1965)

Maxcy, G., and A. Silberston, *The Motor Industry* (1959)

McMillan, J., and B. Harris, *The American Take-over of Britain* (1968)

Millott-Severn, J., *The Life Story of a Phrenologist* (Brighton, 1929)

Montagu, Lord Montagu of Beaulieu, *Lost Causes of Motoring* (1960)

Mooney, J.D., *The Principles of Organisation* (New York: Harper, 1947)

Overy, R.J., *William Morris: Viscount Nuffield* (London: Europa, 1976)

Peters, P., and H. Thornton Rutter (eds.) *Who's Who in the Motor Trade* (1934)

Platt, Maurice, *An Addiction to Automobiles* (London: Warne, 1980)

Plowden, William, *The Motor Car and Politics* (Harmondsworth: Penguin, 1971)

Pomeroy, Laurence (Jnr), *The Grand Prix Car 1906–1939* (1949)

Rhys, D.G., *The Motor Industry: An Economic Survey* (London: Butterworth, 1972)

Richardson, K., *The British Motor Industry: A Social and Economic History 1896–1939* (London: Macmillan, 1977)

Scott-Moncrieff, David, *Veteran and Edwardian Cars* (London: Batsford, 1955)

Sedgwick, Michael, *Vauxhall: A Pictorial Tribute* (London: Beaulieu Books, 1981)

Seth-Smith, Michael, *The Long Haul: A Social History of the British Commercial Vehicle Industry* (1975)

Seymour, W.J., *An Account of our Stewardship* (Luton: Vauxhall Motors Ltd, 1946)

Skefko Limited, *The First 50 Years, 1910–1960* (Luton: Skefco, 1960)

Sloan, Alfred P., *My Years with General Motors* (London: Sidgwick and Jackson, 1965)

Stern, E., *The Bedfordshire County Development Plan* (Bedford: Beds. County Council, 1952)

Turner, Graham, *The Car Makers* (Harmondsworth: Penguin, 1963)

Turner, H.A., G. Clark and G. Roberts, *Labour Relations in the Motor Industry* (London: Allen and Unwin, 1967)

Ullyett, Kenneth, *The Vauxhall Companion* (London: Stanley Paul, 1971)

Vauxhall Motors Ltd, *Bedford Buses and Coaches since 1931* (Luton, 1979)

Vauxhall Motors Ltd, *The Car Super Excellent: The Catalogue of the Vauxhall Motor Carriage* (Luton, 1914)

Vauxhall Motors Ltd, *A History of Vauxhall* (Luton, 1980)

Vauxhall Motors Ltd, *IBC Vehicles: Home to the Vivaro and Frontera* (Luton, 2001)

Vauxhall Motors Ltd, *The Story of the Churchill Tank* (Luton, undated)

Vauxhall Motors Ltd, *This is Vauxhall* (Luton: Vauxhall Public Relations Dept., 1966)

Vauxhall Motors Ltd, *Vauxhall Cars since 1903* (Luton, 1973)

Vauxhall Motors Ltd, *Vauxhall Motor Carriages* (Luton, 1911)

Vauxhall Education Service, *The Vauxhall Story* (Luton: Vauxhall Motors Ltd, 2001)

Vauxhall Motors Ltd, *You See Them Everywhere: Bedford Commercial Vehicles since 1931* (Luton, 1979)

Ward, I. (ed.), *The World of Automobiles: An Illustrated Encyclopaedia of the Motor Car* (undated, late 1970s)

Whisler, Timothy R. *The British Motor Industry, 1945–94: A Case Study in Industrial Decline* (Oxford: Oxford University Press, 1999)

Whiting, R.C., *The View from Cowley: The Impact of Industrialisation upon Oxford 1915–1939* (Oxford: Oxford University Press, 1983)

Who's Who (1963)

Who's Who in the Motor Industry (London: Temple Press, 1963)

Who Was Who, Vol. V: 1951–1960

Wighan, Eric, *The Power to Manage: A History of the Engineering Employers' Federation* (London: Macmillan, 1973)

Wyatt, R.J., *The Austin Seven: The Motor for the Million* (Newton Abbott: David and Charles, 1968)

Zweig, Ferdynand, *The Worker in the Affluent Society* (London: Heinemann, 1961)

Theses and dissertations

Bassill, Phillip, 'The City on the Hill: Municipal Housing Policy in Luton 1918–1950' (unpublished B.A. Dissertation, University of Sheffield, 1976)

Bonsall, J., 'The Derby Borough Development Committee 1906–1933' (unpublished Ph.D. thesis, Nottingham University, 1975)

Chamberlain, John, 'The Development of the Trade Union Movement and Labour Movement in Luton, from 1904 till the General Strike 1926' (unpublished dissertation, Luton College of Technology, 1972)

Holme, A., 'Some Aspects of the British Motor Manufacturing Industry during the Years 1919 to 1930s' (unpublished M.A. thesis, University of Sheffield, 1964)

Pinder, D.A., 'The Luton Hat Industry: Aspects of the Development of a Localised Trade' (unpublished Ph.D. thesis, University of Southampton, 1970)

Smithies, E.D., 'The Contrast between North and South in England 1918–1939: A Study of Economic, Social and Political Problems with particular reference to the experience of Burnley, Halifax, Ipswich and. Luton' (unpublished Ph.D. Thesis, University of Leeds, 1974)

Whiting R.C., 'The Working Class in the "New Industry" Towns between the Wars: The Case of Oxford' (unpublished D.Phil. thesis, Oxford University, 1977)

Seminar papers

Claydon, Tim, 'Trade Union Recruiting Strategies in the Car Industry 1920–50' (unpublished paper presented at the London School of Economics Car Workers' Group, 4 December 1981)

Fishman, Nina, 'The Problem of Trade Union Organisation at Dagenham 1933–45' (unpublished seminar paper presented at King's College Research Centre, Cambridge, February 1981)

Lewchuk, Wayne, 'Management Control in the British Car Industry 1900–1920s' (unpublished seminar paper, London School of Economics Car Group, March 1981)

Lewchuk, Wayne, 'Technology, Pay Systems and Motor Companies' (unpublished seminar paper presented to the SSRC Conference on Business and Labour History, London School of Economics, February 1981)

Littler, Craig, 'Rationalisation and Worker Resistance in Britain between the Wars' (unpublished seminar paper presented at King's College Research Centre, Cambridge, February 1981)

Tolliday, Steven, 'Government, Employers and Shop Floor Organisation in the British Motor Industry, 1939–1969' (unpublished seminar paper presented at King's College Research Centre, Cambridge, September 1982)

Tolliday, Steven, 'Management Strategy and Shop Floor Organisation: Standard and Austin Motors 1920–1960' (unpublished seminar paper presented at King's College Research Centre, Cambridge, November 1981)

Taped interviews

Adair, Tom (Jock), assembly line worker 1938–1960 (interviewed April 1981)

Bates, Eric, Engineering Records Office, Vauxhall, 1930–1979 (interviewed March 1980)

Burns, Keith, tool maker, Vauxhall, 1942–1980 (interviewed January 1982)

Cowell, Les, capstan operator, Vauxhall, 1937–1978 (interviewed March 1980)

Dalley, Sid, body shop worker, Vauxhall, 1933–1970s (interviewed by Steve Tolliday, June 1981)

Davies, Glyn, Press Officer, Vauxhall, 1935–1979 (interviewed July 1978)

Horne, Harold, Convenor AUEW, Vauxhall, 1940–1968 (interviewed July 1978)

Morgan, Glyn, tool maker, began at Vauxhall in 1940, AUEW Convenor (interviewed December 1979)

Pearson, Sir Reginald, Director Vauxhall Motors, worked at Vauxhall 1919–1962 (interviewed February 1979)

Reed, Ernie, body shop worker, Vauxhall, 1939–1920s (interviewed by Steve Tolliday, June 1981)

Smith, Fred, rivetter, Vauxhall, 1935–1979 (interviewed March 1980)

Smith, Don (Jock) and Eve, assembly line workers, Vauxhall, 1938–1944 (interviewed March 1981)

Tylee, Bill, vehicle builder in body shop, Vauxhall, 1933–1970s (interviewed by Steve Tolliday, June 1981)

Vigor, Peter, Editor of *Vauxhall Mirror*, began work at Vauxhall in 1927 and from 1940 until 1978 (interviewed October 1978)

West, Jack, started with General Motors, Hendon, 1920 and stayed with Vauxhall until 1962, foreman in body shop (interviewed January 1981)

Unpublished printed sources

Chrysler UK Ltd, 'Dodge Trucks and Chrysler UK Ltd – A Brief History', PR Dept. typescript (Luton, 1979)

Electrolux Ltd, 'Electrolux – Historical Notes', PR Dept. typescript (Luton, 1977)

General Motors Ltd, 'About General Motors Corporation', PR Dept. typescript (London, 1977)

General Motors Ltd, 'About General Motors Ltd', PR Dept. typescript (London, 1977)

George Kent Ltd, 'George Kent, 1838 to Today', PR Dept. typescript (Luton, 1979)

Laporte Group, 'A Brief History of the Laporte Group', PR Dept. typescript (Luton, 1979)

SKF Ltd, 'History of SKF', PR Dept. typescript (Luton, 1979)

Vauxhall Shop Stewards, 'Vauxhall Shop Stewards AUEW Contact', 4th ed., AEU–NUVB–ETU (Vauxhall, Luton, June 1966)

Index

Please note: references to tables and chart numbers are in italics; those to illustrations are in bold type.

A.B.B. 225
Abercrombie, *Prof.* Patrick 155
Abercrombie Plan 155
Absenteeism 196
A.C. Cars Ltd. 19
A.C. Delco European Replacement Parts Operation 52, 54, 57
Acreage, *178 Table 39. See also* Floor Space
Acres, F.A. 151
AC Spark Plug Company 35
Accident Scheme 197
Adair, Tom 'Jock' 129–30, 152–3, 193
Adamant Engineering 164–6, 231
Adam Opel 31, 173
Adams Motors 21
Admiralty 1, 17
Advertising/Advertisements 32, 67, 69, 71, 83, 108, *Chart 1*
Aeronauts 67
Africa, East 78, South 85
Aircraft 104, 131, 143, 146, 148, 151, 199, 231
Albania 78
Alcock (Peroxide) Ltd. 146
Alden, John 190
Alexandra Palace 73
Allen, *Mr.* 106
Allen, W.H. 231
Allens Engineering Company 161
Allenby, *General* 17
Amalgamated Engineering Union (AEU) 102, 105–10, 117, 121, 125–7, 129–31, 164–9, 176, 194, *Tables 24, 26, 27*
Amalgamated Society of Engineers (ASE) 5, 88–9, 92, 101, 104
Amalgamated Society of Joiners and Carpenters 88
Amalgamated Society of Railway Servants 88
Amalgamated Union of Engineering Workers (AUEW) 120, 176, 193
America, South 78
America, United States of, 28–36, 38, 40, 43, 51, 55, 59–61, 64, 66, 69–70, 74, 76, 78–9, 81–4, 102, 134–5, 173, 177, 179–81, 187–92, 194, 200, 203, 205, 208, 210, 213–16, 218, 220, 222. *See also* Detroit and Flint
American Chamber of Commerce 80
Ampthill 186
Annual Reports, Vauxhall Motors 86
Anritsu 226
Antwerp, Belgium 221
Apprentices 19, 92, 111

Arabia/Arabian 78, 204
Argyll [car manufacturer] 3, 11
Army, Armed Forces 92, 101
Ash, Alfred E. 2, 5, 12, 90
Asia, East 217, 221
Assembly Line/Conveyor Belt 24, 37, 42, 48, 50, 68, 114, 116–17, 123, 125, 129, 157, 171, 192, 194, 196, 213–14, 225, **Plate 42**
Assets, Vauxhall Motors 63, *Table 18*
Aster and White and Poppe 11
Astra Zeneca 226
Austin, Herbert 26, 29
Austin 15, 19–20, 24, 27, 29–31, 37–8, 40, 42, 45, 47, 52, 54, 56–7, 60–4, 66, 69, 73, 76, 115, 123, 128, 172–3, 203. Vehicles: Austin Seven: 20, 38; Austin Morris: 20; Austin 12: 38, 41; Austin 16: 39; 10hp: 40; 12hp: 40
Austin Advocate 69
Austin-Nuffield 57
Automatic Dutch Auction 75
Automation 213, 216
Auto Motor Journal 12
Automobile Engineer 24, 113
Australia 68, 85–6, 189, 214
AWD 218

Bagshaw, John G. 230
Bakers 73
Ball Bearings 142, 146, 231
Balmforth and Company 141
Bank overdraft 19
Bankruptcy/Insolvency 26–7, 44, 69, 204, 218
Barclays 226
Barlow Commission 155
Barnes, *Mr.* 89
Barrow-in-Furness 137
Bartlett, *Sir* Charles John 34, 36–7, 40–1, 43, 50, 52, 54–5, 57–9, 76, 84, 86–7, 117–19, 121–3, 129–36, 152, 162, 170, 173–5, 186–91, 194, 196–7, 201, 229
Basingstoke 11
Batch Production 93
Bates, Eric 34, 39
Bath Technical College 34
Beaverbrook, *Lord* 74, 130
Bedaux System 112
Bedford 21, 73, 103, 116, 152, 159–61, 170, 231
Bedford Engineering Company 160

Bedford Engineering Employers' Association (BEEA) 103, 159–60
Bedfordshire, 72–3, 124, 149, 160, 171, 225, *Chart 2, Table 36*
Bedfordshire Engineering Employers' Association (BEEA) 103, 106, 112, 116–19, 156, 159–60, 166–71, 176, 232, *Tables 37 and 38*
Beickler, Ferdinand P. 230
Belgium/Belgian 85, 212, 222
Bentley 13, 26
Bicycles 67, 137
'Big Three' 54
'Big Six' 34, 37, 52, 57, 86, 118, 173, 186, 217
Birmingham 88, 101, 125, 146
Bisgood, *Mr.* 30
BL *see* British Leyland Motor Corporation
Blair, Tony 220
Bleaching 139, 141, 231
Blockmakers 139
BMC 57, 128, 193
Boaters 140
Body Building Shop/Assemblers, Vauxhall Motors **iv**, 48, 50, 129, 165, **Plate I**
Body Shell 173
Boiler Water Feeders/Boilers 1, 141
Bonus Payments/System 102, 106, 113–16, 119, 121, 130, 135, 160, 162–3, 168–70, 174, 193, 195, 197. *See also* Group Bonus System
Bourgeois 200
Bradford, Yorkshire 5, 89, 90, 142
Brick Industry 140
Britain/British 32, 35, 43, 69, 72–6, 81–4, 86, 112, 125, 134, 136, 149, 177, 179, 186, 188–9, 191–2, 194–5, 200, 203, 208, 213–14, 218, 222
'British Disease' 203
British Dominions/Empire 30–32, 45, 77, 80–2, 85–6, 173, 187
British Gelatine Company 142
British Leyland Motor Corporation (BLMC) later British Leyland (BL) 44–5, 203–5, 209–13, 217–18 *Table 48*. Vehicles: Metro 211; Mini 211
Brooklands 68
Brown, J. 106–7
Brown Bouvri 225
B.T.H. Company Ltd. 54
Budget 1947, 57
Buick 29, 35, 39, 42, 71, 79
Buildings/Land/Plant 17, 52–3, 62, 155 *Table 16. See also* Griffin House; K Block
Building Trade 140, 199, *Table 45*
Burnley, Lancashire 169
Burns, Keith 131
Buses and Coaches 44, 47–8, 172
'Buy at your own price' 75
'Buy British' 76
Byers, Stephen 220

Cadet 31, 38–40, 43, 45, 48, 59, 69, 82, 173, **Plate 15**
Cadillac 29, 35, 41–3, 51, 71, 179
Cambridgeshire 72
Canada 32, 78–9, 81
Canals: Grand Union 7
Canteen 130, 133, 136, 161, 175, 197
Capital 16, 18–20, 24, 29, 42, 53, 61–2, 111, 173, 187, 191, 210, *Tables 4 and 16*
Capstan Lathes/Operators 101, 106, 116, 119–20, 210
Card Index/Kardex 16, 73
Car Tax 57
Cars 2–3, 6–8, 10, 17, 19, 21–2, 26, 33, 37, 41, 56–7, 82, 178, 181, 200, 205, 209, 231
For specific vehicles see under name of maker
Catalogue 78
Central Conference 232
Central Moulders' Union 88
Chambers, John H. 2–3, 8, 229
Chappell, A.E. 125, 166
Chassis 46, *Table 10*
Chaul End Munitions Factory *see under* Munitions
Chelmsford 112
Chemicals 146, 198–9, *Table 45*
Cheshire 72, *Chart 2*
Chevrolet 29–31, 35, 41–3, 45, 70–1, 79, 84, *Chart I.* Vehicles: Nova 213
China 85
Chrysler 203–4, 209, 215, *Table 48*
Churchill Tanks 52, 55, 86, 129–30, 183
Citroen 29, 221
CKDs (Completely knocked down parts of cars) 28, 42, 81, 85
Clark Machine Tool Company 90, 100
Clarkson, Jeremy 221
Clement [car manufacturer] 11
Closed Shop 131
Closures 108, 113, 116, 220
Clothing Firms *see* Textiles
Coatalen, Louis 13–14, 26
Collective Bargaining 167
Commer Cars 46, 48, 90, 100, 105, 140, 142–3, 146–7, 162, 164, 231, *Tables 31 and 35*
Commercial Cars Ltd. 7, 142, 144
Commercial Motor 83–4, 174
Common Market 208. *See also* Europe
Communist Party 117, 123, 130, 136, 151–2, 164, 193
Components 48, 54, 185
Computerisation 216
Concealed Stitch Machine 139
Confederation of British Industry (CBI) 161
Conferences 105, 157, 168, 232, *Table 38*
Conservative Party 201
Construction Work 140, 225
Conveyor Belt *see* Assembly Line
Copelin, Philip 189–90, 229, **Plate 40**
Coulter Electronics 224
County Development Plan 148

Coventry 7, 88, 101, 123, 125–6, 137–8, 146, 148, 150–1, 161, 170, 195
Cowell, Les 115, 119, 132
Cowley 48
Crewe 137
Cripps, Stafford 57
Crossley Car Company 18–19, 21, 23–5, 26
Crown Agents for Colonies 77
Croydon 8
Cundall Folding Machine Company 145–6
Customer Service/Customers 11, 67, 73
Cyprus 85
Czechoslovakia 184–5, **Plate 37**

DAF 217
Dagenham 38, 40, 50, 54, 60, 221
Daily Mail 105
Daimler Motor Company 3–4, 7, 19, 26
Dalley, Sid 127
Dangerfield, Edmund 32
Datsun 209, *Table 48*
Davies, Glyn 117
Davis, Reg. 71, *Chart 1*
Davis Gas Stove Company 141–3, 147–8, 157, 160, 164, 166, 169, 171, 231, *Tables 31, 34 and 35*
Day Work 113, 162. *See also* Measured Day Work
Dealers/Retailers 69, 77
Debentures 16, 24, 29
Debts 20, 70
Defence of the Realm Act 100
Demonstrations 109
Denmark 85
Dennis, *Sir* Raymond 44
Dennis Motors 5, 11, 44, 46
Department of Trade and Industry 204
Depreciation 61–2, 64
Depression 32, 43, 68, 81–2, 84, 87, 104–5, 109, 131, 135, 137, 144–7, 153, 160–1, 172, 174–5, 199
Derby 212
Derbyshire 132
Deskilling 196
Detroit, U.S.A. 30, 33, 51, 125, 134, 187, 189–90, 211, 222
Devon 72, *Chart 2*
Devonshire and Dorsetshire Regiment 34
Diamond Foundry 89
Dilutees/Dilution 87, 92, 100–2, 104, 167
Direct Control 111, 113, 116
Directors 30, 33
Dismissals 196
Disputes 90, 197
Distribution 67
Dividends 17, 65, *Table 20*
Donner, Frederic G. 66
Downgrading/-sizing 196, 217
Drawing Office/Room 92, 113
Dunstable 53–4, 56, 135–6, 163, 183, 185, 191, 199, 215, 218, 223
Durrant, W.C. 34–5

Durham 72, *Chart 2*
Dyeing 139

Earl, Harley 179, 181
East Anglia *see* England
Easy Jet 225
East London Technical College 11
Ebbert, William A. 230
Economic Development Areas 185
Economics of Installment Selling, The 74
Edinburgh 72 *Chart 2*
Edwardes, Michael 205, 210–11
Efficiency System 113–14, 116, 174
Electricians' Union 194
Egypt 78
Electricity 7
Electrolux 145–8, 155–6, 161, 164, 166–7, 169, 171, 199, 224, 231, *Tables 34 and 35*
Ellesmere Port 136, 183, 185, 197, 207, 214–16, 222–4
Employees *see* Workforce
Engine Assembly Shop 94, **Plate 23**
Engine Tax 179
Engineering/Engineers 92, 101, 125, 131, 140–1, 143–8, 154–8, 160–1, 165, 174–5, 198–9, *Table 45*
Engineering Centre 185
Engineering Employers' Association 104, 163–6. *See also* Bedfordshire Engineering Employers' Association and Luton Engineering Employers' Association
Engineering Employers' Federation (EEF) 5, 89–90, 101–2, 104–8, 113, 116, 127, 157, 159–61, 164–6, 169–71, 174, 195, 231–2
Engines 3, 79. Aeronautical 8, Diesel 185, Donkey 1, Marine 1, 3, 7, 67, 77, 90, Petrol 1, 3, Steam 1
England/English 43, 68, 74, 77, 81; East Anglia 149, 169, *Table 36*; Home Counties 149, 163; Midlands 116, 130, 144, 149, 165, 185, 192, 199, 201, 226, *Table 36*; North/ern 124, 138, 146, 149, 165, 169, *Table 36*, South 149, 165, 185; South East 149–50, 225, *Table 36*; South West 149
English and Scottish Joint CWS Factory 141
Erecting Shop, Vauxhall Motors 95, 98, **Plates 24 and 27**
Ernst and Young 226
Essential Works Order 154, 167, 171
Essex 72, 166, *Chart 2*
Ethnocentric Policy 190
Eton 8
Europe/Europeans 30–1, 38, 55, 74, 78, 81, 85–6, 141, 187, 191, 203, 208, 211–13, 216–17, 220–3, 225
Evans, Bob 33
Everett, Robert 3
Exchequer, Chancellor of 57
Exhibitions 73
Expansion 62, 116, 120, 124, 133, 162–3, 174, 185–6, 210

Exports 38, 55–6, 77–86, 155, 173, 177–9, 208–9, *Tables 21, 22, 23, 39 and 47*

Federation *see* Engineering Employers' Federation
Female Employment *see* Women
Fiat 221
Fieldmen 70–1, 73, 173, *Chart 1*
Films 79, 85
Finishing Shop 129
Fisher, Charlie 30
Fisher, Fred 30
Fisher Body Company 30, 35
Fishing 197
Fitters *see* Machine Fitters
Flanders 78
Flash Welding 53
Fleming, John M. 230
Flint, Michigan 35
Floor Area 19, 21, 41, 52–3, 56, 59, 178, 185, *Tables 2, 5, 9, 13 and 39*
Foden 45
Ford, Henry 26, 35, 40, 47
Ford 19, 24, 26–8, 34–5, 37–40, 42–4, 48, 50, 52, 54, 56–7, 59–61, 66, 68–9, 73–6, 84, 93, 112, 115, 117, 120, 123, 128, 208–9, 214–15, 217, 221–2, *Table 48*. Vehicles: Consul 179; Cortina 214; Eight 173; Model A 40, 59, 173; Model T 15, 40, 43, 45; Model Y (8hp) 40, 59, 173; Sierra 214; 2-ton truck 45–6; Zephyr Six 179
Fordism, Fordist 111, 116, 174, 196
Fordson (Ford) 50
Foremen 90, 92, 107, 111, 113–15, 119, 132
Forge Shop, Vauxhall Motors 93, **Plate 22**
Foundry 141
Fountain, Eric 222
France/French 28–9, 68, 78, 81, 191, 214; Grand Prix 68
Franchise 75–6
Fuel Economy 51
Fuses 17–18
Frigidaire Company 35, 52

'Gadgetsville, U.K.' 200
Gardner, William 2–3, 7, 229, **Plate 2**
'Gaffers' Committees' 123
Gas Stoves 231
Gears/Gearboxes 77, 179, 185, 207, 214; Synchromesh 39, 41, 48, 173, 184, 231
'Gemini' 210–11
General Motors (G.M.) 1, 25, 27–35, 37–8, 41–4, 46–7, 51, 58–9, 61, 65–6, 69–70, 72–7, 80–2, 84, 117, 132, 134, 146, 155, 161–2, 173, 179–82, 186, 189–91, 194, 204, 207–8, 210–11, 213–16, 218, 220–3, 229
General Motors Acceptance Corporation (GMAC) 46, 74, 173
General Motors Export Company 31, 81
General Motors (Hendon) Ltd. 34, 66, 81
General Motors News, The/GM News 69, 72, 74, 77, 173

General Motors Overseas Operations (GMOO) 28–30, 33, 36, 45, 58, 76, 134, 187–90, 210
GM Europe 211–12, 216, 218, 220, 223
GM USA 211
General Strike *see* Strikes
Generators 231
Germany/German 28–9, 31–2, 39, 68, 79, 81–2, 132, 154, 177, 191–2, 207–9, 211–14, 218, 220–2. *See also* Rüsselsheim
Gillies, *Mr.* 164
Glasgow 152, 200
Glasgow to London Run 67
Gloucestershire 34
Golden, Charles E. 230
Government Training Centres 152
Grading Appeals Committee 195
Grant, Richard 69–70, 74–5
Great Depression *see* Depression
Greece 78
Greenock 200
Griffin House 190, **Plate 41**
Grosvenor 50
Group Bonus System 114–16, 119–21, 132, 135–6, 152, 174–5, 191–2, 194
Guildford, Surrey 5

Halifax 169
Hall, R.J. 71, *Chart 1*
Hancock, Alfred J. 10, 12, 33, 67, 90, 104–7, 114, 116–17, 174, 229, **Plate 7**
Hancock, E.W. 90, 92
Hartnett, Laurence 30, 71, 80, 84–5, *Chart 1*
Hat Trade 87, 110, 135, 138–48, 150–1, 153–9, 161, 174–6, 198–9, 231, *Table 45*
Hayward Tyler 89–90, 100, 141–3, 166, 231, *Table 31*
Health Insurance 197
Heat Treatment Department, Vauxhall Motors 121, 165
Hegland, David L. 229
Helmets 55
Hemel Hempstead 152
Hendon 28–30, 34, 42–3, 52, 66, 69–70, 72, 76, 81
Hertfordshire 72, *Chart 2*
Hewlitt and Blondeau 104, 143–4
High Wycombe 130
Hill, Walter 188–90, 229
Hillman 46, 161. Vehicle: Wizard 39
Hire Purchase 47, 74, 173, 178
Hodges, Frank William 3, 8–9, 11–13, 15–16, **Plate 6**
Hoffman's of Chelmsford 112
Holidays 122, 171–2, 220
Holland/Dutch 85, 217–18
Holtom, T.W. 4, 7
Honda 209, 212–13, *Table 48*
Hooter 110
Hopkins, R.R. (Hoppy) 194
Horne, Harold 110, 117, 120–3, 125, 130, 132–3, 136, 152–3, 169, 193

Houses/Housing 19, 172, 200
Humber 3, 7, 15, 21, 23–4, 26, 67, 144, 161
Hungerford, R. 71, *Chart 1*
Huntingdonshire 72, *Chart 2*
Hydraulic Machinery 7
Hydrogen Peroxide 141, 231

IBC Vehicles 218, 224
Immigrants/Immigration 225
Imports 203
India 83, 85
India Office 77
Industrial Relations 32, 34, 100, 134, 191–5, 203–5
Inflation 204–5
Installment Selling *see* Hire Purchase
Institute of Automobile Engineers 33
Interbrew 226
Ipswich 169
Isle of Man Tourist Trophy 26, 67
Isuzu 218
Italy/Italian 81, 132, 138, 191

Jaguar 194
Japan/Japanese 85, 177, 191, 203, 212–16, 218, 221–2
Jerrycans 55
Job Demarcation 92
John, Dai 224
Joint Engineering Shop Stewards' Committee 101
Joint Production Committees 122
Jones, Daniel 190, **Plate 41**
Jones, Russell ('Taffy') 152
Journal of Industrial Economics 120

K Block, Vauxhall Motors 52
Kaizen 213
Kanban 213
Kardex *see* Card Index
Karrier 46
Keens, Thomas 140–1, 145
Kennedy, Dominic 221
Kent, *Mr.* 161, 165
Kent, *Sir* Walter 162
Kents (George Kents) 102–3, 112, 126, 142–3, 147–8, 156, 160–3, 166, 170–1, 199, 225, 231, *Tables 31, 34 and 35*
Kent Instruments/Meters 117–18, 225
Kents Process Control 225
Kerry Muir 152
Kidner, Percy 8, 10, 12, 16, 30, 33, 67, 78, 107, 117, 174, 229, **Plate 7**
King, C.E. 21, 26
Knudsen, Bill 43

Labour *see* Workforce
Labour Party/Government 55, 86, 193, 201
Laing, F.C. 71, *Chart 1*
Lancashire 72, *Chart 2*
Lancaster, John 4
Lanchester, Frederick 9, 13, 25

Laporte Chemicals 141–2, 147, 155, 200, 224, 231, *Tables 31 and 34*
La Salle 29, 42, 71, *Chart 1*
Laskey, A.W. 55
Lawson, Henry 3
Layoffs *see* Redundancy
Leaving Certificates 102, 159
Leicester 73, 138, 165
Leighton Buzzard 7
Licensed Bar 197
Life Insurance Scheme 197
Local Food Committee 103
Lock-outs 100, 107–9
London 7–8, 68, 72, 76, 80, 88, 124, 127, 146–9, 151–2, 155, 163, 169, 195, 199, 201, 226, 232; Fenchurch Street 3; Great Portland Street 68; Lambeth 1; Leadenhall Street 67, St. Olave's Grammar School 12; Vauxhall Bridge 1; Vauxhall Gardens 1; Wandsworth Road 1, 229, *Chart 2, Table 36*
London Borough Polytechnic 12
London Transport 152
Losses 20, 31
Lucas 54
Luton 4–5, 7, 11, 41–3, 45, 52–5, 67, 87–8, 92–3, 100–3, 108–9, 112, 115, 117, 123–8, 130, 135–41, 143–53, 155–61, 163, 165–6, 169–71, 174–7, 183, 185–6, 191, 195–8, 200–3, 205, 207, 214–16, 218–22, 226, 229, 231; Capability Green 226; Football Ground 101; Kimpton Road 19, 53, 220; Luton Airport 148, 225; Town Hall 103, 135, 174; Wardown Park 103. *See also* Chaul End
Luton Association 100–3
Luton Borough/Town Council 103, 140, 146, 162–3, 175, 226
Luton Chamber of Commerce 88, 140, 155, 175, 224
Luton Chamber of Commerce Journal 161
Luton Employment Committee/Office 107–8, 110, 144, *Table 32*
Luton Engineering Employers' Association 102
Luton, Mayor of 101, 154, 162
Luton News 41, 77, 105, 108, 110, 143, 150, 154–5, 163, 172
Luton Trades Council 88, 103
Luton University 224–5
Lynmouth **Plate 8**

M1 Motorway 186, 226
Machinery/Machines/shop/Fitters/ Mechanisation 53, 62, 66, 90, 92, 100–1, 104, 111, 114, 116, 121, 166, 170, *Table 66*
McKenna Tariff 32, 81
Maitland, John 16–17, 229
Malaya 85
Malta 85
Management Advisory Committee (MAC) 7, 122–3, 129, 133, 135–6, 175, 193–5, 198
Manchester 14

Manufacturing 225–6
Marquette 42
Marker Off 92
Marketing *see* Sales
Marshall Aid 177
Mass Production 24, 38, 54, 68, 172–3
Material Production Control (MPC) 216
Measured Day Work 114–51, 119–21, 135, 171, 191, 193, 197
Men/Male 138–41, 143–5, 149, 151, 153, 156–7, 175–6, 198–9, *Tables 44 and 45*
Mercedes 221
Mersey, River 185
Meters 142, 147, 231
Midlands *see* England
Migrants/Migration 124, 148–53, 165, 171
Millbrook 186
Millott-Severn, J. 88
Ministry of Labour 164–5
Minister of Supply 130
Models *see under name of manufacturer*
Mooney, James D. 29–32, 34, 45, 58, 76, 80–3, 134, 173, 187
Morgan, Glyn 115, 119–20, 124–5, 176
Morgan and Company 5
Morris, William 26, 28, 173
Morris 12, 19, 24, 26–8, 31, 37–8, 40, 42, 45, 47–8, 52, 54–5, 60–4, 66–70, 73, 76, 115, 123–4, 128, 152, 172–3, 203. Vehicles: Cowley 20, 38; Eight 38; Minor 48; Morris 12 41; Oxford 20, 23, 39. *See also* Austin
Morris Commercial 44–6, 48, 50
Morris Owner, The 69
Mortgage 24, 29
Motor, The 25, 32–3, 65
Motors Accounting Company 76
Mountain Ash 152
Mounting Shop, Vauxhall Motors 99, **Plate 28**
Mullins, *Mr.* 106
Munitions 92, 100, 143, 158
Munitions Act/Bill 100, 102
Mussolini 132

Nacano 226
National Amalgamated Society of Operative House and Ship Painters and Decorators 89–90
National Cash Register Company 69
National Federation of Women Workers 101. *See also* Women
National Union of Vehicle Builders (NUVB) 121, 125, 127–9, 131, 194, *Table 28*; *NUVB Quarterly Reports* 127
New Industries Committee 5, 7, 137, 140, 142, 145, 147, 153–6, 175–7, 198
New United Motor Manufacturing Inc. (NUMMI) 213
Newport Pagnell 50
New Zealand 68, 77, 84–6, 189–90
Night Shift 89–90, 103, 121
Nissan 209, 212, 221, *Table 48*
Nordiska G.M. 31

Norfolk 72, *Chart 2*
North London Locomotive Works 11
Northram, W.A. 71, *Chart 1*
Northumberland 72, *Chart 2*
Norway 85
Nuffield 56–7, 59

Obsolescence 179
Oil Crisis 186, 203–4
Oil Producing Countries (OPEC) 204
Olds 35
Oldsmobile 42, 220
Olley, Maurice 51
Olympia Show 54, 67, 154; 1905 11; 1938 55
Opel 35, 81–2, 207–8, 211–14, 218, 221–2. Vehicles: Ascona 214; Kadet 39, **Plate 15**; Vivaro 218
Over-Capacity 221
Output 14, 21, 41, 56, 215–17, *Tables 2, 5, 9, 13, 49 and 50*
Overdraft 24
Overtime 104, 107–9, 121, 168, 174, 197–8, 200, 205
Oxford 124, 146, 148–52, 166, 170

Paint Shop, Vauxhall Motors 96, 129, 184, **Plates 25 and 36**
Painters 90
Palestine 78
Palmer-Phillips, A.F. 51, 55, 70–1, 73, 84, *Chart 1*
Paris 21
Park End Clothing Company 164
Parliament 219
Paternalism 112, 175, 194
Pattern Makers 164
Pay/Wages 87, 90, 100, 103–6, 114–15, 117–18, 122, 130, 135–6, 157, 159, 165–9, 171, 175–6, 191–3, 195, 197–200, 204–5, 220
Pearson, *Sir* James Reginald 43–4, 55, 115, 117, 120–1, 123, 132–3, 182, 190, 194, **Plate 30**
Pedals 207
Penn, A. 129
Pension Scheme 122, 197
Percival Aircraft 129, 148, 167, 170–1, 231
Perry, *Sir* Percival 40, 173
Petch, *Mr.* 30
Petrol Rationing 204; Tax 81
Peugot 209, 221, *Table 48*
Piecework/Rate 112, 114, 164
Pinnaces 1
Plait *see* Hat Trade
Platt, Maurice 33–4, 134, 179–80, 188–90, **Plate 41**
Polycentric Policy 186, 190
Pomeroy, Laurence [son of L.H. Pomeroy] 15, 25
Pomeroy, Laurence H. 4, 9, 11–14, 16, 21–2, 25–6, 33, 67, 79, 90, 100–2, 113, 172, **Plates 8 and 10**
Pontiac 35, 42. Vehicle: Oakland 29, 35, 42

Population 137–9, 148–9, 198–9, 226, *Tables 29, 30 and 44*
Portugal 85
Prague 185
Press *see* Newspapers
Pressed Steel 151
Price, Bob 210–11
Price, Walter R. 229
Prices 10–11, 20–2, 26–7, 54, 68, 83, 108, 181, 204, 222, *Table 40*
Process Operation Sheets 92
Production 19, 31, 42, 44, 53, 111, 122, 167, 178, 193, *Table 39*
Productivity/Performance 24, 90, 216, 220, 222
Profits 16–18, 27, 38, 53, 62–4, 70, 163, 172, 191–2, 208–9, 213–14, *Tables 3, 4, 7, 17, 18, 41, 47 and 50*
Profit Sharing Scheme 121, 132, 136, 169
Promotion 136
Public Administration 199
Public Relations 117
Publicity 73
Pumps 7, 231

R.A.C.Trials 12, 68
Racing/Race Trials 16–18, 26, 67–8, 73, 78, 172
Radiators 141, 231
Ranfurly, *Lord* 11
Railways 124, 127, 138, 140, 142, 152, 165, 169; London–Midland 7, 138; Luton–Dunstable 138; Luton–Welwyn 138
Rationing 177–8
Recession *see* Slump
Recreation Facilities *see* Social Facilities
'Red Clydeside' 103
Redundancy/Dismissal/Sacking/Layoffs 105–6, 109–11, 114, 116–17, 152, 196–7, 205, 217
Refrigerators/Equipment/Plant 1, 7, 146, 231
Regus 226
Reilly, Nick 219–20, 230, **Plate 49**
Relaxation Agreement 167
Renault 218. Vehicle: Trafic 218
Re-organisation 16, 48, 53, 174
'Responsible Autonomy' 111
Retailers *see* Dealers
Rhea, Alexander D. 229
Rhondda Valley 151
Ricardo, *Dr.* H.R. 26
Riley, Edward 30, 36, 58, 134, 188–9
Road Traffic Act 47
Robotics/Robotisation 213, 216
Rochdale 101
Rolls, Charles S. 9
Rolls Royce 24, 26, 173. Vehicle: Silver Ghost 12
Rootes 37–8, 41, 56–7, 144, 161, 193–4
Rover 15, 23, 67, 112, 193–4, 203, 212, 218. Vehicle: Land Rover 218
Royce, (Frederick) Henry 13
Rowan and Halsey System 102

Running Shop, Vauxhall Motors 17, 97, **Plate 26**
Rüsselsheim 207, 221
Russia 18, 68, 78

St. Petersburg/Petrograd 68, 78
Sacking *see* redundancy
Sales/Marketing/distribution 17–18, 32, 37, 41–2, 47, 52, 66, 68–73, 76–7, 83, 173–4, 191, 197, 199, 203–4, 206, 208–9, 221, *Tables 3, 4, 41, 47; Charts 1 and 2*
Sales Speeder 70
Salmons-Tickford 50
Salter Report 47
Scandinavia 68
Scientific Instrument Makers 88
Scotch Colony 141
Scotland 72, 124, 141, 146, 149, 152, *Chart 2, Table 36*
Sebastopol 78
Second Hand *see* Used Cars
Seligman, *Professor* Edwin 74
Selz, Rudolph 4
Service Sector 199, 225–6
Setter 104
Sewing Machine 139
S.F. Edges 19
Shares/Shareholders 16–17, 24, 30, 32, 42, 61–2, 65–6, *Tables 16 and 20. See also* Stock
Shaw and Kilburn, *Messrs.* 68
Sheffield 101
Shift System 53, 157
Shipley 141, 231
Shop Stewards 105, 117, 125, 129, 157, 193, 195, 232
Shop Stewards and Works Committee Agreement (20 May 1919) 105–7, 116
Short Time 106
Shows *see* Exhibitions
Singer 12, 23, 46, 67
Skefko Ball Bearing Company (Later SKF) 100, 118, 142–3, 147–8, 155–7, 160–4, 169, 171, 199–200, 225, 231, *Tables 31, 34 and 35*
Sloan, *Miss* 101
Sloan, Alfred P. 30–1, 34–5, 38, 43, 69, 72, 74, 81, 173, 187
Slough 152
Slump/Recession 18, 28, 52, 79, 84, 147, 154, 159, 161, 163, 165–6, 177, 215, 217, 221
Smith, *Sir* Allan 104
Smith, Don 'Jock' 129–30, 152–3
Smith, Fred 121, 124, 150, 152, 169
Smiths 54, 57, 90
Snowden, Philip 74
Social/Recreation Facilities 132–3, 136, 161, 175; Choirs 197; Dramatic Society 197; Orchestra 197
Société Lorraine de Dietrich 21
Soda Syphons 141, 231
South of England Economic League 126
South Wales Mining Federation 151
Soviet Union 130. *See also* Russia

Spain/Spanish 78, 85, 212, 220
Spare Parts 83
Sporting Clubs/Facilities 19, 161, 197; Cricket 197; Football 197; Rugby 197; Tennis 132–3, 197
Springing 51
Stacey, J. 71, *Chart 1*
Stalker, J. 71, *Chart 1*
Standard Motors 3, 37–8, 41, 46, 52, 57, 170
Standardisation 57
Star 23
Statistics 72
Steam Engine Makers' Society 88–9
Steam Vehicles 45
Sterling Area 32
Stint 120
Stock 24, 29, 65, *Table 20. See also* Shares
Stockholm 31, 80
Straker Squire 23
Straw Plait *see* Hat Trade
Strikes 89, 100–3, 105–6, 117, 121, 129–30, 135, 143, 157, 164, 171, 193–4, 203–5, 216–17, 222, *Tables 43 and 46*
Styling Centre 186
Suggestions Committee 122
Sunbeam 13–17, 20–1, 23–5, 26, 172, *Table 3*
Sunderland 212, 221
Sussex 72, *Chart 2*
Svenska Arbetsgivare Foreningen (SAF) 161
Svenska Kullager Fabriken 142. *See also* SKF
Swallow, William 190, 229, **Plate 41**
Swayne, Alfred 30
Sweat Shop 110
Sweden/Swedish 78, 85, 100, 142, 161
Swindon 124, 150, 152, 165, 169, 212
Switzerland 212

Talbot 209, *Table 48*
Tanks *see* Churchill Tanks
Tariffs/Taxation 28–9, 31–2, 81, 83, 85, 138, 192, 201, 208, *Table 41*
Taub, Alex 51
Taylor, C. 71, *Chart 1*
Textiles 137, 139, 150, 155, 199, *Table 45*
Thames, River 1
Time and Motion Studies 160
Toddington 186
Todhunter, Benjamin 7
Tools 53, 62, *Table 16*
Toolmakers' Society 88
Tory Party *see* Conservative Party
Tosch, Paul J. 230
Town and Country Planning Act 1947 155
Toyota 212–13. Vehicle: Corolla 213
Tractors 35
Trade, Board of 77, 85, 101
'Trade Card' 101
Trade Unions *see* Unions
Transport and General Workers' Union (TGWU) 127, 127
Transport Committee 122
Treasury 101

Trials *see* Races/Racing
Trimmers/Trim Shop, Vauxhall Motors 90, 104, 129
Trunchion, W.T.F. 167
Tuckwell, Alec 152–3
Tugs 1
Turners 166, 170
'Turnip Patch' 117, 135, 151, 174, 193
Twort, *Mr.* 127
Tyres *see* Wheels

Unemployment/Unemployed 59, 88, 109–10, 131, 144–5, 147, 149, 153–4, 158, 162–3, 170, 225–6, *Tables 25 and 32*
Unions/Unionism 87–90, 92, 100–2, 104–8, 110–16, 120–5, 127–8, 130–1, 135–6, 143, 151–3, 159–60, 163–71, 174–6, 191, 193–6, 198, 205, 216–17, 220, 222–3, 232
UK Open Marketing 52
United Automobile Workers 34, 134
United Builders' Labour Union 88
United Kingdom (UK) 211–14, 220–3. *See also* Britain/British, England, Scotland and Wales
Used Car Market 74–5, 173, 182

Vacuum Cleaners 146–7, 231
Valves 22
Vauxhall and West Hydraulic Company Ltd. 7, 77, 89–91, 229, **Plate 21**. *See also* West Hydraulic Engineering Company
Vauxhall Iron Works (later Vauxhall Iron Works Co. Ltd.) 1, 3, 5, 7–8, 12, 89, 229
Vauxhall Motors (1914) Ltd. 16, 90, 146, 229
Vauxhall-Bedford News 173
Vauxhall Mirror 111, 134
Vauxhall Motors Dealer Council 77
Vauxhall Vehicles: A Type 10; A11 Type 10; A12 Type 10; Ambulances 50, 184; AO9 Type 10; Astra 211, 213–15, 223, **Plate 46**; Bedford Truck 37, 46, 55, 72–3, 173, 182–3, 215, 217–18, **Plate 16**, *Table 12, Chart 2*; B11 Type 10; Big Six 40, 50; BO9 Type 10, B10 Type 10; B12 Type 10; Camper Vans 184–5; Carlton 214–15; Cavalier 211–16, 223; Chevette 209–10, 214, 223, **Plate 45**; Commercial Vehicles 41–8, 50, 52–3, 55–6, 60, 65, 70–4, 82–4, 131, 142, 146–7, 162, 173, 178, 182–5, 207, 217–18, 221, *Tables 9, 11, 14 and 39, Chart 2*; Corsa 215, 221; Cresta 179–82, **Plate 31**; C10 Type 10, C Type *see* Prince Henry; D Type 10, 17, 19, 22; E Type 10, 22, 179; Fourteen 55; 14/40 22, 80; Frontera 215, 218, 221; H Type 40, 50–1, 179; HA Type 181; I Type 40, 179; J Type 40, 179; K Type 183; L Type 179; Light Six 37, 40–42, 48, 50, 58–9, 69, 173; LM Type 22–3, 31; Multi Purpose Vehicle (MPV) 215; M Type 22, 183; Nova 214–15; N Type 14/40 21; O Type 183; OD Type 21–2; OE Type 21–2; Omega 215; Prince Henry 10, 12–14, 68; Rascal 218; Royale

214; R Type 22; Senator 215; Silent 80 22, 50; Sintra 215; Sporting Vehicles 67; Staff Cars 18, 78; S Type 10, 23–4, 183; Ten 55, 57, 59, 69, 84, 86, 173; 30/98 13–14, 19, 22–3, 28, 31, 68, 80, 172; Tigra 215, 221; Trucks 45–7, 50, 84, *Table 10. See also* Commercial Vehicles; Twelve 55, 57, 188; 12/14 10–11; 12/16 10–11; 20/60 31; 25/70 22–3; Vectra 215, 220–1, 223–4; Velox 57–9, 179, 181–2, 196, **Plate 20**; Ventora 181–2, 205, 207; Viceroy 214; Victor 179–82, 200, 205–8, **Plates 32, 34, 44**; Viscount 181; Viva 181–3, 185, 190, 197, 206, 209, **Plates 35, 41, 43**; Vivaro 218; VX 4/90 181; Waveney (Bus) 47, **Plate 17**; Wensum 22; Wyvern 57–9, 179, 181; Zafira 215
Ventilation System 41
Vigor, Peter 111, 116, 120–2, 132, 134
Voiturette 3, 9, 15
Volkswagen 221

Wages *see* Pay
Wages Temporary Regulation Act 105
Waggoner, Rick 220
Wale, Kevin E. 230
Wales/Welsh 124, 138, 149–152, *Table 36*; North 72, *Chart 2*; South 72, 146, 151–2, 212, 224, *Chart 2*; Welsh Society 150
Walton, Alfred 16
Walton, Leslie 8–9, 16–17, 20, 24–5, 30, 32–3, 43, 86, 117, 121, 163, 229, **Plate 14**
War: Napoleonic 138; First World War 4, 7, 11, 13, 16–18, 28, 34, 40, 44, 50, 52, 65–6, 68, 77–8, 81, 86–7, 89–90, 100, 103–4, 110, 113, 124, 129, 131, 135, 139, 141–5, 147–8, 155–6, 158–9, 161, 172, 174–5; Second World War 35, 55–6, 58, 60, 117, 119, 122, 124, 130, 133, 143, 146, 148, 151–8, 163, 167–9, 175–7, 179, 183, 187, 194, 196, 198, 203, 210
War Department 55, 78, 188
War Office 17
Warships 1
Warwick 72, *Chart 2*

Welfare Benefits, Welfarism 112, 136, 161, 175, 194, 197
Welfare State 177
Welwyn 138
West Hydraulic Engineering Company 4–5, 7, 90, 142, 229. *See also* Vauxhall and West Hydraulic Company
West, Jack 28
West Indies 85
Westminster 100
Wheels/Wheel Base/Tyres 45, 179–80
Whitworth Exhibition 11
Willy's Overland 46
Wilson, Alexander 1–3, 229
Wilson, Alexander and Company 1, 3, 229
Wilson, Harold 201
Wilson, Quentin 221
Windows/Windscreen 179–80
'Winter of Discontent' 204
Wiseman, Edmund 139
Wolseley 15
Women/Female 87, 92, 100–1, 125, 137–9, 141, 143–5, 149–51, 153–9, 161, 171, 175–6, 198–9, *Tables 44 and 45*
Workers' Union 88, 104
Workforce/Labour/Employees 21, 31, 87, 90, 100, 106, 108, 111, 113–15, 132, 136, 146–7, 163, 174, 192–3, 195, 197, 199, 206, 208–9, 215, 217, 222–4, *Tables 5, 9, 30, 33, 39, 47, 49, 50*
Working Hours/Man Hours 103, 135, 193, 197, 206, *Table 43*
Working Week 102, 135
Works Committee 195
'World Car' 208

York 5, 89, 104–5, 232
York Memorandum 106
Yorkshire 72, *Chart 2*
Young, A.P. 54

Zenith Carburettor Company 51
Zurich 212, 220